A GAMES CHANGER

A GAMES CHANGER

THE INTERNATIONAL OLYMPIC
COMMITTEE, TOKYO 2020 & COVID-19

STEPHEN R. WENN
ROBERT K. BARNEY

THE UNIVERSITY OF ARKANSAS PRESS
FAYETTEVILLE · 2025

Copyright © 2025 by the University of Arkansas Press. All rights reserved. No part of this book should be used or reproduced in any manner without prior permission in writing from the University of Arkansas Press or as expressly permitted by law.

ISBN: 978-1-68226-276-4
eISBN: 978-1-61075-840-6

29 28 27 26 25 5 4 3 2 1

Designed by William Clift

Cataloging-in-Publication Data on file at the Library of Congress.

In recognition of Tokyo 2020's Olympians, their coaches and trainers, as well as Tokyo's volunteers, who persevered and, in the end, prevailed over COVID-19, giving us all a needed respite from our thoughts in a difficult time. Special thanks, too, to Damian Warner for sharing his story with us.

CONTENTS

Preface	*ix*
Abbreviations	*xvii*
1. Quest for Gold	3
2. Troubling Signs for Tokyo	25
3. Postponement	49
4. "Here We Go"	69
5. The Stretch Run	93
6. Two Days in Tokyo	123
7. Reflections: Tokyo 2020 and History's Long Lens	143
Notes	*159*
Bibliography	*201*
Index	*229*

PREFACE

In early February 2020, my wife, Martha, and I (Stephen) departed our home near Waterloo, Ontario, headed down Highway 401 to the Queen Elizabeth Way, and crossed Buffalo's Peace Bridge into the United States. It was the initial leg of the pleasant seven-hour drive to State College, Pennsylvania, one I have made many times over the years, and a welcome diversion for us, only two weeks removed from the passing of Martha's mother. We encountered some snow along the way, but we were committed to the drive. My PhD adviser, Ron Smith; his daughter, Penny; and son, Dan, were holding an eightieth-birthday celebration for Ron's wife, Sue, the person whom my mother "entrusted" with my well-being thirty years earlier when I attended Pennsylvania State University in pursuit of my doctoral degree. It was a party not to be missed.

With two teenagers back home, we treasured the chance for three days together on our own, but we felt an odd sense of foreboding during those days away. The party was wonderful, our walks around State College and the mandatory visit to the "Nittany Lion" statue elicited fond memories for me, and we reveled (as onsite spectators) in the Penn State men's basketball team's 83–77 win over Minnesota—the sixth win in what became an eight-game winning streak, fashioned mainly through the superlative play of forward Lamar Stevens as the season wound down. However, it was difficult for our thoughts not to be drawn back to recent stories emerging from China about a still poorly understood novel coronavirus, 2019-nCov (renamed SARS-CoV-2 some weeks later), something the World Health Organization (WHO) had labeled a "Public Health Emergency of International Concern" on January 30.[1]

Meanwhile, Bob, after his seventh trip to China over a span of forty years, was still reflecting on this latest sojourn four months earlier, when the country stood on the brink of hosting the 2022 Olympic Winter Games. A joyous feeling of anticipation penetrated almost every nook and cranny of the country. Most Chinese citizens knew lots about the Olympics. Hosting the 2008 Summer Games had seen to that, especially through media coverage and widely staged Olympic Education programs mounted in the nation's public schools. These programs reached government officials, teachers and administrators, more than 400 million students,[2] and perhaps most critically, multiple millions of their parents. These initiatives elicited a sustained tsunami of "Olympic spirit" in China.

Thus it was that Bob and I, fresh from these experiences, became increasingly alarmed about the veritable flood of reports arriving from Wuhan in the heart of China. Alarm turned to disbelief at the carnage that COVID-19 unleashed across the world over the next two years, including the near wreckage of Tokyo's Games of the XXXIInd Olympiad. As of April 5, 2022, when we began conceptualizing this book, the world had witnessed more than 494 million cases of COVID-19 that claimed 6.17 million lives. In the United States, 24,829 of every 100,000 citizens had contracted COVID-19 and more than 997,000 Americans had died. In Canada, where we reside, the numbers, though chilling, were only minimally less mind numbing—at least 3.5 million cases and 37,350 deaths, something that translated into 100 deaths per 100,000 Canadians. A sampling of countries reveals that few regions escaped COVID-19's clutches, with notably high deaths per 100,000 in Brazil (313), Argentina (285), Colombia (277), the United Kingdom (248), Belgium (269), Ukraine (253), the Czech Republic (373), Montenegro (435), Hungary (467), Bulgaria (525), and Peru (653).[3] Travel bans and aggressive lockdown protocols in New Zealand and Australia help explain their comparatively low death totals—386 and 6,435, respectively (8 and 25 per 100,000).[4] On the other hand, scientists struggled to explain Africa's lower case numbers and deaths.[5]

Lamar Stevens, who did so much to improve the relevance of Penn State's men's basketball program in the National Collegiate Athletic Association's (NCAA) Big Ten Conference, was, like so many other US college athletes in 2020, robbed of the opportunity to see his season through to its natural ending—in his case, what would have been a well-earned appearance in the NCAA Tournament, more commonly known as "March Madness." COVID-19 also deprived Stevens of his chance to become Penn State's all-time leading scorer, falling just seven points shy of Talor Battle's (2007–2011) mark.[6] So, too, did the pandemic alter the trajectory of the competitive seasons and Olympic preparation cycles of thousands of athletes around the globe who aspired to challenge themselves in the often once-in-a-lifetime environment of the Summer Olympics. In late March 2020, after weeks of information gathering, discussion, dialogue, and debate, International Olympic Committee (IOC) President Thomas Bach and Japanese Prime

Minister Shinzo Abe announced the postponement of the 2020 Games, with the new dates in July and August 2021 determined six days later.[7]

As these events played out, Bob and I awaited the release of our most recent book, *The Gold in the Rings: The People and Events That Transformed the Olympic Games*. Work on this book had consumed us both from 2015 through the final editing stages in August 2019. We tapped new sources, primarily via personal interviews with current and past IOC and United States Olympic Committee (USOC) officials, and additional material from the IOC's Lausanne archives, to build on our years of researching the IOC's transformational embrace of commercialism through the pursuit of television rights fees and a worldwide corporate sponsorship program (TOP—The Olympic Partners, formerly The Olympic Program). We crafted a book that blended biography with historical storytelling in a manner designed to make the IOC's economic history accessible to a wider readership. We both concede that our enthusiasm for its release was soon overshadowed by global events well beyond our comprehension or control.

Over the ensuing months, we pursued our respective interests and responsibilities, pivoting to teaching in an online, remote environment. Bob, in his seventh decade of teaching at the university level, had witnessed much change with respect to technology and lecture delivery, but nothing so sudden and sweeping. Both of us prefer to teach people and not faces, but we forged ahead, longing for a different reality. We tackled a number of our own research projects that we set aside while collaborating on *The Gold in the Rings*. As Canada dealt with its fourth COVID-19 wave in late 2021, my thoughts wandered to a project that might interest me and also justify applying for a sabbatical in early 2023. With *The Gold in the Rings* bringing our effort to chronicle the IOC's economic history through the late Jacques Rogge's presidency (2001–2013), along with more modest treatment of Thomas Bach's first seven years in office (2013–2020), it seemed wise to cast my gaze in a different direction.

With COVID-19 dominating our lives and consuming the IOC leadership—especially regarding Beijing's prospects of successfully staging the 2022 Olympic Winter Games in a mere three months—I contemplated writing an assessment of the IOC's oversight of Tokyo's hosting efforts that had played out just four months earlier. A litany of questions crossed my mind: What was the nature of the IOC's consultation process with the world's health authorities in judging the need to postpone the 2020 Summer

Olympics? What was the extent of the dialogue with Olympic partners, such as television broadcasters and corporate sponsors, in establishing a path forward? How did IOC officials and Japanese organizers function as a team when facing the challenge of providing the world's elite athletes the chance to convene in Tokyo? What steps did these parties take to assure Tokyo's Olympians that they had prioritized their health and well-being beyond the requirements of a Games site absent a global pandemic? It seemed an inviting exercise for this researcher, but without Bob on board, it did not seem "right." Thankfully, when I floated him the idea, he responded with enthusiasm, and we discussed our next steps.

While journalists charted the key events through Tokyo 2020's postponement to its ultimate staging sixteen months later, we knew that the record of their efforts alone could not permit us to complete the desired analysis. We therefore reached out to Maria Bogner, head of the IOC's Olympic Studies Centre, who had so ably assisted us in pursuing archival material and personal interviews as we wrote *The Gold in the Rings*. We conveyed our desire to assess the preparations for, and execution of, Tokyo 2020, realizing that IOC documents and personal interviews with key historical actors would be central to our efforts. Maria reported that the IOC, in committing itself while events unfolded to having this history written, had maintained an organized approach to storing information in the months leading up to Tokyo 2020. She pledged to assist us in presenting our request to IOC officials for access to the sources that would advance our mission. Some weeks later, with such permission granted,[8] our work commenced.

Central to completing this work were the personal interviews we conducted with numerous IOC officials at Lausanne's Olympic House in January 2023, including President Thomas Bach; Olympic Games Executive Director Christophe Dubi; Sports Director Kit McConnell; former Director, Television and Marketing Services, Timo Lumme; (now former) Medical and Scientific Director Richard Budgett; and Pau Mota, the former Head, Medical and Rescue, for the Fédération Internationale de l'Automobile (FIA), who transitioned to work for the IOC (senior manager, Medical and Scientific Department) in January 2021 for the run-up to the Tokyo Olympics that July and August. We appreciate the time they gave us to explore their experiences before and after the postponement of Tokyo's Olympics in March 2020 and during the months of work involved in creating a safe and secure environment for the athletes. We are grateful to Maria for her support and the work she did on our behalf to facilitate the interviews that, in our opinion, added so much to the texture of the history we have written on this subject. We also appreciate Dave Deevey's swift turnaround on the work necessary to transcribe the interviews. Greg Sennema, a reference librarian at Wilfrid Laurier University, contributed to our efforts in compiling an extremely helpful newspaper and magazine database that guided us in our early research. Dr. Anthony Clarke, Dean, Faculty of Science, Wilfrid Laurier University, assisted the authors with the funds necessary for the production of this book's index. James Fraleigh's meticulous approach on the copyediting front enhanced the quality of the finished product. And we are grateful to Julie Trepier (IOC), Andrea Gordon (Canadian Press Images), Elena Novikova (Postmedia), and Tom McConnell (Bell Media) for assisting us in securing photo permissions for the images employed.

For the last thirty-five years, Bob and I have witnessed, and in some ways contributed to, the expanding interest in Olympic history and the increasing volume of published research in the area, especially relating to the membership of the North American Society for Sport History. We are blessed with many friends in this organization, and we thank them for these relationships that we both cherish. We must thank our spouses, Martha Wenn and Ashleigh Barney, for their continuing support for what we do—which, at times, consumes us. We also acknowledge that this research was supported by Wilfrid Laurier University and Canada's Social Sciences and Humanities Research Council.

As you begin to engage with this book, it is advisable that we, its authors, convey what we believe it to be, and what we know it is not. This work is (to the best of our knowledge) the first book-length examination of the process involved in delivering the Tokyo 2020 Olympics amid the challenges posed by the onset of a global pandemic.[9] It does so, admittedly, from the IOC's perspective, looking out to the Olympic world, and is substantially based on interviews with several central historical actors, specifically IOC officials—including (now former) IOC President Thomas Bach—who labored in pursuit of this goal from their homes and occasionally, Olympic House, the IOC's headquarters in Lausanne. We drew the backdrop for the events described from an extensive review of published English-language media coverage of the IOC's efforts to wrestle with the question of cancellation versus postponement, its subsequent efforts to wind down Tokyo 2020 from its scheduled opening that July, and its push to ramp up the staging of the Games in 2021.

This is therefore an administrative history of how the IOC managed a difficult-to-foresee, never-before-encountered threat to its staging of the Olympic Games. As COVID-19 gripped the world, the environment was ever changing and dynamic, necessitating a coordinated and purposeful response. In gauging their work toward ensuring Tokyo 2020's celebration, IOC officials prized the strength of relationships they formed with Japanese organizers on the ground. First and foremost, Thomas Bach and Prime Minister Shinzo Abe built a trusting relationship, from the time Tokyo had pursued and eventually was awarded the right to host the Games in 2013, through to 2020. Their approach filtered down through the ranks of IOC officials and their Japanese counterparts, especially when dealing with the cauldron of issues caused by COVID-19. Someday a fuller examination of events may replicate our work from a Japanese perspective, using Japanese-language sources (and voices). Until then, our interviews and research have provided us avenues for assessing the collaborative spirit that permeated the shared commitment of Japanese Olympic officials and the IOC's leadership team to find a path forward, as well as the roller-coaster ride of Japanese public opinion over holding Tokyo 2020.

While this book is an administrative history, we mix in the stories of a few Tokyo Olympians, who, as did IOC officials, confronted COVID-19 with the hopes that their Olympic dreams would not be dashed. As COVID-19 raged at varying levels around the world in 2020 and 2021, all athletes, their coaches, and their personal support networks were forced to exhibit flexibility and a steely-eyed measure of resilience to reach Tokyo ready to compete and excel. This reality has been a focus of investigation for our colleagues engaged in sport psychology research.[10] These stories of human interest merited such treatment in this book, because without the athletes' collective resolve, there would have been no Olympics, or at least not one with such a panoply of exceptional performances. Yasuhiro Nakamori, Acting Director General of the Aichi-Nagoya 2026 Asian Games, stated, "During the Tokyo Olympics themselves, the athletes' performances really moved people, not just in Japan but around the world too."[11] We hope including their stories might lead others to expand upon this approach. Considering the number of Olympic or world records equaled or broken in London (101 and 45, respectively) and Rio de Janeiro (87, 25) with those set in Tokyo (145, 28), across archery, athletics, track cycling, modern pentathlon, swimming, shooting, and weightlifting, the athletes clearly triumphed collectively in their battle with the difficulties and trials imposed by COVID-19.[12]

We also drill down on the Olympic journey of Damian Warner, Canada's decathlon gold medalist in Tokyo, whose Olympic appearances in London (fifth place) and Rio (bronze) fueled his drive to reach the top of the Olympic podium. Warner and his coach, Gar Leyshon, sat for two interviews, and this book benefits from their time and willingness to help add a human element from an athlete's perspective to this wider story. Though the need for Warner and his coaching team to devise a path forward is not unique versus other such teams, their pursuit of an adequate training facility in the winter months of 2020 and 2021 underscores the ingenuity, determination, and adaptability demanded of Tokyo 2020's Olympians when they transformed their training approaches.

We sought to write a narrative history accessible to general readers, academics, and Olympic scholars alike. To readers seeking a book that examines the events described through the lenses of race, class, political economy, or gender—all popular and often useful points of embarkation for analyzing the "Olympic project" in our academic field—this is *not* that book. The path remains clear for others to launch such an endeavor, this book perhaps being a useful source in that quest. And while some quarters of our field view narrative history as "less than" history, we do not subscribe to this belief. We assert that our approach broadens the possible readership for this history and offers value for academics and general readers. In welcoming the latter, we depart from the conventional methodology pursued when targeting a book manuscript for a university press. We are grateful to the University of Arkansas Press—most particularly, Dave Wiggins and Christine O'Bonsawin, former series editors of Sport, Culture, and Society—and Editor in Chief David Scott Cunningham, all of whom understood and supported our intent.

The core of our argument is that Tokyo 2020 represents the success of a team of officials in Lausanne and Tokyo who devised ways to work with the needed focus while attenuating sources of noise from Japan and abroad, specifically from some in the medical and media communities who questioned the wisdom of the officials' shared resolve to stage the Games. In the end, the Games were staged. The athletes performed. The much-feared outbreak of an Olympic COVID variant never occurred. People around the world, whose daily existence had been constrained by varying degrees of lockdowns or restrictions, watched and, for a brief period, could escape their personal circumstances. Given the world's plight, has any series of Olympic broadcasts had more "entertainment value"?

Last, in launching this project, and ultimately throughout the research and writing phases involved in the production of this book, we drew a measure of motivation from the counsel provided to historians by Professor Esyllt Jones, a University of Manitoba researcher of infectious disease in society, regarding the need to generate a comprehensive record of COVID-19's myriad influences and impacts on the world. Jones stated: "For everyone out there now who's living through COVID, who's lost people or who's had really negative economic impact in their lives, it's important that that experience be honored by placing it into the story of our history."[13]

What follows is our contribution to that record: our story of the history of persistence and determination of IOC officials and Japanese organizers to deliver Tokyo 2020 in the face of those who doubted their ability to do so, or openly questioned the risks of the enterprise. Perhaps on several occasions, even the IOC leaders wondered about their own prospects for success. Yet the months and weeks before Tokyo 2020 presented a cascade of challenges and a learning experience that left the IOC better informed and prepared to tackle the task of delivering the 2022 Beijing Olympic Winter Games in collaboration with Chinese officials. In terms of the effort needed to stage an Olympic festival, however, Tokyo 2020 was without parallel.

ABBREVIATIONS

AIBA	Association Internationale de Boxe Amateur
ARD	Arbeitsgemeinschaft der öffentlich-rechtlichen Rundfunkanstalten der Bundesrepublik Deutschland
CBC	Canadian Broadcasting Corporation
F1	Formula One
FIFA	Fédération Internationale de Football Association
FIA	Fédération Internationale de l'Automobile
GAVI	Global Alliance for Vaccines and Immunization
IOC	International Olympic Committee
ISF	International Sport Federation
MLB	Major League Baseball
NBA	National Basketball Association
NHL	National Hockey League
NOC	National Olympic Committee
OCOG	Organizing Committee of the Olympic Games
SARS	severe acute respiratory syndrome
TMS	Television and Marketing Services (IOC)
TOP	The Olympic Partners
USOPC	United States Olympic and Paralympic Committee
USOC	United States Olympic Committee
ZDF	Zweites Deutsches Fernsehen

A GAMES CHANGER

1
QUEST FOR GOLD

INTRODUCTION

On March 24, 2020, after weeks of discussions among International Olympic Committee (IOC) leaders, Japanese government officials, and representatives of the Tokyo 2020 Organizing Committee, as well as extensive dialogue with Olympic stakeholders, including television rights holders and corporate sponsors, all of which played out against the increasing specter of COVID-19 and amid a rising chorus of trepidation from athletes about their safety and diminishing abilities to train for elite athletic competition, IOC President Thomas Bach and Japanese Prime Minister Shinzo Abe announced the postponement of Tokyo 2020. A conference call between Bach and Abe that day, attended by several IOC executives and Japanese bureaucrats, brought speculation and media coverage concerning the prospects of staging a multicountry, multisport mega-event amid a global pandemic in 2020 to a close.[1]

"We have no blueprint for this," Bach told Olympians around the world via a recorded video message later that day, regarding the need to resurrect the Games one year after their intended date, but he pledged in heartfelt fashion to seek the solutions needed to make their Olympic dreams a reality. He asked the athletes to "give us a little bit of time now to put this huge jigsaw puzzle together." In describing the "dark tunnel" in which citizens around the globe found themselves, he offered that in 2021, "these Games could then finally be the celebration of humanity after having overcome the unprecedented crisis of the coronavirus." In closing, Bach wished the athletes and their families "good health" and encouraged them to "keep going and stay united in the Olympic spirit."[2]

Our book explores and assesses the efforts of the IOC to assemble the jigsaw puzzle Bach referenced. It is an administrative history of the IOC's decision making and actions that provided the pathway to staging the Games a year hence (July 23–August 8, 2021). Winding down an Olympic festival within four months of its starting date, then pressing forward with it again sixteen months later, had never been done. Yes, the Games were canceled in 1916, 1940, and 1944 because of World Wars I and II, but after these conflicts, sites for 1920 and 1948 were hastily chosen. The years 2020 and 2021 were destined to be learning experiences for IOC leadership and staff—and no doubt also valuable for the fast-approaching 2022 Winter Games in Beijing. The IOC had to generate, on the fly, a playbook (there were ultimately three versions)[3] for delivering the Olympics *for* the athletes and *to* the global sport community within a highly compromised, global-pandemic-infused environment. The human effort in Lausanne and Tokyo to achieve such a goal leaned heavily on adaptability, flexibility, and resilience, all in a pervasively uncertain environment.

While uncertainty cast a shadow over the IOC's efforts, so too did expressions of doubt concerning the wisdom of proceeding with hosting the Games, even delayed until 2021. A chorus of public questioning of the IOC's determination to bring the world's Olympians to Japan ensued. Jules Boykoff, a professor at Oregon's Pacific University, and author of *Power Games: A Political History of the Olympic Games* and *NOlympians: Inside the Fight Against Capitalist Mega-Sports in Los Angeles, Tokyo, and Beyond*, typified the alarm in some quarters: "The decision to press ahead with the Tokyo Olympics in 2021 is truly a matter of life and death. We're talking about an optional sporting spectacle, not some essential service to humanity, and when you throw public health into the mix, the calculus can become uncouth pretty quick."[4]

Journalists Charlie Campbell, Mayako Shibata, and Madeline Roache highlighted an October 2020 poll commissioned by *Kyodo News* revealing that only 38 percent of the Japanese people favored moving forward with the Olympic Games in 2021. "[There's] the question of how to keep thousands of officials, judges, dignitaries, journalists and sponsors safe in one of the world's most crowded cities," they added, "let alone placate 38 million embattled citizens faced with a potential catastrophic super spreader event."[5] A second poll taken in January 2021 showed 80 percent of the Japanese public behind cancellation or a further postponement of the Games. At the time, what turned out to be the country's slow vaccination rollout had not yet even commenced, and daily case counts had peaked at 7,800.[6] In May 2021, two months from the late-July opening of the Games, a mere 14 percent of those polled in Japan wanted them to proceed. The Japan Doctors Union stood opposed, as did *Asahi Shimbun*, one of the country's leading newspapers. An online domestic petition called Stop Tokyo Olympics boasted 450,000 signatures. Michael Osterholm, director of the Center for Infectious Disease Research and Policy at the University of Minnesota, identified the prevailing worry for those beyond Japan's borders: "The worst thing that would happen is that the Olympics becomes a superspreading event that goes around the world."[7] All of this compounded the challenge for Olympic officials.

ATHLETES' STORIES

Before launching our assessment of the IOC's efforts, we stress that as Olympic historians, we are mindful that the athletes themselves are the "show." The IOC, the Organizing Committees for the Olympic Games (OCOGs), and their partners—the National Olympic Committees (NOCs) and the International Sport Federations (ISFs)—facilitate the Olympic Games, but it is the athletes who bring people to the Olympic venues and, even more importantly, deliver them to television screens and (via video streams) cell phones, tablets, and computers. How did athletes adapt and demonstrate both flexibility and resilience while pursuing a newly crafted, unanticipated training cycle, one dominated by the need to establish novel training methods because facilities around the globe had closed and opportunities to compete had evaporated?

US shot putter and two-time Olympic gold medalist Ryan Crouser is a big man. He stands six foot seven and tips the scales at 310 pounds. His daily food intake is four meals comprising some 5,000 calories. Deprived of the stimulation and exhilaration his normal competitive schedule would have provided, and the anticipation of an impending Olympic Games, Crouser filled the gap with bass-fishing tournaments. Absent the normal travel tied to competitions, and able to let injuries heal during a suddenly extended training phase, Crouser's regimen delivered results. He lifted weights in his garage, threw a medicine ball against a cement bridge abutment, and trained with a homemade plywood throwing ring. For Crouser, training broke the "monotony" and kept him "sane." In July 2020, he drove ten hours to one of the few meets staged at the time. He threw the shot 75'2" (22.9 m) for a new personal best.[8] In Tokyo the following year, he won gold with a new Olympic record, 76′5.3″ (23.3 m), falling just short of the 76′8.08″ (23.37 m) world record he achieved at the US Olympic Trials that June.[9] For the first time in the Olympics, three individuals—Crouser, Joe Kovacs (United States), and Tomas Walsh (New Zealand)—finished in the same gold, silver, and bronze podium positions as they had in the previous Games (Rio 2016).[10] In early 2023, Crouser broke his own world record with a mark of 76′8.47″ (23.38 m).[11] He departed Paris in 2024 with his third gold medal in the event.

Forced rest from the pandemic also benefited Uganda's Joshua Cheptegai, who entered the Olympic cycle as the gold and silver medalist in the 10000 m at the World Athletics Championships in Doha (2019) and London (2017), respectively. Locked down in his hometown, Kapchorwa, near the Kenyan border, without his scheduled five or six twenty-hour trips to Europe for competitions, Cheptegai relaxed with his family, assisted his grandparents with gardening, and helped with some painting at a nearby school. Once lockdown ended, Cheptegai headed to a high-altitude training camp with greater reserves of energy and engaged in productive speed-training sessions. Travel restrictions made for an eighty-hour trip to an August 2020 meet in Monaco, where he lowered the sixteen-year-old world record in the 5000 m to 12:35.36. In Tokyo the following year, Cheptegai captured gold in the 5000 m and silver in the 10000 m. Cheptegai's brilliance was further demonstrated in Paris when he captured a gold medal in the 10000 m.

In July 2019, Great Britain's Adam Peaty, a dominant force in the 100 m breaststroke and an Olympic champion at Rio 2016, became the first swimmer to break 57 seconds (56.88). By December 2020, Peaty had recorded nineteen of the fastest twenty times in the event. Fueled by coach Mel Marshall's "Project Immortal"—the pursuit of "a performance so good it's almost inhuman and will never be beaten"—Peaty continued a weightlifting regimen during the pandemic in his garage that took his weight from 88 kg (Rio) to 94 kg by the end of 2020. Ninety-minute training sessions in a backyard water tank he installed helped him maintain his technique, though all of this followed a period during lockdown when he cycled, rested, and even enjoyed the occasional alcoholic beverage. In November 2020, he set a new world record in the short-course 100 m breaststroke, and all indications were that something special awaited in Japan.[12] In Tokyo, Peaty, then unbeaten in the event since 2014, became the first Briton to capture the gold medal in the same swim event in successive Olympic Games. He fell short of the "immortal" swim he craved, but still posted the fifth fastest time in history (57.37 s). It seemed not to bother him. The relief Peaty felt at the close of the race was palpable, as he revealed during a post-race press conference the extent of the pressure he was under as such a heavy favorite.[13] Peaty departed Tokyo with a gold medal in the 4 × 100 m mixed medley relay and a silver medal in the men's 4 × 100 m medley relay. Within days, he knew he needed some time away from the sport, as COVID-19 and the expectations for Tokyo he and others had placed on him had taken a toll on his mental health.[14] In Paris, Peaty missed out on a third gold medal in the 100 m breaststroke by a slim margin (.02 s), his performance perhaps impeded by having contracted COVID-19 in the buildup to the final.[15]

The calendar and Father Time were US open-water swimmer Ashley Twichell's biggest challenges. Twichell grew up in Fayetteville, New York, took to the water at age three, and began her competitive swim career at seven. She landed an athletic scholarship at Duke University and subsequently earned all-American status in the 1650 yd freestyle. She tried without success to qualify for the 2008 Beijing Olympics (400 m freestyle) but began her transition to open-water swimming in 2010, winning her first 10 km US open-water swim title in 2012. However, Twichell failed to make either the US open-water or pool teams for the 2012 London Olympics. While rebounding from 2014 shoulder surgery, Twichell again failed to make the US team for Rio 2016. Undeterred, she swam on, winning the 5 km world open-water championships and the USA Swimming 1500 m freestyle title the following year.

With time running out on her Olympic dreams at age thirty, Twichell looked to a superior performance at the 2019 world open-water swim championships in Gwangju, South Korea, as her last best chance to qualify for Tokyo 2020. Midway through the 10 km event's final lap, she stole a peek at the bodies in front of her and realized her current position (thirteenth) would not secure a spot in Tokyo. With 800 m of open water remaining to propel herself into the qualifying top ten, she began to reel in her fellow competitors; her sixth-place finish made Twichell the second oldest rookie swimmer to represent the US in the Olympics since 1908. Though she had to wait an additional year, her seventh-place finish in Tokyo (where she made her Olympic debut at thirty-two) and the blessings of her pregnancy later that year meant that 2021 was especially memorable for her and husband, Derek Wall.[16]

Helen Glover, a gold medalist in the 2012 London and 2016 Rio Olympics in rowing's coxless pair event, along with her Great Britain teammate, Heather Stanning, was a mother of three young children and had been retired from the sport for some four years when COVID-19 lockdowns hit. She looked at her home rowing machine and asked herself, why not?[17] In Tokyo, Glover, the first mother ever named to the British Olympic rowing team, and her new partner, Polly Swann, finished fourth in the event.

Vigo, Spain's Susana Rodríguez Gacio, a medical doctor and (then) three-time world champion paratriathlete, suffered from "mounting fear and anxiety" when COVID-19 burst forth in early 2020. Rodríguez is visually impaired due to albinism. She combined long shifts at her hospital in service to COVID-19 patients with a determination to continue three hours of daily training on a treadmill, exercise bike, and rowing machine supplied by the Spanish Paralympic Committee. Strict lockdowns limited her to indoor training, specifically on the machines at her apartment that she shared with two other healthcare workers. Meanwhile, she faced many daily concerns: How could her hospital meet demands for patient beds day to day? How could she assist patients who survived COVID in rehabilitating from their illness? How many people could she aid over the phone in discerning their need for a COVID-19 test? "I think sports helped me to be able to recover and face the next day at work," Rodríguez concluded. With only ten days for her body to adjust to Tokyo's elevated humidity in August 2021, Rodríguez pushed through to win the gold medal in her event.[18]

In October 2019, Canadian Paralympian Alison Levine achieved the distinction of the world's number one ranking in boccia (BC4 category), powered by steadily improving performances and her win at Montreal's World Open five months earlier.[19] She entered Tokyo 2020 with that top ranking but faced immense challenges in her preparation, having to train in her apartment for six months by throwing the balls on her linoleum floor and then collecting them with a homemade contraption her father constructed. Levine also used a hand bike to help maintain her conditioning. While she was eventually able to return to a boccia court at Institut National du Sport du Québec in March 2021, it was far from ideal, as she was permitted to interact with only one teammate because of social distancing measures. Because her neuromuscular disorder affects her spinal cord, diaphragm, and lung function, she was identified as high risk for COVID-19. Levine knew that Canada's restrictions made her preparations unequal to those of her eventual rivals in Tokyo, but she remained undeterred. "If it means me not doing as well at this Paralympics but being alive for the next one, I'm okay with that," she stated in sanguine fashion.[20] She bowed out in the preliminaries in Tokyo without the satisfaction of improving on her fifth-place finish in the 2016 Rio Olympics, but responded powerfully four months later by capturing the gold medal at the World Boccia Americas Regional World Championships in São Paulo, Brazil. The win punched her ticket for the 2022 World Championships, where she finished fourth in the individual event and won the bronze medal in pairs with her partner, Iulian Ciobanu.[21]

Some athletes invested their energies during lockdown in trying to lift and inspire people around the globe through the IOC's #StayStrong online campaign, which launched in early April. Jan Frodeno, Germany's gold medalist in the 2008 Olympics triathlon, completed (and shared for fans on Facebook) an Iron Man competition at home using his countercurrent pool (3800 m), stationary bike (180 km), and treadmill (marathon). Frodeno, who was the first athlete ever to win both a gold medal in the Olympic triathlon and the Iron Man World Championships title (2015), raised over €200,000 for charity.[22] Welshman Geraint Thomas, a two-time Olympic gold medalist in team-pursuit cycling (Beijing and London), completed three twelve-hour rides over seventy-two hours on a turbo bike in his garage, a feat that raised £350,000 for Great Britain's National Health Service. Thomas thought this challenge on par with eight- or nine-stage races in the Tour de France, an opinion he was well qualified to offer as the Tour's 2018 champion.[23]

Renaud Lavillenie, France's two-time Olympic medalist in the pole vault (London 2012, gold; Rio 2016, silver), organized the "Ultimate Garden Clash," an online competition streamed by World Athletics via Twitter, YouTube, and Facebook, that pitted Lavillenie against his fellow competitors Sam Kendricks (United States) and Armand Duplantis (Sweden, though American born) that drew "hundreds of thousands" of viewers.[24] The bar in their respective backyard training grounds was set at 5 m, and the three men competed to see how many clearances they could compile in two fifteen-minute sessions. Duplantis and Lavillenie racked up thirty-six clearances, while Kendricks cleared the bar twenty-six times.[25] Duplantis, who captured gold in Tokyo (and three years later in Paris, setting a new world record), holds the indoor and outdoor world records. Lavillenie finished eighth in Tokyo, while Kendricks, a 2017 and 2019 world champion and the bronze medalist in Rio, missed the competition due to a positive

COVID test in Tokyo.[26] Fellow pole vaulters Katerina Stefanidi (Greece), Katie Nageotte (United States), and Alysha Newman (Canada) replicated the event two weeks later with the bar set at 4 m, though they had access to their training facilities. Collectively, they aimed to beat the men's ninety-eight clearances, but fell short with eighty-five (Stefanidi, 34; Nageotte, 30; Newman, 21).[27] Stefanidi, the gold medalist in Rio, finished fourth in Tokyo, while Nageotte captured the gold medal; however, Newman, whose preparations were impeded by a concussion suffered in April 2021, did not emerge from Tokyo 2020's qualification round (but rebounded to win bronze at the 2024 Paris Olympics).

DAMIAN WARNER'S TOKYO 2020 OLYMPIC JOURNEY

Damian Warner, Alison Levine and Alysha Newman's fellow Canadian, and a bronze medalist in Rio 2016's decathlon (as well as a three-time medalist at the World Championships in 2013, 2015, and 2019), proved in the months preceding Tokyo the maxim that individuals may win Olympic medals, but it is a committed, engaged team behind the athlete that fosters the environment for such success.

Born and raised in London, Ontario, Warner's path to the Olympic Games was nontraditional. He had little involvement in organized sport as a youth, as his single mother lacked the resources to support these endeavors. Warner knew his mom would have found the money, but, sensing it was best directed elsewhere, he did not push for such opportunities. He recalls being very active with road hockey, basketball at the local playground, and hide and seek with his neighborhood buddies, but he did not try out for a team until Grade 8, when he made his elementary school softball and basketball teams. It was his first exposure to organized sport. "I wasn't very good," he concluded.[28]

In high school, "scared to get cut" from a team, Warner avoided trying out for basketball or football by telling friends he and his Mom lacked money for team fees. Then a friend put forward the funds, which quashed further excuses. He made the junior basketball team at London's Montcalm Secondary School in Grade 10, showed up for few practices, skipped too many classes, and eventually lost his standing on the team.[29] He played football in Grade 11, then, determined to put forth a better effort, used that positive experience as a springboard to try out for Gar Leyshon's senior basketball team.

Leyshon and his assistant basketball coach, Dennis Nielsen, heard about Warner and his athletic potential before he showed up for tryouts.[30] "Damian was like a mythological creature. You never saw him," recalled Leyshon. Nielsen taught Warner in a Grade 10 English class, but nothing stood out, other than "school wasn't his priority."[31] But when Warner appeared in his Physical Education class, Nielsen immediately ran to Leyshon and said, "This kid's great."[32] Leyshon had heard it before from Nielsen; he was "always pumping people's tires." However, Leyshon and Nielsen soon agreed that the reports and school hall gossip were accurate. Warner possessed a high degree of natural athletic talent—a "different level of athleticism," stated Leyshon, who observed at the first tryout, "It looked like he was wearing roller skates and everybody else was in snowshoes." Once he gained confidence, Warner helped Leyshon and Nielsen achieve a goal for Montcalm's basketball program by getting a team to the Ontario high school championships.[33]

At this same time, Dennis Nielsen decided to start a track and field team and pushed Leyshon to assist. He'd been helping Leyshon with basketball, Nielsen told him, and now it was his turn to reciprocate. "Dennis is a hard guy to say no to," said Leyshon, who then pushed his basketball players to come out for the newly minted track and field team. He rationalized that he could "keep an eye on them" this way, as several of his players faced challenges away from school. With an old dirt track and "sand pits full of dog shit and broken glass," as Leyshon recalled, the early days of coaching track and field presented a stiff challenge.[34] Warner, as part of the parade of Leyshon's basketball players to Nielsen's track and field team in Grade 11, gravitated to long jump, triple jump, and high jump, events he pursued through senior year.

With his high school studies concluding, Warner did not have US scholarship offers because he had not prioritized his schoolwork. "I wasn't a great student. My grades weren't that good. I skipped school all the time," he confessed. Still, he had left an impression on Leyshon and Nielsen, who presented him with the idea of taking up the decathlon after high school. "I had no idea what the decathlon was, but I trusted those guys," stated Warner, who resolved to "give it a try" in 2010.[35] Leyshon and Nielsen still considered themselves neophytes at coaching track and field, so they called Vickie Croley, the head coach of the track and field team at Western University of London, Ontario, and Dave Collins, who handled pole vault for Croley's team, to sound out their interest in working with Warner.

"Damian was really shy," recalled Croley. "I saw the dynamic power and speed he had. Just such a talented athlete. But he had to learn how to run better mechanically." She was on board. Collins was stunned when he got his first look at Warner using a pole vault: "I remember day one, the second Damian got off the ground with a pole my jaw dropped. I turned to Gar and said, 'What was that?'... To see something that athletic and that explosive, you knew instantly that this was different."[36] Collins needed no push as, like Croley, he was both intrigued and enthusiastic.

With Team Warner assembled and functioning well, Warner's ascent in the track and field world was rapid, as he finished fifth in the decathlon at the 2012 London Olympics at the age of twenty-two. More success soon followed: third at the 2013 World Championships (Moscow), first at the 2014 Commonwealth Games (Glasgow) and the 2015 Pan-American Games (Toronto), second at the 2015 World Championships (Beijing), and third at the 2016 Olympics (Rio).

Warner's early exploits attracted the attention of B2ten, a Montreal-based, privately funded organization dedicated to supporting Canadian athletes identified as having serious opportunities for Olympic and World Championships podium finishes.[37] Its genesis dates to the push for medals at the 2010 Winter Games in Vancouver. B2ten's budget derives from donations from a select number of individuals with ties to Canada's business world who have been likened to "alumni boosters at top NCAA schools."[38] These "members," though anonymous, have included the likes of Stephen Bronfman (heir to the Seagram's distillery fortune) and André Desmarais, who stepped down in 2020 as co-CEO of Power Corporation, a high-profile financial services company, after twenty-four years in the role. In its first eight years, B2ten, which has "no office, no computers and no land lines," raised C$30 million in support of these select Canadian athletes.[39] "We're not claiming we're building athletes from scratch," stated B2ten's cofounder and CEO Dominick Gauthier. "We're a conversion organization. Take top athletes, find what's missing and convert that to medals. Because that's what Canada is really bad at."[40] In 2015, Warner's athleticism was on full display at a B2ten event in Mont Tremblant, Quebec, when the invited participants were involved in an activity called PürInstinct.

Leyshon, who accompanied Warner to Mont Tremblant, was the oldest participant, lined up against a bevy of Canada's best athletes. He was named a team captain and permitted to make the first pick. "Damian," stated

Leyshon matter-of-factly. Hold on, said the organizers of the activity, we haven't explained the rules yet. "I don't care," answered Leyshon, "we're winning."[41] The participants soon learned PürInstinct challenges an athlete's decision making, determination, and fitness. The field is 27.4 m (80'10.7") long and 11.88 m (38'11.7") wide. At opposite ends of this field of play, there are end zones that are each 6.5 m (21'3.9") long. Competing teams are each composed of six players. Three players must move the ball collaboratively through passes the length of the field in sixteen seconds or less against two defenders without dropping the ball or being touched while in possession. When an offensive foray concludes, the other three players go on offense while two new defenders take the field. The game is divided into innings, so that both teams play on offense and defense, and lasts between fifteen and forty-five minutes.[42] "It's so much fun to play," reported Leyshon, while also affirming the wisdom of his first pick: "[We won]. We kicked the [expletive] out of everybody because I got to pick Damian first."[43]

Despite Warner's success, Athletics Canada, the country's national sport-governing body for track and field, believed for some time that he would be better served with more experienced coaching and tried to sideline Leyshon. "They named Vickie as head coach because they wouldn't accept me as his head coach because I didn't have any experience. Then, they didn't want her as head coach [after the Rio Olympics] because she wasn't good enough, apparently." Athletics Canada also pushed Warner to leave London. "They took his funding away and said he had to leave, right?" asserted Leyshon. "They did everything in their power to get him out of London. For years."[44] Warner, caught in the middle of the politics following the 2016 Rio Olympics, left London, along with his partner, Jen Cotten, to live in Calgary, so he could train with Athletics Canada's choice, Les Gramantik.[45]

Gramantik's place within the ranks of Canada's track and field coaching community was well known, and Leyshon regards him as a "great coach."[46] He was the Canadian national team's head coach at the 2008 Beijing Olympics, three Pan-American Games (2003, 2007, 2011), two Commonwealth Games (2006, 2010), and three World Championships (1999, 2001, 2007). Gramantik praised Warner's coaches in London but believed the group to be too big: "The only problem was there were too many of them. In a sport like decathlon, you need one voice. You can't have too many people talking to you all the time. Then you never know which way to turn your head."[47] However, after two years in Calgary, a fifth-place finish at the 2017 World Championships, and two wins at the prestigious Hypo-Meeting in Götzis, Austria, Warner pined for the familiar and his London team. Warner's calls to Leyshon commenced in 2017 and extended into early 2018. He missed his family, especially his mom, sister, and uncle. He batted away Leyshon's efforts to convince him to extend his stay in Calgary. Warner was coming home. The time away, reflects Leyshon, was very important, and benefitted Warner going forward: "People have to grow up and they have to be reborn sometimes ... he came back a different person."[48]

Warner was clear with Leyshon that he wanted more input into decisions regarding his training regimen and competitive schedule and sought a more collaborative relationship on this front. "I don't want to drive the bus," said Warner, "but I want to sit in the front seat."[49] Given he had been training for the decathlon for eight years, Leyshon understood that Warner "had his own ideas on what works" and heartily accepted his terms. And from a personal standpoint, he added, in his future interactions with Warner in training sessions and meets, "I had to understand that it wasn't basketball where you're yelling all the time"; Leyshon needed a focused, calmer approach to his coaching.[50]

However, Leyshon could not step aside from his job as a full-time high school teacher and its accompanying salary without remuneration for coaching; he and Warner needed to shore up their financial support back in London. Much of it came from Vito Frijia, a London-based construction engineer and president of the Southside Group. Frijia also owns the London Lightning of the National Basketball League of Canada (while also serving as the league's president since 2015). "He has done everything for us," said Leyshon.[51] In explaining his support for Warner's athletic endeavors, Frijia spoke of his personal qualities, especially his humble nature: "He's a world-class athlete and you would never know it from his attitude. His heart is in the right place so you want to help out a person like that. He loves London and London should love him back."[52]

Leyshon and Warner envisioned a two-year runway for takeoff to Tokyo. They held training bouts at International Management Group's facilities in Bradenton, Florida, once in 2018 and twice in 2019. They visited the Elite Athletic Training Facility in Chula Vista, California (near San Diego) in 2018, partly through Leyshon's friendship with Kris Mack, the Olympic Training

Damian Warner practicing for the pole vault at Western University's Thompson Athletic and Recreation Centre on May 1, 2019. Credit: 2019/ London Free Press, a division of Postmedia Network Inc./HENSEN, Mike.

Center residence program coach for USA Track and Field. They also had training stints at Louisiana State University and in Santa Barbara, California.

Warner's home training facility is Western University's Thompson Arena. "It is a hockey arena. It's not a track facility, really," confirms Leyshon. "It's a flat track around a hockey arena that's kept at ten degrees year-round. So, it's just possible to train there. But to train there for an entire winter is to invite injury. And, honestly," states Leyshon, "it's boring, it's cold, it's dark. [...] It's not a perfect setup for somebody who's trying to be the best in the world at an outdoor sport." This explains the emphasis on inserting regular training in warm weather environments into Warner's pre-Tokyo 2020 calendar. However, they backed off the travel schedule after the first year, as it seemed to be just too much. Though Warner appreciated the warmer weather settings and training sessions, as compared to his daily routine at Thompson Arena throughout Canada's winter months, he found himself drained from the travel.[53]

In 2019, Warner dealt with a measure of disappointment when sprains of both ankles, one a mere six weeks before the competition, compromised his performance at the World Championships in Doha (September 27–October 6).[54] Warner had been bullish on his prospects in Doha given his

Damian Warner completes a warm-up heave before practicing the shot put in July 2020. At the time, Warner drove daily to Strathroy, Ontario, some twenty-five miles from his home in London, to work out on a field behind Strathroy District Collegiate Institute. *Credit: 2020/London Free Press, a division of Postmedia Network Inc./HENSEN, Mike.*

strong momentum building toward the gold medal.[55] Despite hardly being able to walk, Warner still captured bronze, a success and result that Leyshon dubbed "crazy." Tendonitis and Achilles problems took a toll on his training in 2019 too.[56] With a significant break before the 2020 Olympics, Warner relished the thought of getting "back on the horse" with his training "for the Olympic year."[57]

In February 2020, the two were at Louisiana State University in Baton Rouge for an indoor track and field meet where Warner competed in the shot put, hurdles, and long jump. His performances confirmed he was on a good path and had left 2019's injury problems behind.[58] On an off day, they headed to New Orleans, coincidentally on the first day of Mardi Gras, and were startled by the small crowds. Soon they heard reports about COVID-19 and understood much change was afoot.[59] They returned home and continued to train. On March 13, Western University moved to remote learning and restricted access to its facilities, including Thompson Arena. Uncertainty prevailed in Damian Warner's world as well as in the lives of thousands of other elite athletes and their coaches around the globe who harbored dreams for Tokyo 2020 when the World Health Organization's (WHO) declared COVID-19 a worldwide pandemic that March 11.[60]

"This is going to change things," Gar Leyshon recalls thinking in the early days of March. Local elementary and secondary schools closed on March 13, as did Western University. Little did he know what awaited him and Warner. Leyshon's immunocompromised child fell ill and was isolated in a local hospital with his wife.[61] Warner, now dispossessed of his training facility, went outside to a local high school, Saint André Bessette Catholic Secondary School, but its public track was soon closed down. He then headed off to nearby Strathroy District Collegiate Institute (40 km from London), where he could work out behind the school without being seen from the road (as he was not supposed to be using the facility). When the IOC and Japanese organizers announced the postponement of the 2020 Tokyo Olympics on March 24, Warner had just completed an "awesome" discus practice before checking his phone for messages or updates, ultimately spotting a notification of the postponement. "It's kind of like someone like just popped the bubble," recalled Warner.[62]

The news startled Warner. He'd believed the IOC and Tokyo organizers would push through with the original schedule because "too much money was on the line." His immediate thought was, "So, do we come to practice tomorrow?" He and Leyshon resolved to take two weeks off "just to kind of wrap our heads around it."[63]

Mindful of the situation with his child, Leyshon stepped back from daily contact with Warner,[64] who picked up his training in Strathroy in the company of his partner, Jen Cotten, an accomplished former national-level track and field athlete, who ran with him and pushed him. Cotten's help aside, Warner reported, "those were some tough months, it just seemed like the weather was colder, and like the wind was stronger."[65] He was unable to train for the 110 m hurdles, pole vault, long jump, or high jump in Strathroy.[66] They were strange days: "I remember being downtown [in London] and seeing windows and doors boarded up and it was like from a movie, it was the weirdest thing. I was expecting zombies."[67]

His mind also raced with questions that had no answer. "How are we going to keep training?" he wondered. Could the Games go forward in a year? If so, he would then be thirty-one—what might that mean for his chances for a gold medal? If not, and the Games went back on schedule in Paris in 2024, he would be thirty-four. "It's like the further down the road it gets, maybe like, the less likely [a gold medal performance] could potentially be." Financial considerations also surfaced, as he had secured sponsor deals with "two or three really good companies" in the pre-Tokyo window and had even filmed commercials in Florida. What would happen to those deals? Would the sponsors still be there in a year's time if the Games proceeded in 2021? In the ensuing weeks, he viewed Instagram posts that confirmed his competitors, especially those situated in Europe, had access to their training facilities.[68] Though he understood and fully accepted the decisions made by national and provincial authorities, as well as Western University, he asked, "Even though we're doing the right thing, are we at a disadvantage? Your mind starts to go wild," concluded Warner.[69]

Warner's recollections of the uncertainty and doubt that pervaded his thoughts mirror the feelings of many athletes who aspired to participate in Tokyo 2020 and, for some, the precarious nature of their financial situations. "It was an extremely uncertain environment across the whole world," stated the IOC's sports director, Kit McConnell. "Athletes largely couldn't travel. Some of them couldn't train. They didn't know if they would still have a contract centrally from their National Federation, the sponsors, everything else." And everyone was concerned about any prospective qualification process in the face of travel bans.[70] COVID-19 severely tested their resilience.

During summer 2020, Ontario residents had access to golf courses, though restrictions were imposed on the number of tee times in a day, arrival-time windows at a course before scheduled tee times, the use of power carts, and the need for masks. Clubhouse entry was limited to paying green fees and using washrooms; holes were modified so that flags were not removable, and no one needed to pull their ball out of a hole. Still, golfers in the province flocked to the courses. One such golf enthusiast was Leyshon, who met up for a round with Nielsen and fellow teacher, Ryan Stafford, in late summer 2020. Leyshon spent some time lamenting to his golf partners about the limitations on Warner's training in the upcoming winter months and the unknowns going forward. We had "nothing," stated Leyshon glumly. Stafford floated the name of his cousin, Scott Stafford, London's managing director for parks and recreation. Maybe he'd have an idea or two, offered Ryan.[71]

Ryan facilitated a conversation between Leyshon and Scott, who was willing to assist if possible. Leyshon's late father, Glynn,[72] was one of Scott Stafford's former physical education professors at Western. Stafford also knew Nielsen through local track and field circles because one of his daughters was accomplished in the sport. Damian Warner's accomplishments were certainly well known to him too.[73] With more than thirty years of experience working for the city in roles including arena operations, roads and transportation, community sports, and parks and recreation,[74] Stafford was as well positioned as anyone to brainstorm a possible solution.

Stafford concluded the options were few. The city's staff maintained ice in a few indoor arenas during the summer months and would do so going forward because of the uncertainty over youth hockey schedules in the upcoming fall and winter months. Of those arenas with no ice installed, or "dry pads," Stafford quickly struck Silverwoods Arena from his list, as the ceiling was far too low to throw a discus or javelin. This left only Farquharson Arena, the city's oldest arena, a building constructed more than sixty years prior and that had been once targeted for demolition. No ice had been installed, as its small dressing rooms precluded social distancing for youth hockey players, coaches, and parents should play in the sport be greenlighted in the months ahead.

Leyshon and Nielsen met Stafford at Farquharson Arena.[75] "We thought, 'This is great,'" recalled Leyshon, "because [we've] got nothing."[76] Stafford ensured, along with the city manager, that all occupational health and safety issues were addressed, and he pored over provincial legislation to confirm that those athletes who planned to use the arena in addition to Warner were exempt from restrictions established as a result of the pandemic.[77] User fees were agreed upon with the London-Western Track and Field Club (as a number of its athletes also would use the facility),[78] and the planning process advanced, with Team Warner being granted access in October. Stafford and Mike Vandertuin, who managed financial allocations for sport within Stafford's unit, fielded requests from Team Warner as the work on the conversion unfolded, and did their best to assist with financial support when possible.[79] Six weeks later, after much heavy lifting, Warner was training in Farquharson Arena.

Many hands played a role in converting Farquharson Arena to Damian Warner's training facility for the winter months preceding the rescheduled

2020 Tokyo Olympics—in fact, as many as one hundred individuals. The process had a community feel to it and it generated significant pride within Team Warner.[80] All members of the team, including Warner, contributed to the labor required, as did those outside the team. Scott MacDonald, who recently had been hired to manage the London-Western Track and Field Club, recruited athletes to assist. Vito Frijia stepped up with money and equipment required for the work—perhaps most importantly, the offloading of rolled-up Mondo track left over from the 2015 Pan-American Games staged in Toronto, a 2.5-hour drive from London. John White, a father of one of London-Western's athletes, sent one of his company trucks to pick up the Mondo from Toronto, after Athletics Canada said it had no way to get it to London.[81] Vickie Croley marshalled a few coaches and a number of her athletes to offload John White's cargo when it arrived at the arena. The Mondo had been rolled up for more than five years, so it resisted any efforts to attach it to the floor of the arena pad until Leyshon and Nielsen devised a plan to glue the Mondo to sheet metal that could then be attached to the floor, a project taken up by Leyshon, Nielsen, Warner, and Taylor Ehrhardt, a London-Western athlete. Ehrhardt and Nielsen built an eight-meter-long jumping pit. Frijia supplied ten tons of sand and the front-end loader needed to move the six tons that were ultimately used. Ehrhardt hand-crafted the wooden throwing rings for shot put and discus in one assembly that could be turned over easily, depending on the discipline being practiced. Warner praised Ehrhardt's creativity and ingenuity.[82] Scott MacDonald had the long jump runway and pits for pole vault and high jump delivered from Western University.[83] To enable discus and javelin training, Warner, Leyshon, and Nielsen fussed with the suspension of tarps from the arena ceiling on a trial-and-error basis.[84] A renewed sense of hope and purpose prevailed.

Vito Frijia's continuing financial support was crucial, but Leyshon bristled at the rules governing Warner's training budget and wrestled with Athletics Canada officials to authorize expenditures for procuring needed equipment. Expense rules precluded use of the budget for equipment purchases, as it was targeted for travel and accommodations. Well, Leyshon argued, we can't go anywhere, so do we just lose the money? Athletics Canada relented.[85] Proprietors of "The Ceeps," a tavern haunt for generations of Western University's students, supplied tents and heaters, because there was no escaping that Farquharson Arena was just that—an arena—and the city was unable to heat the facility comparably to a home.[86] "If someone

It was certainly nothing fancy, but the conversion of Farquharson Arena to a decathlon training facility in fall 2020 permitted Damian Warner to continue preparations for competition in the Tokyo Olympics from November 2020 through early April 2021. *Credit: 2020/CTV News London, Ontario, a division of Bell Media/LALE, Brent.*

had told us, 'You're going to be running inside [Farquharson]' we probably would have cried. But," said Warner, "we [came] together with the community and all the athletes to put together as good a training situation as we [could]."[87] When Team Warner entered its new work environment in November, enthusiasm was running high. The will to make it work had been amply demonstrated and remained evident going forward.

The mere fact that the "end boards" of the hockey rink pad were 52 m (170′7.2″) apart limited Warner's training. He had about 40 m (131′2.8″) of Mondo track on which he could operate at full speed, so crash pads were installed at each end. For a hurdles workout, Croley designed a three-hurdle course Warner could clear after a start; then he could bounce off the pads and clear the same three hurdles on a return leg. "The boards would move, and it's got a big echo," reported Warner, "I hated those down-and-backs. You hit, then you have a second, reset and go the other way. It's extremely hard to do."[88] Though a 400 m workout was not possible, the team invested in a curved treadmill, and Warner did what he could inside a tent. To build up "speed endurance," he would do repeated runs up and down the track, punctuated by hitting the crash pads. Training for the grueling 1500 m had

Damian Warner's Olympic odyssey truly began with the 2012 London Olympics, where he finished fifth in the decathlon. Here, Warner is shown in competition at the 2012 Canadian Track and Field Olympic Trials in Calgary, Alberta, in June 2012. Credit: 2012/Calgary Sun, a division of Postmedia Network Inc./CHAREST, Al.

to wait until a return to outdoors training in 2021. Workouts for the 100 m were limited to 40 m sprints. The team emphasized his technique and starts. While discus and javelin practice were possible, there was a complete absence of results feedback for his javelin throws, as all that could be seen was the missile's contact with the tarps. Warner had to go by "feel." "It was like throwing in the dark," concluded Leyshon. Though compromised by a shortened runway, Team Warner saw long jump training as "closer to normal training." Pole vault training was shelved for some weeks as Warner did not like his poles and COVID-19 wreaked havoc on the delivery time for new poles. High jump practice proved challenging because of the compact setup and limited Mondo available for the run-up, but Warner persevered.[89]

As this phase of his training unfolded, Warner used an app called Coach's Eye extensively. Many of his training sessions were filmed so he could spend his afternoons and evenings at home comparing past meet performances with his training progress. He drew encouragement from this exercise, especially by analyzing his starts. He knew he was progressing with the long jump, shot put, high jump, and—once the new poles arrived—pole vault. "I'm getting better as an athlete," he told himself. Warner's resolve held for three months.[90]

Though local temperatures were unusually mild in December and January, the thermometer plunged in early February 2021. Even before the cold snap, the temperature in the facility had been wearing on Warner. Leyshon confirmed, "You couldn't get warmed up. [Warner] didn't sweat once in three months." His feet had been cold for weeks, given he was often in spikes with no socks.[91] In late February, recalled Warner, "I just had a couple of rough pole vault practices in a row, and I was just like . . . I don't think this is conducive to winning a gold medal at the Olympics." He was "worn down and tired," and thought perhaps he and his coaches were fooling themselves that his training would position him to perform well. His competitors were completing full decathlons and seemed "in awesome shape."[92] France's Kevin Mayer, the world record holder, organized a decathlon as early as December 2020 on Réunion Island near Madagascar in the Indian Ocean in order to achieve the Olympic standard for qualification.[93] Meanwhile, there Warner was in London, grinding out his days at Farquharson Arena, "just like being inside this, this box with no windows and freezing cold," remembered Warner. His mind was also occupied with thoughts of impending fatherhood, as Jen Cotten was expecting their first child in early March. This welter of feelings coalesced to bring Warner to a critical juncture, a "breaking point" in his mind, and he felt "overwhelmed."[94]

Leyshon, who knows Warner as well as anyone, had no consoling, uplifting words. "I was like, 'Dude I got nothing else. I don't know what to say . . . I got nothing here. We're here another five weeks, so don't tell me you're done because you can't be [expletive] done. There isn't anything else to do."[95] There was no escape to a warm weather training facility. It was a hard message for Warner to hear.[96]

Two "really rough weeks" followed. His "energy levels were dropping," noted Leyshon, "and he was moody, and he was complaining about stuff,"[97] but the gloomy atmosphere disappeared immediately with the safe arrival of his son, Theo, on March 11. "It was so amazing how it changed," recalled

Leyshon.[98] "After that," affirmed Warner, "it didn't matter, you know . . . I still trained, so I knew that I only had a little bit of time" to get the work in. Then, it was time to get home to his son. "It just all went away. Different motivations at that point." The weather improved, he got outside for training, "and things just started to like, even out a bit," Warner said.[99] The move outdoors in March 2021 instilled new life into Warner's training pursuits and gave him a brighter outlook toward what lay ahead. His 2020 Tokyo Olympic odyssey entered its final chapter.

2

TROUBLING SIGNS FOR TOKYO

In summer 2019, with the Tokyo 2020 Olympics some twelve months distant, preparations for the Games followed a familiar pattern of enthusiasm versus skepticism. "Critics are dubious," wrote the *Los Angeles Times*' Olympic beat writer, David Wharton, but "Japanese organizers are doggedly optimistic."[1] This "Olympic divide" separating critics and supporters plays out in most host cities in the run-up to the Olympics. Tokyo 2020's critics decried exploding costs, viewed as exceeding $20 billion (when the Olympics bidders in 2013 pledged costs of $7 billion), while the boosters pointed to record-setting domestic sponsorship of more than $3 billion, more than double London 2012's record-setting $1.2 billion. Japanese organizers also celebrated encouraging ticketing developments when 7.5 million Japanese citizens registered for the opportunity to procure some of the 3.2 million tickets made available in a first public sale.[2] "The fact that the talk is so much about not being able to get tickets," offered a buoyant Yuriko Koike, Tokyo's governor, "is a symbol, a representation of the enthusiasm and expectations that a lot of people have toward the games."[3]

This enthusiasm had withstood challenging moments. In 2015, Japanese officials discarded Tokyo 2020's original logo amid charges that its design was lifted from one employed by a theater in Liège, Belgium.[4] Mere months earlier, Tokyo 2020 organizers had abandoned British architect Zaha Hadid's design for the new Olympic Stadium when estimated costs surpassed $2 billion. They transitioned to a less extravagant and costly plan ($1.2 billion) submitted by Japan's Kengo Kuma.[5] In early 2019, Japanese Olympic Committee President and IOC member Tsunekazu Takeda resigned both of his positions.[6] Allegations resurfaced that he was involved with a bribery scheme connected to the Tokyo bid committee, in which $2 million was allegedly transferred to Papa Massata Diack, a reputed fixer from Senegal, and his father, Lamine, the former head of the International Association of Athletics Federations (1999–2015, now World Athletics), via a Singaporean company, Black Tidings. The money was allegedly meant to sway votes from certain IOC members. Takeda denied any wrongdoing.[7] Despite these trials, the affinity for the Olympics the Japanese people had developed over decades held firm. COVID-19 would test this bond in ways corruption allegations and cost overruns could not.

RESPECT AND ADMIRATION: JAPAN AND THE MODERN OLYMPIC MOVEMENT

Any account of Japan's century-plus association with the Olympic Movement, including the trying circumstances of hosting the 2020 Tokyo Olympics in 2021 amid the ravages of COVID-19, begins with Jigoro Kano, who, in addition to being the founding father of ju-jitsu (the forerunner to judo carried out in a sport context), pioneered his nation's introduction to the world of international sport. Kano exemplified a philosophical mien directly in tune with those sport-driven values that stirred Baron Pierre de Coubertin's motivations to reestablish in modern times what he perceived to have been glorified in Greek antiquity: a quadrennial Olympic festival that contributed greatly toward culturally binding together the Greek world. Coubertin hoped for the same in a modern, global context.

Jigoro Kano, the third of three sons, born in May 1860 to a sake-brewing family, grew up to be an undersized (5′2″), shy, studious individual. Bullied at school, he sought physical confidence and defense strategies from his modifications to the ancient art of samurai combat. In time, Kano's newly crafted system of martial arts became known as ju-jitsu; it eventually became the first of several martial arts disciplines to gain Olympic event status (contested for the first time in Tokyo in 1964) following its transition in a sport context to judo. Through higher education at Tokyo Imperial University (1877–1882), a scholarship grant supporting study abroad (Paris, London, Amsterdam, Brussels, and Berlin, 1889–1890), and subsequent directorships of school and governmental physical exercise programs, Kano made his way to the brink of Japan's earliest brush with Olympic matters.

Kano was coopted to the IOC by Pierre de Coubertin in 1909, the first Asian to gain such distinction. Subsequently, he journeyed to the 1912 Olympic Games celebrated in Stockholm to attend his first IOC Session meetings. In Kano's charge were two athletes, history's first Japanese Olympic competitors.[8] He also attended the first post–World War I Olympics (Antwerp 1920). Though he missed attending the 1924 Games in Paris, he culminated his "Olympic life" with his presence in Amsterdam (1928), Los Angeles (1932), and Berlin (1936). It was largely through Jigoro Kano's rising stature and influence within the IOC, coupled with his steadfast devotion toward Tokyo's quest to gain "honored Olympic Games host city status," that Japan was awarded the Games of the XIIth Olympiad, to be staged in Tokyo in the summer of 1940, and, as well, the Fifth Olympic Winter Games scheduled for Sapporo in early February.[9] Preparations commenced immediately following the 1936 Games. Unhappily for Japan, the devastating events of September 1939 and the opening of hostilities in World War II mirrored the cancellation measures Berlin faced in 1916 due to World War I.[10]

Hand in hand with Jigoro Kano's rising influence in IOC matters was Japan's expanding excellence in Olympic athletic competition. In a tally of total medals (in men's and women's events) achieved by all countries between Japan's debut in Stockholm in 1912 and the 1992 Summer Games in Barcelona, Japan ranked first in judo, second in gymnastics, second in volleyball, seventh in swimming, and eighth in wrestling. Beginning with the very first Olympic Winter Games in Chamonix, France, in 1924 to those in Albertville in 1992, Japan competed consistently and strongly, with occasional medal performances in ski-jumping and speed-skating.[11] The world first became aware of Japan's now fully recognized Olympic athletic-performance excellence in men's swimming at the 1928 Amsterdam Games, when five freestyle swimmers achieved a silver medal in the 4 × 200 m freestyle relay and a bronze medal in the 100 m freestyle event, giving an advance hint of what was to come.[12] At the Games of the Xth Olympiad in Los Angeles in 1932, a Japanese team of thirteen young men dominated the men's competitions as no other country ever had or would. Astoundingly, Japanese men won the gold and silver medals in every individual swimming event except one, the 400 m freestyle, in which Japan achieved bronze. Then, too, the team won the gold medal in the only relay event, the 4 × 200 m freestyle competition.[13]

Beyond all doubt, though, Japan's most historic "Olympic moments" occurred when the country hosted Olympic festivals themselves, primarily 1964's Games of the XVIIIth Olympiad in Tokyo, and secondarily, the Thirteenth and Twentieth Olympic Winter Games in Sapporo (1972) and Nagano (1998), respectively. The 1964 Tokyo Summer Games served as a

Japan's prime minister, Shinzo Abe, delivers an impassioned plea for IOC members' support of Tokyo's bid at the IOC's 125th Session in Buenos Aires, Argentina, September 2013. Credit: 2013/International Olympic Committee/JUILLIART, Richard.

debutante ball for democratic post–World War II Japan after completing a twenty-year transformation of one of the world's largest cities from a "firebombed ruin to an ultra-modern metropolis."[14] A new sewer system, a new port, two new subway lines, an eighteen-mile metropolitan expressway with double and triple elevated crossings, and a bullet train linking Tokyo with Osaka were among the more glamorous infrastructure projects. Tokyo 1964 marked the birth of the satellite era for Olympic television coverage, a development that leveraged greater revenue in future years from the sale of Olympic television rights for the International Olympic Committee (IOC), Organizing Committees of the Olympic Games (OCOGs), International Sport Federations (ISFs), and National Olympic Committees (NOCs). Olympic financial support totaling $2.8 billon was generated from the Tokyo Metropolitan Government, the treasuries of the nation's various prefectures, and the National Government's strongbox.[15] Through advanced standards and application of technology and technological expertise, striking individual and organizational efficiency—indeed, to world acclaim—the Tokyo Olympics symbolized Japan's return to the "civilized world."[16]

Japan has hosted two editions of Olympic Winter Games: Sapporo in 1972 and Nagano in 1998. In 1972, Sapporo, with a population slightly exceeding one million, was Japan's seventh largest city and the most populated urban center that had ever hosted the Winter Games. The Sapporo Games saw the debut of satellite transmission of the Olympic Winter Games in color. The finals of the 70 m ski-jumping event resulted in rapturous Japanese celebration as Yukio Kasaya (gold), Akitsugu Konno (silver), and Seiji Aochi (bronze) ascended the victory podium.[17] The Nagano Games in 1998 were marked by television revenues amounting to $513.5 million, the largest broadcast-revenue figure yet in Olympic Winter Games history, and an increase of 150 percent relative to the Games in Lillehammer in 1994.[18]

Thus, with a vibrant century-long Olympic genealogy established, the nation's major metropolis, Tokyo, realizing what its 1964 hosting experience had accomplished for Japan in both global political and economic consequence, and in measures of national pride and social cohesion, sought once again as 2020 approached to place itself "before the eyes of the world."[19]

THE IOC'S TOKYO 2020 (PANDEMIC) JOURNEY BEGINS

In 2019, Kit McConnell, the IOC's sports director, who serves as its point person with the ISFs, did not know much about the Chinese city of Wuhan. This soon changed. Born in Australia but raised in New Zealand, McConnell holds a BA in history and politics and a master's in business studies in sport administration. His involvement with the Olympic Movement began as an IOC intern in 1996 and 1997, which he leveraged into a position with the 2000 Sydney Olympics Organizing Committee. He returned to the IOC to assist with the 2002 Salt Lake City Olympic Winter Games and then spent eleven years as the tournament director for the Rugby World Cup, only to return to Lausanne as sports director in 2014. McConnell is centrally involved in the delivery of the sporting events at the Olympic Games from qualification plans through event scheduling. He oversees the Sport and Medical and Scientific Departments, (until recently) Esports, and boxing,[20] a sport the IOC took control of in 2019 because of the Association Internationale de Boxe Amateur's (AIBA) governance and finance issues, and its demonstrated unwillingness to effect needed reforms.[21]

AIBA's $16 million debt (which some projections held would rise to as much as $29 million), continuing questions about refereeing standards, and its election in November 2018 of Uzbek Gafur Rakhimov—an individual on the US Treasury's sanctions list for alleged involvement with "a global crime network"—raised alarm bells. Serbian IOC member Nenad Lalovic, who led the task force charged to investigate AIBA's operations, concluded in his damning report that AIBA "exposed the IOC and its commercial partners to unacceptable reputational, legal, and financial risks." The IOC Session formally sidelined AIBA on the recommendation of the IOC Executive Board in June 2019.[22] Boxing now fell within McConnell's purview. With the Asia/Oceania Olympic qualifying boxing tournament scheduled for Wuhan from February 3 through 14, 2020, he soon became much more familiar with this city of more than eleven million inhabitants in China's Hubei Province.

On January 3, the BBC published one of the first news items on a "mysterious viral pneumonia" that numbered forty-four cases, with eleven of them categorized as "severe." The World Health Organization (WHO) confirmed it was monitoring the situation.[23] "We started to get messages, media alerts, questions from national federations and National Olympic Committees about that event," stated McConnell, "and the stories that were coming of an outbreak linked with the fish markets in Wuhan." Frequent discussions with Chinese officials ensued.[24] Meanwhile, in Canberra, Australia's lightweight boxer Harry Garside was finishing preparations before traveling to Wuhan. One of the cleaners at Canberra's Australian Institute of Sport, who happened to be Chinese, warned Garside, "Ooh . . . there's a big, big problem over there with sickness." Garside shrugged off the warning. Mike Loosemore, the IOC Boxing Task Force's chief medical officer, was monitoring advice from Great Britain's Foreign and Commonwealth Office. Neither it nor the IOC was advancing travel bans.[25] However, in late January, with Chinese authorities reporting 9 deaths and 440 cases, the IOC Boxing Task Force, under the leadership of Japan's Morinari Watanabe, canceled the qualifying tournament in Wuhan.[26] Within days, it was moved to Jordan, where it was staged in early March.[27] "We dodged a bullet," said Garside a year later, mere weeks before winning a bronze medal in Tokyo.[28]

WINTER YOUTH OLYMPIC GAMES LAUSANNE 2020

While IOC officials deliberated on the prospect of staging the Asia/Oceania qualifying boxing tournament in Wuhan through the first three weeks of January, Switzerland hosted the Winter Youth Olympic Games (YOG) Lausanne 2020. More than 1,800 athletes from 79 countries descended on

Christophe Dubi, executive director, Olympic Games, fields a reporter's question at the IOC's press conference staged in conjunction with the Winter Youth Olympic Games Lausanne 2020, January 20, 2020. Credit: 2020/ International Olympic Committee/MARTIN, Greg.

Lausanne,[29] a city of some 140,000 on the shore of Lake Geneva. The downtown was "rocking," noted the IOC's Olympic Games executive director, Christophe Dubi. A native of Lausanne, and the son of Swiss hockey legend Gerard Dubi, he has always considered Lausanne a little on the "boring side," but from January 3 through 22, it shed its staid image. "The city was amazing," recalls Dubi. The streets and venues were teeming with people and the city was alive.[30] COVID-19 was a story but not a perceived threat.

Richard Budgett, the IOC's medical and scientific director and an Olympic gold medalist in rowing (Los Angeles, 1984), confessed his thinking was that COVID-19 was, much as had been the case with the SARS outbreak eighteen years earlier, not likely to reach Europe. "I'm probably too much of an optimist," concluded Budgett in explaining his contemporary thoughts. "I remember the Chinese team arriving [for the YOG in Lausanne] and people, we knew there was an outbreak in China, but it was over there."[31] Maria Bogner, head of the IOC's Olympic Studies Centre, served as a volunteer for the YOG and recalled one of the somewhat odd duties she was assigned: to smell the contents of water bottles of athletes returning to the Olympic Village, as a means of preventing underage athletes from sneaking alcohol

Members of the Netherlands delegation walk past the Vortex, the Athlete's Village for the Winter Youth Olympic Games (YOG) Lausanne 2020, on January 7, 2020. Lausanne's citizens as well as other Swiss residents filled the city's streets and venues during the competitions. Meanwhile, the first stories were surfacing in China about a new coronavirus. *Credit: 2020/International Olympic Committee/RUTAR, Ubald.*

into their residences. Though she recalled thinking this was not particularly hygienic for anyone, a particular risk linked to COVID-19 did not cross her mind, nor did it for those who tasked the volunteers with this duty.[32]

Christophe Dubi's role is to "increase the Olympic Games' value proposition" as a means of attracting the interest of prospective host cities, and then, once Games have been awarded, to "make sure we deliver." It is a position of immense responsibility with novel, robust challenges, as the IOC is in a "seller's position" with the Olympics, especially with respect to the Winter Games—"something new" for the IOC, which for years could anticipate multiple bid cities in any given cycle. Dubi graduated from University of Fribourg (Switzerland) with a degree in economics after he washed out as a student at Lausanne University. He comes from a family of hard-working entrepreneurs, shop owners in the Lausanne area, so he was one of the first to pursue a university education, partly because his father suggested this path instead of taking over the family business. When Dubi received his degree, Joseph Deiss, a member of the Swiss federal council from 1999 to

2006, and a past president of both Switzerland itself and the United Nations General Assembly, told him his degree was a "very, very cheap license, but you have your own opinion, and it matters." Deiss's counsel convinced him he had a chance to make a success of himself despite his less-than-prolific accomplishments as a student. He taught for a time at a private school following graduation, then worked for a finance company, but he understood his niche was eluding him. He also sensed "something was wrong" with the management of the company, so he left. A year later, he noted, its leader "was in prison."[33]

Dubi returned to teaching, but his father, who represented Switzerland at the 1972 Sapporo Olympic Winter Games, said he knew someone at the IOC, Gilbert Felli (who would become the Olympic Games executive director). Considering he could chart his connection with the Olympic Games back to his father's competition, when he was only three years old, maybe now things were coming full circle for him. Felli took Dubi on as a "trainee" in the late 1990s, and he benefitted from Felli's mentorship. Future IOC President Jacques Rogge supported hiring Dubi to assist with the Coordination Commission of the 2000 Sydney Olympic Games, which he chaired. He thrived during Rogge's presidency, eventually taking on the role of sports director (McConnell's current position). He replaced Felli as Olympic Games executive director when Felli stepped down in 2014 to become a senior IOC adviser for the 2016 Rio Olympic Games. When the University of Fribourg celebrated its 125th anniversary and Dubi was well into his tenure as a member of the IOC's staff, he was profiled in a university-produced booklet. "Okay," he thought, "if I have achieved one thing in a university context, it is to be in that booklet," he laughed.

Following the Winter YOG Lausanne 2020, Dubi took some vacation time. While away, the level of alarm over COVID-19 in media reports increased, and communication among IOC officials intensified. One of the biggest challenges facing Dubi, McConnell, and others in the weeks ahead was "clarity on information," McConnell observed. "Having enough information to make what would seem to be the right decisions, and finding that balance between all of the information that gives you comfort to make a decision and the time pressures of making that decision . . . finding that balance between making a decision with enough informed framing of the decision early enough to allow it to be successfully implemented, but late enough for it to be the right decision," posed a thorny problem.[34] That "point of tension," said McConnell, challenged politicians and health officials around the globe. Dubi, McConnell, and other members of the IOC's senior leadership team prioritized "constant communication and engagement" as well as "transparency" with Olympic stakeholders, something deemed vital to fulfilling the IOC's leadership role.

For IOC President Thomas Bach, coming to terms with the seriousness of the situation was a "gradual" process. He, too, fondly remembers Winter YOG Lausanne 2020 and a celebration held at the Olympic Museum in its wake to mark the Chinese Lunar New Year with members of the local Chinese community and visitors from Beijing. With the increasing numbers of media reports concerning cases in China and other nations, his thinking shifted to, "Okay, what does it mean? What does it mean for us? . . . From the very beginning," Bach said, the focus rested on asking, "How can we make the Games happen for the athletes?"[35]

Timo Lumme, the IOC's former director of television and marketing services, recalled distinctly the moment he believed the situation in China posed a possible global threat. Several days after the Winter YOG Lausanne 2020 concluded, he was watching the evening news and learned of a hospital having been built in Wuhan "in seven days. . . . At that stage, you realize that something big was going on."[36] His days were soon filled with conversations with broadcast and TOP sponsor senior officials who, "were already knee-deep in investment in terms of whether it was on-site stuff, whether it was campaigns, whatever it was." Senior executives of the Olympic partner firms needed to make decisions—"Well, do we carry on spending, do we do this?" Questions coming from the lower managerial ranks of these companies were reaching senior leadership, and the senior executives were turning to Lumme for answers. It was a frustrating time, he reports, given the immense pall of uncertainty and the fact that his department was unable to give clear direction on whether "it's going to happen, it's not going to happen. Spend, stop, you know, shut the taps off, put it off. Whatever."[37]

THE *DIAMOND PRINCESS*

As the Lausanne's Winter Youth Olympic Games closed, *The Economist* reported that the novel coronavirus identified by Chinese authorities a month earlier had spawned more than 600 cases in 6 different countries, leading to 17 fatalities. Scientists and health specialists were still assessing its transmissibility; what concerned them, however, was the early data on its mortality rate, because it mirrored that of the world's last encounter with a global pandemic, the Spanish influenza of 1918.[38] In their next issue, the magazine's staff provided a further indication that spread of COVID-19 (still called 2019-nCov) would prove challenging. China's reported 282 cases on January 20 mushroomed to nearly 7,800 within the next nine days.[39] In the same period, 4 cases outside of China grew to 105 in 19 countries. The unknown that remained in projecting the trajectory of COVID-19 was how many people experienced mild symptoms and thus didn't consider themselves sick, which could lead to additional spread.

On January 20, the same day that Chinese authorities reported 282 cases, Princess Cruise Line's *Diamond Princess*, with 2,666 passengers and 1,045 crew members, eased out of Tokyo's Yokohama Port for its planned six-day voyage, with scheduled stops in Hong Kong, Vietnam, Taiwan, and Naha (Okinawa), Japan, before a scheduled return to Tokyo on February 4.

Italy's Gennaro Arma was three years into his captaincy of the ship, an eighteen-story ocean liner built for approximately $500 million and operating since 2004. Unknown to Arma and his crew was the fact that one of its passengers, who disembarked in Hong Kong on January 25, had brought the novel coronavirus aboard with him. By the time the *Diamond Princess* returned to Tokyo one day early on February 3, the spread of COVID-19 from this passenger made clear the dangers of the contagion.[40]

Though a twenty-plus-year veteran with Princess Cruise Lines, Arma confessed that dealing with directives from the Japanese government and the cruise line during this period, while trying to limit the spread of the virus on board, meant that he and his crew were trying to transform the ship "into a colossal luxury hospital and oversee the logistics of food delivery, sanitization, and health care for a small city" with "no playbook, no dedicated training, [and] no dedicated protocol."[41] On the evening of February 3, Arma informed his passengers of the individual who disembarked in Hong Kong and that all passengers would be required to stay on board an additional day for screening. The crew had earlier commenced more frequent sanitizing of public areas, made hand sanitizer available, and more frequently changed buffet utensils, but it was not nearly enough to blunt the spread of the virus. When a number of gowned and masked Japanese healthcare workers boarded the ship later that evening, crew members became concerned. Following the workers' consultation with Arma, the captain instructed all passengers to return to their cabins.

By the next morning, initial testing revealed that nine passengers and one crew member had tested positive. Passengers were required to remain in their cabins for the next two weeks, by order of the Japanese government. The ship remained moored in the harbor. The number of positive cases climbed to 20 on February 6, 61 on February 7, and 135 on February 10. On February 13, the case count reached 218, a number larger than any recorded by the world's nations other than China.[42] Eventually, the ship's case count topped out at 712, with mitigation measures proving more effective for the passengers than crew.[43] As news about the *Diamond Princess* worsened, Olympic officials looked on with interest and concern.

THE GAMES WILL GO ON

With the ship's passengers and crew still under quarantine, IOC officials met with Japanese Olympic organizers in Tokyo for a two-day session commencing on February 13. Despite the 218 cases aboard the *Diamond Princess* and the appearance of COVID-19 in the Japanese population, carried by Japanese nationals flying home from Wuhan (taking total Japanese cases close to 250), Tokyo Olympic officials maintained a brave face and expressed their commitment to stage Tokyo 2020 in July and August. "They were very determined" to proceed, confirmed Thomas Bach.[44] The torch relay was scheduled for March. "I would like to make it clear again that we are not considering a cancellation or postponement of the games," stated Tokyo Organizing Committee President Yoshiro Mori, "let me make that clear."[45] The mayor of Tokyo 2020's Olympic Village, Saburo Kawabuchi, offered some hope: "Based on the various pieces of information we receive, it seems this virus is not as strong as the influenza virus. The virus is susceptible to humidity and heat. In Japan, we have a rainy season, which could defeat the virus."

John Coates, the chair of the IOC's Tokyo 2020 Coordination Commission, informed press conference attendees that the IOC expected reports from the Japanese government, the city, and Olympic organizers to assist the IOC in ensuring "necessary precautions" during the run-up to the Olympics. The presence in Tokyo of Richard Budgett, the IOC's medical and scientific director, signaled the IOC's concern over the burgeoning complexity of the situation.[46]

Meanwhile, as the end of the quarantine period on the *Diamond Princess* neared, various governments, including those of the United States, Australia, Great Britain, Canada, and Hong Kong, scrambled to establish logistics for getting their citizens home.[47]

John Coates, Tokyo 2020 Coordination Commission chairman; Christophe Dubi; Yoshiro Mori, president, Tokyo 2020; and Toshiro Muto, Tokyo 2020's CEO, are peppered with questions about the spread of COVID-19 and its possible impact on Tokyo 2020 at a press conference in that city on February 13, 2020. Credit: 2020/International Olympic Committee/TAKEMI, Shugo.

Mori's pronouncement and Kawabuchi's projection stood at odds with an opinion offered the previous week when Tokyo 2020's CEO, Toshiro Muto, said he was "seriously worried that the spread of the infectious disease could throw cold water on the momentum toward the Games." Muto softened his stance the next day; however, his initial thought was not without justification. China's F1 Grand Prix, scheduled for Shanghai in April, was scrubbed; the World Rugby Sevens rounds set for Hong Kong and Singapore were bumped from April to October; and even the SportAccord Conference, the annual gathering of international sport federation and business leaders—all of whom possessed Olympic ties—planned for Beijing in April was canceled.[48] In less than a week, organizers of the 2020 Tokyo Marathon, scheduled for March 1, pared the field from 38,000 runners to 176 elite runners and a few dozen para-athletes.[49]

Despite these developments, a period Thomas Bach labeled a "traumatic time," the IOC president recalled "unity" among the NOCs, ISFs, and the athletes who were consulted to continue planning for the Games in the summer. The athletes' focus was on the fallout for the qualifications process, not so much the prospect of the Games being affected schedule-wise. "And,

Some of the first passengers permitted to disembark from the *Diamond Princess* are driven away on a bus on February 19, 2020. Credit: 2020/Canadian Press Images/Associated Press/HOSHIKO, Eugene.

there was still great unity that we continue the preparations for 2020," recalled Bach. "And that we see how it evolves. It was not yet a pandemic. Nobody knew when it would finish. Nobody knew how it would spread, how far it would spread."[50] Bach confirmed that IOC officials were trying to "stretch out the clock"; "We were closely monitoring, hoping that time would play in our hands. That it could get under control."[51]

The following day, February 14, Coates, Mori, and Muto appeared "glum" while fielding a string of journalists' questions related to the emerging coronavirus. By this time, there were nearly 64,000 cases around the globe, punctuated by close to 1,400 deaths in China. Coates indicated nothing the IOC had received from the WHO was moving it to alter course, and he remained "100% confident" that Tokyo 2020 would be staged as scheduled. Mori said the Games would go ahead without any changes in modes of delivery.[52] In these early days, IOC officials wrestled with the knowledge that delaying the Games until the fall would wreak havoc with professional sport events to occur later in the year previously contracted by Olympic television partners (most especially NBCUniversal in the United States). What about the logistical planning and financial expense undertaken by

TOP (The Olympic Partners) and domestic sponsors for brand promotion in Tokyo during the summer? And what of all the tickets sold to prospective spectators living in Japan and abroad and their associated hotel bookings? These concerns help to explain the early steadfast commitment to staging Tokyo 2020 on schedule. Still, an economic tsunami was stirring, and Coates and his Japanese partners surely knew it, even if they were not yet prepared to acknowledge it publicly. A "question mark," stated Shigeru Omi, a former official with the WHO, hovered over the Games, as there was no means of foreseeing COVID-19's status in five months.[53] Coates, Mori, and Muto's trepidation is understandable.

Mori, a seasoned politician and former prime minister (April 2000–April 2001), and Muto, a former deputy governor of the Bank of Japan, were painfully aware of their country's struggling economy. Significant further disruption to the economy from fallout tied to COVID-19 and the threat to the scheduled Tokyo Olympics concerned them. Japan boasts the world's third-largest economy; however, several factors had conspired in late 2019 to trigger a decline of the country's GDP by 1.6 percent in the final quarter (annualized rate of 6.3 percent). An increase in the country's sales tax (from 8 percent to 10 percent as a means of dealing with the country's debt), severe "collateral damage" from the ongoing US–China trade war,[54] and October's major weather incident, Typhoon Hagibis (and its damage, estimated at $15 billion), were at the root of the rough fourth quarter. With recession fears sparked, and consumer spending dropping by 2.9 percent, COVID-19 merely added to officials' pessimism surrounding the months ahead.[55]

OR WILL THEY GO ON? DOUBTS EMERGE

Though Coates, Mori, and Muto espoused the IOC's and Japanese organizers' shared confidence in the unfolding of the Games on schedule, the likelihood of this happening became the subject of discussion and speculation within the wider Olympic community and beyond. Terrence Burns, who had vast experience in the world of Olympic marketing through his work with US-based Meridian Management (and the IOC's TOP program) in the late 1990s and early 2000s, and was an adviser to numerous past Olympic-bid cities, highlighted the difficulties of any internal debates among IOC officials and Tokyo's organizers on a path forward for Tokyo 2020. Cities, asserted Burns, certainly planned for contingencies in the case of "natural disasters such as earthquakes [and] fires," and past incidents like the Munich Massacre (1972), the Centennial Park bombing (Atlanta 1996), and 9/11 had forced them to game-plan possible terrorist attacks, but he had "never seen an Olympic organizing committee asked, 'Are you ready for a global pandemic?' "[56] David Hughes, Australia's Olympic team medical director, stated bluntly that there would be no "vaccine for coronavirus before the Olympics. We would need to know it is safe to take athletes into Japan."[57] Hitoshi Oshitani, a Japanese virologist with Tohoku University, stated that "we don't have an effective strategy [for dealing with COVID-19], and I think it might be difficult to have the Olympics [now]. But by the end of July, we may be in a different situation."[58] Yasuyuki Kato, a professor who specialized in infectious diseases at the International University of Health and Welfare in Narita, Japan, concluded what many feared: that Tokyo 2020 might become "a hub to disseminate the virus to other countries."

Dick Pound, the longest-serving IOC member and a former vice president (now an honorary member having celebrated his eightieth birthday in 2022), predicted that if conditions did not permit staging the Games in 2020, a cancellation was the more likely end result, versus postponement or changing location. He estimated a final decision on Tokyo 2020's fate could be delayed until late May.[59] "I'm sure somewhere within the walls of the IOC headquarters, there's a big board with various scenarios on it where people are thinking about, 'OK, what do we do in the worst case situation?' "[60] A few weeks later, John Coates rejected the need for the deadline proposed by Pound when he returned to Australia from Europe, duly compelled by government mandate to isolate for two weeks.[61]

As for what might have appeared on the "big board" Pound postulated, cancellation was the "cleanest alternative" in a legal sense, as consensus for such a decision between IOC officials and Japanese organizers was not required, and the Host City Contract granted the IOC the unilateral right to cancel Tokyo 2020. Some parties would have dealt with risk mitigation by securing insurance in the event the Games were canceled (for any reason by the IOC). The parties "might not have been entirely made whole" through insurance payouts, but it would have represented a somewhat palatable resolution as opposed to losing "their sunk costs and revenue flows." While the IOC possessed the legal authority to cancel the Games, "it was not an attractive option," stated Pound, "either for the host country, which had invested heavily in the Games, or the current generation of Olympic athletes who [were] preparing for the Games."[62] It was most assuredly not "an attractive option" for the television broadcasters and corporate sponsors, travel companies engaged in the sale of Olympic packages, or their clients planning to visit Japan to attend the Games.

Kit McConnell emphasized the plight of the athletes in this period of uncertainty and any consideration of canceling the Games. "If you're an athlete, 70 percent of the athletes at the Summer Olympic Games only ever go to one Games," stated McConnell. "And, we hear about the Michael Phelpses and everyone else, but 70 percent of the athletes go to one Games. So, this was their Games."[63] "There was a real intent to make the Games happen the whole way through," McConnell affirmed, and the "mission" remained clear.[64] "Our responsibility is to organize Olympic Games," stated Thomas Bach, "not to cancel them."[65] In this commitment, Christophe Dubi praised President Bach's leadership and resoluteness: "You don't cancel the Games. Yes, you can according to the Host City Contract," confirmed Dubi, "but you don't cancel the Games. This is not what the organization is designed to do. This organization is designed to deliver for the athletes the best world stage possible."[66] So, while canceling the Games was an option, it was one that the IOC consigned to the bottom of the list.

Pushing forward with the Games for their scheduled July 24 start despite the proliferation of COVID-19 around the globe "[could] put lives at risk" and force any "contracting parties and partners" to gauge whether to fulfil their obligations or "abandon them as part of [mitigating] financial and employee risk," concluded Dick Pound.[67] "There is no canceling an investment of 3 trillion yen (about $28 billion)," said Munehiko Harada, a professor at Waseda University's Faculty of Sport Sciences. "What can be considered," he continued, "is holding the games without spectators." Perhaps events deemed more susceptible to the spread of the virus such as judo or wrestling could be scrubbed from the event schedule, Harada suggested. Hideomi Nakahara, a visiting professor with Yamano College of Aesthetics who specialized in infectious diseases, was far less hopeful. He could not foresee COVID-19 being tamed on a global basis, and if athletes from regions rife with the disease were permitted to attend, others would pull out of the competition.[68] Might the Games, as Yasuyuki Kato feared, serve as a destructive superspreader event, even if spectators were not permitted? Staying the course might easily be deemed reckless and expose the IOC and Japanese organizers "to legal responsibility for, at the very least, negligence."[69] Would NOCs pull their teams from the competition? Would athletes be able to adequately prepare for competition and would the training environments possible around the globe differ in such a way as to alter the fairness and integrity of the competition?

Postponing the Games, perhaps by one calendar year, was, on the surface, a more appealing option. A delay would provide the world's scientists time to grapple with COVID-19, grant citizens around the globe the tools (principally, a vaccine protocol) and knowledge to combat the pandemic, *and* supply the Japanese the chance to showcase their efforts to give thousands of Olympians the opportunity to compete in what for most would be a once-in-a-lifetime opportunity. It was also the most complicated solution of the three options. However, while many journalists and sport officials considered the possibility of postponing the Games, IOC officials didn't openly discuss it with Japanese organizers until the proliferation of COVID-19 cases forced them to do so. Introducing such a topic early in the discussions in January and February, stated Thomas Bach, would have undercut the confidence of Tokyo's organizers. "We did not speak with the Japanese about it," observed Bach. "Because . . . confidence. If we would have raised this with the Japanese, they would have interpreted this, that we have lost confidence in them, that they can do it. And, then you would have the domino effect."[70]

Unwinding an Olympic festival, with all of the preparations required in their final stages, while realizing the process would need to be ramped up again at a distant date, had never been done before. There were many wild cards. First and foremost, any decision to postpone the Games had to be shared by the IOC and the Tokyo organizers.[71] Would the world's plight be substantially different in one year's time? What cascading effect would postponement have on the renegotiation of myriad contracts tied to staging the Games, such as those for television broadcasts, corporate sponsor programs, security, hotel rooms, ticket sales, medical services, and special arrangements with the Japanese government for athletes' access to Japan without visas?[72] Significant among these contractual arrangements was the presale of some 4,100 apartments comprising the Olympic Village for occupancy following the Games.[73] What about the pledged access to Olympic event venues following the staging of the Games in 2020? What would the impact be on ISFs and their schedules long established for 2021? The "Olympic contractual web," concluded Pound, is "immensely complex and interconnected across a broad range of issues."[74]

While these debates unfolded, medical experts in Japan, as was the case for their colleagues around the globe, were wrestling to unlock some keys to mitigating the spread of COVID-19. They sought to delay any further spike in cases to permit the country's medical system to manage patients who required hospitalization. A task force established by Abe's administration suggested people with mild symptoms remain at home, though the notion that COVID patients should be seen at hospitals at hours other than those assigned to people without COVID seems, in hindsight, a less-than-robust mitigation strategy. Companies were advised to permit work from home whenever possible and to stagger hours at workplaces to reduce the likelihood of jammed commuter trains.[75] Dentsu, Japan's behemoth advertising and public relations firm, announced on February 25 that 5,000 employees at its Tokyo office would shift to teleworking when an employee in his fifties tested positive, while a cosmetics firm, Shiseido Co., confirmed that 8,000 workers would begin to work remotely, though its storefront operations and production line would continue.[76]

Abe's administration absorbed repeated serious blows and withering criticism in the Japanese press over its early management of the COVID-19 crisis: "The administration was ill-prepared to cope with a crisis of this kind and public discontent is evident," concluded Hiroshi Hirano, a political psychology professor at Gakushuin University. Support for Abe's administration tumbled more than 8 percentage points to 41 percent, while the disapproval rate climbed to 46.1 percent.[77] Koichi Nakano, a professor of political science at Tokyo's Sophia University, labeled the Abe administration's performance "staggeringly incompetent." Although Japan confirmed its first COVID-19 case on January 28, and WHO identified COVID-19 as a concern two days later, more than two weeks drifted by before the country's Ministry of Health informed Japanese citizens how to alert medical officials of suspected cases.[78] Nakano noted with incredulity the government's decision to permit Japanese nationals to depart the *Diamond Princess* without a fourteen-day quarantine period as was imposed by the US, Australian, Israeli, and British governments following the transfer of their nationals back home. Some ninety officials who boarded the *Diamond Princess* during the quarantine period were released without a test even though four had become ill. The Ministry of Health reconsidered the situation and tested forty-one of them, but not "medical professionals and quarantine officers," who were judged to have taken necessary "precautions." As February drew to a close, the government's COVID-19 task force had met thirteen times, but Prime Minister Abe's attendance averaged a modest twelve minutes.[79] Japan was testing only 900 people a day while some surrounding nations had moved their capability to 10,000.[80] Abe, judged Nakano, was "largely invisible." He and China's Xi Jinping, stated Nakano, likely wished to keep their "distances from the crisis for fear of being held responsible for its consequences."[81]

Should one think that Nakano was a lone voice, Yoichi Masuzoe, a former governor of Tokyo, and minister of health during Abe's first tenure as prime minister, judged the government's response to COVID-19 "disastrous." Ben Dooley, a *New York Times* reporter specializing in Japanese business and politics, concluded that Abe's approach to COVID-19 had "rapidly drained the reservoir of goodwill he had built up over seven years in office."[82] Reports also surfaced that some Tokyo residents, shaken by the government's performance and subpar communication concerning the pandemic—most especially a recent decision to close Japan's schools—were squabbling in queues outside pharmacies in their pursuit of masks, and that a wave of "panic-buying of toilet paper" had set in.[83]

SHINZO ABE AND THE 2020 TOKYO OLYMPICS

Much was on the line for Shinzo Abe and Japan concerning the staging of Tokyo 2020. The Games were to be the "crowning event" for Abe as the end of his second presidential term neared (2021). No other Japanese prime minister has served nine years in the position. In 2012, when the Tokyo bid committee readied its plans under the banner, "Discover Tomorrow," nearly two-thirds of Japan's population and Tokyo's residents supported the project. Even more, 78 percent and 81 percent, respectively, expressed confidence that Tokyo 2020 would "leave positive legacies in Japan."[84] Japan's resilience in the face of the "Triple Disaster of 2011," when the country weathered an earthquake, tsunami, and the Fukushima nuclear disaster, was to be on full display.[85]

When the IOC awarded the Games to Tokyo in 2013, the bid team projected the cost of hosting the Games at $7.3 billion. By December 2019, Tokyo organizers confirmed this figure had ballooned to $12.6 billion. However, Japan's National Audit Board ventured in a lengthy report that the true costs would exceed $20 billion. Government agencies and Olympic organizers have long sparred over what represents "Olympic-related" costs. *Nikkei*, a Japanese financial newspaper, and *Asahi Shimbun*, a daily newspaper, pegged the costs at $28 billion.[86] In March 2019, Tsunekazu Takeda's resignation filled much of the domestic and international news cycles tied to Tokyo 2020.[87] The athletes, the crowds, and the energy and enthusiasm that accompanies the Olympic Games had promised to chart a different, more positive narrative for Tokyo 2020. Then, amid scandals over costs and votes, COVID-19 hit and "changed everything"[88] for the Japanese people and Shinzo Abe.

There is little doubt that the close, personal relationship that Abe and Thomas Bach forged amid the backdrop of the Tokyo 2020 Olympics factored prominently in (ultimately) moving Japan to stage the games in 2021. In Abe, Bach found an individual cut from much the same cloth as he had been, a learned individual of energy, dedication, and humanistic qualities. The two supreme leaders of the primary forces behind ensuring the Games indeed would take place, despite the severely trying conditions of global health, were both men of substance.

Shinzo Abe was born on September 21, 1954, in Tokyo, a vast, sprawling metropolis still bearing some of the ravages inflicted by American B-29 bombers during the closing stages of World War II. That year and through much of Abe's youth, Tokyo, like greater Japan, existed under American occupation and governmental authority. An examination of young Shinzo's ancestry foreshadowed a life in politics, but the ideological underpinnings of his lineage actually presaged two possible callings. His maternal side beckoned him toward a political career underscored by an enthusiastic approach to Japanese nationalism. During World War II, his maternal grandfather, Nobusuke Kishi, had been vice minister of armaments in the cabinet of Prime Minister Hideki Tojo. In postwar Japan, Kishi served as the nation's prime minister (1957–1960). Alternatively, from Abe's paternal side sprang a more liberal-democratic wellspring. Though his paternal grandfather, Kan Abe, served in the Japanese House of Representatives during the war, he was a stalwart pacifist, a vigorous antagonist to military conflict and Tojo's expansionist designs. Abe's father Shintaro, born in 1924, experienced the high and low moments of World War II during his high school years. Immediately following graduation in 1944, he entered naval flight training to become a fighter pilot in the Pacific theater. As a desperate Japan staggered through the last phases of the war in the spring and summer of 1945, Shintaro Abe volunteered for and commenced training to become a kamikaze pilot. Fortunately, this deadly mission ended abruptly with Japan's surrender shortly before he completed his training. The catastrophic life-ending atomic explosions over Hiroshima and Nagasaki in early August 1945 terminated the war and almost certainly spared Shintaro's life—and, of course, led to the eventual birth of his son, Shinzo.[89]

With both grandfathers having carved out careers in politics (including as prime minister), and his father having served in Japan's House of Representatives with ministerial appointments over a thirty-three-year government career—including four years as minister of foreign affairs (1982–1986) under Prime Minister Yasuhiro Nakasone—Shinzo Abe followed his distinguished forebears. Following high school, Abe attended Tokyo's Seike University, graduating in 1977 with a degree in political science. Sent abroad to America, he studied English, history, international relations, and political science over three semesters at the University of Southern California. A three-year stint working for manufacturing giant Kobe Steel preceded his initial foray into politics, first in several lower-rank government positions, followed by a lengthy tenure as private secretary to his father, a leader in Japan's Liberal Democratic Party.

Shintaro Abe died in 1991; two years later Shinzo Abe was elected to the House of Representatives, commencing a political career that ended with his assassination on July 8, 2022, at the hands of an angered zealot whose mother had suffered bankruptcy from investments made in conjunction with the Unification Church, to which the Abe family had political ties. Abe's professional career was marked by two terms as Japan's prime minister (2006–2007, 2012–2020), cut short by resignation because of medical issues in August 2020. His near-decade in that position marks him as Japan's longest-serving prime minister. In encapsulating Abe's life, little doubt remains that he, like his father, Shintaro Abe, and grandfather, Nobusike Kishi, was a nationalist, intent on building and securing Japan's status, particularly in the Asian world: economically by trans-Pacific partnerships; politically by engaging in energetic dialogue with both domestic and foreign authorities on problem areas; and militarily by reforming Japanese defense forces, revising Article 9 of the constitution (outlawing declarations of war), and pursuing treaties of collective security.

A central thrust of Abe's political leadership involved efforts to reform Japan's stagnant economy. At its core, Abe's economic agenda, dubbed "Abenomics," reflected three priorities: (1) easing monetary policy and lowering interest rates so that consumers and businesses could more readily borrow (and spend) money; (2) enhanced government spending on infrastructure and tax breaks for companies to provide fiscal stimulus; and (3) a pledge to facilitate corporate reforms,[90] specifically by dealing with nepotism, "changing unhealthy work cultures,"[91] and pushing for the entry of more women and migrant workers into Japan's workforce.[92] While most credit Abenomics with improving and lending a measure of stability to the nation's economy, his lofty goals for corporate reform proved elusive.[93]

Throughout the 1980s Abe accompanied his father on some eighty visits to foreign countries, experiences that educated him on the art, science, and importance of building relations with foreign leaders. In that last realm, his connection with Thomas Bach and commitment to Tokyo's Olympic mission was to be the closing chapter in a distinguished prime ministerial career, though a controversial one for some Japanese citizens in light of his perceived "hawkish" approach to defense and foreign policy.[94] As the 2020 calendar turned to March, despite the worrying early ripples of the newly isolated coronavirus, Abe, Tokyo 2020 organizers, and the IOC remained resolute in their determination to stage the Tokyo 2020 Olympics in five months' time. But COVID-19 continued to churn.

With a better understanding of the significance of the pandemic's threat in mid-March, Abe's government amended Japanese law to permit a state of emergency to be declared, on the advice of an advisory panel, if conditions warranted. An emergency represented a "situation in which the capacity to provide medical care will reach its limit and people's lives and health will be put at risk unless measures are taken."[95] All previous measures enacted to mitigate the spread of COVID-19 in Japan had required the cooperation of the country's population. With an emergency declaration now within Abe's reach, what would be Tokyo 2020's fate?

3

POSTPONEMENT

On February 20, 2020, deaths due to COVID-19 surpassed 2,100 worldwide. Four days later, China reported 77,000 positive cases, while the number of deaths in the country had climbed beyond 2,500. Later that same day, Tedros Adhanom Ghebreyesus, the World Health Organization's (WHO) director general, stated, "Using the word pandemic does not fit the facts, but it may cause fear." Still, the rising number of infections outside China, especially in Iran, South Korea, and Italy, informed everyone that "the increasing signs of transmission outside China show that the window of opportunity for containing this virus is narrowing."[1]

IOC Medical and Scientific Director Richard Budgett recalled, during that February, continuing support for staging the Games among his counterparts affiliated with the International Sport Federations (ISFs) and National Olympic Committees (NOCs). "We all talked about COVID-19," said Budgett, "but no one thought it would really affect the Games. And, then slowly you began to realize, and it wasn't really until March, I believed it was a serious threat."[2] By March, the "unity" that IOC President Thomas Bach had highlighted within Olympic stakeholder groups toward pressing forward with plans to stage the Tokyo 2020 Olympics dissipated. Budgett was one of the first IOC officials to witness some Olympic stakeholders' resolve to stay the course begin to fracture.

Budgett had studied medicine for three years at Cambridge University, where he took up rowing (though not for Cambridge), before moving on to London Teaching Hospital, where he seriously pursued the sport at the University of London. He surprised himself with his ability to withstand the physical demands and the prolonged tryout with University of London's rowing team, thinking over the course of three months, "it will be over soon." But Christmas arrived and he "had not been thrown out."[3] He raced in the coxed pairs at the 1981 World Championships and captured a bronze medal. This achievement steered him to continue his rowing pursuits while furthering his medical education. He rowed at the 1984 Los Angeles Olympics and, along with the legendary Sir Steven Redgrave (who won the first of his five gold medals at consecutive Olympic Games), Andy Holmes, Martin Cross, and coxswain Adrian Ellison, won the gold medal in the coxed fours event. However, his professional goals in medicine precluded extending his time as an elite athlete.

Upon Budgett's return from Los Angeles, the British Olympic Medical Center somewhat fortuitously opened at the same hospital where he was training. Following completion of research projects there, he branched out into sport medicine. Over sixteen years, he served as the chief medical officer for several British teams at the Olympics before being named chief medical officer for the 2012 London Olympic Games. This job took him to Beijing and Vancouver as part of the London 2012 delegation. He could not contain his excitement at being named the IOC's medical and scientific director in 2012, but his wife counseled him to "take two weeks off" before assuming his new duties. He accepted her advice, later noting, "Little did I know how much excitement there would be" over the ensuing ten years. His primary duties involved protecting the health of athletes at the Olympic Games (in part through educational initiatives), overseeing the process in doping control at the Olympics (though much of the technical work has passed to the International Testing Agency in recent years),[4] "raising the level of sport and exercise medicine through the world," and working with colleagues in sport medicine to generate "consensus statements" concerning accepted practice with athletes with issues as they continue to evolve.[5]

In early March 2020, Shinzo Abe took additional steps to lessen the spread of COVID-19. Visitors from South Korea and China were required to quarantine at certain facilities and avoid the use of public transportation for two weeks. This touched off immediate concerns about the country's tourism industry given that South Korea and China provided 40 percent of Japan's tourists in 2019. Japanese citizens returning from China and South Korea were similarly required to isolate for two weeks. Abe "requested" that Japanese schools close until the end of the normal spring break in early April. He discouraged the staging of sport and/or entertainment events with large crowds.[6] As noted, Parliament also granted the government the power to declare a state of emergency, in serious situations and with an advisory panel's concurrence, so Abe was no longer compelled to ask for the public's cooperation with restrictive measures.[7]

Although Olympic organizers were steadfast in their commitment to stage Tokyo 2020 on schedule, Jonathan Finnoff, Team USA's chief medical officer, soberly noted that athletes, coaches, and trainers needed to be mindful that "it is a dynamically changing situation."[8] Budgett confirms that March 2020 marked a turning point when many fellow medical officers who were aligned with the NOCs and ISFs—and who, mere weeks earlier, had possessed few concerns about staging Tokyo 2020 on schedule—changed their thinking. Consensus evaporated swiftly. Some said, "Look, let's make this work, let's make it happen," related Budgett, while others said, "No, no this is irresponsible. We can't do it." This "division of opinion," he observed, "was hard" and posed a challenge, as did the wait, he concluded, for the WHO to "stick their neck out" and declare a pandemic.[9]

Finnoff's assessment, an accurate one and obvious to many observers, prompted fissures in the consistency of messaging from Japanese officials, especially when a Tokyo Organizing Committee member, Haruyuki Takahashi, went off script and speculated on the possible need for a one- or two-year delay, something he was even prepared to recommend. Yoshiro Mori, Tokyo 2020's President, swiftly called a press conference, labeling Takahashi's thought as "outlandish"[10] and dismissing the possibility of a delay. Takahashi's opinion, stated Mori, ran counter to that of the Organizing Committee. Takahashi was required to express regret for his comments. Seiko Hashimoto, Japan's Olympic minister, backed Mori's thinking, telling the Japanese parliament that a delay was "impossible." And, yet, Takahashi was only assessing things as they were rapidly evolving in early March.[11]

A CLIMACTIC DAY: MARCH 11, 2020

The IOC continued to prioritize open lines of communication with the Japanese government, the Tokyo metropolitan government, the 2020 Tokyo Olympic Organizing Committee, and the Japanese National Olympic Committee. "There still wasn't a single source of truth for what COVID meant and what particularly COVID meant in Japan," stated Timo Lumme, former IOC director of television and marketing services,[12] but leaning on the partnerships IOC officials had established with Japanese contacts was important. The two weeks leading to postponement were challenging, stated Christophe Dubi, "because in these two weeks no one knows what happens in the world. Everybody is in panic."[13] Rampant media speculation swirled about the future of Tokyo 2020. Pressure mounted on IOC officials, though in assessing this period, Kit McConnell believes the pressure on IOC decision makers was even higher after the Games were postponed. Before the postponement, commented McConnell, "you didn't have to have any, every answer"; after the IOC committed to holding the Games in 2021, "you did."[14]

Within hours of the drama involving Haruyuki Takahashi having played out in Tokyo on March 11, Dr. Anthony Fauci, director of the US National Institute of Allergy and Infectious Diseases, appeared before the House Committee on Oversight and Reform. His would become a familiar face and voice for Americans in the months ahead. Revered by some for his honesty, and reviled by others for symbolizing perceived government overreach into their personal lives in his attempts to control the virus, Fauci stated that COVID-19 "would get worse." Professional sport events, he observed, should they proceed, should do so without spectators. Ninety minutes later, in Switzerland, Tedros Ghebreyesus declared COVID-19 a global pandemic.[15] Global stock markets tumbled, with the Dow Jones dropping 2,352.6 points (9.9 percent).[16]

A flurry of sport cancellations and postponements soon followed. The International Tennis Federation delayed the Federation Cup finals scheduled for Budapest in April. The World Figure Skating Championships in Montreal, due to open the following week, were canceled. Europa League soccer matches that pitted Italian and Spanish sides were canceled due to newly announced travel restrictions.[17] As the "climactic" day closed, the National Basketball Association (NBA) suspended its season, following the announced positive test of Utah Jazz center Rudy Gobert.

Those whose lives were tied to the global sport calendar as administrators, athletes, participants, spectators, or workers were reeling. Even President Donald Trump, who had spent much effort over the preceding weeks downplaying the virus, appeared to accept the gravity of the situation in his remarks during a hastily scheduled address from the White House that evening.[18] The National Hockey League (NHL) suspended its season on March 12, while Major League Baseball (MLB) closed training camps the same day with the hope of reopening them in two weeks (though by March 16, Commissioner Rob Manfred concluded that the best-case scenario would be a restart in mid-May).[19] US Senators Jerry Moran (R-KS) and Richard

Blumenthal (D-CT), while calling cancellation of the Olympics "a last resort," jointly put Thomas Bach and Olympic leaders on notice: "If not handled properly, this year's Olympic Games present a dangerous opportunity for COVID-19 to spread at unprecedented levels throughout the globe."[20] The flurry of sport cancellations became a frenzy. Haruyuki Takahashi, though shamed in the aftermath of the March 11 press conference, must have been somewhat heartened by the knowledge that he had seen what was coming for the sports world.

Despite the tumult, Japanese resolve at the highest levels concerning the prospects for the Games remained strong: "There is no change to the government stance that we will make preparations for the Tokyo Games as planned," stated Chief Cabinet Secretary Yoshihide Suga, "by keeping close contact with the International Olympic Committee, organizers, and the Tokyo metropolitan government."[21] This resolve clashed with the fact that Japan had reported 1,300 COVID cases in thirty-four of the country's forty-seven prefectures.[22] Yet Japan's Olympics minister, Seiko Hashimoto, conveyed measurable determination in stating, "Neither the IOC nor the Tokyo Olympics organizing committee are considering postponing or canceling" Tokyo 2020, nor were "downsizing or shutting spectators out of events" under discussion. Abe shared similar sentiments in a telephone conversation with Trump on March 13.[23] That day, Tokyo's Nikkei Index, already ravaged by COVID-19 fears, dropped a further 6.03 percent, hitting 17,435.05—its lowest point since November 2016.[24] The Japanese government and Tokyo Olympic officials expressed confidence going forward, but Japan's citizens were shaken. By mid-March, nearly 70 percent believed the Games would not proceed as planned in July.[25]

THE EUROPEAN BOXING QUALIFYING TOURNAMENT IN LONDON

Against the tide of cancellations and postponements, the IOC's Boxing Task Force pressed forward with the European qualifying tournament starting on March 14. Seventy-seven Olympic spots were to be contested, fifty for men and twenty-seven for women, and participants exceeded three hundred. At the time, some sport events continued in England (though Premier League football suspended its season on March 13). Public Health England was centrally involved in discussions with IOC Boxing Task Force officials concerning mitigation, temperature checks were mandated, and hand sanitizer was liberally available. The ten-day event soon shifted to not admitting spectators within three days of its opening, but as a result of the spiraling number of travel restrictions and quarantine protocols, and a desire to permit the participants to return home, the Boxing Task Force suspended the event.[26] British Prime Minister Boris Johnson announced the same day that he "advised against mass gatherings." As of March 17, Johnson effectively shut down the United Kingdom's sport schedule, as "mass gatherings requiring emergency workers are something 'we are now moving emphatically away from.' "[27]

Ten days later, Eyüp Gőzgec, president of the Turkish Boxing Federation, openly questioned the wisdom of starting the event, announcing that three Turkish boxers and a coach had tested positive for COVID-19 (though one boxer's test later proved to be a false positive) and charging that they contracted the illness in London. There were no firm means of confirming this was the case given the timeline. Still, Gőzgec charged that "athlete health was absolutely not considered first—that's the whole reason for our frustration."[28] The Croatian Boxing Federation reported positive tests registered by two coaches and one boxer, and the organization's epidemiologist opined that the individuals likewise were infected in London. An indignant Gőzgec piled on with his criticism of the IOC officials: "This is the disastrous result of the irresponsibility of the IOC Boxing Task Force."[29] Gőzgec's frustration is understandable, though the depth of his public anger was likely fueled in part by his status as a member of AIBA's Executive Board, the organization whose power the IOC had stripped. The entire scenario highlighted the challenges, noted by McConnell, to make the right decisions in real time in an uncertain environment.

THE COVID-19 SPIRAL CONTINUES

The cascading series of postponements and cancellations concerned aspiring Olympians who had pinned their hopes of journeying to Tokyo on the yet-to-be-staged qualifying events. Disruptions swept through regional rowing, judo, weightlifting, and badminton qualifiers scheduled worldwide.[30] In the wake of President Trump's announcing a thirty-day travel ban on twenty-six European countries, members of the US biathlon team attending a competition in Finland were roused from their beds and rushed to the airport. The departure was hastily arranged, admitted Max Cobb, president of the US Biathlon Federation: "We didn't ask them. There wasn't time."[31] The Boston and London Marathons, the latter serving as an Olympic qualifier for British runners, were postponed to September and October, respectively.[32] The Paris and Barcelona Marathons were similarly delayed.[33] Cam Levins, Canada's record holder in the marathon, and in pursuit of a place on his nation's Olympic team, lost his qualifying chance when the Rotterdam Marathon was also postponed. "If the Tokyo Olympics do indeed take place this summer," stated Levins, "I urge the International Olympic Committee, World Athletics, and Athletics Canada to take this global crisis into consideration when naming all competing athletes."[34] Veteran Australian track and field coach Nic Bideau sensed the need for a year's delay for Tokyo 2020 because the increasingly ravaged qualification process had left so many countries unable to select athletes.[35] Belief in the likelihood of a delay also permeated the senior ranks of British sport officials.[36] Speaking to the inability of his country's athletes and those in some other nations to train as a result of closures of "gyms, pools, and training centers," together with the IOC's and Japanese organizers' resolve to push forward, Alejandro Blanco, long-time president of the Spanish Olympic Committee, spotlighted how the inequities present in the global athletic community would skew the competitive landscape.[37]

Coincident with these events, Richard Budgett announced the postponement of the scheduled IOC World Conference on Prevention of Illness and Injury in Sport scheduled to open within days in Monaco. He had just concluded meetings there with the ISF and NOC medical directors, but attendees who planned to attend the follow-up World Conference departed the city-state.[38] Other prospective attendees, facing travel bans invoked by their institutions, were unable to make the journey. "It begs the question," wrote the *Sydney Morning Herald*'s Phil Lutton, "that if the IOC-hosted medical conference in Monaco could not be held without significant disruption, what hope does the IOC have of staging an Olympic and Paralympic Games that would see almost 15,000 athletes, tens of thousands of officials and media, and up to a million fans descend on Japan in a few months?"[39]

In a March 17 press release, the IOC's public posture remained steadfast: "With more than four months to go before the Games there is no need for any drastic decisions at this stage; and any speculation at this moment would be counterproductive."[40] Bach and the IOC still did not wish to undercut the confidence of 2020 Tokyo officials in their ability to stage the Games by discussing the possibility of a postponement.[41] "Everything" in

Tokyo, stated Christophe Dubi, IOC executive director, Olympic Games, "was designed to be rocking the world in probably one of the most exciting metropolises of the world."[42] The work of the Tokyo organizers had been "top grade," affirmed Timo Lumme, with the Tokyo 2020 Olympics ready to "set new benchmarks."[43]

There were reasons to extend the IOC's period of consideration for the effect of COVID-19 on the Games. Retired Canadian race walker Iñaki Gómez, a member of his country's Olympic Athletes' Commission, sympathized: "I recognize they are treading a tight line. They're conscious of the brands, they're conscious of the Japanese economy, and they're in a precarious position." Still, for Gómez, COVID-19's threat was undeniable. "For me, I think that has to all go out the window. We're trying to contain something that is unprecedented in the last 100 years."[44] Japan's case count remained low in early March, and this, too, factored into the IOC's reasoning for not expediting a decision when the event was some months distant. However, media reports appeared later in March indicating that these numbers might be underrepresenting the situation because of constraints placed by the Japanese National Institute of Infectious Disease on individuals' eligibility for a COVID-19 test.[45]

Also on March 17, Thomas Bach encouraged NOCs and ISFs to contemplate needed adaptations for selecting Tokyo's Olympians, noting that 43 percent of the expected contingent had yet to qualify or be named. In an effort to calm frayed nerves within the athlete community, he further stated that the IOC's decision-making process concerning Tokyo 2020 would be governed by two principles: (1) "to protect the health of everyone involved and to support the containment of the virus," and (2) "to safeguard the interests of the athletes and Olympic sport."[46] Lord Sebastian Coe, president of World Athletics, the international governing body for track and field, was firmly on the same page as Bach, exuding confidence in the managing parties' ability to move forward with Tokyo 2020. When queried whether it was premature to state that Tokyo 2020 could not be held in July, Coe responded, "I do think that. We are spending the lion's share of our working hours on how to figure this out."[47] In this task, Coe was focused on efforts to facilitate a level playing field for track and field athletes regarding their ability to prepare for Olympic competition in a world where restrictions on gatherings differed by region.

Away from Lausanne and Tokyo, doubts intensified. Nick Green, Australia's chef de mission for London 2012, was blunt: "I actually can't see how the Games can go ahead, to be frank."[48] British cyclist Callum Skinner said athletes needed, at minimum, three months to foster the opportunity for peak performance.[49] He envisioned boycotts by NOCs "if the situation in Japan or in their own country remains serious."[50] In a measured opinion piece, Tony Minichiello, the coach of Irish heptathlete Kate O'Connor, revealed the challenges involved in her preparations with the closure of her training site at Sheffield Hallam University. "It means we're kind of stuffed," he wrote. While sympathetic to the logistical nightmare for IOC and Japanese Olympic officials of a postponement, Minichiello asserted that "those in power need to realise that such disrupted preparation will affect the integrity of the sport. You can't seriously expect Premier League footballers to pick up where they left off if they have been unable to train properly for weeks, and it's no different for athletes across other sports."[51] Tim Hinchey, USA Swimming's CEO, and his Australian counterpart, Leigh Russell, CEO of Swimming Australia, echoed Minichiello's views concerning COVID-19's threat to the integrity of sport competition in Tokyo.[52] Meanwhile, doping officials in the United Kingdom and the United States said they would be forced to reduce their testing program in advance of Tokyo 2020. Further compromising the IOC's hoped-for July opening of the Games was the news that Kozo Tashima, vice president of the Japanese National Olympic Committee, had tested positive for COVID-19.[53]

Canada's Hayley Wickenheiser, a six-time Olympian, four-time gold medalist in ice hockey, and a member of the IOC Athletes' Commission, tweeted on March 17, 2020, "To say for certain they will go ahead is an injustice to the athletes training and global population at large. We need to acknowledge the unknown. . . . From an athlete perspective, I can only imagine and try to empathize with the anxiety and heartbreak athletes are feeling right now."[54]

Wickenheiser was well positioned to opine on COVID-19's emerging virulence. In her last year of medical school at the University of Calgary, while a medical resident in Toronto and fulfilling her duties as the assistant director of player development for the NHL's Toronto Maple Leafs, she served in February and early March 2020 in the emergency departments of four Toronto hospitals. "I saw a shift from thinking this will blow over, everything will be O. K. to a scenario where it was a little bit more panic." While not treating COVID patients directly, as mandated by her university, she witnessed a great deal. The day before tweeting her thoughts, she watched as a young, otherwise healthy airline pilot "enter[ed] respiratory distress" and required intubation. Her experiences in those emergency rooms brought on a "free-floating anxiety about going to the hospital" that wouldn't subside until she removed her hospital clothing in her garage after each shift and headed directly for the shower to lessen the risk of contaminating her home. Soon, she and other medical school students were removed from "all acute emergency scenarios" and reassigned to call centers to expand efforts at contact tracing. Within Canadian sporting circles, Wickenheiser possesses a good deal of gravitas; interestingly, less than a week later, as COVID-19 continued to cut a swath around the world, the Canadian Olympic Committee would be one of the first NOCs to announce its decision to keep its athletes home from Tokyo 2020, while simultaneously advocating a year's delay in its staging.[55]

Unease and concern prevailed during a massive conference call March 18 among Thomas Bach; several other IOC officials, including Richard Budgett and Christophe De Kepper, the IOC's director general; and two hundred athletes from the global Olympic community. The realities the athletes faced in their attempts to maintain training regimens in a world increasingly gripped by COVID-19 were squarely juxtaposed with the IOC's continuing message of its desire to press forward on schedule. US table tennis player Han Xiao encapsulated the thinking of many athletes: "It's clear people are getting to a breaking point. I'm seeing almost a critical mass of athlete voices expressing frustration or asking the question, 'Should this be postponed?'" Canada's Seyi Smith, a member of his country's track and field team in London (2012), while cognizant of the IOC's responsibility "to make the event happen," reminded "everyone on the call that [COVID-19] is a deadly disease and that secondary deaths and overloading the medical system are the issues here, and we need to take this seriously."[56]

While members of the athlete community were rattled and apprehensive, so, too, were some journalists who tried to understand the thinking of the likes of Bach and Coe, both of whom resolutely maintained that staging an Olympic festival with eleven thousand athletes from all over the globe, along with media personnel, judges, and officials was viable that July. Journalistic criticism grew harsh. Wrote the *Sydney Morning Herald's* Andrew Webster:

> Indeed, the IOC won't even consider the possibility of a postponement. Hasn't happened before, not happening now, only time we've cancelled is for the world wars, next question, please. The Olympic movement's position speaks to an arrogance. That is special. That a different set of rules applies to

them and not the rest of us. It suggests the IOC is pandering to broadcasters and sponsors and the billions of dollars they have paid. It certainly doesn't speak to the athlete, who is now caught in a bizarre no-man's land, training and trying to qualify for an event that may not happen. And it certainly doesn't speak to the rest of the globe that is being locked down, with borders shut, with international flights cancelled, with death rates climbing.[57]

Still, for Bach and the IOC's leadership team, maintaining focus during periods of intense media scrutiny was not new territory. "If you are listening in this job to newspaper headlines," Bach observed, "you are lost."[58]

While Andrew Webster and other journalists were increasingly restive about the public messaging from Bach, Coates, and other IOC officials, they were unaware of the extensive and ongoing dialogue between the officials and Japanese organizers. A postponement had been on the IOC's "white board" for some time, but such a decision had to be determined jointly by Tokyo organizers and the IOC. Though the Host City Contract accorded the IOC the power to unilaterally cancel the Games—something Bach had clearly stated it would not do[59]—it did not grant the IOC the authority to impose a postponement on their Japanese partners without triggering a breach of contract.

Calls for a postponement came from the NOCs of Brazil, Norway, Germany, Slovenia, and the United States, while the Australian Olympic Committee informed its athletes that training for an Olympics staged in July 2020 was not possible (and to expect a delay).[60] Andy Anson, CEO of the British Olympic Association (BOA), stated that Abe, Mori, and Bach had no other option. Neither was the BOA prepared to move forward with the July 2020 date. "It would have been unthinkable for us [the BOA]," stated Anson, "to continue to prepare for an Olympic Games at a time, the nation, and the world no less, is enduring great hardship."[61]

United States Olympic and Paralympic Committee (USOPC) Chair Susanne Lyons, and its CEO, Sarah Hirshland, released survey results from 1,780 American athletes that showed 68 percent of them felt the Games could not be staged fairly in July. "It's more clear than ever," stated Lyons and Hirshland, "that the path toward postponement is the most promising, and we encourage the I.O.C. to take all needed steps to ensure [that] the Games can be conducted under safe and fair conditions for all competitors." Even Lord Coe reversed course and advised Thomas Bach that staging the Games in July "is neither feasible nor desirable."[62]

COVID-19's spread around the globe was unrelenting. A week before the postponement of Tokyo 2020 was jointly announced, the worldwide number of COVID cases exceeded 179,000, with a majority (98,006) registered outside of China for the first time. Of the 7,426 COVID-related deaths reported worldwide, those outside China (4,105) now exceeded the 3,321 within. On the eve of the postponement, the WHO reported that the worldwide case count stood at 332,935; the number of deaths had nearly doubled (14,510). The pace of COVID-19's spread was alarming. WHO's Tedros Ghebreyesus announced that sixty-seven days had passed from the report of the first COVID-19 case to the 100,000th. In just eleven more days, the total reached 200,000; four days later, infections surpassed 300,000.[63] Japan's case count now numbered 1,700.[64]

IOC and Japanese officials felt both relief and disappointment at Shinzo Abe and Thomas Bach's March 24 decision to postpone the Games. Though Yoshiro Mori confessed some disappointment, he firmly believed that "to be on course with a certain direction is a sigh of relief."[65] The Tokyo venues, noted Christophe Dubi, were world class, and Tokyo 2020 had promised to provide a promotional boost for new sports designed to engage the world's youth, such as skateboarding, surfing, sport climbing, BMX freestyle, and 3-on-3 basketball. "And, then BAM!, everybody goes down. Everybody is in fear. The morale is eight feet under."[66] However, the IOC reacted quickly, launching efforts to retool its operations by establishing an internal team dedicated to advancing the IOC's crisis efforts over the coming months. Known as the "Here We Go" Task Force, it functioned alongside the All-Partner Task Force (which involved IOC officials and Olympic stakeholders) that had been active from the early days of the pandemic.[67]

While some journalists and athletes declared that the IOC and Japanese organizers had dithered in resolving the dilemma, a few American athletes, who lamented that the leadership of the USOPC had sidestepped an opportunity to take charge, leveled the same charge at that body. "We did have the opportunity to be leaders on the issue," stated Han Xiao, chair of the USOPC's Athlete Advisory Council, "and I feel like it was a little bit of a missed opportunity." Christian Taylor, two-time Olympic (triple jump) gold medalist (London 2012 and Rio 2016) and four-time world champion, believed the USOPC's leadership group was late in taking a stand: "I really think, at some point . . . the Olympic committee should have recognized that the Games should not have gone on."[68] In the days leading up to Bach and Abe's joint announcement, Lyons and Hirshland noted concerns from USA Swimming's Tim Hinchey, and Max Siegel, CEO of USA Track and Field, on behalf of their athletes who pressed for a delay.

Lyons and Hirshland, in trying to satisfy the US sport community, also acted as responsible partners within the wider Olympic Movement.[69] They were constrained by the tendency in years past of the United States Olympic Committee (USOC; renamed USOPC in 2019) to throw its weight around in Olympic decision-making circles. This factor, as well as its large share of Olympic television and sponsorship revenue (as a result of the Amateur Sports Act, a 1978 US federal law that had assigned exclusive rights to the use of the Olympic rings, marks, and emblems to the USOC), had compromised the USOC's relationships with the IOC and the world's NOCs. This tension reached its apogee in the 1990s and most notably in the early 2000s, when the USOC realized, in the wake of Chicago's first-ballot dismissal in the contest to host the 2016 Olympics (Copenhagen Session, 2009), it needed to repair its relationships. The USOC deferred nominating any further host cities until it established a revised revenue-sharing agreement with the IOC. Two years of dialogue (2010–2012) and a good deal of work from Christophe De Kepper and former USOC CEO Scott Blackmun resulted in such an agreement and placed interorganizational relations on better footing.[70] Lyons and Hirshland knew, given the place of US television networks and corporate sponsors within the funding model for staging the Olympics, that if the USOPC declared that US athletes would not travel to Tokyo, the USOPC would be postponing the Games unilaterally. Their posture was thus understandable and defensible if one considers the track of IOC–USOPC relations through this historical lens.

The opinions offered by Han Xiao, who served as chair of the USOPC Athletes' Advisory Council from 2017 through early 2021, and Christian Taylor, former London and Rio medalist and founder of the Athletics Association (an advocacy group for the world's track and field athletes, which was already engaged in lobbying for more Olympic revenue to flow to the pockets of the athletes),[71] as well as the advice provided by Hinchey and Siegel, underscored the anxiety and tension within the Olympic athlete constituency and in administration and coaching communities. These emotions likewise permeated Olympic hopefuls across the globe. Some athletes had secured Olympic qualification spots and could train; others were stymied in their efforts to pursue meaningful training; and still others in search of an Olympic roster spot were clearly unsettled, as their remaining scheduled opportunities to do so were steadily disappearing from the competition calendar. Coaches struggled to tailor their athletes' training regimens to their unique circumstances. With no playbook for guidance, Olympic administrators searched for a way forward.

Even though each athlete's circumstances differed, all shared the unease and uncertainty tied to COVID-19 and the prospects for Tokyo 2020. Two-time Olympian Kaarle McCulloch's dilemma was instructive. Named to Australia's cycling team on March 19, McCulloch loaded her Toyota Yaris with three bicycles and two suitcases on March 24—hours before the postponement was announced—and set out on a twelve-hour trip from Adelaide in the state of South Australia, eastward across the continent's lower tip, to her mother's home near Sydney. Already on the cusp of lockdown, South Australia closed its borders later that day, which would have made any effort to head home in the days ahead more difficult. Even though Adelaide served as her training base, McCulloch stated, "if things go into lockdown, I need to be home I think."[72] Once home, she established a "gym" on her mother's back porch and pondered her future. She had planned to retire after Tokyo 2020 so that she could complete her university degree. Now, she knew the nineteen-week journey to possible retirement and life's new chapter had been extended by a year.

The uncertainty wore on McCulloch and other athletes. In assessing her mood over the preceding week, she confessed to having been "a little bit short-tempered and quite anxious. Not my normal self because as an athlete we have plans put in place all the time, we know exactly what we're doing six weeks from now at 2 pm." This reality no longer governed her life as an athlete or the lives of other aspiring Olympians. COVID-19 delivered a gut punch, and she needed time to decompress and think.[73] Ultimately, McCulloch pushed through to Tokyo 2020 the following year and finished ninth and thirteenth in the women's keirin and sprint events, respectively.

SHINZO ABE AND THOMAS BACH MAKE A HISTORIC DECISION

What finally pushed the needle toward postponement? How did the joint decision of the IOC and 2020 Tokyo Organizing Committee unfold in real time? Without question, the WHO's March 11 declaration of COVID-19 as a global pandemic pushed the IOC closer; as Richard Budgett recalled, "that was it."[74] His reflections revealed his understanding of the manner in which the WHO's action would further erode confidence within the community of NOC and ISF medical officers with whom he collaborated. There was still the matter of how Thomas Bach would broach discussing a postponement with the Japanese. On March 17, the IOC signaled publicly, though not explicitly, that postponement was a possibility given that athletes' health, preservation of Olympic sport, and the fight to contain COVID-19 would be its governing principles moving forward. Bach was mindful that within the Japanese media, the talk centered on cancellation, not postponement. For Bach, the catalyst in moving forward with Japanese organizers was news that he received in the late afternoon of March 21 concerning the further spread of COVID-19 across the continent of Africa.

The first COVID-19 case in sub-Saharan Africa was reported in Nigeria on February 28, but in the days after the WHO released its "COVID-19 WHO African Region—External Report 3" on March 18, the agency noted rapid spread to eleven new countries there, pushing the affected total to thirty-eight, and the total case count from 345 to 1,716.[75] WHO officials warned Bach and other IOC leaders of the threat that COVID-19 posed to Africa as temperatures likely would encourage its spread past the capabilities of its healthcare system. "Okay, now that's it," Bach said to himself. "If you don't have the African athletes coming to the Games, these are not the Olympic Games anymore ... end of the story."[76]

Bach conferred with Christophe De Kepper to set up an IOC Executive Board meeting on the following day (Sunday, March 22). Christophe Dubi was delegated to raise the issue of cancellation or postponement with the Japanese organizers, informing them that the board would be discussing the subject, so they did not learn of it secondhand. Similarly, Dubi informed Tokyo Organizing Committee President Yoshiro Mori about the meeting. Mori and his colleagues expressed that this planned discussion was not "a problem" for them.

At the IOC Executive Board meeting, it took just "30 seconds"[77] for attendees to dispense with the thought of cancellation. Christophe Dubi confirmed that the IOC had done its due diligence, closely studying its insurance and commercial contracts; certainly, it could have unilaterally canceled the event. Dubi even ventured the thought that it would have been easier for the IOC to cancel rather than to postpone. However, Dubi recalled, "the boss always said, with the support of the Executive Board, 'we're just going to [stage the Games] and find the ways and means.'"⁷⁸ The Executive Board meeting ended with the stated resolve to move forward with postponement.

Bach; his spokesperson, Mark Adams; De Kepper; and Dubi then called the Japanese organizers to discuss the results of the board's deliberations. The Japanese placed one condition on the impending discussion. "I got scared," said Bach, "Now it comes," thinking that they were immediately jumping to financial matters. But the Japanese simply said, "No cancellation." Bach breathed a sigh of relief. He assured the Japanese this was not the path going forward. But he wished to discuss issues tied to postponement directly with Shinzo Abe, with whom he had constructed "a relationship of mutual confidence and trust."⁷⁹ Bach was also aware that any decision required the agreement of the Japanese government. Tokyo organizers indicated that they would be in touch about the possibility of scheduling a discussion between Abe and Bach.⁸⁰

While these events unfolded, Kit McConnell was engaged in completing forty-seven different conversations with ISFs, the Paralympic Committee, and other involved organizations, among them the Union of European Football Associations. "Here's the considerations," McConnell informed his contacts, "here's the likely direction. Does it work for you? Here's the timeline of communication. Do you have any questions? Do you have any input?" The degree of outreach was vital, stated McConnell, "as it couldn't be seen as an IOC decision where we're sitting in isolation, where white smoke goes up and we send out a press statement saying, 'Here's the decision we've taken.' We needed everyone on that journey with us." McConnell duly reported to Bach that the ISFs were on board with the IOC's decision. Similar support flowed from the NOCs and the Athletes' Commission. The key stakeholders linked arms to move forward. "This alignment between all parties," including the Japanese, stated Christophe Dubi, "really helped us make the right decision at the same time."⁸¹

The Japanese informed Bach on Monday (March 23) that the telephone call could be arranged with Shinzo Abe for the following day. Abe's comments to members of the Japanese parliament that same day, which received much attention in Japan, conveyed his mindset and signaled the track of the dialogue between Japanese officials and the IOC's leadership team. Abe's desire was to hold the games in their "complete form." He was clearly aware that the onset of the pandemic had compromised athletes' ability to prepare for competition. "If it is difficult to hold the games in such a way, we have to decide to postpone [them], giving top priority to (the health of the) athletes."[82] In consultation with Bach and De Kepper, Christophe Dubi and Tokyo 2020 Coordination Commission Chair John Coates tended to the necessary planning or scripting of the call between the two leaders. Meanwhile, word was received from Japan that Abe agreed with the postponement. The call was duly scheduled for the next day, Tuesday, March 24.[83]

Olympic House, the IOC's new headquarters in Lausanne since 2019, should have been abuzz with the activities of scores of its more than five hundred employees, but because of COVID-19 restrictions, only a few people occupied the building on that cool, crisp morning. The sun shone brightly. Abe, in Japan, and Bach, seated in the IOC executive boardroom, spoke over the telephone. The connection was momentarily lost, but IOC staff swiftly reconnected them.[84] As they conversed, Abe queried Bach on the new dates: "Postponed to when?" Bach replied that the IOC would have to engage its partners via a stakeholders call; consultation was especially important with the ISFs, given that the international sport calendar is laid out months in advance. "Okay," responded Abe, "but not later than the summer" of 2021.[85] While Abe did not express his reasoning to Bach, most observers (including IOC officials) assumed upon reflection that Abe wanted the Games staged before national elections scheduled for the later months of 2021. In his assessment of the process, Mark Adams offered, "There was no need to lead the Japanese, no need for the Japanese to lead us. We [came] to a kind of similar conclusion that postponement was kind of the only way to go . . . there was no need to put anything in writing because both sides understood that they needed to trust."[86]

Discussion, as usual, eventually turned to finances. "You know," recalled Bach, "you cannot start a financial negotiation with a Prime Minister in such a call. Impossible." However, he believed the personal relationship he had forged with Abe over the previous eight years might keep such discussions from getting mired "in the bureaucracy." Too many lawyers and bureaucrats would get involved. Disputes were best avoided. Bach suggested to Abe that "we should keep the name as, as it is, 'Olympic Games, Tokyo 2020.'" Bach and Abe "shook hands over the phone." The Host City Contract had been "preserved," meaning, "in the end, they have to take all the costs which they would have to take for 2020, and we would have to take all the costs we would have to take for 2020," Bach confirmed. "There was never a signature"—that

IOC President Thomas Bach is shown moments after hanging up the phone, following his discussion with Japanese President Shinzo Abe when the two men agreed to postpone the Tokyo 2020 Olympics.
Credit: 2020/International Olympic Committee/MARTIN, Greg.

is, no signed document—"there exists only the transcript" recorded by both parties but never exchanged.[87] He concluded, "We were lucky to have a partner, a like-minded partner in Prime Minister Abe, at the time, who saw it as an opportunity for Japan. And, we saw it as the opportunity and responsibility for the Olympic Movement. And, so we came together."[88]

Now the heavy lifting began. Where to start? "Let me put it this way," said Bach. "I think if we had been aware of the challenges of organizing, the full scale of challenges, of organizing postponed Games, we, both Prime Minister Abe and I, and my team here, and everybody, we would have thought twice."[89] "It's excruciating ramping up a second time," observed Christophe Dubi. "Can't imagine. We were ready to go. The venues were perfect... the financing of these Games was monumental. Most successful sponsorship program ever.... It was ready to be rocking the world with full venues. The ticketing campaign was successful. The hospitality was brilliant," he stated. And then, at the eleventh hour, COVID-19 derailed the mission of the Japanese organizers, IOC officials, and Olympic stakeholders. "There was no blueprint," acknowledged Dubi, for the "mammoth task" ahead.

While the COVID-19 challenge placed the IOC on a massive learning curve, Dubi believes its performance in 2020 and 2021 demonstrated its functionality. "This organization that is perceived from the outside as being a mono block or a monolith, which is impenetrable," said Dubi, "which is in a Golden Tower here along the lakeshore, is amazingly agile." COVID-19 demanded such agility from "the whole Olympic community."[90] And, in the end, Bach, noted Dubi, was resolute. He told all Olympic stakeholders, "Listen, whatever happens in the next few months [...] we will be together in Tokyo."[91]

4
"HERE WE GO"

QUESTIONS NEEDING ANSWERS

Questions abounded following the decision to postpone the Tokyo 2020 Games. What dates made the most sense for hosting them in 2021? In a reconfigured hosting cycle, would Japanese organizers be able to retain key personnel who had made commitments through the close of the Paralympics in September 2020? How could the IOC and Japanese organizers redeploy staff to deal with the unprecedented challenge of winding down an Olympic festival and effectively restaging it at a future date? How would TOP sponsor contracts due to expire at the close of TOP IX (2017–2020), or agreements with companies onboarding in 2021 for TOP X (2021–2024), be managed? Could the Japanese renegotiate the contracts governing the use of all Olympic venues? What process would permit the IOC to best tap the expertise of medical and public health officials with the goal of establishing a "playbook" of policies and procedures for hosting the Games safely in a COVID world? The days ahead appeared daunting, but the work commenced without delay.

A SNAPSHOT OF THE FALLOUT FOR ATHLETES AND COACHES

"Of all the characters in the NBA," wrote *Bleacher Report's* Josh Cohen in 2013, "no one is more layered and more fascinating than Gregg Popovich... he is the league's best coach and its most interesting man... it's not close on either front... eclectic, acerbic, and downright hysterical—sometimes intentionally, sometimes not."[1] Former Chicago Bulls and Los Angeles Lakers coach Phil Jackson has eleven NBA titles to his name, but by the time he stepped away from the sidelines in 2011, Popovich had four NBA titles as coach of the San Antonio Spurs, adding another in 2014.

Jackson's departure left most basketball analysts comfortable in sharing Cohen's take. Following Popovich's appointment as San Antonio's head coach during the 1996–1997 season, his teams recorded twenty-two straight winning seasons, a feat besting even Jackson's record. He received the league's Coach of the Year award in 2003, 2012, and 2014. Since NBA players became eligible for Olympic competition, only Chuck Daly (1992, gold medal), Lenny Wilkens (1996, gold), Rudy Tomjanovich (2000, gold), Larry Brown (2004, bronze), and Mike Krzyzewski (2008, 2012, and 2016, all gold) had served as the head coach of the US men's Olympic basketball team. Popovich, a late cut during his playing days with the 1972 men's team—the same team that was embroiled in controversy in the gold medal final with the Soviet Union—served as an assistant on Larry Brown's staff. The team's 5-3 overall record, with losses to Puerto Rico, Lithuania, and Argentina, dulled the sheen on the bronze medal won. "The Olympics," wrote Jack McCallum, turned into Popovich's "personal bête noir."[2]

Jerry Colangelo, managing director of USA Men's Basketball, who NBA Commissioner David Stern tasked to turn the ship around at USA Basketball following the Athens Olympics, selected Krzyzewski over Popovich at the final interview stage. But in 2015, with Krzyzewski opting to step down after the Rio Olympics, Colangelo named Popovich the men's team's head coach for Tokyo 2020. He assumed the role following the third straight gold medal performance by Krzyzewski's teams.[3] Now Popovich, like all coaches and athletes who had been within months of traveling to Tokyo, needed to pivot and plot a new path forward in an uncertain environment.

Arizona native MyKayla Skinner was not selected to attend the US women's gymnastics Olympic Trials in 2012 (as a fifteen-year-old). She harbored some bitterness after posting the fourth-best overall score at the 2016 US Olympic Trials when selectors named her an alternate to the five-women team for Rio (Simone Biles, Aly Reisman, Gabby Douglas, Laurie Hernandez, and Madison Kocian). Following the Rio Olympics, Skinner focused on her University of Utah studies and participation in National Collegiate Athletic Association competition. Unfulfilled dreams, however, brought her back to international competition. She finished ninth at the 2019 US Championships, which was her springboard for promising performances in early 2020 and gave her hope of serious pursuit for a place on the Tokyo 2020 team. And then COVID-19 hit. Skinner's possible path to Tokyo a year later became even more trying in December 2020 when she contracted the virus. "For two weeks I felt like I couldn't move off the couch," she recalled. "I was sick, tired, and exhausted." She missed six weeks of training, leaving her only five months to compete for a place on the Tokyo 2020 US women's gymnastics team.[4]

For some athletes, the postponement of Tokyo 2020 turned out to be a blessing. In speaking of a COVID-19 outbreak on the US women's rowing team in March and April 2020, when at least twelve rowers contracted COVID-19 at their Princeton University training camp, team physiotherapist Mark Nowak said, "Learn from us, and what we've gone through." The afflicted rowers "battled symptoms for weeks." Rower Kendall Chase of Evergreen, Colorado, reported "a searing headache that lasted for six days." She felt "like [her] brain was being destroyed by [her] sinuses." Chase barely left her bedroom for more than a week. "One day I tried to go for a walk, and I made it maybe 30 seconds out the door before turning around," she said. "I just couldn't do it. The sun hurt my eyes so much that I couldn't take it." Reaching peak condition before competitions in July and August 2020 with such complications would have been challenging. The rowers were lulled into believing a common narrative that maintained young and healthy people were less likely to contract COVID-19, and if they did, the effects would be mild. The team's direct experience snapped them out of this false belief. When team doctor Peter Wenger stressed the need for vigilance in protecting each other's health going forward, as well as mitigation strategies such as masking to ensure the "four or five training blocks" needed to facilitate success in a year's time, they understood.[5]

Great Britain's Tom Daley, a three-time Olympian (now five-time) in diving who won bronze medals in London 2012 (10 m platform) and Rio 2016 (10 m synchro), targeted Tokyo 2020 for redemption because of his failure to make the finals in the 10 m platform event in Brazil. Daley and his husband, screenwriter Dustin Lance Black, and their infant son, Robbie, went into lockdown at their London apartment. Daley's mother entered their "bubble." Though only a short distance from his training base, the London Aquatic Centre, he was still out of the water in early June. Time away from training made him more conscious of "stretching," "mobility," and "flexibility." Yet Shinzo Abe and Thomas Bach's shared postponement decision was a bit of good fortune for him: In early 2020, Daley fractured a hand. "I wasn't off to the best start [with training]," he explained. "So maybe I'm lucky that I can start again next year." His body benefitted from the down time: "Lockdown," he concluded, "has given me a massive chance to stay away from the pool and not repeatedly have to hit the water. Not having that impact on my body makes a real difference." Daley's experience as an elite athlete left him stoic about the future. A measure of acquired wisdom and the power of positive self-talk came to the fore. "Everyone is in the same situation, so it will make for an interesting Olympic Games next year," said Daley. "If you are able to stay calm and, in the moment, that can be a positive. Older athletes with more experience probably don't need as much training; we have done all the repetitions, we know what our bodies require to compete and we know how to prepare mentally."[6]

COVID-19'S PATH AND THE IOC'S PIVOT

Even though US President Donald Trump suggested delaying the 2020 Tokyo Olympics after the World Health Organization (WHO) declared COVID-19 to be a global pandemic, on March 24—the day the Games were officially postponed—he advocated "opening up" the United States by Easter (April 12).[7] US medical experts were appalled.[8] New successive weekly case counts in the United States in March 2020 numbered 487 (21 deaths), 2,618 (48 deaths), 64,258 (491 deaths), and 146,155 (4,555 deaths).[9] India was in lockdown. Great Britain was in lockdown.[10] In its April 1 situation report, the WHO reported that the total number of confirmed global cases since the outset of COVID in China stood at 823,626 (40,598 deaths).[11] Only one month earlier, recorded cases worldwide had rested at 87,137 (2,977 deaths).[12]

For Thomas Bach, the deteriorating situation in Africa offered a lever to advance postponement discussions with Japanese organizers; however, within two days of that joint decision, conditions in Japan worsened. Katsonobu Kato, Japan's health minister, suggested that the country was on the cusp of "high infections." New case counts in Tokyo set records for four straight days.[13] Within two weeks, Shinzo Abe declared a state of emergency for the country's largest cities, which collectively encompassed 56.1 million of the nation's 127 million inhabitants. Kenji Shibuya, director of the Institute for Population Health at King's College, London, pulled no punches in his analysis: In its commitment to mitigation strategies, "Japan has been screwing up." The current numbers were "just the tip of the iceberg." The emergency measures implemented in the urban centers depended on voluntary compliance, as Japan's constitution precluded the imposition of a mandatory lockdown. Abe's pronouncement had no teeth. "It's possible," commented Hiroshi Nishiura, an epidemiology professor at Hokkaido University and government adviser, "that Tokyo has entered a period of explosive and exponential growth" in infections. Asking the Japanese people to "exercise self-restraint" was no solution for the accelerating spread, he added.[14]

Still, as was the case in other countries, medical officials had diverging opinions. Hitoshi Oshitani, Nishiura's fellow government adviser and Tohoku University professor of virology, speculated that the infection rate would be low if people avoided "hot spots," defined by the government as "closed spaces where crowds meet in close proximity."[15] Abe soon announced the country's move to enlarge its testing capacity to 20,000 per day; meanwhile, Japan was scarcely conducting 50 percent of its 7,500 possible daily tests.[16] All this, despite the immense task ahead, left IOC officials feeling a sense of relief. "I often think," said IOC Medical and Scientific Director Richard Budgett, "if you take a decision and then think, phew, then it's probably the right one."[17]

One of Budgett's immediate concerns was soon resolved. He felt strongly confident in Tokyo 2020's chief medical officer, Takao Akama. But would Akama be able to steadfastly pursue his path for the next eighteen months, given that he, like all people working on behalf of the Organizing Committee, assumed that their terms of service ended at the close of the originally scheduled Paralympic Games in early September 2020? Akama, "quiet, considered, very senior and respected in Japan," said Budgett, "is what you need in a chief medical officer, [someone] who can open the doors and knows the right people to approach."[18] A medical doctor and an exercise immunologist at Waseda University, Akama was well known in Olympic circles, having served as the chief medical officer for the Japanese Olympic teams in Beijing and London, and before that as a team doctor for the Japanese delegation in Athens.[19] Budgett received swift reassurance that Akama and Medical Director Tetsuya Miyamoto, with whom Akama partnered closely, both would remain in place through the rescheduled Olympic and Paralympic Games. "The people there," observed Budgett, "were totally committed. This was the biggest thing in their lives."[20]

Budgett judged the preparations in Tokyo on the medical side, especially concerning the Olympic Polyclinic (medical center), to be excellent. Medical officials certified that the infrastructure was "more or less ready" by March;

however, with the postponement came the need to preserve the Polyclinic's functionality for eighteen months. Foremost among the challenges was the need to retain and continuously operate two rented onsite MRI machines. "An MRI machine," stated Budgett, "you have to keep it running . . . [or] the magnets go." In terms of their rental fees and the need to continuously operate the units, "I dread to think," said Budgett, "what that would have cost." The temporary antidoping laboratory required similar consideration in terms of extending its life (as plans were to convert it to office space after the Paralympic Games). Tokyo and Japan, said Budgett, came through with the necessary resources to support Akama and his team.[21]

Christophe Dubi outlined one of the immediate human resources challenges for the Tokyo 2020 Organizing Committee. The committee was "ramping up exponentially" in early 2020, bringing staff members on board to see the operations through until September 2020. Now, with the postponement, this ramping-up phase screeched to a halt. Tokyo 2020 officials needed to engage with "hundreds of people" to say, as Dubi put it, "With the work we have to do now, you're not needed. But hang in there. We're going to be back to you." Such negotiations, he concluded, were "amazingly complex."[22]

Meanwhile, Dubi and his fellow IOC directors established an internal task force, called "Here We Go," to begin addressing the myriad challenges the postponement posed. It first met on April 1, two days after the new dates for the Games were settled (July 23–August 8, 2021).[23] Japanese organizers established their own internal task force named "New Launch."[24] Tokyo's governor, Yuriko Koike, who joined Olympics Minister Seiko Hashimoto and Tokyo 2020 President Yoshiro Mori on the postponement call between Abe and Bach,[25] focused on the year that the world would have to tame COVID-19 before the Games could be staged. Abe, too, championed this thought, stating that staging Tokyo 2020 in 2021 would "offer proof that humanity had beat the coronavirus."[26] And, like her IOC counterparts, Koike well understood Japanese officials were entering new territory: "We will have to examine how the postponement will affect us," offered Koike, with this task falling to New Launch.[27]

One of New Launch's early priorities involved resolving issues tied to the status of Organizing Committee staff members who had been seconded from jobs with the Tokyo Metropolitan government or corporate sponsors.[28] Could their positions be extended? Were all personnel needed for the next few months, or not until mere months before the rescheduled Games? A joint steering committee, cochaired by John Coates, IOC's 2020 Tokyo Olympics Coordination Commission chair, and Yoshiro Mori, included Christophe Dubi and Tokyo 2020 CEO Toshiro Muto. The steering committee began its dialogue and problem solving[29] with an aim to "optimize and streamline the scope and service levels at the games" to control costs.[30] The added expense of postponing the Games was estimated in the early weeks of discussion at $2.8 billion.[31]

While multiple dates were considered for rescheduling the 2020 Olympics, the IOC's consultation process resolved things rapidly. Pushing the Games back only a few months, given the accelerating spread of COVID-19, did little to enhance hopes of staging them. A date early in 2021 posed difficulties for ISFs that had their competition calendars set and would have needed to reschedule many World Championships.[32] Prime Minister Abe imposed only one condition: no later than the end of the following summer.[33] Stretching out the period of postponement to the maximum length sanctioned by Abe gave "science time to deliver," reported Christophe Dubi, while extending the time needed to complete the qualification events that would fill the Tokyo 2020's Olympian complement.[34]

On March 30, Bach and Abe confirmed the new dates on a conference call, also attended by Mori and several other IOC and Japanese officials. World Athletics pushed its World Championships scheduled for August 6–15, 2021, to the following year.[35] Other ISFs followed with necessary shifts in plans. While the Olympic community took time to breathe and evaluate events of recent weeks, the United States Olympic and Paralympic Committee's (USOPC) former executive director, Harvey Schiller, placed things in perspective. "Everyone wants the opportunity for people to participate and be a champion," he observed, "but we suffered through world wars, and we are going to suffer through this, and we will get a chance to compete, but this is just going to have to wait."[36] Ensuring the availability of the venues in a year's time fell to New Launch. Tokyo Big Sight, a convention center to have been repurposed temporarily as the main press center and broadcast facility, was just one of the structures already booked by other users on the newly established dates for the Games in 2021. Toshiro Muto conveyed the challenge going forward: "It will all come down to negotiations with each venue, so we cannot tell at the moment."[37]

Japanese athletes who had eagerly anticipated Tokyo 2020 on home soil seemed relieved by the postponement decision. Tennis star Kei Nishikori,

NBA player Rui Hachimura, sprinter Abdul Hakim Sani Brown, and Ritsu Doan, who toiled for PSV Eindhoven, all expressed a favorable view of the decision taken by Abe and Bach. Sport climber Akiyo Noguchi's immediate thoughts likely reflected those of Olympians around the globe as she sought a personal reset: "It's not going to be easy dealing with this. I'll use this time to grow mentally and physically, so that I can become someone who can help build excitement for the games."[38] While the Japanese athletes looked for a new path, the nation's sport federations scrambled to extend the contracts of a legion of foreign coaches who had been hired to place Japanese athletes and teams in a position to challenge for medals in 2020.[39]

Meanwhile, in early April, the Japanese government, as a means of confronting the shock to the country's economy, approved a $990 billion stimulus plan—nearly twice the size of the package authorized to ease the 2008 financial crisis—aimed at assisting households and businesses. "I'm resolved to overcome this crisis, together with Japanese citizens, by mobilizing all possible policy means," stated Abe. He labeled the COVID-19 health crisis and its economic fallout the greatest challenge faced by Japan in the post–World War II era.[40]

Richard Budgett hoped that the need to push the Games back might reopen discussions around one of his driving concerns with the original dates: Japan's summer heat and its implications for the athletes. But the matter soon disappeared. Issues tied to the sport calendar, media rights calendar, and Abe's scheduling (and political) stipulation meant that a summer date prevailed. "I thought this is a fantastic opportunity to hold the Games in May or late September," recalled Budgett. "But . . . it was like a juggernaut, isn't it? And there was no turning it round from being in July [and] August as it was."[41]

Complex issues immediately arose for Timo Lumme and his managerial team in Television and Marketing Services (TMS). Lumme confirmed that immediate concerns included the status of the Olympic Village and the athletic venues in a year's time, as well as whether members of the Organizing Committee with whom relationships had been forged would be able to remain in place. "And my piece of it was really to make sure that the revenue source is carried on, that the taps didn't get shut," recalled Lumme, "so, that's really what [TMS] focused on."[42] Different issues prevailed for broadcasters and TOP partners. For broadcasters, said Lumme, "there were operational, financial, legal, [and] sometimes tax elements that had to be considered." In some cases, money had already been spent on Olympic Broadcasting

Services (OBS), the host broadcaster, "so those [considerations] had to be managed." For TOP sponsors, different issues surfaced for those firms that were centrally involved in delivering the Games: "So, if we take Omega, for example," said Lumme, "timing, scoring, venue results, [the] Games can't happen without that." This necessitated a "technical assessment" with Omega executives to gauge the issues stemming from postponement—what additional costs were entailed, and what impact was there on "manpower" or "equipment"? IOC officials led a "contractual construct discussion" with the broadcasters and TOP sponsors to make sure "everyone was on board and happy."[43]

Allianz, a German insurance giant, was onboarding for TOP X (2021–2024). Having reached an eight-year agreement (announced in 2018) to enter the TOP program in the insurance category,[44] Allianz was eligible to activate its TOP status in all Olympic nations in 2021. However, with the Games postponed a year, what were the implications for the two Japanese domestic insurance sponsors of the Tokyo 2020 Organizing Committee, let alone any insurance sponsors in NOC territories through the TOP IX cycle (2017–2020)? Did their rights expire? With the overlap, said Lumme, "the tectonic plates were shifting," and the IOC lacked precedent on which to lean. Working with Allianz negotiators to reach an understanding, the IOC authorized an extended window for the two domestic sponsors in Japan. Allianz's entry into the Japanese market was delayed, and the issue was similarly managed in several NOC territories. Depending on the situation, the window was extended nine months or one year. "It was a complicated equation or chess game as to make sure how we managed that," Lumme concluded.[45]

Olympic television partners, facing emerging COVID protocols, advanced their conception of the Games as an experimental environment for testing use of cloud technology to transmit the broadcast signal to one where global cloud delivery of Olympic telecasts was crucial. Yiannis Exarchos, OBS's CEO, characterized this shift, made in conjunction with TOP sponsor (and cloud partner) Alibaba, as "perhaps the biggest technological change in the broadcast industry for more than half a century, since the introduction of the satellite."[46]

In trying to assess the nature of the overall challenge at a macro level, Christophe Dubi recalled three imperatives. First, a way forward was needed to "resecure" the venues, hotels, and all elements of the infrastructure necessary to deliver the Games. These amenities included the Olympic Village that was to be "delivered to the new residents" after the Olympics, as well the

International Broadcast and Main Press Centers, both housed in a massive trade show and convention center—to be transferred back to the operators of the building. This process involved "thousands of contracts," said Dubi,[47] but the Japanese, undeterred, attacked the problem and resecured all forty-three competition venues, the Olympic Village, the International Broadcast Center, and the Main Press Center by July 2020.[48]

Second, the IOC and Japanese officials needed to determine how to run the Games—an admittedly complex undertaking, even in normal times—"in a COVID context." Thus, they needed to wrap the Games within a COVID framework without certainty that spectators would be present or whether a vaccine would be available. This extended to re-envisioning the ticketing program and how to deal with the unknowns with respect to spectators. This aspect of the work necessitated ongoing, close cooperation with the WHO.

Third, the operating parties needed to "train and deliver," stated Dubi, "which means rehearsing the operations, but the operations in a COVID protocol," reliant as they were on buy-in from athletes and volunteers, who had to be convinced to conduct themselves in a manner that "would not put anyone else at risk." This last element necessitated "constant briefing to the whole Olympic family," even when some answers to their questions were unknown. "The exercise in this period of time," Dubi recalled, was "to be clear about what we know, and what we don't know, while giving confidence that at some point we will have an answer to all pending questions." This transparency was central to "getting the Olympic family constantly in the tent."[49]

Given the situation and revised timeline, the day-to-day demands on Dubi's Olympic Games team in Lausanne were transformed. No longer were they consumed with questions about transportation, accreditation, security, technology, and finance. Now, for instance, they were exploring the prospects for a vaccine. Yet what were the various vaccine technologies at play? What was mRNA? How might they capitalize on COVID protocols activated by other sport authorities, such as the NBA and NHL, that continued their paused seasons? What was the status of travel restrictions imposed by governments? "We [had] to open ourselves up to what we're not designed to do, which [was] to work with the medical and scientific community to understand how [COVID-19 would] evolve and maintain constant communication with [the] WHO," stated Dubi. "Super, heavy decisions" were needed "a year and a half out" in concert with Japanese officials, using knowledge sharing from the WHO and representatives of the pharmaceutical industry. "By multiplying touch points" in 2020, stated Dubi,

The IOC Executive Board convenes virtually with IOC President Thomas Bach and the IOC directors on May 14, 2020. Credit: 2020/ International Olympic Committee/MARTIN, Greg.

"you could form an opinion that something was coming on, that a vaccine would be coming." Then the job was to deliver this information to Olympic stakeholders in transparent fashion so, despite the "unknowns," the Games would be "safe and secure." In this assessment of his team's operations, Dubi concluded, "being in a crisis always helps [you] to reshape and restructure."[50]

"Transparency" and "engagement," stated Kit McConnell, were central to consultations with the ISFs: "Not pretending to know what we didn't know. Not pretending we even knew the right questions to ask every time, because no one had gone through this before." Days were long and challenging, he observed, in an environment of relentless media scrutiny, and—as was the case for many around the world, himself included—punctuated by separation from family (specifically his relatives in New Zealand).[51] Dubi credited Thomas Bach's leadership with bolstering the spirits of IOC officials: "[It] is one thing to say, 'Okay, this is how we're going to work, and this is how we can address the situation.' But for that person to walk in the unknown and say, 'We [will] all do that, we agree, and follow me. Follow me. Connect, we're going to get there' " exemplified "courage," said Dubi, and this courage from "the very top of the organization" filtered down through the ranks.[52]

The IOC was also trying to decipher the cost implications of postponement. On May 14, the IOC Executive Board established a ceiling of $650 million to handle the IOC's share of additional costs, and up to $150 million to support the needs of the ISFs and NOCs.[53]

TWO STORYLINES

Two narratives, each with significant implications for the Tokyo 2020 Olympics, ran parallel through early 2020 and converged by midyear. First, could scientists and vaccine manufacturers unlock the necessary science and generate the global distribution network required to rapidly produce and share effective vaccines, when the record for fastest-produced vaccine (for mumps) was four years?[54] Second, would the IOC and their Japanese partners be able to construct the COVID protocol, dubbed the "playbook," needed to deliver the Games in Tokyo safely and securely while preventing both further spread and what some scientists speculated might result from such a mass gathering of thousands of athletes from all over the globe—a new Olympic COVID variant?

In the short term, three governing principles guided the IOC and Japanese officials in their efforts. First, they decided to replicate, to the best of their ability, the competition event schedule approved for delivery in 2020, one reached in agreement with the ISFs and other stakeholders, and which included the venue operators, whose cooperation was also required. Second, the IOC, Tokyo 2020, and all stakeholders would "explore all opportunities to optimise and streamline the scope and service levels at the Games and reduce the costs that have been caused by the postponement."[55] Third, the Games Delivery Plan already in place would be modified to include measures designed to address the challenges posed by COVID-19.[56] In June, Tokyo organizers shared a roadmap to the Tokyo 2020 Olympics with the IOC Executive Board based on their deliberations to that point. They understood COVID-19 was an unprecedented challenge, but also considered that continuing the 2020 Tokyo Olympics project presented "a huge opportunity for Japan, the Olympic Movement, and the whole world." The Games offered "a milestone in the world's shared journey of recovery."[57]

Because COVID-19 ultimately required purposeful and careful reflection among Japanese organizers and members of the joint steering committee, they established three tenets: (1) "prioritiz[e] the health and safety of athletes, spectators, stakeholders, volunteers, and staff," (2) "reduce the cost impact of postponement and promote public interest," and (3) "simplify and reduce the complexity of the Games to ensure they can be organized efficiently, safely, sustainably in this new context."[58] Moving forward, the operating parties deemed it essential that stakeholders and delivery partners invest in seeking "creative solutions" to "simplify Games delivery from the viewpoint of reducing cost and [the necessary implementation of] COVID-19 countermeasures." In a debrief with reporters following the May 14 IOC Executive Board meeting, Thomas Bach indicated that some two hundred ideas for reducing costs were under consideration.[59]

Soon after January 11, when Chinese officials released the genetic sequence of SARS-CoV-2 online, scientists around the globe pushed ahead with their work on vaccines.[60] Unprecedented amounts of public and private money were directed to vaccine research, with countries buying doses before a vaccine was even available, a situation that facilitated rapid progress.[61] Noted Stephen Evans, a professor of pharmacoepidemiology at the London School of Hygiene & Tropical Medicine, "The fact that governments pre-bought the vaccines meant that people could take greater risks with what they did at an earlier stage without having to take one step at a time."[62] Work conducted over five decades on coronaviruses, stated Eric Yager, an associate professor of microbiology at Albany College of Pharmacy and Health Sciences in the United States, gave scientists "existing data on the structure, genome, and life cycle of this type of virus."[63] These years' worth of research informed scientists that the key for any "antibody therapies and vaccines" was a means of confronting the S (spike) proteins that were central to "viral attachment, fusion, and entry."[64]

The two most well-known COVID-19 vaccines to emerge in 2020, those from Moderna and Pfizer/BioNTech, were linked to messenger RNA (mRNA) technology, which allowed for the genetic material of COVID-19's S protein to be injected into its recipient without the use of live virus. The human body employs the mRNA to produce S proteins, which enables the immune system to identify these proteins and position the body to confront any "future attack" from the real virus.[65] The last step central to the vaccines' rapid delivery was the decision of government agencies tasked with approving vaccines to sanction the use of a "rolling review," under which pharmaceutical companies could submit data from their clinical trials on an ongoing basis.[66]

Rumors suggested, recalls Thomas Bach, that early progress on a COVID-19 vaccine was encouraging. Bach established communication with a representative of one of the numerous companies pursuing a vaccine. During the rep's visit, Bach probed for an indication of the company's progress and received heartening news: The official felt that the vaccine's development would not take "too long" and pledged an update soon. Bach also sounded out his visitor on whether the IOC might be able to eventually acquire vaccine doses and received a hopeful response. He also learned that although the various vaccine makers were in competition, because of the unprecedented challenge of COVID-19, they "were talking to each other." Bach understood that more than one vaccine would be available before "the end of the year." He was also advised to explore the possible acquisition of vaccines from the different producers as a means of safeguarding the IOC's ongoing efforts.[67] By early May, he also secured from a group of Turkish epidemiologists the opinion that COVID-19 case numbers would rise rapidly in summer 2020, but there was a strong likelihood of diminished virulence by the following summer; the situation would be better understood in two months' time. "And, of course," observed Budgett, "it just kept being unpredictable, didn't it?"[68]

Over the ensuing weeks, Bach was put in touch with the three cofounders of BioNTech:[69] the German-based Turkish husband-and-wife team of Uğur Şahin and Özlem Türeci, and Christoph Huber. Şahin, said Richard Budgett, "is a brilliant scientist," who is a humble, "really cool guy," and as a team Şahin and Türeci are "extraordinary and admirable."[70] The IOC's Medical and Scientific Commission chair, Uğur Erdener, who also served as president of Turkey's NOC, as well as president of the International Archery Federation, facilitated this connection and functioned as a valuable liaison with Şahin and Türeci over the months ahead due to their shared Turkish roots.[71]

Meanwhile, Christophe Dubi connected with Moderna's CEO, Stéphane Bancel, who shared with Dubi that "these days ... I'm speaking with presidents and prime ministers, this is my day-to-day life ... what is happening is incredible."[72] Jean-Claude Killy, the French alpine skiing legend and former IOC member, expedited Dubi's conversation with Bancel, a conversation Dubi highlights as reflecting the goodwill the IOC enjoys with leaders and decision makers worldwide.[73] IOC officials, confirmed Bach, were much heartened by this dialogue with Pfizer/BioNTech and Moderna executives: "We said, 'Okay, if [a vaccination program] can start early in the year [2021], we are pretty safe.'"[74] Outside of Lausanne's Olympic House, confidence in the ability of the IOC and Japanese organizers to move forward (or the wisdom of even doing so) was lacking, but the work they were completing daily, as well as the up-to-the minute knowledge they were receiving on vaccine manufacturers' progress, sustained Bach and IOC officials and bred conviction that the Games would be a reality.

Two of BioNTech's three cofounders, the husband-and-wife team of Uğur Şahin and Özlem Türeci, are shown at the Axel Springer Award ceremony in March 2021, held online. *Credit: 2021/Canadian Press Images/dpa via AP Pool/von JUTRCZENKA, Bernd.*

The IOC membership, stated Dubi, in conjunction with the organization's operation through the work of its commissions, permits the IOC to leverage "an amazing network of individuals." Rarely is the IOC refused when it reaches out for assistance. "Whatever the topic," observes Dubi, "you have [a connection to] some of the very top-notch experts from around [the globe]." IOC heads could access the likes of officials with Moderna, BioNTech, and eventually Pfizer, BioNTech's partner organization on a COVID-19 vaccine, with "one or two phone calls." The IOC, offers Dubi, "is surrounded by tremendous goodwill," and at this critical juncture of Olympic history, this goodwill was both advantageous and prized.[75] "No one ever shuts a door when you speak about the Olympic Movement or Olympics Games," he added.[76]

One expert who provided the IOC with valuable counsel and leadership at this time was epidemiologist Brian McCloskey, who brought a wealth of experience to the IOC in its efforts to meet the COVID-19 challenge. He generated and led the London 2012 Olympic Organizing Committee's public health services initiatives and had since served as an adviser to the IOC's Medical and Scientific Commission. He has been a long-time member of the WHO's mass gatherings unit (2008–), cochaired the WHO's Novel Coronavirus-19 Mass Gatherings Expert Group, and upon being tapped by the IOC, had recently completed a six-year term (2013–2019) as director of global health for Public Health England.[77] Along with Richard Budgett, Brian McCloskey played a central role in formulating mitigation strategies that provided the foundation of the "playbooks" designed to deliver a safe and secure environment for Olympic athletes and all occupants of the Olympic Village.

McCloskey's work with Budgett on this portfolio commenced before it was known if a vaccine would be delivered in time for the Games and whether spectators would be present; it also pre-dated the October 2020 appearance of the Delta variant. McCloskey pledged to IOC officials that he would recruit throughout "the whole network" for the "best of the best" to advise the IOC. He explained his thinking in securing a team of advisers: [We tapped on people from a] "range of fields, including public health, travel and hospitality, theme parks, crowd management, economy and behavioural sciences."[78] Budgett applauded McCloskey, who also chaired the Independent Expert Panel that supported the IOC's and Tokyo 2020's efforts,[79] for his wisdom and energy: "I think that the playbooks really benefitted from having not just the Brian McCloskeys of the world, these superb public health doctors and scientists, but also people who were running theme parks and had other roles trying to keep things going through the pandemic."[80] The approach served the IOC and ISFs well. Subsequently, stated McCloskey, "we scenario-planned the Games and anticipated challenges involving virtually all aspects of the Games."[81]

The pathway of Bach's discussions with BioNTech also required consultation with Pfizer executives, given the two companies' March 2020 cooperation agreement. BioNTech took responsibility for producing several "vaccine candidates" for clinical trials by leveraging its "proprietary mRNA vaccine platforms," while Pfizer weighed in with support on research and development along with manufacturing and assumed control of the distribution plan for a successfully produced, approved vaccine.[82]

Shortly after his most recent briefing with BioNTech officials, Bach received a call from Paul Deighton, the chairman and CEO of the 2012 London Organizing Committee. Following an exchange of pleasantries, Deighton related that a "contact" at Pfizer had made it known to him that its CEO, Albert Bourla, wanted to speak with Bach. Could Bach take a call "in a few minutes?"

"Sure, Paul, he can call me in a minute," replied Bach.

Sensitive to the relationship he forged with BioNTech, and not fully conversant with the tenor of relations between Pfizer and BioNTech, Bach wondered if Bourla's outreach to him was a good or bad sign. He assumed if things were falling off the rails, BioNTech would have delivered the news. He scrambled to contact BioNTech before Bourla called, not wanting them to think he was pulling an end run with Pfizer. Fortunately, Bourla's call was delayed, and Bach received reassurance from a BioNTech official that the Pfizer–BioNTech relationship was "good," and it was simply a matter of "bureaucracy." If Bach could reach a deal with Pfizer, BioNTech officials "were more than happy." Bach and Bourla agreed "to come together" (i.e., establish a deal), subject to further negotiations.[83]

It was one thing to reach agreement with Pfizer, but Pfizer could not initiate distribution of Olympic vaccine doses unilaterally, as federal governments controlled the prioritization of vaccine recipients. But the IOC learned that the WHO had its own unit, GAVI Alliance (Global Alliance for Vaccines and Immunization), that organized the fair distribution of vaccines with its member states.[84] Bach connected with GAVI's CEO, Seth Berkley, to request vaccines for those elite athletes involved in qualifications for Tokyo 2020 and those who were already set to participate in the rescheduled Games. For every vaccine dose GAVI directed to athletes, the IOC would supplement GAVI's holdings with two doses for distribution around the globe. Bach also pledged an awareness campaign in support of vaccination headlined by famous Olympians. GAVI's executives expressed support for the plan but needed backing from their board of directors, and said they would renew discussions in "three days or one week."[85]

However, GAVI did not follow up with the IOC. Thus, the IOC turned to final negotiations with Pfizer, which Bach classified as "pretty tough," because "too many lawyers [were] involved." Once the negotiations concluded, Pfizer and BioNTech queried the IOC on the number of vaccines it needed. The number Bach presented did not make executives with either party blink. "If you need more, tell us," they said.[86]

The IOC still needed to work with countries and NOCs to develop a place in the distribution chain for Olympic athletes. This mission took Bach to Brussels to engage with the European Union. "The athletes do not, we do not want, to be in the first line," stated Bach. "The first line is about life and death and there we are out." He hoped countries would look at distributing vaccines to athletes in the second wave of vaccinations, with a

Thomas Bach, IOC president, and Tedros Adhanom Ghebreyesus, director general, World Health Organization (WHO), are shown socially distanced on exercise bicycles, following the signing of the IOC/WHO Co-operation Agreement in Geneva, Switzerland, in May 2020. Ghebreyesus shared Thomas Bach and the IOC's resolve to stage the Tokyo 2020 Olympics.
Credit: 2020/International Olympic Committee/MARTIN, Greg.

clear understanding that these doses did not diminish the vaccines available within each nation, but were supplied by the IOC in addition to the country's stockpile.

Athletes and their advocates walked a delicate line in those countries that did not place them in a priority group for vaccination. "We're saying while we don't want to jump the queue, we would be thankful for our athletes to get vaccinated as soon as possible," offered Michael Schirp, a spokesperson for the German Olympic team. "So, you try to give a signal, but don't want to come across greedy," he acknowledged. In Germany, 73 percent of the Olympic athletes did not want "special treatment," and accepted that the German government had not advanced their place in the nation's queue; however, if the IOC announced at a future date that vaccination was a requirement for participation, 70 percent said such priority should be granted.[87] The USOPC's CEO, Sarah Hirshland, agreed to follow the US government's policies, but proposed "a hopeful best-case scenario in which athletes could be vaccinated before the [US Olympic trials] events in mid-June."[88]

Thomas Bach believes, in the end, it all "worked very well."[89] The IOC encountered little "pushback" around the globe, reported Richard Budgett.[90] India, Hungary, Israel, Serbia, Mexico, Denmark, and the Philippines were a few of the countries to advance Olympians in their respective vaccination queues.[91] "There was general acceptance that this [was] a tiny number of people doing an important thing in Tokyo. They should have priority of vaccines," stated Budgett.[92] Some countries where priority was given to Olympic athletes volunteered to help out Olympians from countries where this was not the case.[93] Approximately 85 percent of the occupants of the Olympic Village in Tokyo were vaccinated before departing their home countries.[94]

PAU MOTA: "CHARGING ON A WHITE HORSE OVER THE HORIZON"

Riding the crest of enhanced popularity stemming partly from the wildly successful Netflix documentary series, *Drive to Survive*, which debuted in March 2019, Formula One (F1) declared revenues of $2.02 billion and an overall profit of $17 million following the 2019 season. F1's revenues for the previous year, 2018, were $1.83 billion.[95] *Drive to Survive* offered viewers a behind-the-scenes look at the drivers and teams pursuing the 2018 F1 World Championship. "Behind it all, you have powerful people and brands fighting it out," said the show's producer, Paul Martin. "We used to say in the early days it was *Game of Thrones* in fast cars."[96] The 2020 race calendar loomed as an important one, a season that placed F1 squarely at a "crossroads," said *Forbes'* Christian Sylt. While F1 fended off threats from its own teams to launch a rival racing series, investors in its parent company, Liberty Media, lacked patience regarding its stock price target for January 2019 ($47), which still had not been reached in early 2020. Of the three largest sources of revenue (broadcasting rights, sponsorship, and race hosting fees), F1 executives believed that the most growth potential rested in the sponsorship realm. As Lewis Hamilton prepared to chase his seventh straight driver's title with the first Grand Prix scheduled for Australia in March 2020, investors stood poised to judge whether Liberty had F1 "back on track" in second and third quarters of that year.[97]

And then, COVID-19 burst forth. The racing calendar was thrown into chaos, and the season's launch was pushed back until July. Despite a reconfigured seventeen-race schedule, revenues sank to $1.15 billion, and F1 posted an overall loss of $386 million. The McLaren racing team alone lost $225 million in the first quarter of 2020.[98] It could have been worse, much worse, especially if F1 had not been able to push forward safely with its revised race schedule.

Central to F1's efforts to navigate the pandemic in the 2020 racing season was a Spanish-born, Lausanne-based doctor, Pau Mota. Since 2018, Mota had served as the head of Medical and Rescue for the Fédération Internationale de l'Automobile (FIA).[99] He completed his medical training in Spain and later obtained a PhD in public health and epidemiology at St. Andrew's University in Scotland, where he also pursued a postdoc. Mota was also a youth handball player who pursued the sport up to the junior level with FC Barcelona. With FIA and F1 already reeling from the canceled Chinese Grand Prix scheduled for April, FIA and Formula One Management tasked Mota and his medical department to learn as much as they could about COVID-19 and the challenges it posed.[100]

Mota read as much as he could, but beyond this, his professional training, and news of exploding cases in China and COVID's spread to Italy, informed him by mid-February that a lockdown would arrive in Switzerland and other countries within a few weeks. One of the telling clues for Mota as to what awaited the world came from his study of international flight bookings: He noticed cancellations were starting to appear six weeks in advance. He and his colleagues constructed a "wall map" for all of FIA's competitions tied to F1, Rally, and Endurance racing and examined government-imposed restrictions at all race sites. With some F1 personnel already in Australia ahead of the Grand Prix scheduled for Sunday, March 15, Mota spoke to FIA Secretary-General Peter Bayer on March 10. Mota was convinced the last flights out of Australia would occur within the next few days.[101] No further personnel were to be sent to Australia. Then, a McLaren F1 team member who worked in the race paddock tested positive sometime between the late evening of Thursday, March 12, and the early morning of Friday, March 13. Race officials scrubbed the Australian Grand Prix a mere two hours before the engines would have started for the first practice session.[102] F1-affiliated personnel scrambled to exit Australia on the thirteenth. Cancellation of large numbers of international flights followed on March 14.[103]

During a March 15 online meeting with FIA President Jean Todt and members of FIA's board, Mota was tasked to establish the mitigation strategies needed to convey approximately two thousand people among race sites for the 2020 F1 season, a schedule that needed to comprise twelve races. "I like challenges ... I like emergencies," said Mota, so he launched into the work. He had thirty-minute daily online meetings with team engineers. He discussed epidemiology, virus transmission, and the latest developments tied to COVID-19, as well as ways the Grand Prix race protocols would have to change. Mota consulted with his peers employed by Fédération Internationale de Football Association (FIFA), the NBA, and the NFL to educate himself on strategies under consideration by others seeking the means to stage sport events safely. He also reached out to Richard Budgett shortly after the 2020 Tokyo Olympics were postponed.

Budgett told Mota that the IOC was working with the WHO on protocols and risk assessment. WHO officials subsequently passed on to Mota the current knowledge and mitigation strategies generated by Budgett, McCloskey, and other medical experts, which Mota refined for a Grand Prix race environment. "The protocols and countermeasures" were modified to keep them in line with any restrictions activated in individual host countries. Mota managed the onsite testing, building confidence with in-country public health officials that he and his team could isolate and safely remove individuals who tested positive. In the end, F1 staged seventeen races in twelve countries.

Mota's taxing work schedule—eighteen-hour days for four months straight since the onset of COVID-19—caught up with him by the summer. The travel schedule was backbreaking, and the prolonged periods of separation from his wife and children bothered him. Mota's circumstance coincided with Budgett's feelings of being overwhelmed by the workload in leading the Medical and Scientific Team during the COVID-19 crisis. In Budgett's case, his team consisted of a small number of members, none of whom were doctors.[104] In late July, when he had a brief break in Lausanne from the Grand Prix race schedule, Mota reached out to Budgett to share his thoughts on the challenge facing the IOC: "Richard, your protocol was fine in March, but to put that on the ground, you need a lot of flexibility. You need a huge, big team of people who know very well what they are doing. And you need a medical doctor on site." He offered Budgett his services going forward to Tokyo. "Richard, you will need people for Tokyo. I'm available for Tokyo if you need someone. And I am the only one who has experience with 2,000 people in another sport," said Mota.[105] All of this and more was discussed between Budgett and Mota over a socially distanced coffee in Lausanne in August. For Mota, working alongside Budgett (and staying with his family) in Lausanne in 2021 was a possible exit strategy from F1 and its travel demands. During a meeting with Christophe Dubi and his fellow directors, Budgett lobbied for adding Mota to the IOC team as senior manager of its Medical and Scientific Department, effective in January 2021. Budgett needed support—"I can't do this alone." Christophe Dubi signed off on Budgett's request.[106]

Mota fulfilled his duties with FIA through December 2020 but volunteered his counsel for Budgett and the IOC through the waning months of the year during online sessions primarily dedicated to generating the playbooks.[107] By this time, given media reports and Bach's interaction with BioNTech officials, Budgett and Mota understood the strong likelihood that vaccines would be available by the end of year. However, the layers of protection built into the earliest version of the playbook did not include the vaccine; it would be regarded as a bonus. Those who collaborated on the playbook's production did not assume its availability. Based on his deliberations with Budgett and his advisers as well as his personal experience with F1, Mota concluded that "we could run the Games without having the vaccines."[108] What was necessary, in his mind, "was the political will from the Japanese government."[109] Mota was convinced that the Japanese were resolute in their determination to go forward,[110] despite the headwinds from opposition politicians and pockets of the Japanese media. His contribution in the months ahead, including his onsite work in Tokyo during the Games, when he assisted in conducting thirty thousand COVID-19 tests per day,[111] was much valued by Richard Budgett, who commented that the ensuing nine months "must have seemed like two years for him ... [but, Pau, in the end], came in ... charging on a white horse over the horizon and saved the day."[112]

THE CHALLENGE AHEAD

In gauging the nature and depth of the organizational and managerial challenges the IOC faced in dealing with COVID-19 and its fallout for Tokyo 2020, Thomas Bach recommended caution in comparing Tokyo 2020 to other Games. "Never compare editions of the Games," said Bach. "It's human [nature] that you always think the challenges you are facing are very important." Bach reflected on the difficulties Pierre de Coubertin faced in generating interest and support for the Olympic Movement following the inaugural Games in Athens (1896), compounded by the eight-year interruption (1912–1920) caused by World War I. Sigfrid Edström and Avery

Brundage faced similar challenges following World War II in renewing interest in the Olympic Games after a twelve-year pause (1936–1948). Boycotts began to plague the Games in the 1970s on the heels of the terrorists' attack on Munich in 1972, and the financial debacle at Montreal 1976 diminished interest in hosting the Olympics. "No money," said Bach, with the Games dependent on governments to bankroll them. "The Games," he said, "were on the brink." Juan Antonio Samaranch "[saved] the Games," he concluded.

COVID-19 threatened to severely diminish the Olympics in global consciousness. "Memories are becoming shorter and shorter, and I don't know who would have remembered in '24," said Bach. This concern, among others, pushed Bach and his team at Olympic House forward in the days and months ahead. "If you're a global organization," he observed, "you will always have a problem somewhere."[113] COVID-19 was their problem. Surely it is justified to underscore the challenge confronting the IOC and Japanese organizers in resurrecting the Games in 2021 with the label of *unprecedented*.

5

THE STRETCH RUN

Thomas Bach is not the only IOC president to have participated in the Olympic Games. Avery Brundage competed in the pentathlon and decathlon in the 1912 Stockholm Olympics, and Jacques Rogge was a three-time Olympian in sailing (Finn class, 1968, 1972, and 1976). Until Kirsty Coventry's recent election as his successor, Bach was the only IOC president to have won a medal—in his case, gold, as a member of West Germany's foil fencing team at the 1976 Montreal Olympics. Great Britain's Barry Paul, a two-time Olympian and one of Bach's former competitors, recalled he "was difficult to hit because he was always moving, fighting, [and] scrapping."[1] "He would keep coming at you with the blade—bah! bah! bah!—just relentless," recounted US fencer Ed Donofrio, a fellow Olympian in Montreal.[2] The US-led boycott of the 1980 Moscow Olympics curtailed Bach's competitive career, but not before he and other members of the West German foil fencing team captured the 1977 World Championships in Buenos Aires.[3] He leveraged a degree in law and politics at the University of Würzburg (1978) into formal training experience as a lawyer, leading to the establishment of his own law firm (1982) and a PhD in law (1983). He was an athlete representative at the 1981 Baden-Baden Olympic Congress and a founding member of the IOC's Athletes' Commission (1981–1988), having also served on the West German NOC before Juan Antonio Samaranch recruited him to the IOC in 1991.[4]

Bach's diverse educational and professional path, combining law, business (as a member of various boards of directors for European-based firms, including Michael Weinig AG, Siemens Schweiz AG, and Melius GmbH), and sport and its connection to politics (through his years as an IOC member, a member of the IOC Executive Board—including eleven years as a vice president, and director of promotion for Adidas under Horst Dassler from 1985 to 1987), served him well when he was elected IOC president in 2013.[5]

"It's like a person having three feet and being able to put one in each camp," observed the IOC's former marketing director, Michael Payne.[6]

Although he first stepped onto a piste at age five or six, maneuvered into the activity by his parents who sought to "channel"[7] his "rambunctious"[8] ways, Bach's first sporting love was not fencing. As was the case with most young German boys, and certainly those in his hometown of Tauberbischofsheim (a 117 km drive north of Stuttgart), it was football. Bach recalls "coming home every day with bloody knees or bloody elbows" he'd earned on the pitch.[9] His parents, thinking he was a little obsessed with the game, but realizing his need for physical activity, floated the idea of him joining a sporting club.

Young Thomas responded enthusiastically: "Oh, fantastic, finally joining a football team."

"No, no, no, not football," said his parents, "you go to fencing."

"No way," said Bach.

His parents tried to sell him on the idea. They had heard good things about the young fencing coach, Emil Beck; boys who had recently taken up the sport at the club had had positive experiences. But Bach stood firm, at least for several weeks, until his parents arrived at a different approach. They told him if he joined the club he did not have to commit to fencing, but they believed that the all-round sport approach at the club, which included gymnastics and endurance training, would "benefit" him. This was a message he was willing to heed, so off to the club he went, where he met a few new friends. It was not long before he gravitated to fencing and Emil Beck.

Beck, a barber whom Bach described as "charismatic" and "self-taught," became, in his mind, "the most successful fencing coach in the world."[10] Nine of the fencers from Beck's training facility, including Bach, won eleven individual and team fencing medals at the 1976 Summer Olympics in Montreal (five of them gold). Eight years later at the 1984 Los Angeles Olympics, eleven of his charges captured twelve medals (seven gold). In Seoul in 1988, thirteen of the twenty-member West German fencing team trained under Beck in Tauberbischofsheim.[11] Beck coached high-profile German fencers Matthias Behr (four Olympic medals, one gold), Alexander Pusch (four Olympic medals, one gold), and Anja Fichtel (four Olympic medals, two gold). He was a demanding coach, but his approach delivered results, engendering great dedication among his athletes. Matthias Behr, who succeeded Beck as the German national fencing team leader, once commented: "There was a saying: If Emil Beck tells you to sit down, you don't look to see if there is a chair behind you."[12]

Thomas Bach celebrates an individual success as a member of West Germany's gold-medal-winning foil fencing team at the 1976 Montreal Olympics. *Credit: International Olympic Committee/President's Office.*

Bach credits former IOC president Juan Antonio Samaranch with three important lessons gleaned from his years of watching and learning under the Spaniard's IOC leadership from 1980 through 2001. " 'Never stand still,' or be caught flat-footed," maintain steady communication with "allies and opponents alike" while placing a priority on "managing relationships," and constantly safeguard the "universality of the Games" by nurturing collegiality among the International Sport Federations (ISFs).[13] In managing the COVID-19 challenge, Bach leaned into Samaranch's advice, especially with respect to building and managing relationships with many partners and stakeholders, as well as communication. For Bach these priorities were important if the IOC was to succeed, along with the Japanese organizers, in staging the Tokyo Olympics in 2021. It was "all about gaining confidence and trust," he said, adding, "You could have the most perfect project ... [but] if tomorrow five NOCs are saying, 'Under these circumstances I cannot send my athletes.' And, if then, 100 others will follow, then you are gone. Or if the World Health Organization [WHO] would say, 'Uh, uh, no way,' you are gone. Or, if the Japanese would say, 'No, no,' you are gone."[14]

As IOC president, one attracts supporters and critics, the stark reality of leading a global organization encompassing NOCs in more than 200 countries. One makes decisions under the glare of worldwide media attention. Some see in Bach "a clairvoyant strategist." Others consider him an "autocrat," who has been "maligned as a friend of dictators."[15] Some point to his important work as an athlete's advocate at the close of his own Olympic career. There is little doubt he, along with members of Timo Lumme's team in Television and Marketing Services (TMS), delivered the revenue needed to keep the Olympic Movement afloat and solvent during the pandemic.[16] Some critics believe that Bach assumed too soft a stand against Russia when investigation revealed its state-sponsored doping program. He also became embroiled in a charged debate on the possible terms of participation of Russian and Belarusian athletes in the 2024 Paris Olympics. Many opposed their participation because of the war Vladimir Putin launched in Ukraine. Further, Bach and the IOC have been criticized heavily for their unwillingness to confront China concerning its treatment of its Uyghur population in its northwestern Xinjiang Province.[17] Though Bach and other IOC officials emphasized that the IOC's commitment to staging the Games in Tokyo revealed its commitment to athletes, some in the academic community do not believe the body's priorities tilt toward competitors.[18] When he did not dismiss out of hand suggestions made by a number of members at the IOC's Mumbai Session in October 2023 to extend his twelve-year term as president beyond 2025—an eventuality requiring a change to the *Olympic Charter*—it touched off much chatter in Olympic circles and among journalists assigned to the "Olympic beat."[19]

In a reflective moment, Bach pondered whether his communications prior to the postponement could have been more "transparent" with the athletes, many of whom were anxious and unsettled while heeding his words to train at "full steam." Nevertheless, Bach and his colleagues plowed forward in an uncertain environment, ultimately one that forced the IOC to reconfigure and supplement its organizational flowchart. Once engaged in the mission to bring the Games to fruition in 2021, Bach remained stoutly resolute. In the face of continued opposition from many Japanese citizens and certain quarters within the domestic media to staging the Games in 2021, Bach stated with conviction, "You cannot take a decision regarding the Olympic Games, which is followed by billions of people worldwide, which is being longed-for by athletes around the globe, by having a poll."[20] Bach was, according to the *New York Times*' Andrew Keh, "the centrifugal force in propelling [the Games] ahead."[21]

Through the wider lens of crisis communications, and in extending their analysis from the weeks leading to the Games' postponement through their staging the following year, Donna Wong (Waseda University) and Yue Meng-Lewis (The Open University, Milton Keynes, UK) found the crisis communication strategies of the Japanese organizers and the IOC to have been ill conceived. They believe the organizers' collective approach, especially in the earliest days of the pandemic—when fears grew amid ongoing denials of COVID-19's possible impact on the Games proceeding on schedule in 2020—risked institutional damage to both parties and revealed a communications approach reflecting "indecision, incoherence, and policy backtracking."[22] Our own research reveals that a layer of complexity was added to information sharing, at least from the IOC's perspective, given prevailing uncertainty about COVID-19 and Tokyo 2020's determination to proceed on schedule at the outset of the crisis, along with the fact that postponing the Games required Tokyo 2020's consent.

Still, as the sixteen months of preparation unfolded, key IOC officials became increasingly convinced that the Tokyo Olympics would occur in a safe and secure environment. "I never felt it wasn't going to happen," stated Kit McConnell.[23] When Christophe Dubi was asked if he ever doubted that the IOC could carry off its mission, he replied, "No, not [for] one second." He did wonder if the possible "asymmetric" evolution of COVID-19 would have greater impact on the ability of some athletes from certain regions to participate in the Games. "We knew we would hold them. Now, in what shape and form? Couldn't tell."[24] Richard Budgett, the IOC's medical and scientific director, exuded similar confidence. "I never really doubted [that the Games] would happen." Encouragement from the trusted counsel of Brian McCloskey, described by Budgett as "always a glass half-full person," soothed concerns. Said McCloskey to Budgett, "You know, with the right mitigation, and people do[ing] the right thing, you can hold this safely."

Though Budgett did wonder if the necessary buy-in with the mitigation measures would be endorsed and practiced by all those in the Olympic Village, his doubt did not extend to whether the Games would take place.[25]

As Dubi asserted, Bach demonstrated his leadership skills through his efforts to bolster the morale and confidence of the team at Olympic House in Lausanne, especially those he relied on extensively (Dubi, Budgett, Lumme, and McConnell), along with the Japanese organizers, NOCs, ISFs, athletes, Olympic broadcasters and sponsors, and the WHO.[26] The doggedness Bach displayed in leading the IOC's mission to provide the world's Olympians their opportunity in Tokyo was generated on the pistes in Tauberbischofsheim and owed something to his own lost opportunity in Moscow in 1980.

And, yet, while Bach's public face and statements conveyed confidence throughout the buildup to the rescheduled Games, in quiet, private moments, he often experienced deep concern. "Every day you were wondering. You know, nobody knew what would happen . . . and the situation changed all the time [due to] new information," he said. Bach heard about problems from the Americans one day, the Africans the next, and later from the Europeans. "But the most challenging in all of this was not one of these doubts," said Bach, "it was that you could not share these doubts with anybody." If he had revealed these doubts others would lose confidence. "So, you had to manage this within yourself. . . . I was praying every day and I had my doubts every day," he concluded.[27]

It would be eighteen months (through the staging of the Paralympics) in the life of the IOC like no other.

ECONOMIC HEADWINDS

Though economists had predicted a recession in Japan prior to the outbreak of COVID-19, it was hoped that Tokyo 2020 and the influx of business and tourism would reverse the economy's course.[28] Japan indeed suffered the two successive quarters of economic contraction that herald a recession, seeing an annualized decline of 3.4 percent in the first three months of the year. The decision to delay Tokyo 2020 denied Japan its anticipated immediate backstop. Many questioned whether the government's $1.1 trillion stimulus plan would be sufficient.[29]

Hiroaki Yamamoto was one of countless business owners in the Tokyo region looking to the 2020 Olympics as a significant revenue opportunity. The outbreak of the pandemic disrupted the revenue streams of Galaxy Express, his commuter bus company, and he estimated that the postponement, once it had been finalized, might cost him $370,000. He was hoping to stay afloat until May.[30] Yamamoto was still operating his firm in early June, having launched free service in March from Higashimurayama on the outskirts of Tokyo, to the downtown core. "Business-wise," said Yamamoto, "we are barely hanging in there. But precisely because everyone is having a rough time now, I want to repay them for their loyal patronage." Passengers who were fearful of taking a train switched to the bus, which was frequently sanitized and operated at half capacity. In return for Yamamoto's generosity, travelers offered him "rice, vegetables, and sometimes cash."[31] It was not the first time Yamamoto had placed his community's needs ahead of his company's profits. In the wake of the 2011 Tohoku earthquake and the tsunami it spawned, Yamamoto's buses transported approximately two thousand volunteers to aid in the relief efforts at no cost.[32] Yamamoto's industry and benevolence during COVID were rewarded. He maintained the service to the downtown core through September 2020, but then phased in a return to the company's pre-pandemic routes. Galaxy Express survived the shroud of COVID-19.[33]

One of the early goals in the wake of the postponement was the generation of measures by IOC and Japanese officials to simplify the delivery of the Games and reduce the costs to Tokyo 2020. A review of pre-pandemic costs slashed expenditures by $4.3 billion (in accordance with policies outlined in the IOC's Olympic Agenda and New Norm policies). However, an additional $280 million was cut by eliminating team welcoming ceremonies at the Olympic Village, asking stakeholders to reduce their delegations by 10 percent to 15 percent, modifying transportation plans, staging several pre-Games meetings online as opposed to in-person, "and scaling back on the overall look and overlay of the venues." Tokyo 2020 also reduced its expenditures on the Opening and Closing Ceremonies.[34]

WORK CONTINUES IN IOC TELEVISION AND MARKETING SERVICES

While Shinzo Abe's administration grappled with COVID-19's fallout for the Japanese economy, those in TMS labored to sustain the IOC's revenue sources. Timo Lumme's team restructured or amended existing contracts with television networks and TOP partners in light of the postponement. They also needed to advance ongoing discussions about new agreements or possible renewals. While constantly communicating developments concerning the emerging "playbook" for COVID-19 management in Tokyo to the broadcasters and sponsors, and also soliciting their input, Lumme pushed forward for TOP renewals with Atos (through 2024)[35] and Procter & Gamble (through 2028).[36] "The impression is that everything ground to a halt and we were all stuck in our homes, but the reality is . . . that a lot of world commerce and . . . the rest of it kept on going but it was all managed remotely. We all became avid users of Zoom or Microsoft Teams," stated Lumme. Though the transition went smoothly, he was quite content to end that mode of operations. "It was sometimes 14 hours of nose pressed to the screen," Lumme recalled. When the situation shifted such that numerous people within the IOC secured access to his Microsoft Teams' calendar as a means of booking conference time with him, "it was relentless" and "full on." "Get a sandwich quickly," he said of his chaotic schedule, "and carry on."[37]

In the months ahead, TMS negotiated a new TOP partner agreement with Deloitte from 2022 through 2032, a deal covering three Summer Olympics and two Olympic Winter Games.[38] With the partnership, the IOC planned to leverage Deloitte's "deep expertise in management and business consulting to help enhance the IOC's digital ecosystem supporting the Olympic Movement."[39] All negotiation meetings save one were completed remotely.[40]

In some ways, COVID-19, and the restrictions it imposed on how people might interact, aided the function of Lumme's team. More frequent "core leadership team meetings" were made possible (if only remotely) because members of his team were not traveling. This allowed TMS to "turbocharge the level of managerial attention to issues and processes." "We were much more effective in terms of making things happen," said Lumme, "coming to decisions, having clarity on issues, reaching consensus, whatever it may have been, by working together as a team." While much of his time was devoted to reaching these agreements, and liaising with executives of television and TOP partners, he was also centrally involved in generating the playbook, "the Bible by which the Games could happen in these extraordinary circumstances."[41] As the playbook took shape, Lumme gained confidence that the Games would happen, "and also that certain things [beyond the Games themselves] could be delivered to the commercial partners."[42] In the end, a separate playbook was generated for the sponsors and broadcasters. The broadcasters' playbook was tweaked depending on the venue (indoors vs. outdoors) and the form of competition (individual vs. team).[43]

Timo Lumme, director, IOC Marketing and Television Services S.A. is shown at the daily meeting of IOC officials with members of the Tokyo 2020 Organizing Committee on July 24, 2021. Lumme retired at the close of 2022 following eighteen years of service to the IOC. He was succeeded by Anne-Sophie Voumard.
Credit: 2021/International Olympic Committee/THOMPSON, Dave.

Broadcasters realigned their production plans for the Tokyo Games. In terms of output, stated Gary Zenkel, president of NBC Olympics, there would be no reduction in its coverage, but "if you look under the hood and how it's all coming together," much more on the production side would be occurring in the United States, with a 10 percent reduction in onsite Tokyo employees. CBC, Canada's Olympic broadcaster, had had 285 staff members in Sochi with a 1,100 m² footprint in the International Broadcasting Center, but in Tokyo these figures were cut back to 130 and 900 m². Across its Montreal and Toronto operations, CBC would have another 250 employees engaged in delivering the Tokyo broadcasts, though live play-by-play commentating in Tokyo for Canadian viewers would take place only in the swimming, athletics, gymnastics, and basketball venues. ZDF and ARD, the two public broadcasters in Germany who shared the Tokyo rights, planned to produce the vast majority of their coverage at home. Like CBC, ZDF and ARD scaled back significantly their number of onsite commentary positions.[44]

LEADERSHIP ISSUES AND THE TOKYO 2020 OLYMPICS

A wave of relief flowed through a sparsely populated Olympic House on Sunday July 5, 2020, when news arrived of Yuriko Koike's reelection as Tokyo's governor, having prevailed over twenty-two challengers. Several of her chief rivals advocated a further postponement, or even cancellation, of Tokyo 2020. Koike, a former minister of the environment under Prime Minister Junichiro Koizumi, and a minister of defense in Shinzo Abe's first administration, broke with Abe's Liberal Democratic Party in 2017. However, on the matter of the Tokyo Olympics Abe and Koike stood united in their desire for the Games to be held in summer 2021. Kit McConnell reported that her support for the Games remained steadfast throughout the effort to reschedule and stage Tokyo 2020.[45] A pre-election poll commissioned by the *Asahi Shimbun* revealed that 59 percent of those polled desired the Games to be postponed or canceled. Her resolve concerning the staging of the Games in 2021 did not penalize her on election day; she captured close to 60 percent of the vote. Voters gave Koike high marks for her steadying daily media presence during the early months of the pandemic when she "anchored near-nightly news conferences."[46]

Following her reelection, Koike met with Abe to discuss strategies and possible measures to tackle COVID-19's continuing threat. "I would like to lead the Olympics and Paralympics next year as proof that we have overcome the coronavirus," she told reporters.[47] At the same time, in Lausanne, Thomas Bach sought patience from a group of American athletes who wished for more "concrete communication" and answers from the IOC as to how the Games would unfold. "How can you know already in detail maybe the most complex event to organize in the world? You can put potential developments together," said Bach, "but you cannot have a solution today."[48] IOC staff and Japanese organizers were focused squarely on the task of running the Games in 2021. The less churn in the political leadership scene in Tokyo, the better from the IOC's perspective. Within days of Koike's reelection, IOC officials and Japanese organizers announced that all venues had been secured and the same competition schedule would be employed in 2021.[49] Still, despite this positive development, Japanese citizens lacked enthusiasm for holding Tokyo 2020 in 2021. *Kyodo News* revealed its national poll showed only 23.9 percent wanted the Games staged in 2021, 36.4 percent supported an extended delay, and 33.7 percent believed canceling the Games was the better course of action.[50]

Thomas Bach and Shinzo Abe forged a close friendship over Tokyo 2020. Bach greatly valued Abe's resolve when the IOC and Japanese organizers wrestled with the earliest days of the pandemic and eventually moved along the path toward postponement. Yet, in the domestic realm, in terms of his administration's response to COVID-19, Abe's support had much diminished, as measured by volume of media criticism and public polling. The nation's GDP contracted by 28.1 percent (annualized rate) in the second quarter.[51] By August 2020, Abe's approval rating had fallen below 40 percent. Amid this decline, Abe sensed his health becoming increasingly fragile, induced by a return of the ulcerative colitis that had forced him to resign in 2007. He now recognized that the condition impeded his performance, and on August 28 announced he was stepping down to focus on the treatment plan devised by his doctors. Stated Abe: "I don't want to make mistakes in important political decisions . . . I decided I shouldn't continue sitting in this seat as long as I cannot respond to the mandate of the people with confidence."[52]

To succeed Abe, Chief Cabinet Secretary Yoshihide Suga emerged from a collection of candidates, including the Liberal Democratic Party's policy chief, Fumio Kishida, and former Defense Minister, Shigeru Ishiba.[53] Suga inherited a pandemic-ravaged economy, the postponed 2020 Tokyo Olympics, worsening relations with China and North Korea, and the challenge of the mercurial Donald Trump, whose diplomatic backing was needed in the region.[54] Abe had been able to establish a means of dealing with Trump.[55] Could Suga find a similar formula of "personal diplomacy" with the controversial president?[56]

Suga's elevation came ten days after the first of a series of meetings of a government task force, headed by Deputy Chief Cabinet Secretary Kazuhiro Sugita, that had been assigned the responsibility of setting policy for admitting athletes to Japan the following summer, knowing the likelihood that the pandemic would have run its course was very slim. Members of Tokyo 2020 and the Tokyo Metropolitan government also served on the committee with Sugita and other federal-level politicians. Policy questions included, What proof would be required to ensure an athlete was not actively dealing with COVID-19 upon entry? How would matters of border control be handled? What isolation/quarantine procedures were needed? What countermeasures were best advised for the Olympic Village and athletic venues, and what limitations on transportation would be placed on athletes, coaches, and support staff?[57] The mandate was daunting and reflected the multiple issues confronting those in Japan determined to provide a safe environment for Olympic visitors in a COVID-19 world (and protect the domestic population).

Thomas Bach's first opportunity to meet face to face with Yoshihide Suga occurred in November when Bach and the IOC's director of spokesperson services, Mark Adams, traveled to Japan to discuss Tokyo 2020's preparations with Suga, Koike, and Tokyo 2020 officials.[58] Japanese public opinion continued to weigh against holding the Games in 2021, with a *Kyodo News* poll revealing only 38 percent favored staging the Games (though this percentage reflected an uptick from the 23.9 percent voicing this thought in the poll taken in July) in 2021.[59] Nearly 60 percent wanted a postponement or outright cancellation. Interestingly, while much gloom and doom prevailed concerning the prospects for Tokyo 2020 when Bach and Adams departed Switzerland, the Japanese stock market was celebrating a massive ongoing recovery, resulting in a 15 percent jump in November alone, and by the close of the year, its highest yearly close since 1989. Experts cited monetary easing policy, the Japanese government's stimulus package, optimism concerning COVID-19 vaccine development, and greater clarity on matters tied to the US election as factors fostering the recovery.[60]

At one point in their discussion, Bach wished to share with Suga some encouraging information flowing from his recent conversations with Pfizer/BioNTech and Moderna executives. "I'm coming here with excellent news." Bach told Suga. "I can assure you, Mr. Prime Minister, that when it comes to the Games next year, the vast majority of participants who will come to Japan will be vaccinated." Suga received the news stone-faced. "No reaction," recalled Bach, still somewhat perplexed over two years later. "Thank you for the discussion," said Suga, "we will continue to prepare, thank you for coming." "I didn't understand his reaction," recounted Bach, "I thought it was maybe his personality or his culture?"[61]

The group departed the meeting room and engaged with the press corps assigned to the prime minister. Thinking the news on the vaccines was something to be shared with the Japanese people, and Tokyo citizens in particular, Bach reported that he, Suga, and Koike had a "very fruitful discussion," and he expressed his gratitude for the "full commitment of the Prime Minister" for Tokyo 2020. Bach's opening remarks began with the news on the likely vaccination rate of Olympic participants next year. He

IOC President Thomas Bach meets with reporters following his discussions with Japanese Prime Minister Yoshihide Suga on November 16, 2020. Bach would soon be hustled away from the microphone by one of Suga's press attachés, who sought to curtail discussion of the IOC's plans for the vaccination of Tokyo 2020 athletes and officials, given the anticipated slowness of Japan's vaccine rollout. *Credit: 2021/ Canadian Press Images/Pool photo via AP/NOGI, Kazuhiro.*

was immediately cut short by a tug on his arm from Suga's press attaché, who was attempting to curtail any further discussion of the subject. Bach learned later that Japanese officials did not expect a swift rollout of the vaccine on the home front, certainly not as swift as would be witnessed in other regions of the world. The reason: Japan would not approve a vaccine or recognize data from clinical trials without the vaccine first being tested on "Japanese people only." Still, Bach was confident that he and the IOC could count on Suga's support moving forward. Critically, Abe had urged his successor to ensure that the Games were staged.[62]

Within weeks of Bach's visit to Japan, Suga shut down the arrival of foreign nationals from late December 2020 through the close of January 2021 as a mitigation strategy to stem an outbreak of a new COVID-19 variant, Alpha (SARS-CoV-2 VUI 202012/01) first detected in Great Britain,[63] and then declared a state of emergency in early January for Tokyo and three neighboring prefectures (Chiba, Kanagawa, and Saitama) in response to climbing case counts and a doubling of the number of recorded COVID-related deaths (3,700). It was a move Suga fundamentally resisted, as he was committed to maintaining economic activity, but he relented in early January in the face of lobbying from politicians and medical officials. Then, too, the fact that his administration's approval rating had fallen 30 percentage points since he took office in September likely contributed to his action. Hospital beds were scarce in Tokyo. "We are having too many cases to trace right now, and the state of emergency is coming too late. It's better now than never, but it should have been declared probably in the fall last year," commented Fumie Sakamoto, who served as an infection control manager at Tokyo's St. Luke's International Hospital.[64] Meanwhile, officials from five hundred towns across Japan that had stepped up as far back as 2016 to host athletes for two-week training periods prior to the Olympic Games (to allow them to both acclimatize to their new environment and demonstrate the country's enthusiasm for the Olympics) wondered openly about the measures that would be enacted to prevent the spread of COVID-19—and if the athletes would even end up staying in their towns.[65]

North Americans would not have even classified the Suga-declared state of emergency as a "soft lockdown." Restaurants in Tokyo and the three prefectures were asked to shut down operations at 8 p.m. nightly, while employers were to encourage their employees to work remotely. Citizens were asked to leave their homes only after 8 p.m. to complete "essential tasks." Meanwhile, "schools, museums, movie theaters, gymnasiums and stores [would] remain open." The system relied on voluntary compliance. Shigeru Omi, the head of the government's expert panel, conceded that "stronger measures might be needed."[66] Shinzo Abe's biographer, Tobias Harris, at the time a political-risk analyst at Teneo Intelligence, highlighted the difference in Japan's approach to COVID-19 to those countries that adopted more stringent measures: "It just shows you how hard it is to break away from this mind-set that [Japan has] had pretty much for the last year that we're going to find a balance between public health and economic growth and we're going to keep trying to thread that needle." It might work, offered Harris, but "it's running a pretty big risk."[67]

Rising COVID-19 case counts in Japan and around the globe in early 2021 sparked renewed doubts for the future of the 2020 Tokyo Olympics. Taro Kono, a member of Suga's cabinet, felt the Games "could go either way." In two months, the rate of Japanese polled who were pressing for a second postponement or cancellation had climbed past 80 percent.[68] Suga and Bach remained resolute. The Games would go on, with Bach stating, "There is no

Plan B," while also drawing attention to the knowledge gained concerning COVID-19 and advances in science and on the vaccine and testing fronts.[69] For those Japanese citizens opposed to the Games, one of the central fears was a "collapse of [Japan's] health care system" in light of their worries that the Games would serve as a superspreader event.[70] Corporate giants in Japan, such as Toyota, SoftBank, and Rakuten expressed concern about the negativity enveloping the Games and/or the health risks in staging them.[71]

Kaori Yamaguchi, a member of the Japanese Olympic Committee's Executive Board, viewed the situation as a dilemma: "We have been cornered into a situation where we cannot even stop now. We are damned if we do, and damned if we do not."[72] Kazuki Shimizu, a researcher in the Department of Health Policy at the London School of Economics and Political Science, together with a number of colleagues, expressed grave reservations: "Plans to hold the Olympic and Paralympic games this summer," they wrote, "must be reconsidered as a matter of urgency. The whole global community recognises the need to contain the pandemic and save lives. Holding Tokyo 2020 for domestic political and economic purposes—ignoring scientific and moral imperatives—is contradictory to Japan's commitment to global health and human security."[73] US social commentators Dave Zirin and Jules Boykoff identified the possible knock-on effects of the 2020 Tokyo Olympics: "If the situation in Tokyo remains the same, or tragically worsens, there will be a rebellion against these Games and that rebellion will have a reverb effect in Paris and in Los Angeles, the sites of the next two Summer Games. Tokyo's willingness for the Games to go on, even if it means worsening the pandemic, raises the stakes dramatically for Olympic boosters and demonstrators alike."[74]

Despite the media raising further doubts, Kit McConnell noted it was at moments like these that IOC officials stayed riveted to the "mission" to host the Games in a "safe and successful environment." "The clarity of the mission, I think, allowed us to, not ignore all of the noise and everything," said McConnell, "[but most of it]." "Every time you turned on CNN, whatever they're talking about, and a lot of the time through that period, it was COVID, and a lot of the time it was Tokyo. Because . . . the combination of COVID and the Olympic Games is catnip for the media, right? Just throw out some speculation, get a commentator to go on TV and call in to doubt the Games." He understood the ratings game within the cable news industry, but the approach, "cause[d] increasing uncertainty and concern for everyone in the system."[75]

Yoshiro Mori, president of Tokyo 2020, pushed back on the gloomy atmosphere enveloping the Games. "Spring will definitely come. After a long night, there will definitely be a morning. Believing so, I would like to work hard to the end so that we can give joy and hope to many people," stated Mori as he tried to rally members of the Organizing Committee. Thomas Bach, too, believed Tokyo 2020 would be "the light at the end of the tunnel."[76] As the release date for the first version of the Tokyo 2020 playbooks neared in early February 2021, Bach, the IOC, and Japanese officials hoped to change the narrative.

THE PLAYBOOKS

As information changed during the pandemic, operators of sports leagues around the globe adapted and relaunched their competitive schedules. The IOC expanded its knowledge base and generated playbooks for Tokyo 2020 on the basis of best practices. Three versions emerged (February 3, 2021; April 28, 2021; and June 15, 2021). Pau Mota's experience with Formula One was an important resource in 2020. The Independent Expert Panel chaired by Brian McCloskey leaned into the project, as did the All-Partner Task Force that drew on the expertise of Dubi, McConnell, Budgett, and Pierre Ducrey, the IOC's director of games operations, as well as representatives of multiple IOC departments, the WHO, Olympic Broadcasting Services, Tokyo 2020, and the Japanese national and Tokyo Metropolitan governments.[77]

The mountain in front of the IOC and Japanese organizers was not comparable to those faced by sports leagues in specific domestic environments. "A sport-specific event in a specific country, you can develop a framework around that," stated Kit McConnell. The size and scope of Tokyo was unmatched: 33 sports, 339 events, 11,000+ athletes arriving from all over the world, multiple venues, 5,000 officials, along with the Olympic Village. "Absolutely no template [existed] for how to do that and give confidence that it would be done in a safe way. So, the development of the framework for the delivery of the Games was the biggest challenge," opined McConnell.[78] All guidelines had to be aligned with existing restrictions and COVID-19 policies in the host country. Extensive consultations took place with the ISFs and Japanese authorities to craft protocols for indoor sports, which necessarily differed from those held outdoors, as did those for sports such as judo or wrestling where "close contact" was required, as opposed to golf or tennis where distancing was a matter of fact. Team and individual sports likewise were subject to different regulations, especially in regard to dressing rooms and ventilation, and rules to govern both training and competitive environments were devised.[79]

Pau Mota stressed the need for "the latest science and the best science" in the playbooks, which not only served as the outline for health protocols, but also functioned as a "communication tool" with athletes and stakeholders.[80] Nakamura Hidemasa, Tokyo 2020's games delivery officer, echoed Mota's thoughts at the time of Playbook #1's release: "The COVID-19 pandemic has impacted the daily lives of people around the world, and the Olympic and Paralympic Games need to adapt accordingly. Safety and security have become everyone's top priority, and this summer's Games will be no different. . . . The purpose of this first edition is to communicate 'what we know at this time' to a large number of people in an easy-to-understand manner."[81] Hidemasa, who Christophe Dubi praised for his commitment and described as a "remarkable gentleman,"[82] pledged that guidelines and policies were subject to ongoing modification.[83] Building confidence, an overarching goal emphasized consistently by Thomas Bach, was at the heart of Dubi's view that the playbooks provided the "rules that will make each and every one of us a sound, safe and active contributor to the Games."[84] For athlete and coaching communities experiencing significant anxiety, the playbooks represented a means of building confidence with both cohorts that their health would be prioritized and that both the IOC and Japanese organizers were prepared and capable of meeting the challenge.

Rohan Taylor, Australia's head swimming coach, believed the playbook might put his athletes on a better path. As he anticipated its release, Taylor confirmed that Australia's swimmers had demonstrated a good deal of resilience thus far, but "real, tangible organizational scaffolding ahead of Tokyo would be a blessing" and a means of reducing "uncertainty." "We have to be able to move into that space [in Japan] and be compliant but also we want some of that certainty," he concluded. Guidance from the IOC at this time would "help settle the nerves a bit."[85]

The ISFs and their delegates, as well as judges and technical officials, comprised the target audience for the first playbook published (versions for athletes and team officials, broadcasters, sponsors, press, Olympic and Paralympic Family, and workforce soon followed). It established three central principles: "Minimize Physical Interaction," "Test, Trace, and Isolate," and "Think Hygiene." Officials were advised to limit physical interaction, avoid handshakes and hugs, steer clear of "spaces that are closed, crowded, or involve close contact," follow the daily activity plan they were to file prior to the Games, and travel only on Games transport, using public transport only with permission. Frequent handwashing and use of sanitizing agents was advised. Masks were required unless outside and a minimum of two meters away from people. Athletes could receive support from clapping but singing and chanting was discouraged. Individuals were asked to ventilate rooms and closed spaces every thirty minutes, and Olympic visitors were required to download the COVID reporting app used in Japan.[86] "If you have been to the Games before," advised Kit McConnell, "we know this experience will be different in a number of ways. For all Games participants, there will be some conditions and constraints that will require your flexibility and understanding."[87] The playbook also outlined policies under headings such as "Before You Travel," which listed the need for a negative COVID test taken within 72 hours of departure; "Entering Japan"; "At the Games"; and "Leaving Japan." Much coordination was required between those arriving and their assigned COVID liaison officer (individuals appointed by NOCs and ISFs), who served as the point of contact with the IOC and the International Paralympic Committee, Tokyo 2020, and the local Japanese health authorities.

Whatever positive press coverage the IOC might have anticipated from the delivery of the playbooks failed to materialize, as focus shifted to the sexist remarks delivered by Yoshiro Mori following a meeting of the Japanese Olympic Committee. Limits needed to be placed on the speaking time of women at these meetings, stated Mori, "or else we'll never be able to finish."[88] Japan's tennis superstar Naomi Osaka called Mori's remarks "really ignorant." Two of Japan's national daily newspapers called for him to resign. Despite Yosihide Suga labelling Mori's comments as "not in the national interest," Japan's power structure rallied around Mori and dismissed calls for his resignation. Even Seiko Hashimoto, Japan's Olympics minister, and Yuriko Koike, the two most prominent women involved in preparations for Tokyo 2020, pledged their continued support if Mori retained his position. Mori retracted his remarks and hoped the firestorm would blow over.[89] It did not. Mori resigned eight days after his controversial comment.[90] Early handicapping pegged Saburo Kawabuchi, a former President of Japan's soccer federation, as his replacement. He was Mori's preferred choice, but Hashimoto, a seven-time Olympian, who competed in both the Summer (cycling) and Winter Olympics (speed skating), capturing a bronze medal in the 1500 m speed skating event in Albertville (1992), emerged as Tokyo 2020's new President.[91]

The IOC's sports director, Kit McConnell, briefs reporters online concerning the release of the third "playbook" containing mitigation measures to govern life in the Olympic Village and athletic venues in June 2021. Also visible are Christophe Dubi, Brian McCloskey, Craig Spence (chief marketing and communications officer for the International Paralympic Committee), Pierre Ducrey, and an unidentified IOC official. *Credit: 2021/Canadian Press Images/Pool photo via AP/MEHRI, Bherouz.*

Across the three versions of the playbook (February, April, June) for all constituencies, the policies were updated, enhanced, and augmented. Guidelines for the use of dining facilities as well as planned countermeasures were added. The text displayed a clear priority on intercepting people positive for COVID via testing protocols before they entered the Olympic Village. As the playbooks were revised, it was determined that all people arriving in Tokyo would require two negative COVID tests on separate days within ninety-six hours of departure, and they would be tested at the Tokyo airport, with results known when they cleared immigration.[92] Comfort would come with the identification of positive cases upon arrival. "We want hundreds of cases upon arrival," Pau Mota told several IOC officials a week before departing for Japan. "Because if we have them at arrival, the issue is not to have positive cases." The challenge, in Mota's mind, was how they managed the positive cases.[93] Athletes, coaches, ISF officials, NOC officials, and specified volunteers were also subject to daily rapid-antigen testing in Tokyo (with results available within twelve hours). Others, such as volunteers, and broadcast, marketing, and press personnel, would be tested every four days.[94]

This comprehensive testing protocol translated into 30,000 tests per day, with the necessary follow-up on the 20 to 60 positive tests per day to confirm it or identify a false positive. This required a staff of sixty people in the COVID testing facility at the Tokyo Olympic Complex, comprising equal representation from the Ministry of Health, the Tokyo Metropolitan Government, and the National Institute of Infectious Disease.[95] Pau Mota was embedded with this group. Mota, who concluded his work for the IOC in December 2022 and now works as an emergency room doctor in Lausanne, said an appreciative Richard Budgett, was at the "coalface with the really big firehose," along with his colleague (and now Mota's good friend) Satoshi Shimada, who co-managed operations in the test facility. During the Olympic and Paralympic Games, this dedicated group processed slightly more than a million rapid antigen tests. PCR tests were also conducted at the Olympics (3,426) and Paralympics (1,918) for individuals who were deemed close contacts.[96]

MORE DOUBTS

The playbooks did not impress all journalists, Olympic observers, or scientists. Motoko Rich, Andrew Keh, and Matthew Futterman, all reporters who were heavily covering Tokyo 2020, found the first version of the playbook underwhelming. "At only 32 pages, and conspicuously light on details, the document may do little to assuage the concerns of critics who question whether the Olympics can proceed safely amid a pandemic," they offered. "And the raft of questions left unanswered in its colorfully illustrated pages highlights just how many complicated feats of logistical planning and execution remain ahead for organizers of the world's largest sporting event."[97]

Craig Tiley, the Australian Open tennis tournament director, reflected on the playbook's content in the wake of staging the 2021 Grand Slam event in Melbourne two weeks earlier. Tennis Australia projected a loss of $78 million[98] from the cost of flying 370 players from more than 100 countries to the tournament, which operated with reduced spectator capacity. Adding to the financial misery, Tennis Australia also paid for the two-week mandatory quarantine period for all players. Players were required to remain in their rooms for nineteen hours per day for two weeks prior to the tournament's first match but could use the other five hours for training within a "bubble" environment. Seventy-two players were kept under

Dr. Richard Budgett, director, IOC Medical and Scientific Department, addresses audience members at the tenth International Athlete's Forum in Lausanne, May 2021. Credit: 2021/International Olympic Committee/MORATEL, Christophe.

full-day isolation for two weeks because they were deemed to have had close contact with passengers on their flight who tested positive. Tiley questioned why Olympians were not being isolated upon arrival. Only one player tested positive in Melbourne. "Compared to what we've done, we've had a far more rigorous programme than what is being proposed. I love the Olympic Games," said Tiley, "I'd like to see it be successful, but with the experience we had, I cannot see it working."[99]

A research team led by Dr. Annie Sparrow, then–assistant professor of global health at the Icahn School of Medicine at New York's Mount Sinai Hospital, questioned the plans announced in May to manage COVID-19 during the Games, highlighting that only 5 percent of Japan's population had been vaccinated. Their conclusion was damning: "The IOC playbooks," they wrote, "are not built on scientifically rigorous risk assessment, and they fail to consider the ways in which exposure occurs, the factors that contribute to exposure, and which participants may be at highest risk." Sparrow and her colleagues advised that events be classified on the basis of low, moderate,

Brian McCloskey, Public Health England's director of public health (2013–2019) and the chairman of the World Health Organization's Novel Coronavirus-19 Mass Gatherings Expert Group, provided vital support to IOC officials in generating the "playbooks" that outlined policies governing conduct of athletes, officials, and members of the Olympic Family in Tokyo during the Olympics and Paralympics. Credit: 2022/International Olympic Committee/MARTIN, Greg.

and high risk. They also called on the WHO to convene an emergency meeting to address needed elements of a revised risk-management approach for Tokyo 2020.[100] Christophe Dubi recalled that follow-up conversations with Sparrow and her team also revealed a desire for "special filters" to be retrofitted to the ventilation systems in the Olympic Village. It simply was not possible, stated Dubi.[101] Their concerns moved the WHO to re-engage with the Tokyo Organizing Committee and Japanese government officials prior to the release of the third playbook. This dialogue resulted in further refinement of the antigen testing procedure, additional restrictions on athletes and officials' ability to interact with members of the Tokyo population, and detailed sanctions for violating established rules.[102]

The authors of an editorial in *The Lancet* questioned the silence of the US Centers for Disease Control and Prevention and the European Center for Disease Prevention, neither of which offered an opinion on the wisdom of pushing forward with the Tokyo 2020 Games.[103] While the editorial's contributors noted the "extraordinary measures" adopted by the IOC and

Japanese organizers to limit the possibility of transmission, they argued that the "global community" had an interest in how the situation was managed. Too much of the decision making, they said, rested in the hands of the IOC and Japanese government, both of which had "huge economic and reputational incentives" attached to forging ahead. It was time for a "global conversation." *The Lancet*'s editors also reported that the Tokyo Medical Practitioners Association had called on Yoshihide Suga to halt the Games because the Tokyo healthcare system lacked any additional capacity.[104] Richard Budgett indicated that the IOC and Japanese officials prioritized outreach to members of the medical community who offered such criticism (as was the case with Annie Sparrow and her group) to engage in conversation, not with the expectation of winning them over, but to listen to their views and assure them that "we were doing everything possible."[105] As the playbook for the athletes and officials moved through second and third iterations, it doubled in length, a clear reflection of the expanded regulatory approach.

THE FINAL NUMBERS

When the media pressed Brian McCloskey about COVID-19 testing in Tokyo when positive cases emerged at the airport and the Olympic Village (fifty-eight Olympic-related positive cases between July 1 and 19), he calmly responded that he and his team were seeing what they had expected. "If all the tests that we do were going to be negative, we wouldn't bother doing the tests in the first place. We do the tests," he stated, "because they are our way of filtering out people who might be developing infection, who might become a risk later."[106] A major outbreak was avoided on South Africa's men's football (soccer) team early in the Games,[107] though in the later stages of the competition calendar, six members of the Greek artistic swimming team tested positive, withdrew from the Games, and entered fourteen days of isolation.[108]

Months later, McCloskey reflected on officials' ability to maintain control over COVID-19 cases and avoid what some were projecting as a superspreader event. He had drawn his motivation to persevere from the athletes who deserved their Olympic opportunity, but he also realized that the Olympic Games, because of their worldwide profile, had "to demonstrate that, if we pulled together as a global community, people could start to see that the pandemic did not have to control their lives forever."[109] There were 33 positive cases among the 11,300-athlete cohort, and 464 positives at the

Games in total, a small number when considering the tens of thousands of stakeholders present. The positivity rate in the Olympic Village and the "closed loop" (the restricted area that athletes, trainers, officials, team delegation members, volunteers, and workers could enter but not leave) was a very low 0.02%.[110] McCloskey well understood that those outside Tokyo and looking in on preparations had rattled nerves. "What was more difficult to understand," he wrote, "were some experts' alarming comments and unwillingness to see the diligent work we did. Hundreds upon hundreds of hours were put into the preparations. We knew the Games needed to be safe; we knew this wasn't a situation where we could take a gamble—we had to get it right first time."[111]

McCloskey's team of experts—the one he'd pledged to IOC officials to recruit—hailed from Japan, the United States, the United Kingdom, and Switzerland. Its members spent more than two months working through computer simulations of how athletes interact with their peers in such an environment, a process designed to generate robust mitigation strategies. One significant result of this initiative was to switch from testing athletes every four days to testing them each day. McCloskey's team shelved the original plan for 3,000 tests per day in favor of administering more than 25,000 daily tests (which grew to 30,000).[112] Data generated through genomic sequencing and shared by Japanese government officials in late 2021 showed that Olympic visitors neither introduced new strains of COVID-19 to Japan nor transmitted the dominant strain of Japan's Delta variant (AY.29) abroad.[113] If, in questioning the doubters and voicing these thoughts, McCloskey took a bit of a delayed victory lap, it can be understood.

SPECTATORS OR NO SPECTATORS?

"We have to take decisions that may need sacrifice from everybody." With these words, Thomas Bach confirmed his acceptance of the decision made by Japanese authorities in March to close its border to overseas visitors planning to attend the Tokyo 2020 Olympics.[114] A decision on the status of Japanese spectators was delayed until late June when the IOC and the Tokyo Organizing Committee announced they would permit 50 percent capacity at Olympic venues. In no case could the crowd size exceed ten thousand; however, the Japanese reserved the right to modify the plan if conditions dictated such action.[115]

Bach departed for Japan in early July 2021. Hardly on the tarmac following his flight, Bach learned that the Japanese had urgently requested a stakeholders' call that evening. "I knew what was coming," said Bach; "it was not a welcome call."[116] During the discussion, the Japanese declared that spectators would not be permitted. "We were not happy with this approach," stated Bach, "not happy at all," given ten thousand spectators were attending baseball games in Tokyo and all over Japan. "How can this happen?" IOC officials asked their hosts. Baseball games allowed spectators in large numbers. No foreigners were involved, was the reply.

Bach still wonders whether he should have lobbied harder with the Japanese, but with Shinzo Abe gone, and the IOC dealing "with a very different prime minister," such a debate might not have been wise and could have harmed the IOC's relationship with the Japanese government. Bach and his colleagues well understood the anxiety pervading Tokyo's citizenry and the reality that, "it's a killer argument to say, 'We have to do it for health reasons.'"[117]

The decision coincided with Prime Minister Suga's declaration of yet another state of emergency earlier in the day that would take effect the following week.[118] Christophe Dubi believes the late, ponderous vaccine rollout in Japan likely doomed the possibility of spectators. "It was hard to take," said Dubi, because the atmosphere clearly would be different. Dubi opined that the IOC could have engaged earlier with the Japanese on the need to push forward with their vaccination program as early as possible.[119]

Upon his own arrival in Japan, Michael Payne, the IOC's former marketing director, was struck by the juxtaposition of empty Olympic venues against baseball stadia and sumo wrestling halls replete with spectators. "It slowly became apparent," wrote Payne, "that the decision to ban spectators from the Games was perhaps more about political expediency than COVID health protocols." Payne also questioned Yuriko Koike's order to remove "all forms of Olympic pageantry and flags" adorning Tokyo's cityscape. For Payne, these events marked one of the last chapters in the hijacking of the Olympic agenda by a hostile domestic media and "the political opposition and other groups with an eye on scoring points in the lead up to the upcoming general election."[120]

The decision to ban spectators, as well as the prevailing public opinion in Japan toward the Olympics, triggered moves by a number of Olympic

Thomas Bach, shown with Tokyo 2020 President Seiko Hashimoto (left) and Yuriko Koike, Tokyo's governor (on Bach's left), during a visit to Tokyo's Olympic Village on July 18, 2021. Hashimoto replaced Yoshiro Mori in February 2021 and guided Tokyo 2020 through the final months of preparations for the 2020 Tokyo Games. *Credit: 2021/International Olympic Committee/MARTIN, Greg.*

sponsors. Toyota pulled Olympic-themed television ads in the domestic market and announced that its CEO, Akio Toyoda, would not attend the Opening Ceremony.[121] Panasonic's CEO, Yuki Kasumi, likewise decided against attending. Chief executives from Nippon Telegraph & Telephone Corp, Fujitsu Ltd., NEC Corporation, Meiji Holdings Co., Asahi Group Holdings, Nippon Life Insurance Co., and Sumitomo Mitsui Financial Group did the same.[122] At least a dozen firms scaled back or canceled their onsite promotions plans.[123]

THE OPENING CEREMONY

Two hours before the Opening Ceremony on July 23, Christophe Dubi was asked to sit for two television interviews, one of them with CNBC Asia. He was unaware that CNBC had recruited a second guest, Dr. Annie Sparrow, who sounded the alarm. Dubi summed her accusations as, "You, sir, you are probably responsible for what will be an Olympic variant of COVID. And how proud will you be of that?" Dubi was able to get through his interview by taking the mindset, as he recalled, that "you have a line, you have an escape." At the same time, however, he realized that the real test for the mitigation measures was Tuesday, July 27. Brian McCloskey informed Dubi that based on pre-departure testing protocols and tests administered at Tokyo's International Airport, they would know the bubble was holding if positive cases did not climb after that Tuesday. "From Tuesday," McCloskey shared, "when the system is under tension, you should see cases declining." If the numbers ramped up, certain sports or the Games themselves would be under threat.[124] In the end, the established procedures prevailed.

Dubi has witnessed numerous opening ceremonies during his IOC tenure, but the one that perhaps resonates the most with him, he did not see; he was only three years old. During his childhood, a framed photograph of the Swiss delegation at the Opening Ceremony of the 1972 Sapporo Olympic Winter Games hung in the foyer of his family's apartment. Looking closely at the photograph, Dubi could see his father, Gerard, a member of the ice hockey team. It was a constant reminder of his connection with the Olympic Games, in which his family took much interest over the years. At most Olympic Games, the Opening Ceremony has stood as one of the few moments he could relax, as he is otherwise constantly on call for last-minute problems and issues. "If it's to report on how great the Games are, I'm not the one," concludes Dubi. While it was a much more subdued and somber ceremony in Tokyo, it was exceedingly emotional. Dubi sat next to Pierre Ducrey. The two men took their seats and exhaled, but even after counting to ten, when they looked at each other, they both had "tears in [their] eyes because it was a mammoth effort to get there."[125]

Neither Timo Lumme nor Richard Budgett thought that the Opening Ceremony was a vivid, memorable occasion.[126] About a thousand people, predominantly Olympic officials, dignitaries, and journalists, populated what was a cavernous Olympic Stadium built to seat sixty-eight thousand. National Public Radio (US) described the proceedings as a "delicate mix of celebration and solemnity."[127] Yes, there were fireworks and a parade of athletes—though, with a much reduced number of participants, only twenty athletes per country.[128] Nevertheless, Opening Ceremony directors were successful in crafting pieces within the staged production that permitted the global audience to reflect on the challenges and sense of isolation COVID-19 had imposed on the world. Brazil withheld its athletes from the ceremony, judging the risk too severe.[129]

His Majesty the Emperor Naruhito and IOC President Thomas Bach wave to spectators at Tokyo 2020's Opening Ceremony. *Credit: 2021/International Olympic Committee/HUET, John.*

When the ceremony concluded, Thomas Bach rose from his seat on the dignitaries' stand and bade Emperor Naruhito adieu. Moments later, he convened with members of his leadership team. He greeted those on whom he had relied so heavily in 2020 and 2021, including members of the Executive Board, in a room under the stadium grandstands. The overriding feeling was "we did it." The "very emotional moment . . . still gives [him] goosebumps."[130] Now, it was finally time for the athletes to take center stage.

6

TWO DAYS IN TOKYO

DAMIAN WARNER RETURNS TO COMPETITION

Following the birth of his son in early March 2021, and the appearance of spring weather in southern Ontario that permitted him to train outdoors, Damian Warner entered the final phase of his preparations for the 2020 Tokyo Olympics. His life had changed. He was a father. He was in a positive frame of mind with a renewed sense of purpose, unburdened of the monotony of training in the COVID world of 2020 and the early weeks of 2021. He was also free from the confining walls of Farquharson Arena, happily anticipating a return to competition and an assessment of his progress. "He [was] happy and he [was] healthy," recalled his coach, Gar Leyshon.[1]

As a (then) five-time winner of the prestigious Götzis (Austria) Hypo-Meeting for decathletes in 2013, 2016, 2017, 2018, and 2019, Warner and his coaches viewed the upcoming event in late May as a means of gauging his progress going forward. At Götzis, he could size up the condition and preparation status of some of his rivals. When Team Warner learned that the Hypo-Meeting was "on" as scheduled, the emotional lift it provided "was like magic." With the meet scheduled for May 29 and 30, Leyshon and Warner got their vaccines, secured airline tickets, and prepared to depart for Austria.[2]

Arriving at Toronto's Lester B. Pearson International Airport, Warner and Leyshon proceeded to the Air Canada kiosk to "check in" his vaulting poles.[3] There they were informed that they would not be permitted to fly to Zurich, their jumping-off point for ground transportation to Götzis. They were completely mystified. They had the required documents, evidence of vaccination, and tickets from Air Canada, yet received no explanation for being held off the flight. They made phone calls and sent emails. Thoroughly agitated and discouraged after several hours of chasing a solution, Leyshon told Warner, "I don't think we're going to get there."

Persistence finally paid off. After eight hours of inquiries and traipsing up and down the airport's entry hall, Leyshon discovered that Lufthansa could get them to Munich. He threw down his credit card with palpable relief.[4] They rearranged ground transportation with the Hypo-Meeting's organizers for the trip's final leg to Götzis.[5] When they arrived in Austria, Warner felt a measure of normalcy prevailed there, given the chaotic events of the previous day,[6] though it all made even less sense when they learned that other Canadian competitors and support staff bound for Götzis took the following day's Air Canada flight with no roadblocks.[7] It took Leyshon a full year to extract a refund from his country's national airline.[8]

Leyshon was bullish on Warner's prospective points total at the Hypo-Meeting. Before departure he shared with his friend, US track and field coach Kris Mack, that he would be disappointed with anything less than 8800 points. Mack was incredulous, thinking that 8500 or 8600 points would be more realistic for Warner's reentry to competition.[9] Warner, who later related he'd had some "doubts," was energized by pre-competition chatter among his rivals, whose hope was "to beat Damian after three events" and "win this competition." Warner's competitive juices started to flow.[10]

Warner's performance in the first two events, the 100 m (10.14 s) and long jump (8.28 m/27′1.98″), went well. Warner's long jump resulted in a new world decathlon record for the event. He rode those performances to a world-record decathlon performance in the 110 m hurdles. Ultimately, he achieved an eye-popping 8995 points—a personal best (surpassing his previous best—8795), a Canadian record, and the fourth-best points performance ever registered by a decathlete.[11] He fell just short of becoming the fourth athlete to surpass 9000 points, identifying his javelin and shot put results as having held him back. That number could wait. The message delivered at Götzis to his competition and the world was that his preparation under the shadow of COVID-19 had been sound. He was the first six-time winner of the event (and now an eight-time winner, having won the event in 2024). Warner emerged from the competition healthy and focused on Olympic gold. He returned to Canada and quarantined for two weeks, finally arriving home to Jen Cotten and his infant son, Theo. All was well!

NEXT STOP: GIFU CITY, JAPAN

Warner and Leyshon's arrival at Tokyo 2020's Olympic Village was a two-stage process that required an initial eleven-day stay at a hotel in Gifu City, a five-hour drive from Tokyo. The accommodations there were good, though Warner said the food "wasn't that great."[12]

A quarantine-like atmosphere prevailed. They spent sixteen to eighteen hours each day in their rooms. They were driven to the track in a minibus, barely 300 m from the hotel—they were not permitted to walk the route. Outside of training and time in the cafeteria, those at the hotel were restricted to their rooms except for one hour when they were allowed to sit on the hotel's rooftop.[13]

Warner occupied his time with Netflix, three puzzles, coloring books, and LEGO bricks that were supplied in his room. It was like "a "pre-school prison," he recalled. When in the cafeteria, diners were separated from those across the table by Plexiglas partitions. One could not converse meaningfully with anyone other than the person next to you.[14] Leyshon recounts that the emphasis was clear: Keep all foreign visitors separated from Japanese nationals. The only Japanese people they mixed with were those who served them food, escorted them out of the hotel to the minibus, or drove it. They were not permitted to use the hotel's main escalators or elevators, being restricted to the use of the service elevator. Before athletes left the hotel for the track, the lobby was cleared.[15] Masks were always worn, except when eating and while in their rooms. They submitted COVID tests each day, days they counted like inmates awaiting their release.

Despite the challenging experience in Gifu, Warner affirmed that Team Canada officials and athletes were vigilant and followed the rules. Too much was on the line for the athletes, and the Canadian delegation certainly did not want to see any of the country's athletes dismissed from the Games. No one "wanted to be the person that tests positive by doing something silly that gets somebody else sick and then they can't compete," stated Warner. No one wanted to "ruin somebody's dream that they have been training years and years for, right?"[16]

COVID-19 controls and the rigid rules in place at Gifu extended to similar training centers throughout Japan, all supervised by local health authorities. The officials who managed these facilities did so under the auspices of the Tokyo 2020 Organizing Committee. Airport COVID testing and testing protocols in Gifu and other training centers functioned in two ways: to winnow out positive cases and create a secure bubble for athletes at the Olympic Village, and to protect the Japanese citizenry. "There was real anxiety amongst the [Japanese] public health officials, the public themselves, [and] the [federal] government, and local governments about these people coming in. And so, they would have been really tightly controlled," confirmed Richard Budgett. As an element of the mitigation plan, despite his and the IOC's confidence in the protocols activated in the Olympic Village, Budgett worried that the training camps would be canceled.[17]

Warner transitioned from life in Gifu to a controlled but less constrained atmosphere in Tokyo's Olympic Village. One of the biggest challenges he faced, because his event was staged on August 4 and 5 in the second half of the Olympic event calendar, was steering clear of those who had completed their events and felt less restricted in their personal behavior. Many "were letting their guard down," recounted Warner, "and we had our guard fully up." He had journeyed too far over the past sixteen months to be sidelined at the final moment.

ASTOUNDING PERFORMANCES: ATHLETES AMAZE

Damian Warner has been asked if athletes' accomplishments in Tokyo should be marked with an asterisk. He countered any such notion with the thought that, "if anything," when one considers the uncertainty, the delay, the COVID protocols, and the absence of spectators, an "exclamation mark" is more appropriate.[18] As the forty-eight hours set aside for the decathlon competition neared, many Olympians had already delivered superlative performances.

Australians rejoiced at the two triumphs of Ariarne Titmus over US swim legend Katie Ledecky in the 200 m and 400 m freestyle events.[19] Titmus had won against Ledecky in the 400 m freestyle at the 2019 World Championships. The swim world, robbed of their ongoing (respectful) rivalry for two years, reveled in their Tokyo performances. Ledecky, who ran her personal career Olympic medal count to seven golds and three silvers in Tokyo, showed her resilience and championship mettle by capturing gold medals in the 800 m and 1500 m freestyle events. In her Olympic debut, Maggie MacNeil, Warner's compatriot and fellow Londoner (Ontario, Canada), won the 100 m butterfly and took home silver and bronze medals in the 4 × 100 m freestyle relay and 4 × 100 m medley relay, respectively. For dominance in the pool, one need look no further than the American Caeleb Dressel, who captured five gold medals (50 m freestyle, 100 m freestyle, 100 m butterfly, 4 × 100 m freestyle relay, and 4 × 100 m medley relay), an astounding collection of Olympic hardware that he proudly showed the people in his hometown upon returning to Green Cove Springs, Florida.

For the sheer joy experienced in victory, it was hard to match that felt by Hidilyn Diaz, who won gold in the women's 55 kg weightlifting competition, and in doing so captured the first ever gold medal for the Philippines.[20] On the same day Diaz made Olympic history, Great Britain's Tom Daley fulfilled his quest for redemption and Olympic gold, when he and partner Matty Lee went to the top of the podium following their win in the 10 m synchro diving event (Daley also won a bronze medal in the 10 m platform).[21] Jamaica's Elaine Thompson-Herah became the first woman to win the 100 m and 200 m on the track in successive Olympic Games.[22] Ethiopian-born, Dutch runner, Sifan Hassan dazzled with gold medals in the 5000 m and 10000 m races, while also capturing a bronze medal in the 1500 m.

US gymnast MyKayla Skinner, an Arizonan who overcame COVID-related pneumonia earlier in the year, experienced a most improbable path toward being awarded an Olympic medal. She was not eligible for the team competition because she was one of two designated American individual-event athletes; however, she competed in the qualifying rounds in all four individual women's gymnastics events (vault, uneven parallel bars, floor exercise, and balance beam). Though she performed well in the preliminary qualifying rounds, her best finish was in the vault, where she placed fourth. Two American teammates (Simone Biles and Jade Carey) finished ahead of her, however, and advanced to the individual vault final. Their results prevented Skinner from qualifying for a berth in the individual vault final (wherein only a team's top two finishers in the qualifying round for each individual event advanced to the final) and representing the United States. Having given it her best, Skinner had no regrets.

However, the circumstances surrounding Skinner's vault teammate, the much-celebrated defending Olympic champion Simone Biles, offered Skinner a "second chance" to appear on the victory podium. Biles, once a teenage gymnastic phenom from Texas, now a twenty-three-year-old veteran competitor, and a winner of four gold medals at the previous Olympic Games in Rio in 2016, plus nineteen more gold medals at several World Gymnastic Championship competitions, sadly and suddenly was seized by what the gymnastics world calls "the twisties"—the loss of a sense of aerial awareness while executing twisting or tumbling routines. Biles's resolve collapsed, triggering significant media treatment of athletes' mental health issues, not just her own. She withdrew from the finals of three individual disciplines, as well as the individual all-around and team competitions. This left only the balance beam, in which she recovered sufficiently to secure the bronze medal. (Biles eventually reminded fans of her championship mettle and placed an exclamation mark on her recovery with four gold and one silver medal at the 2023 World Gymnastics Championships, then captivated fans in Paris with performances resulting in three Olympic gold and one silver medal).

With Biles's withdrawal from the vault event, MyKayla Skinner moved into the final as the second American qualifier, joining teammate Jade Carey. With two exceptional vaults in the final, Skinner captured second place and the silver medal. "I was actually going to get on a plane to go home," she stated in a post-event interview. "This has seriously been so humbling, and I'm just so grateful to be here."[23] Thus does Olympic heroism sometimes arrive in unforeseen ways.

Rivalling Skinner's experience for improbability were the shared gold medals in men's high jump for Qatar's Mutaz Barshim and Italy's Gianmarco Tamberi. Never had more than one man cleared 2.37 m (7'9.3") in the same Olympic competition. In Tokyo, three did, including Maksim Nedasekau of Belarus. However, Barshim and Tamberi recorded no misses before all three attempted 2.39 m (7'10.09"), along with three other jumpers who had passed at lower heights. No one cleared 2.39 m, so the officials called for a jump-off for the gold between Tamberi and Barshim.[24] Barshim proposed the possibility of awarding "co-golds." Following deliberations, the "possibility" was confirmed. After the ensuing celebration, Barshim explained his approach: "For me, coming here, I know for a fact for the performance I did, I deserve that gold. He did the same thing, so I know he deserved that gold." A broken ankle had sidelined Tamberi from participation in the 2016 Rio Olympics, while Barshim had struggled with injuries while preparing for the Tokyo Games. On this day, the two friends delivered a lesson in sportsmanship. "This is beyond sport," Barshim said, "this is the message we deliver to the young generation."[25] Nedasekau took the bronze medal.

As Kit McConnell crossed off the completed events at the end of each day, he reflected on the different vibe in Tokyo, largely created by COVID-19's impact on the participants' lives over the last sixteen months and the absence of spectators. "You could see what it meant to the athletes on the field of play to be competing [in Tokyo] in an Olympic environment," McConnell

Gianmarco Tamberi and Mutaz Barshim celebrate their joint gold medal finish in the men's high jump in Tokyo. Credit: 2021/International Olympic Committee/ DAVIDSON, Alex.

observed. Without friends and family to reach out to after their events, the "athletes turned to each other. . . . That spirit on the field of play," said McConnell, "was incredible."[26] More highlights would follow in the days ahead. Gregg Popovich exorcised his Olympic demons when the US men's basketball team defeated France 87–82 in the final.[27] Canada's women's soccer team captured a spot in the final with a 1–0 semifinal win over their US archrivals, then proceeded to defeat Sweden 3–2 on penalty kicks in the final game, delivering a long sought-after gold medal to one of the best ambassadors for the sport, Canada's Christine Sinclair.[28] Japan rejoiced at its home team's sweep of gold medals over the United States in the baseball and softball finals.[29] In the gripping marathon event, Kenya's Eliud Kipchoge repeated his gold medal performance in Rio.[30] Making her fifth Olympic appearance, thirty-five-year-old US track star and mother, Allyson Felix, won her tenth (bronze, 400 m) and eleventh medals (gold, 4 × 400 m relay). She became the most medal-decorated female athlete in Olympic track and field history, and also surpassed Carl Lewis's ten medals to become American history's most decorated Olympic track and field star.[31]

A FIGHT FOR GENDER EQUITY

Many Tokyo 2020 athletes' narratives, such as Damian Warner's preparation saga for competing in 2021, rhapsodize their demonstrated persistence in seeking training opportunities in their home communities after being compromised by COVID restrictions. Because of when the coronavirus emerged and its varying prevalence across the globe, athletes navigated a qualification process devised rapidly on both sport-by-sport and regional bases. In the Americas, a boxing qualification tournament in Argentina planned for May 2020 could not be staged. In its place, the IOC Boxing Task Force determined that female boxers might base their qualifications for Tokyo on performances recorded at three tournaments held across 2018 and 2019. This decision short-circuited the plans of eleven-time Canadian flyweight champion and Rio Olympian Mandy Bujold, who was returning to the ring following the birth of her daughter in November 2018 (and postpartum complications). Bujold had planned her pregnancy so she might compete in the 2020 tournament in Argentina and lock down a place on the Canadian Olympic team. Given her status as the world's second-ranked flyweight at the time of her plan to begin a family, she was confident in her chances.[32] COVID-19 disrupted her carefully conceived effort to flip the script on her Rio experience when she fell ill the evening before her quarter-final bout, landing her in hospital with an intravenous feed. Despite being so compromised, she made her way from the hospital bed to the ring, losing decisively to China's Ren Cancan, who went on to capture a bronze medal.[33]

In explaining her determination to find a route to Tokyo, Bujold stated, "I want to show my daughter to never give up and keep pushing. I know the IOC is trying to find ways to qualify athletes but it's hard when it's all being cancelled. You need to have the best athletes there to keep the integrity of the Games."[34] With her path to Tokyo 2020 blocked, Bujold pursued an appeal to the IOC, without success. Her case drew the attention of former heavyweight boxing champion Lennox Lewis and tennis legend Billie Jean King, both of whom questioned the IOC's reaction to Bujold's situation. Canada's federal heritage minister, Steven Guilbault, appealed directly to IOC President Thomas Bach; meanwhile, Bujold and her lawyer, Sylvie Rodrigue, took her case to the Court of Arbitration for Sport (CAS).[35] The IOC's handling of Bujold's case, wrote Guilbault, conveyed to "female athletes the world over—you can be an athlete or a mother—but not both at the same time. Hers is a nuanced case that deserves consideration, not rigidity."[36]

The CAS agreed, ruling in Bujold's favor. Perhaps exhausted or distracted by the legal machinations, or simply experiencing "ring rust" during her first competitive contest in eighteen months, Bujold lost her first bout in Tokyo to Serbia's Nina Radovanović.[37] In the bigger picture, however, Bujold was winning a helpful precedent, a "game changer" for future Olympians who also happen to be mothers. In assessing the struggle to secure her place in Tokyo, Bujold concluded, "It was one of the biggest fights of my career. But also the fight with the most meaning."[38]

WARNER'S TWO MEMORABLE DAYS IN TOKYO

Compounding the challenge for Damian Warner and his fellow decathletes in Tokyo—and a constant fear for Richard Budgett—was the searing heat. The temperature in Tokyo reached 33.7°C (92.7°F) on August 4, with a relative humidity of 62 percent that made conditions feel like 109°F.[39] Warner related that the temperature for the pole vault on August 5 was even higher. While he himself did not have a thermometer at track level, an official showed him one that registered 114°F. "Day two," reported Warner, "was hot, hot, hot." It "was the hottest competition I've ever been in." At one point during the pole vault competition, Warner "knelt down and burned [his] knee on the track."[40]

Warner arrived at the Olympic Village five days before his competition, expecting that his coach, Gar Leyshon, would have to stay at a nearby hotel, except for a twenty-four-hour window while he was in competition. However, Warner caught a break. Because competitors whose events had concluded were streaming out of Tokyo daily, space opened up in the Village, and Leyshon was permitted to remain there for the duration of Warner's stay after only one night in a nearby hotel. This simplified and better facilitated their interaction during the final days of Warner's preparations.[41]

Day One

With the first event, the 100 m, scheduled for 9 a.m. on August 4, Warner rose from bed when his alarm sounded at five. He loads multiple alarms on his phone at such times, as one of his recurring dreams is that he misses an alarm and scrambles to a competition that has already commenced. He proceeded outside for some stretching and a run around the Olympic Village. Warner waved to fellow Olympians who were completing similar precompetition rituals, listening to music to help get him into "his own headspace." After visiting the dining hall for breakfast, he returned to his room to pack his equipment bag for the day's competition.

He and Leyshon headed to the stadium, well familiar with the precision of the bus transportation system and the fact that the ride would take 23 minutes and 20 seconds. Armed with his notebook, which he keeps close during competitions to record meaningful cues and focus points, and bolstered by his performance in Götzis two months earlier and solid practice sessions in Japan, Warner exuded measurable confidence. The key word guiding his approach as he entered the competition was "execute." Still, having sat next to Dallas Maverick and Slovenian Olympian Luka Doncic, and having watched NBA legend and China's three-time Olympian Yao Ming walk by his seat in the dining hall days earlier, his tension and excitement were palpable. While you try to convince yourself "it's just a normal competition, it's not," said Warner.[42]

The rooms beneath the grandstands for the decathletes and heptathletes were sizable, the food and drink plentiful; however, several coaches thought one folding chair per athlete was less than desirable in fostering the necessary rest and relaxation between events. Coaches asked Japanese stadium officials for air mattresses for their athletes, and the response was favorable and swift. Warner found the officials "accommodating" and willing to help, while Leyshon ventured that the Japanese response converted the rooms into the "best facilities" he has seen for decathletes in a major competition.[43]

Warner scaled back his warmup for the 100 m because of the high temperatures, then reentered the combined events room to await notification for his heat. He was seeded in the final heat with the fastest runners. Answering the call for his heat, he went to his lane assignment, prepared his starting blocks, and did one run, which he later dubbed "horrible."[44] His calves were cramping; he'd had to wait too long following his warmup and had cooled down. He tried a second start. It was no better. Hastily, he went through some stretching and a rapid warmup routine until his name echoed through the PA system. Warner, in the outside lane, was the last competitor whose name was called before the starter assumed control of the proceedings. No time to think, just go, he told himself. When the gun sounded, he propelled himself forward and barreled down the track, finishing in an impressive 10.12 seconds. It was the start he "was looking for."

Warner had little time to reflect as he headed immediately to the long jump pit. "There's 24 guys trying to find their [marks and] approaches, it's all a little bit rushed," reflected Warner.[45] In his long jump warmup, Warner avoided near disaster. Athletes strive to set the length of their approach to the "takeoff board" with great precision. The routine involves making the approach but running through the landing pit as opposed to launching oneself from the board. Warner has done this countless times; however, on this occasion he had so much speed that when his lead foot hit the soft sand, it sank too deep and threw him off balance. He narrowly avoided crashing into an official and a nearby television camera at the end of the pit. He nimbly slid between the two "threats." Warner's maneuver, thought a relieved Leyshon, was perhaps "the most athletic thing he [would] do that day."[46]

Warner was scheduled to jump following Belgium's Thomas Van der Plaetsen, who had finished third in Götzis behind Canada's Pierce LePage. Unfortunately for Van der Plaetsen, he tore his hamstring in completing his first jump. A delay ensued. The unlucky Belgian required a wheelchair to depart the competition area. Once granted access to the runway, Warner roared toward the board, launched himself, and jumped 8.24 m (27'0.5"). Had Warner achieved this in the Olympic long jump event itself, he would have captured the bronze medal. Leyshon, situated next to the pit at a distance, knew Warner nailed the jump, but Warner wasn't convinced as he scrambled out of the pit. He looked over to Leyshon and other jubilant Canadian officials, concluding that it must have been better than he had at first perceived. It was the second-longest jump in the history of Olympic decathlon. Somewhere, Harry Marra smiled.

Harry Marra had guided retired American decathlete Ashton Eaton to gold medal performances in the London (2012) and Rio de Janeiro (2016) Olympics, and also had coached his training partner and spouse, Canadian heptathlete Brianne Theisen-Eaton, to the bronze medal in Rio. Eaton is one of three men who bested 9000 points in the decathlon prior to the Tokyo Olympics. He is also one of three decathletes to win the coveted gold medal in consecutive Olympic festivals. USA Track and Field named Marra Coach of the Year in 2012. In 2016, World Athletics recognized him as the World Athletics Coach of the Year.[47] A much-respected voice in the sport, Marra believed that the early discipline performances in the decathlon were critical in putting one's competitors in a tough position. Securing a sizable point lead following the 100 m and long jump meant added pressure for one's opponents—they were now chasing. "When people are chasing," says Leyshon, "they tighten up . . . it's the enemy of performance." Warner's exhibited strength in the 100 m and long jump has led him to follow the script established by Marra: Push hard in the 100 m and long jump.[48] In Tokyo, as in Götzis, Warner finished first in both. After two events, Warner was 216 points clear of Australia's Ashley Moloney, who sat in second place.[49] Several of Warner's competitors never recovered.[50]

The last event prior to the midday break was the shot put. Warner's performance in Götzis (14.31 m/46'11.39")[51] and his months of practice had not delivered the desired results. "There are certain events throughout the decathlon," stated Warner, that are "not as locked in as the others." For Warner, shot put is one of those "make it or break it events" that determines if he will meet or approach his overall expectations for performance. His initial throw was 14.2 m (46'7.1"). A second attempt was marginally better. Though these marks left him in good position, he did not want his competitors to sense an opening. Some were capable of throws exceeding 15 m (49'2.55"). Warner's third attempt, 14.8 m (48'6.68"), bettered his result from Götzis by close to 50 cm (1'7.69"), securing him an additional 30 points.[52] Leyshon bore witness to Warner's emotional response to the third throw.[53] It was the type of throw he needed to maintain the gap on the field. Pierce LePage's 15.31 m toss (50'2.67") and the 809 points assigned to it propelled Warner's teammate past Moloney into second place (2773). Warner (2966) led the field by 193 points.[54] His third throw boosted his spirits, and he relaxed on the bus ride to the Olympic Village and some much-needed rest. The high jump and 400 m awaited the competitors later in the day.

Warner opted for the Olympic Village as a midday refuge, where he could clear his head and refocus for the next two events. He wanted to stay clear of the stadium's combined events room and the tension of the competition environment, even though it offered the comfort of good food, refreshments, and the air mattresses. He had confidence in the reliability of the ground transportation and had a wide choice of food at the dining hall. Following lunch, a shower, and a few episodes of *Seinfeld*, he returned to the stadium.[55]

Warner was wary of the likes of Moloney, LePage, and Team USA's Garrett Scantling, while France's Kevin Mayer still lurked as a serious threat. He was keenly aware of Mayer's Day Two strengths in the javelin, 110 m hurdles, and pole vault. Warner jumped 2.02 m (6'7.53") in the high jump, 7 cm (2.76") less than he cleared in Götzis, but Warner had a near miss at 2.05 m. He was still on his pace set at Götzis where he had scored 8995 points.[56] Meanwhile, Moloney surged back into second place (3647) with a jump of

Damian Warner competes in the high jump event on the first day of the decathlon competition at the 2020 Tokyo Olympics. *Credit: 2021/ International Olympic Committee/EVANS, Jason.*

2.11 m (6′11.07″), trailing Warner (3788) by 141 points. Moloney maintained his momentum in the 400 m, capturing first place in a time of 46.29, with LePage (personal best, 46.92) and Warner (season's best, 47.48) finishing close behind in the third and final heat.[57] With 4722 points earned on the first day, Warner was 81 points clear of Moloney, while Kevin Mayer was in fifth, 382 points behind the leader. "I did exactly what I needed to do," Warner recalled. In the mixed zone populated by media personnel, Warner told reporters—whose leading questions hinted at the competition being over—that he would need to bring his best the next day.[58]

LePage's Day One performance was noteworthy. Though he tumbled the following day from third overall to a fifth-place finish, only a select few were aware he was competing with a sizable tear in a patellar tendon. It was a scenario like the one that confronted Warner before the 2019 World Championships, when successive sprained ankles compromised his preparations and results (bronze medal). Tokyo 2020 taught LePage "a lot about resilience." He took those lessons to heart, using the experience as a springboard to a silver medal finish behind Kevin Mayer at the 2022 World Championships in Eugene, Oregon, a meeting from which Warner withdrew after he injured a hamstring in the 400 m. World-class decathletes are blessed with elite athleticism, motivation, and drive, but good fortune also plays a role in their results.

As Warner and LePage rested prior to the 400 m in Tokyo, LePage consumed mustard packets, while Warner took shots of balsamic vinegar. They exchanged a look of shared "disgust" at what they were consuming, but both knew that the goal, as stated by LePage, was to "keep that lactic acid down." LePage's personal best convinced him that mustard packets had a place "in [his] future." He also experimented with Warner's balsamic vinegar. "It might be the only time Damian takes shots," deadpanned LePage.[59]

The heat was, as expected, a major challenge on Day One. Leyshon, distressed that most of the decathletes had no umbrellas for shade during the afternoon events, joined other coaches in their concern, which turned to disgust when they learned that "TV did not want them." Eventually, two large umbrellas appeared. Warner used Leyshon's hand umbrella. He and LePage dipped frequently into coolers with ice and drinks supplied by Athletics Canada. Also adding relief were ice vests and towels that could be soaked in the coolers' ice water.[60]

When they exited the stadium, Warner and Leyshon headed for the bus stand. They were approached by an Athletics Canada official who indicated that there was a car waiting outside the gates to take Warner back to the Olympic Village. Though Warner and Leyshon were comfortable with the thought of a ride on the air-conditioned shuttle bus, Leyshon thought that someone had worked hard, trying to do something "extra nice" for his athlete. They accepted the ride to reward that person for their effort.

When they arrived at the vehicle stand, scores of cars were parked there, but none were designated for Warner. As they searched for his car, the bus drove by. Stymied, they tried to reenter the stadium grounds to catch the next bus but were told the gate that they exited was a one-way egress point, meaning that they had a forty-minute delay caused by a long walk to a designated entry gate and the need to clear security once more.[61] Once back in the Village, Warner and Leyshon resolved to would stick with the reliability of the bus on Day Two. Though Leyshon was agitated, thinking he should have nixed the idea of the car ride, he soon cooled down. Warner brushed it off, not letting the scenario alter his positive mindset.[62] He'd had larger mountains to climb over the past sixteen months than losing forty minutes of rest. Nothing could dim the shine on the success he enjoyed on

Day One. Warner visited the dining hall, retreated to his room to relax with a few more episodes of *Seinfeld*, packed his bag for the next day, and again set multiple alarms on his phone.

Day Two

When Warner headed to the stadium on August 5, he carried with him positive energy from home as Jen Cotten, his coaches back in Canada, and his agent, Jeff Fischer,[63] sent texts, photos, and videos of scenes featuring his friends and family. Fischer had hosted a viewing party in his backyard on Day One. Dennis Nielsen bearhugged people. The atmosphere was celebratory, at times quite loud, loud enough that five-month old Theo was outfitted with earmuffs to prevent him from being scared amid the pandemonium. "They were so crazy," recalled Warner, "that it almost felt like they were in the stands watching"; the support "[meant] a lot." On Day Two, the "Warner fan" group gathered at a local bar where several patrons, neither familiar with Warner nor the decathlon, became avidly engaged and excited viewers.

For Leyshon, all of this explained why Warner smiled so much over the two days of competition. He could feel the embrace and warmth of his supporters thousands of miles distant. It was a valuable way of keeping him relaxed and upbeat. As the competitors marshalled in the combined events room, Warner was eager for the 110 m hurdles, his favorite event, and the first test scheduled for the decathletes that day.[64]

Warner, once again seeded in the third and final heat due to past performances, watched as Kevin Mayer ran the hurdles course in 13.9 seconds in the second heat, a performance well off Mayer's personal best. Warner still viewed Mayer as his chief threat due to the Frenchman's Day Two strengths. Nevertheless, Mayer's hurdles performance opened the door for Warner to put a greater total points distance between the two of them. Warner delivered: 13.46 seconds, an excellent time, even though it was a trifle off his 13.36 seconds (decathlon world record) recorded in Götzis. His time, however, well clear of Mayer's and the rest of the field, awarded him 1045 points, pushing Mayer 58 points further back.[65] Perhaps even more importantly, Warner demonstrated poise in managing a brush contact on one of the hurdles. His body told him to gear down slightly to avoid further complications. If not for this element of his performance, he might have challenged the world record decathlon performance in hurdles that he had achieved in Austria. Leyshon believes that earlier in Warner's career, such a rapid and coolly managed adjustment would have posed a major problem, but Warner's decision to "throttle back" reflected his accrued experience. It was all about "mitigating risks," said Warner. "I don't need to run 13.3 in the hurdles, I just can't run 13.8." When he saw his posted time, he thought, "That's what you're looking for."[66] Warner and Mayer were the only two competitors to run under 14 seconds.[67]

As the decathletes returned to the combined events room after the hurdles event, Warner, in assessing the body language of several of his competitors, sensed that some had conceded him the gold medal. This "sense" provided him with a further jolt of confidence leading into the seventh event, the discus throw.[68] Mayer (5327) remained in fourth place, 440 points behind Warner (5767). Ashley Moloney (5605) stood second overall.[69] If the feeling for some at track side was that Warner, barring injury, had locked down the gold medal in the hurdles event, this feeling was strengthened when he threw the discus 48.67 m (159'8.14"), bettering his Götzis result by 24 cm (9.45").[70] Warner finished third in the event. Of the front runners, Mayer finished sixth (48.08 m/157'8.91") and LePage wound up seventh (47.14 m/154'7.9"). Warner (6610) was now 251 points clear of Moloney (6359), while Mayer remained a distant fourth (6157).[71] Mayer approached Warner after the event and complimented him, admitting ruefully, "If there was an event where I thought ... I had a chance to come back, I thought this was it."[72] Mayer's attention now focused on a silver medal.

Mayer's opportunity for a podium finish rested in the pole vault and javelin throw. As they prepared for the pole vault, the competitors tried to block out thoughts of the stifling heat. The fiberglass poles got so hot in the competition area that Leyshon worried about the effect on their functionality. When Leyshon went down to track level, the heat on the back of his neck "felt like a blowtorch."[73] The athletes, with their poles, waited for their attempts under the grandstands in the shade. The severe heat had one benefit: Warner and several other competitors noted that the hot conditions affected the rubber-encased ends of the bar and their connection with the rubber surface of the small platforms on which the bar rested, adding a bit more adhesion. Some brushes against the bar that ordinarily would have dislodged it resulted in clearances. Warner cleared 4.90 m (16'0.91"), bettering his result in Götzis by 10 cm (3.94") and equaling his personal best.[74] Even though he finished eleventh in the event, his result blunted the modest gains recorded by Mayer (5.2 m/17'0.72"), Scantling (5.10 m/16'8.79"), LePage

(5.00 m/16′4.85″), and Moloney (5.00 m), all of whom finished ahead of him.[75] As the decathletes retreated for lunch and rest prior to the javelin throw and the grueling 1500 m, Warner was 221 points clear of the field.[76]

Warner departed the stadium atmosphere during the midday break. With the pole vault and discus in his rear-view mirror, two problematic events "where technically things can get out of control," Warner now realized the gold medal was well within his grasp. It was an "awesome" feeling. "Don't step off the curb and sprain your ankle. Don't fall down the steps, don't choke on your food and pass out," he told himself. Because of the extended duration of the pole vault competition, the break was shorter than the one enjoyed by the decathletes on Day One.[77]

"Javelin was interesting," recalled Warner, who stated that his warmup "was as horrible as can be." Though he had set his approach length a countless number of times in competition, in Tokyo he struggled in establishing his mark. His warmup throws concerned him; his run-up length appeared not to be in sync with his well-established approach and footwork pattern. The situation proved "super stressful." Warner went back to his notebook in search of an answer. He remeasured his approach and quickly convened with Leyshon to report that he had been off by 2 m (6′6.74″). On reflection, Warner thinks he might have rushed his original measurement for his mark due to the distraction of other track and field events in progress at the same time—or it might have been a simple "mental lapse."[78] With the situation resolved, Warner registered a solid 63.44 m throw (208′1.64″). As expected, Kevin Mayer surged forward, with a personal best throw of 73.09 m (239′9.56″), which left him in the silver medal position (8066), but still well behind Warner (8280).[79] Short of a complete disaster, the 1500 m amounted to four victory laps. That thought aside, Warner set his sights on becoming the fourth man ever to register 9000 points, a total never achieved in Olympic competition.

Warner approached the start line for the 1500 m with "no nerves." This was an odd feeling. At this stage of a decathlon competition, worn down by two days of physical challenges, athletes are often "almost on the edge of being a wreck." Nausea threatens to hamper performance. Warner and Leyshon established split times necessary for Warner to surpass 9000 points. In hindsight, Warner concluded that he was too relaxed entering the race. He encountered difficulty in meeting the split times despite the loud and urging reminders from Leyshon at trackside. Leyshon's description of the first three laps was both colorful and humorous. He "was picking daisies," said Leyshon, but that changed as the bell lap sounded and Warner began to reel in runners over the final 400 m. His speed on the final lap, recounted Warner, was the "coolest thing." With 150 m remaining in the race, a flood of thoughts washed over him, in particular those tied to the challenges resulting from COVID-19. "I did it," Warner told himself,[80] when he crossed the finish line in fifth (4:31.08), well ahead of Mayer's fourteenth-place finish.[81] He was unsure if his pursuit of 9000 points had been successful until the results were posted on the stadium scoreboard.[82] Warner finished with 9018 points and a new Olympic record, ahead of Mayer (8726) and Moloney (8649), who captured the silver and bronze medals, respectively.[83]

Warner went "wire to wire," seizing the lead with his outstanding 10.12 seconds in the 100 m, never relinquishing it over the succeeding nine events. Following the 1500 m he spent some "fellowship time" with his decathlete brethren, circled the track holding aloft a Canadian Maple Leaf flag, and exchanged friendly banter with the female heptathletes, who had remained in the stadium until the decathlon was complete. There was much demand for his time in the mixed zone with reporters from around the globe, followed by a lengthy stay in doping control before his arrival back at the Olympic Village at 3 a.m. Before retiring, Warner and Leyshon enjoyed an extended visit to the dessert bar in the dining hall.[84]

The following day, August 6, Warner stepped to the top of the podium in the medal ceremony, an eleven-year quest fulfilled. Then, the next morning at breakfast, Canada's chef de mission, Marnie McBean, invited Warner to serve as the nation's flag bearer in the Closing Ceremony scheduled for August 8. Warner and Leyshon were part of the mass exodus from Tokyo on August 9, eagerly anticipating the opportunity to reunite with family and friends. It had been some ride.

A FINAL THOUGHT

Like so many of Tokyo 2020's illustrious Olympic champions, Damian Warner further cemented his earned reputation as a superlative athlete, but also revealed himself to the wider world as an exemplar of determination and resilience. COVID-19 challenged Warner and others who aspired to participate in the Tokyo Olympics. Competing in Tokyo was not only a win for them; their courage and exploits provided a "win" for the rest of us too. Reeling from the isolation of a global pandemic, we were afforded the opportunity to escape a measure of its shadow for two weeks. Perhaps never before had a televised Olympic Games delivered such "entertainment value" for the global community.

In the months ahead, Warner withdrew from the decathlon at the 2022 World Championships in Eugene, Oregon, due to an injury incurred in the 400 m race; captured the silver medal at the 2023 World Championships in Budapest, behind Pierce LePage; and stood poised to medal in 2024 for a third time in Olympic competition in Paris before failing to record a result in the pole vault on Day Two. Fellow competitors Kevin Mayer, who would have been competing on home soil, and reigning world champion Pierce LePage withdrew due to injury in July before the Games opened. Like so many elite athletes who challenge themselves and their abilities on the world stage, Warner, Mayer, and LePage have experienced both highs and lows. It is their ability—and the ability of all successful world-class athletes—to manage the highs and withstand the lows that underpins their records of accomplishment.

7

REFLECTIONS: TOKYO 2020 AND HISTORY'S LONG LENS

As we draw the final curtain on the saga of what passed in Japan for the Games of the XXXIInd Olympiad, the sole Olympic Games edition of their now century-and-a-quarter history to be staged in an odd-numbered year, it is appropriate to offer readers our judgment as to what history's long lens will reveal—or, taken another way, what lessons of history might be gained from the so-called COVID Games for future contemplation and guidance. Our Olympic outlook is empirically driven. We depend on facts, and the facts tell us that the Tokyo Games were a success story. They occurred. Athletes performed admirably after having weathered the challenges of preparing in a COVID-19 environment. People around the globe watched them, some while caught in varying degrees of isolation and lockdown, and for a period, found escape from the monotony of their daily lives in a pandemic. The feared further spread of COVID-19, given the numbers of people descending on Tokyo from around the world, did not occur.

That the staging of Tokyo 2020 in the face such of immense challenge was a success story is beyond debate, despite criticism offered by a cadre of Olympics skeptics, some of whom reside in academia and the media.[1] It is true that some ambiguity impinges on assessing the Games' success or failure, because the original goal advanced by Shinzo Abe to display a "vision of a proud, 'reborn' Japan showcasing itself to the world obviously did not come to pass," as Paul O'Shea and Sebastian Maslow wrote, and "neither did the promise of a 'Recovery Olympics' [aid] in the reconstruction of the post-3/11 Tohoku region."[2] In our view, COVID-19 moved the "goalposts" for assessing Tokyo 2020's success or failure. Measuring their success would depend on the Games taking place, if the athletes could rally and perform in competition given the challenges presented during their training and preparations, and if the IOC and Japanese organizers could retrofit the Tokyo venues for competition in a COVID-19 environment without triggering either the feared superspreader event or an outbreak of a new variant.[3]

In the end, Tokyo 2020's success was built precisely on the energy of one fundamental factor. Its dominance from start to finish of the grand project is undeniable. It is simple. It reflects a consistent pattern of cohesion toward achieving a solution to a vexing problem. The success of the Games was borne on the shoulders of *human relationships*, reflecting organizers' great trust in personal communication, cooperation, inspiration, and determination.

HUMAN RELATIONSHIPS

Few doubt the prominent role of human relationships in history's progress. Although irreconcilable personal differences have been root factors in conflicts through the ages, page after page of world history has demonstrated that people working together collaboratively have delivered needed solutions. So it was for the success of the Tokyo 2020 Games. In general, such a feat depended most importantly on the two leaders of Tokyo's Olympic enterprise—Thomas Bach, IOC president, and Shinzo Abe, Japan's prime minister—throughout the periods of bidding on and receiving the Games, their preparations, and their eventual postponement in March 2020. After Bach and IOC officials congratulated Tokyo's bid delegation following Bach's September 2013 announcement of the city's successful bid in Buenos Aires, Argentina, at the IOC's 125th General Session—where Abe had a front-row seat—the two men met next at the Seventieth Session of the United Nations General Assembly in New York, where Abe addressed the august world body. There, in Midtown Manhattan, Bach and Abe each declared their intention "to work closely together to ensure the success of the 2020 Olympic and Paralympic Games in Tokyo."[4]

Over the succeeding months and years, Abe and Bach created a genuinely close relationship, indeed a friendship, based on mutual trust and confidence that Japan and the IOC were up to the task. So, too, did such a relationship of trust and commitment develop between Japanese Olympic and IOC officials charged with the responsibilities of transforming Abe's and Bach's personal resolve into hard-and-fast planning. As we have related in the preceding pages while focusing on the problems created by the onset of the pandemic, this trust and commitment extended to the relationships between Hideki Nidemasa and the IOC's Christophe Dubi and Kit McConnell, and likewise between Richard Budgett and Brian McCloskey with Takao Akama, Pau Mota with Satoshi Shimada, and Timo Lumme with an array of Japanese CEOs and marketing executives whose companies were invested in Tokyo's enterprise.

Both Abe and Bach needed a full measure of expressed "trust and confidence" as Tokyo 2020 drew nearer. There is no doubt that Shinzo Abe's disposition on hosting an Olympic Games became steadfast as time passed. For Abe, the Olympics represented a final bookend to his political career. For Thomas Bach, the Tokyo Games would have been the centerpiece event of the last year of his eight-year tenure as IOC President. As it eventually unfolded, Tokyo 2020 launched his second term. When the IOC met in March 2021, twelve months following the postponement announcement, a resounding vote (93–1) reelected Bach for a final four-year presidential term.

For the (then) sixty-seven-year-old Bach, there was much to accomplish. His acceptance speech reflected the interpersonal tone marked by his past leadership and what he sought to underscore going forward: "You know that this touches me deeply. It also makes me humble. When you elected me for the first time as your President in 2013 in Buenos Aires, I said that I wanted to lead the IOC according to my campaign motto, 'Unity in diversity' and be a President for all of you and for all our stakeholders. This commitment is also true for my second and last term. My door, my ears and my heart remain open for each and every one of you."[5] Still another element of Bach's acceptance speech extended his interpersonal theme: "I would today like to inspire a discussion with you and everybody interested in the Olympic community—on whether we should not complement the Olympic slogan 'faster, higher, stronger' by adding after a hyphen, the word 'altogether': this could be, from my point of view, a strong commitment to our core value of solidarity and an appropriate and a humble adaptation to the challenges of this new world."[6] It is the type of rhetoric that makes Olympic critics cringe, but is melodious to the true believers who have embraced the Olympic Movement's stated mission and its underpinning philosophy of Olympism.

THE DIFFICULT PATH FORWARD IN 2020

With the onset of the coronavirus, which in time caused almost 34 million cases of COVID-19 and more than 74,000 deaths in Japan, an Olympic festival to which the world had been invited quite obviously could not be held in such dangerous health conditions.[7] An alarmed Japanese populace, angry media, embattled layers of governmental authority, and activist-oriented academics would have none of it. Human existence in Japan was at stake. Abe and Bach sought a solution.

In line with the Olympic cases of 1916, 1940, and 1944, when the world was gripped by military conflict, cancellation beckoned. But as we have seen, the forces of persistence prevailed, and a postponement for one year to the summer of 2021 was accommodated. Shinzo Abe made public the outcome of his conference with Bach: "In the present circumstances and based on the information provided by the World Health Organization today, the IOC president and the prime minister of Japan have concluded that the Games of the XXXIInd Olympiad in Tokyo must be rescheduled to a date beyond 2020 but not later than summer 2021, to safeguard the health of the athletes, everybody involved in the Olympic Games and the international community."[8] The rest of that story, of course, is the history that we have examined in this book.

On August 28, 2020, less than a year before the replanned 2020 Olympics were scheduled to open in July 2021, Shinzo Abe resigned his post as prime minister. He had served in that supreme position of authority longer than any other person in Japanese history. Long-festering and debilitating bouts of ulcerative colitis resulting in a persistent inflammatory bowel condition demanding twice weekly hospital visits finally took their toll on the sixty-five-year old Abe.[9] He could go on no longer.

Abe's successor, Yoshihide Suga, assumed the mantle of leadership and, therefore, oversight of Olympic matters. Thomas Bach, undeniably grieving Abe's state of personal health that prompted his retirement, feared a reordering of Suga's agenda priorities that might be unfavorable for the prospect of Tokyo's Olympic Games. Nevertheless, Bach could take a measure of confidence from one of the final thoughts expressed by a severely weakened Abe to his successor as he turned authority over to him: "Please see to it that my friend Thomas Bach gets his Olympic Games."[10]

Thomas Bach did indeed "get his Olympics," and "his friend," Shinzo Abe, witnessed them. However, almost a year following those Games, Abe, in increasingly precarious health, died at the hands of an assassin.[11] At Abe's state funeral, a solemn Bach paid his final tribute to the former prime minister, who, quite possibly, more than any other single person connected with Japan's Olympic project, ensured that there would be a celebration of Olympic Games in modern history's XXXIInd Olympiad. Stated Bach, "We agreed on the postponement of the Olympic Games at the height of the global pandemic. Without his support the Olympic Games Tokyo 2020 would not have taken place. The athletes, the Olympic Movement and fans around the world owe him a huge debt of gratitude."[12]

The power of human relationships doubtless played a fundamental role in the successful conclusion of the Tokyo 2020 Olympic Games. Faced with catastrophic challenges that threatened Abe and Bach's successful solution, the relationship established between the two leaders permeated through the secondary ranks of both the Tokyo Olympic Games Organizing Committee and the IOC. That all-too-important factor should not be lost on future historians of the Modern Olympic Movement.

What can be gleaned about the IOC, its operations, and its decision-making practices when the lens is focused on its response to the onset of COVID-19? Was the IOC's collective determination to stage the Tokyo Olympics simply a "the Games must go on" moment, best reflected earlier in Olympic history by IOC President Avery Brundage's decree that the 1972 Munich Olympics would not be shut down in the wake of the Palestinian terrorist incident (in which eleven Israeli athletes and coaches died, along with several of the attackers)? At one level, yes, and this view is affirmed by Thomas Bach, who stated succinctly during our interview, "Our responsibility is to organize Olympic Games, not to cancel them."[13]

Beyond this, we can conclude that Bach's leadership is valued by IOC staff members in Lausanne. Where he wanted to go, despite the obvious hurdles the IOC officials and Japanese organizers needed to clear, they were committed to follow. He was driven in part by his lost opportunity to compete in Moscow 1980 because of the multi-nation boycott triggered by the Soviet Union's invasion of Afghanistan. Readers of this book will recall well what they themselves faced in shifting to work on a remote basis. There were numerous unknowns, much anxiety, and for many, a measure of despair. IOC officials and staff members were not immune from these thoughts. Still, in the end, the IOC's pivot to this new work environment, and the decision to embrace the challenge of overseeing preparations for staging the Tokyo 2020 Games in 2021, reflected a decided unity of purpose. The overarching goal to stage the Games in 2021—the "mission," as they described it—acted as a glue binding the operation together. It is hard to venture further in assessing lessons learned about the IOC in the run-up to Tokyo 2020, simply because COVID-19 posed such a unique, never-seen-before test. As with many organizations at the time, the IOC relied on flexibility, adaptability, and the resilience of its personnel to "carry on." And without question, the entire exercise served the organization well in pressing forward with the 2022 Olympic Winter Games in Beijing. In terms of lingering impacts, it was also made clear to us in discussions that the IOC has shifted to a greater number of online meetings as a means of reducing expenses on travel. It now is operating in the "Zoom era."

There is measurable loyalty within the IOC membership and among its staff to Thomas Bach. His performance during the COVID-19 crisis and its fallout for Tokyo 2020 has been much praised by those who we interviewed and other staff and former staff members who offered their opinions outside of the interview process. Such esteem likely had fueled discussion of extending his twelve-year term, which required the term limit set on the president's position in the wake of the Salt Lake City bid scandal to be reversed. As scholars looking from the outside in, our view is that organizations with such a global mandate and scope of operations benefit from renewal in leadership. Bach reflected on the IOC's leadership situation and his own future in 2024 and stifled further speculation in confirming his intent to step down in 2025, mere hours before the Closing Ceremony for the Paris Olympics. Bach's successor, Zimbabwe's Kirsty Coventry, was elected as the IOC's first female, and first African, president in March 2025.

Bach navigated several difficult moments before the pandemic, including the controversy concerning anti-LGBTQ legislation introduced in Russia prior to Sochi 2014, lagging preparations by organizers of the 2016 Rio Olympics and the impact of the Zika virus, trying to thread the needle in the IOC's response to Russia's state-sponsored doping program and its attack on the integrity of sport, and declining enthusiasm within the Olympic bid environment. He has overseen significant revenue generation from selling television rights and making record-setting deals with TOP sponsors, revenue that the IOC relied on to fund its operations and support NOCs and ISFs during the COVID-19 crisis. "After 12 years in the office of IOC President our organization is best served with a change in leadership. New times are calling for new leaders," stated Bach, as he cleared the path for those seeking to succeed him.[14]

THE JAPANESE PUBLIC VOICE: IT SAID IT COULDN'T, SHOULDN'T BE DONE!

Amid the widespread alarm the COVID-19 pandemic engendered across the globe, several constituencies embraced the position that sporting festivals such as the Olympic Games should be canceled altogether. The prospect of thousands upon thousands of folks gathering in Japan from the far corners of the world to witness such a spectacle, they said, was a recipe for disaster—even a new Olympic COVID-19 variant.

As we have seen, calls for cancellation were particularly loud in Japan itself. As summer 2020 waned, polls reported that the Japanese public overwhelmingly condemned holding the Games, an opinion that persisted up to the eve of their eventual opening in late July 2021.[15] However, in light of the athletes' superb performances, and with health-protection measures arresting anxieties, Japan's citizens executed an "about face" and watched the spectacle in unprecedented numbers.[16] Domestic television coverage of the Tokyo Games drew 115 million individuals, 91 percent of Japan's population.[17] The Opening Ceremony was the most watched television program of the previous ten years. In the end, Japanese citizens were amply rewarded. The nation's athletes captured fifty-eight medals, twenty-seven of them gold, placing Japan third in the medal count among all countries—distinctly the country's best-ever Olympic performance.[18] Though Japan's pre-Games public voice had said it "shouldn't, couldn't" be done, indeed it had been done.[19]

Prime Minister Yoshihide Suga, who piloted Japan through the Games, paid a price. Popular opinion in Japan weighed heavily against his management of COVID-19; with some citizens opposed to his decision to push forward with the Games even in 2021, his popularity tumbled below 30 percent in opinion polls. He resigned in early September 2021 to clear the path for new leadership of the Liberal Democratic Party, whose vise-like grip on power in Japan virtually guaranteed his successor, Fumio Kishida, the keys to the prime minister's office in the November federal election.[20]

ACADEMICS WEIGH IN

There resides in the world of academia a body of scholars whose disciplines especially invite social activism. In the realm of serious scholarship on the Modern Olympic Movement, sociologists, anthropologists, political scientists, philosophers, and historians have long been part of a vibrant and "publicly conscious" group of Olympic skeptics who have questioned the place and value of the Games. They have plenty of grist for their arguments. Problems galore, of course, have festered in the climate of Olympic festivals for as long as they have been celebrated, in both ancient and modern contexts. In the context of the focal point of our study, the Tokyo Olympics, if one bores in on "problematic incidents" tied to Tokyo's festival alone, one might be astounded by their number and circumstance. From one thoroughly documented list, buttressed by more than 325 references (281 of them drawn from English-language global news sources and newspapers), 52 problematic incidents were identified.[21] Of course, each problem, great and small, had to be addressed, impinging on dwindling energies and resources.

A brief digression from Tokyo 2020 is in order at this point. The less-than-critical issues just noted find themselves diminished in the face of major targets of negativity raised by activists. Among the foremost of these targets is the great financial cost of the Games, at the expense of serving the needs of the local community's disenfranchised and deprived people. As the Games opened in late July 2021, Japan was reported to have spent $15.4 billion in preparation. A Japanese government audit put the figure at much more.[22] Expense aside, the fact remains that Olympic-related urban infrastructure improvements (including those effected in Tokyo) in transportation, telecommunications, personal security, and beautification of public space, among other factors, have improved urban life for those living in the crowded conditions of a city—irrespective, with few exceptions, of which Summer Olympic Games one considers. The IOC has addressed the growth in the number of "white elephant" stadia in recent Olympic host cities, as it emphasized with interested bidders the priority they should place on envisioning temporary facilities. The organizers of Paris 2024 embraced this vision of sustainability by choosing reusable materials.[23]

Another target of activist scholars' questioning relates to the perceived devastation of the physical environment by construction projects devoted to Olympic facilities, especially for the Winter Games. Modern Olympic authorities are aware of this. Olympic bid and organizing committees have attended to this issue and will continue doing so; as noted recently by Amanda Shuman and Philippe Vonnard, however, much work remains.[24] The lessons of Beijing and Sochi were harsh, though Paris's commitment to temporary facilities might offer a path for organizing committees to follow. Still, its $1.5 billion expenditure to clean up the Seine, though a laudable goal, is open to question, given the issues encountered during competition.

Questions have also been raised regarding the treatment of Paris's unhoused population during the run-up to the 2024 Summer Olympics.[25] Olympic finance is channeled to environmental concerns. Though some progress is being made, continuing focus on this issue is admittedly imperative.[26]

Also high on the activist menu of complaint is the perceived problematic marriage of the Olympics Movement with the forces of commercialism. By "getting into business," the Olympics invited the ugly word "materialism" into conversations directed toward the giant revenue-producing character of the Games. The word implies a direct contradiction with the original noble Coubertinian virtues as expressed in Olympism. The subject of Olympic values is doubtlessly one that has long concerned members of the IOC, including, more importantly, its presidents.[27] The figures of total revenue production from television and corporate sponsorship have long since passed the millions and soared into the billions. Given global consumption, and the urge for production and distribution entities to satisfy it, Olympic marketing will most certainly advance in tune with the times. The good news is that 90 percent of such Olympic revenue is directed toward a huge paid and voluntary constituency worldwide, comprising those who serve the interests and affairs of NOCs, ISFs, and Olympic Games Bid and Organizing Committees.[28] Jules Boykoff and Dave Zirin[29] have drawn attention to the lobbying efforts of the likes of Global Athlete, an organization dedicated to accessing some of this money for Olympians. We agree. We noted at the outset of this book that the athletes are the "show." Without them, there are no Games. We support a base payment to all athletes who qualify for the Games, and bonus payments for gold, silver, and bronze medal athletes.

Last, and perhaps the factor that ensures an Olympic critic's most strident response, is what they deem a refusal by the IOC to dent the superstructure of Olympism in support of expression and action against abuses of civil and individual human rights on the part of political regimes, many of which are indelibly tied to the Olympic Movement. If the IOC, in view of its *Olympic Charter*, acts to penalize a member nation for its conduct or political actions (beyond the realm of sport), it establishes a dangerous precedent. What might be earned by any one such precedent-breaching act is overshadowed by what could well be lost—the luster of the Olympic Movement's image. The IOC has (with varying degrees of success) and will for the foreseeable future walk a tightrope on such matters. The Olympics are dedicated to advancing sport and celebrating the achievements of the athletes. In pursuing this commitment, the IOC realizes that the Olympic enterprise is not immune to world geopolitics, but it seeks to minimize its influence to retain focus on its core mission and the sustained promotion of the Olympic values that underpinned the genesis of Coubertin's Olympic vision.

The advance of the Olympics into commercialism itself is damning enough for many; its bowing to political pressure is far more problematic. What is the generally accepted image of the Olympics to the global community? For starters, it is an image related to youth. Second, it conveys a level of physical performance beyond comparison, set in circumstances of fair play, sportsmanship, and dedication. The Olympic image is one of health, vitality, and possibility. The Games are most certainly no longer largely a men's viewing event. They are viewed by men and women; indeed, in most cases, they have become a family viewing enterprise. Much of this attraction is generated by this image and perpetuated by Olympic values; yet neither has this image been ignored by leaders within the world's corporate community, who seek to link their companies' fortunes with the Modern Olympic Movement and its most flamboyant production, the Olympic Games.

Stemming from concern over Japan's award and imminent hosting of the 2020 Games, and including criticism of the Olympics in general, bold organized action took place against the IOC's attempt to stage the Games of the XXXIInd Olympiad. Sociologist and Olympic activist Jules Boykoff led one such attempt, during which the subject of Tokyo's motivations in pursuing the Games received ample discussion. In recounting what he referred to as an "international summit," he stated, "Recently, we've seen a really important development on the Olympic activist front. In July 2019, activists from around the world came together in Tokyo for the first-ever international summit to share ideas, strategies, [and] tactics; to strengthen the bonds among anti-Olympic activists."[30] Boykoff, an energetic multi-cause activist, has written or participated in protests dealing with racial justice, climate change, and homelessness, among other areas. Feelings of the "summit group," reported Ryusei Takahashi of the *Japan Times*, expressed that "all" would "be losers" as a result of Tokyo 2020.[31]

One of Boykoff's colleagues in anti-Olympics activism, Andrew Zimbalist, a professor of economics at Smith College in Massachusetts, similarly expressed a dim view of Tokyo's Olympic aspirations: "Tokyo will not benefit long term from hosting the 2020 Olympics—contrary to the hopes and prayers. I'd be really surprised. You don't have any of the ingredients for that.

At the end of the day, the best way to have a good experience with hosting the Olympics is to not host them."[32] Hiroki Ogasawara, an anti-Olympics activist and sociology professor at Japan's distinguished Kobe University, added: "No longer should we see the anti-Olympics movement as being isolated and divided according to nations and cities because the protest is already worldwide and the Olympics inevitably involve global scale wrongdoings, too."[33]

Following the onset of COVID-19, and in advance of the Tokyo Games' "playing out," Boykoff was particularly active, writing in a *New York Times* op-ed that "for the sake of global public health, the Tokyo Olympic Games should be canceled."[34] Months later, members of the summit group, estimated to be a thousand strong, complemented a greater number of those demonstrating their anti-Olympic activism outside a largely empty stadium for the Games' Opening Ceremony.

The views expressed by Boykoff, Zimbalist, and Ogasawara, and a host of others are heartfelt. On some matters, we share some common ground. Yet following the successful conclusion of the 2020 Tokyo Olympics, a question might be posed: "How many of these activists, often prompted by academic critique, weighing the obstacles posed against the success of a COVID-ridden Tokyo 2020 Olympic Games, joined the mass of Japanese citizens in proclaiming the Tokyo Olympics a success?"[35] Despite the record of success in the face of an unprecedented, unparalleled challenge, we would judge "not many." Tokyo's Olympians, 70 percent of whom, as history shows us, would have only this one chance to mount what is arguably the world's greatest stage for athletic competition, got their shot in what proved to be a safe environment.

Our mission in this book has been to examine the efforts of the IOC and Japanese organizers to deliver the Tokyo 2020 Olympics in the face of myriad challenges posed by a global pandemic. Admittedly, any fully panoramic view of the Tokyo Olympics in a historical sense that emerges in the years ahead not only will reflect on the push to host the Games on a delayed basis, but also will examine the perseverance and performances of Tokyo's Olympians. Though we did provide a glimpse into the athletes' resilience in their preparations by focusing on the experiences of Damian Warner, Canada's gold-medal decathlete, there is more to be written about the challenges that the athletes encountered and overcame. The work of the International Paralympic Committee and the exploits of the world's Paralympians who competed in Tokyo, too, merit attention of researchers.

Where we do share the frustrations of those who question the core of the Olympic Movement relates to the scandals and corruption surrounding some past Olympic bids. Future historians will address scandals tied to Tokyo 2020's bid and domestic sponsorship endeavors alongside other contemporary scenarios that unfolded in Salt Lake City and Rio de Janeiro, as well as the "Slavkov affair"[36] tied to London 2012. Efforts were made to respond to the most well-studied of these situations, Salt Lake City, with fifty changes to the *Olympic Charter*; however, people either attached to bid committees or IOC members themselves who are determined to act dishonorably may still find ways to circumvent established policies.

Although the 2020 Tokyo Olympic Games were a resounding success, especially given the multiple problems faced in preparing for and staging them, one cannot ignore or dismiss the disturbing dimensions tied to Tokyo's bid and the evolution of its domestic corporate sponsorship program. There have been serious allegations and acknowledged shortcomings—indeed, alarming events—that in the end mellowed the congratulatory handshakes exchanged by Olympic officials following the Games. In that regard, two scenarios stand out.

The first of those unsavory episodes relates to what has become "an old tale" during the bidding contest for winning "Olympic Host City" distinction: unethical conduct, personal financial gain, corrupt politics, and utter refusal to abide by established bid rules and regulations. In this vein, Tokyo can add its name to the list of cities that engaged in documented scandalous and dishonorable events to win its bid.[37] In March 2016, French prosecutorial authorities, examining Paris's bid to host the 2024 Games, unearthed alleged activities linking Japan's NOC chief and IOC member, Tsunekazu Takeda with Papa Massata and Lamine Diack, and a Singaporean firm, Black Tidings, geared to securing the winning bid for Tokyo.[38] Takeda resigned. The reputations of Papa Massata Diack, and his father, Lamine, were known in the Olympic world. Both men had also been tied to the bid scandal spawned by alleged actions linked to Carlos Nuzman and other members of the Rio 2016 Games bid committee.[39] Obviously, the lessons learned from the tainted bid-rigging affairs associated with the Games in Salt Lake City (2002), Sydney (2000), Nagano (1998), and Atlanta (1996)—which had prompted inquiry, investigation, indictment, court cases, convictions, and even imprisonment, and had resulted in mass changes to the *Olympic Charter* to ensure ethical conduct, rigorous oversight, and vigorous transparency—once again had been compromised in the face of individual greed and avarice. Particularly galling for Japan was the fact that the disturbing dimensions of the Tokyo 2020 bid dredged up memories of its most recent past Olympic experience, that of the successful bid by Nagano for the Olympic Winter Games of 1998.[40]

The second imbroglio relates frontally to one of the chief reasons why anti-Olympic skeptics and activists rail at the Olympic Movement's exploding size and its need to create the finance necessary for support of the enterprise: the world of television rights and commercial sponsorships linked to global mass entertainment and consumption of goods and services. The billions of dollars involved have proven to be a heady attraction to some with questionable scruples. In Tokyo 2020's case, enter Dentsu, the giant Japanese advertising firm whose tentacles extend into every corner of the globe. Currently the world's fifth largest advertising agency ranked by annual revenues, Dentsu does business from its forty-eight-floor headquarters tower in downtown Tokyo. Enmeshed with practically every major institution in Japan, the firm's activities account for 28 percent of the national advertising budget. It has been referred to at times as "the unofficial communications department of Japan's governing Liberal Democratic Party."[41]

With respect to the bid process, it went unstated that because "Olympic business" rests upon the sale of advertising connected to the Olympic brand (the image of the five rings and its world recognition), Tokyo's aspirations to host the Olympic Games offered an unrivalled opportunity for Dentsu to contribute its energies and resources into the grand project. Winning the bid was crucial to this. Thus it was that Dentsu aided Japan's host-status victory by donating some $6 million to the Japanese Olympic Committee to use in securing the bid. A little more than $2 million of that amount was allegedly channeled to Singapore as payment to Black Tidings (and its owner, Tan Tong Han) and the Diacks for the services provided in acquiring IOC member votes. With the bid secured, however, Dentsu's next step was to ensure that its preferred list of client companies gained the necessary commercial sponsorship opportunities. This quest, of course, could only be achieved by circumventing the public bidding and tendering process enunciated in Japan's Anti-Monopoly Legislation.[42]

With zeal and determination, Dentsu, aided immensely by the services and influence of its former senior executive Haruyuki Takahashi, a prominent and influential member of the Tokyo Organizing Committee—and someone who suggested early on that the events in Wuhan, China, would likely force a delay in hosting the Games—threw itself into the act of circumvention, enlisting fellow advertising firms Hakuhodo, Tokyu, and Ceresto, to avoid tendering and, in turn, award lucrative Olympic-related advertising and marketing contracts to "selected" Japanese goods and service purveyors in return for "considerations" totaling millions of dollars.[43] Takahashi's actions drew the attention of Japanese prosecutors.[44] The volume and results of Dentsu's quest were mind boggling—a record-shattering return of some $3.6 billion raised, a figure doubling the highest domestic sponsorship figure of any previous Olympic Games. The bookkeeping remains unclear on what share of the money raised made its way toward helping to underwrite the cost of the Olympic Games themselves, and what remained with Dentsu and its partners. The fallout from the domestic sponsorship scandal tied to Tokyo 2020 crushed Sapporo's bid for the 2030 Olympic Winter Games. Sapporo's mayor, Katsuhiro Akimoto, and Japanese Olympic Committee President Yasuhiro Yamashita cited diminished support from the local citizenry, "whose trust was largely lost" due to the thicket of ongoing court cases.[45]

A FINAL WORD!

To end on a more pleasant note, despite all resistance, criticism, misgiving, and doom and gloom, in a world pregnant with serious political and military unrest and confrontation—indeed, with a human health epidemic more serious than any in recent history, the Tokyo Games still took place, preserving modern Olympic history's almost complete legacy of regular celebration. Beyond the importance of human relationships that fueled the ability of IOC officials and Japanese organizers to navigate the trials posed by COVID-19, two foundational components were central to the Games going on.

First, Olympic athletes, standing on the brink of being—as they have been in the past numerous times in Olympic history—pawns and sacrificial lambs in the face of crises and the imposition of political events, were given the opportunity to compete. As we have seen, they bent with the hardships and restrictions imposed and performed up to and beyond the standard defining "Olympian." Perhaps Seiko Hashimoto, Tokyo 2020 Organizing Committee president, said it best: "We were able to create a stage where athletes from all around the world came together. The scenes observed every day, together, were about emotional relationships among people, unity in diversity, a symbol of peace and what we call the power of sports. While various opinions were voiced as Tokyo 2020 and IOC officials leaned in on the task at hand, "many people were able to find the essential value of the Games."[46] We will never know for certain, of course, but nevertheless, we have abundant past examples to certify that thousands of youngsters and their parents worldwide have been inspired by the example of such Olympic athletes, enough so as to pursue pathways toward similar pursuits. This legacy certainly extends to the Tokyo Olympians.

Second, the value system Pierre de Coubertin imposed on the Olympic Games some 130 years ago as their raison d'être remained in place. The Olympic credo of peace, fair play, respect, and tolerance, among many other similarly descriptive concepts, which the Olympic Movement has invested millions of dollars to advance, and which, beyond any other sporting movement, has found much success despite ongoing grievances and criticisms, remains the central message that appeals to youth, parents, and, yes, the commercial marketplace, too. These are the Olympic Movement's most important image considerations, and they must be protected if the Movement seeks to remain the world's preeminent sporting movement in the hearts and minds of its adherents.

History reveals that the IOC and the Olympic Games have survived a long list of threats: tepid support for Coubertin's enterprise in the late 1800s and early 1900s; two world wars; the Great Depression; and the encroachment of world geopolitics and its fallout in the form of boycotts, questions concerning the IOC's move to embrace commercial revenue, doping scandals, and host-city bidding crises. Tokyo 2020, and the 2022 Beijing Olympic Winter Games six months later, where athletes pursuing their sporting dreams performed and excelled while in the throes of a global pandemic, showed we can add COVID-19 to that list.

NOTES

PREFACE

1. Sarah Moore, "History of COVID-19," *News-Medical Life Sciences*, updated September 28, 2021, https://www.news-medical.net/health/History-of-COVID-19.aspx.
2. IOC Press Release, June 18, 2008: "Olympic Education a Lasting Benefit for China's Schoolchildren," https://olympics.com/ioc/news/olympic-education-a-lasting-benefit-for-china-s-schoolchildren. See also, IOC Press Release, May 18, 2009: "Olympic Values Reach 400 Million Chinese Children," https://olympics.com/ioc/news/olympic-values-reach-400-million-chinese-children.
3. Henrik Pettersson et al., "Tracking Covid-19's Global Spread," *CNN*, April 5, 2022, https://edition.cnn.com/interactive/2020/health/coronavirus-maps-and-cases/.
4. Pettersson et al., "Tracking Covid-19's Global Spread"; Julia Hollingsworth, "New Zealand and Australia Were Covid Success Stories. Why Are They Behind on Vaccine Rollouts?" *CNN*, April 15, 2021, https://www.cnn.com/2021/04/15/asia/new-zealand-australia-covid-vaccine-intl-dst-hnk/index.html.
5. Maria Cheng and Farai Mustaka, "Scientists Mystified, Wary, as Africa Avoids COVID-19 Disaster," *CTV News*, November 19, 2021, https://www.ctvnews.ca/health/coronavirus/scientists-mystified-wary-as-africa-avoids-covid-19-disaster-1.5673339. While cautioning that acquiring accurate data in Africa poses a challenge, the WHO has been consistent in its messaging that Africa remains "one of the least affected regions in the world." Possible explanations include Africa's lower population age compared to countries in Europe and the Americas, "lower rates of urbanization," Africans' "tendency to spend time outdoors," and the possible "protective effects" of past malaria.
6. Evan Smith, "Penn State Basketball's Lamar Stevens, the 'Heart and Soul' of Cavaliers," *Victory Bell Rings*, January 2022, https://victorybellrings.com/2022/01/14/psus-lamar-stevens-the-heart-and-soul-of-the-cleveland-cavaliers/. Stevens, undrafted, who has played for the Cleveland Cavaliers, Boston Celtics, and Memphis Grizzlies, is trying to find his way back to an NBA roster while toiling in its G League early in the 2024–2025 season for the Motor City Cruise. His final Penn State season ended with a minimum of two games to play.
7. Motoko Rich et al., "I.O.C. and Japan Agree to Postpone Tokyo Olympics," *New York Times*, March 24, 2020, https://www.nytimes.com/2020/03/24/sports/olympics/coronavirus-summer-olympics-postponed.html.
8. María Bogner, email message to Stephen Wenn and Bob Barney, January 13, 2022.
9. Through a media analysis, Aiden George Stead has examined the Canadian Olympic Committee's Tokyo 2020 experience in thesis form. Aiden George Stead, "The Pandemic Olympics: A Thematic Analysis of COVID-19 and the Tokyo Olympic Games" (master's thesis, Human Kinetics, University of Ottawa, 2022), https://ruor.uottawa.ca/server/api/core/bitstreams/649c17fb-0f64-420a-881d-f1a77e28e864/content.
10. See, for instance, Hee Jung Hong and Justine Allen, "An Exploration of the Resources of High-Performance Athletes and Coaches to Cope with Unexpected Transitions," *Sport, Exercise, and Performance Psychology* 11, no. 4 (2022): 412–28, https://doi.org/10.1037/spy0000306; Harry B. T. Lim et al., "The Impact of the Covid-19 Pandemic on

Singapore National Youth Athletes' Mental Health and Potential Protective Factors," *International Journal of Sport and Exercise Psychology* 22, no. 7 (2023): 1569–87, https://doi.org/10.1080/1612197X.2023.2235593; Carolina Lundqvist et al., "When COVID-19 Struck the World and Elite Sports: Psychological Challenges and Support Provision in Five Countries During the First Phase of the Pandemic," *Journal of Sport Psychology in Action* 13, no. 2 (2022): 116–28, https://doi.org/10.1080/21520704.2021.1931594; Inês Miguel et al., "Portuguese Olympic and Paralympic Athletes' Experiences of the Covid-19 Pandemic and the Postponement of the Tokyo 2020 Olympic Games," *International Journal of Sport and Exercise Psychology* 22, no. 8 (2023): 1932–50, https://doi.org/10.1080/1612197X.2023.2238296; Masaki Nishida et al., "Mental Health Services at the Tokyo 2020 Olympic and Paralympic Games During the COVID-19 Pandemic," *Sports Psychiatry: Journal of Sports and Exercise Psychiatry* 1, no. 2 (2022): 36–38, https://doi.org/10.1024/2674-0052/a000005; Morgan Rogers and Penny Werthner, "Gathering Narratives: Athletes' Experiences Preparing for the Tokyo Summer Olympic Games During a Global Pandemic," *Journal of Applied Sport Psychology* 35, no. 2 (2022): 330–48, https://doi.org/10.1080/10413200.2022.2032477; and Antonia Rossiter et al., "Effects of Long-Haul Transmeridian Travel on Physiological, Sleep, Perceptual and Mood Markers in Olympic Team Support Staff," *Chronobiology International* 39, no. 12 (2022): 1640–55, https://doi.org/10.1080/07420528.2022.2139186.
11. "Hosting Asian Games Will 'Wipe Away' Japanese Doubts, Says Top Official," *France24*, June 10, 2023, https://www.france24.com/en/live-news/20231006-hosting-asian-games-will-wipe-away-japanese-doubts-says-top-official.
12. Diego Girod (research coordinator, Olympic Studies Centre, Lausanne), email message to Stephen Wenn, October 5, 2023.
13. Abigail Turner, "The Importance of Preserving the History of the COVID-19 Pandemic," *Global News*, March 12, 2021, https://globalnews.ca/news/7692671/coronavirus-covid-19-pandemic-preserve-history/.

CHAPTER 1

1. "Joint Statement from the International Olympic Committee and the Tokyo 2020 Organising Committee," *Olympics.com*, March 24, 2020, https://olympics.com/ioc/news/joint-statement-from-the-international-olympic-committee-and-the-tokyo-2020-organising-committee. Those on the call were Yoshiro Mori, president of the Tokyo 2020 Organizing Committee; Seiko Hashimoto, the Olympic minister of state for Tokyo's Olympic and Paralympic Games; Yuriko Koike, governor of Tokyo; John Coates, IOC Coordination Commission chair; Christophe De Kepper, IOC's director general; and Christophe Dubi, IOC Olympic Games executive director.
2. "Joint Statement from the International Olympic Committee."
3. "Public Communications around COVID-19 and Games Postponement of IOC and Stakeholders—Knowledge Capture," March 2022. This document was produced by the IOC's Olympic Studies Centre in Lausanne, Switzerland, and was kindly provided to the authors by the Centre's head, Maria Bogner.
4. Charlie Campbell et al., "Tokyo's Olympics Trial," *Time*, January 18, 2021, 44, https://search-ebscohostcom.libproxy.wlu.ca/login.aspx?direct=true&AuthType=ip,cookie,url,uid&db=rgm&AN=147960786&site=ehost-live.
5. Campbell et al., "Tokyo's Olympics Trial" (brackets ours).

6. Kenji Hall, "Tokyo Rift," *Sports Illustrated*, May 2021, 12, https://search-ebscohost-com.libproxy.wlu.ca/login.aspx?direct=true&AuthType=ip,cookie,url,uid&db=rgm&AN=149875978&site=ehost-live.
7. Alice Park et al., "The Pandemic Games," *Time*, July 19, 2021, 58, https://search-ebscohost-com.libproxy.wlu.ca/login.aspx?direct=true&AuthType=ip,cookie,url,uid&db=rgm&AN=151321306&site=ehost-live.
8. Jeré Longman, "The Pandemic's Secret Formula: Backyard Workouts and Lots of Sleep," *New York Times*, August 30, 2020.
9. Tom Goldman, "USA's Ryan Crouser Sets Olympic Shot Put Record and Wins Olympic Gold Again," *National Public Radio*, August 5, 2021, https://www.npr.org/sections/tokyo-olympics-live-updates/2021/08/05/1025012458/usas-ryan-crouser-sets-olympic-shot-put-record-and-wins-gold-again.
10. Sean Ingle, "Ryan Crouser Leads Historic Olympic Podium Repeat in Shot Put," *The Guardian*, August 5, 2021, https://www.theguardian.com/sport/2021/aug/05/ryan-crouser-leads-historic-olympic-podium-repeat-in-shot-put.
11. "Crouser Breaks World Shot Put Record with 23.38m in Idaho," *World Athletics*, February 18, 2023, https://worldathletics.org/news/report/ryan-crouser-world-shot-put-record-2338m-idaho.
12. Matt Dickinson, "Project Immortal Is Not Boastful or an Ego Trip—I Just Want to Aim High," *Times* (Edition 1, Ireland), December 30, 2020, 46–47.
13. Andy Bull, "Adam Peaty Wins GB's First 2020 Tokyo Gold and Makes Olympic History," *The Guardian*, July 25, 2021, https://www.theguardian.com/sport/2021/jul/26/adam-peaty-wins-gold-100m-breaststroke-tokyo-olympics-2020-swimming.
14. David Charlesworth, "Tokyo Olympics: Adam Peaty Dismayed by Some Reaction Since Announcing Month-Long Break from Pool," *The Independent*, August 2, 2021, https://www.independent.co.uk/sport/olympics/adam-peaty-swimming-tokyo-break-b1894897.html.
15. Matthew Henry, "Peaty Tests Positive for Covid After Winning Silver," *BBC Sport*, July 29, 2024, https://www.bbc.com/sport/olympics/articles/crgl6nox39e0.
16. Ben Pickman, "Water Wait," *Sports Illustrated*, May 2020, 480; Mark Spezia, "Denied Three Times, Ashley Twichell Clinches a Spot (Maybe More) at 2020 Tokyo Olympics," *ESPN*, September 20, 2019, https://www.espn.com/espnw/life-style/story/_/id/27643598/denied-three-s-ashley-twichell-clinches-spot-maybe-more-2020-tokyo-olympics. Their son, Lochlan William Wall, arrived safely in late May 2022: Yanyan Li, "Olympian Ashley Twichell Gives Birth to Baby Boy," *SwimSwam*, May 28, 2022, https://swimswam.com/olympian-ashley-twichell-gives-birth-to-baby-boy/.
17. Jane Thornton, "How the COVID-19 Delay of the Tokyo Olympics Helped Some Athletes Break Records," *The Conversation*, July 20, 2021, https://theconversation.com/how-the-covid-19-delay-of-the-tokyo-olympics-helped-some-athletes-break-records-163861. Dr. Jane Thornton, the author of this article, succeeded Richard Budgett as the IOC's Medical and Scientific Director on September 1, 2024.
18. Ciara Nugent, "Athletes on the Front Line," *Time*, July 19, 2021, 84, https://search-ebscohostcom.libproxy.wlu.ca/login.aspx?direct=true&AuthType=ip, cookie,url,uid&db=rgm&AN=151321354& site=ehost-live.
19. Canadian Paralympic Committee, "Alison Levine," accessed December 27, 2024, https://paralympic.ca/team-canada/alison-levine.

20. Rachel Brady, "The Tokyo Olympics Challenge: How Can Canadian Athletes Aim for Gold at Games Compromised by COVID-19?" *Globe and Mail*, March 13, 2021, https://www.theglobeandmail.com/sports/olympics/article-the-tokyo-olympics-challenge-how-can-canadian-athletes-aim-for-gold-at/.
21. "Levine Claims Gold While Dispaltro and Bussière Capture Bronze at the World Boccia Americas Regional Championships," *Boccia Canada*, December 12, 2021, https://bocciacanada.ca/en/news/article/levine-claims-gold-while-dispaltro-and-bussiere-capture-bronze-at-the-world-boccia-americas-regional-championships/; "Alison Levine and Iulian Ciobanu Cap Off the Rio World Boccia Championships with a Bronze Medal," *Boccia Canada*, December 13, 2022, https://bocciacanada.ca/en/news/article/alison-levine-and-iulian-ciobanu-cap-off-the-rio-world-boccia-championships-with-a-bronze-medal/.
22. Sam Price, "Covid 19: The Athlete Response," *Olympic Review* April/May/June 2020, 40.
23. Price, "Covid 19: The Athlete Response."
24. Price, "Covid 19: The Athlete Response."
25. Sean Ingle, "Duplantis and Lavillenie Scale the Heights in Ultimate Garden Clash," *The Guardian*, May 3, 2020, https://www.theguardian.com/sport/2020/may/03/duplantis-and-lavillenie-scale-the-heights-in-ultimate-garden-clash.
26. Tom Goldman, "Coronavirus Knocks U.S. Pole Vaulter Sam Kendricks Out of Tokyo Olympics," *National Public Radio*, July 29, 2020, https://www.npr.org/sections/tokyo-olympics-live-updates/2021/07/29/1022065062/coronavirus-knocks-u-s-pole-vaulter-sam-kendricks-out-of-tokyo-olympics.
27. Doug Harrison, "Reigning Olympic Champ Stefanidi Beats Alysha Newman in Virtual Pole Vault Event," *CBC*, May 16, 2020, https://www.cbc.ca/sports/olympics/summer/trackandfield/ultimate-garden-clash-women-world-athletics-1.5573279. For video, see "Ultimate Garden Clash: Women's Pole Vault Edition," *CBC*, https://www.cbc.ca/player/play/1738892867633.
28. Personal interview, Damian Warner, January 13, 2023, London, Ontario.
29. Personal interview, Damian Warner, January 13, 2023; personal interview, Gar Leyshon, January 10, 2023, London, Ontario; Gar Leyshon, email to Bob Barney, February 15, 2023.
30. Personal interview, Gar Leyshon, January 10, 2023.
31. Devin Heroux, "Team Damian Warner: How 2 English Teachers Helped Turn a London Teen into the World's Greatest Athlete," *CBC*, 19 July 2022, https://www.cbc.ca/sports/olympics/summer/trackandfield/world-athletics-championships-damian-warner-feature-heroux-1.6524281.
32. Personal interview, Gar Leyshon, January 10, 2023.
33. Personal interview, Gar Leyshon, January 10, 2023.
34. Personal interview, Gar Leyshon, January 10, 2023.
35. Personal interview, Damian Warner, January 13, 2023.
36. Heroux, "Team Damian Warner."
37. Cathal Kelly, "Montreal-Based B2ten Is Giving Canadian Olympians a Better Run for Their Money," *Globe and Mail*, February 16, 2018, https://www.theglobeandmail.com/sports/olympics/montreal-based-b2ten-is-giving-canadian-olympians-a-better-run-for-their-money/article38013877/; B2ten, "Our History," accessed December 12, 2024, https://b2ten.com/about-b2ten/.
38. Kelly, "Montreal-based B2ten."

39. Kelly, "Montreal-based B2ten."
40. Kelly, "Montreal-based B2ten." The roots for B2ten extend back to the 2002 Salt Lake City Olympic Winter Games when Jennifer Heil, a Canadian moguls skier, finished fourth in her event. Gauthier, her coach (now husband), believed her training resources fell short of what was needed to pursue a podium place, so the two collaborated, along with J. D. Miller, to raise private funds in the build-up to the 2006 Torino Olympic Winter Games, where she captured the gold medal. The model employed to catapult Heil forward was expanded to encompass a select group of elite Canadian winter and summer athletes in ensuing years. B2ten supported Tessa Virtue and Scott Moir, two of Canada's most decorated figure skaters; cross-country skier Alex Harvey; and Vancouver 2010's gold medalist in moguls, Alexandre Bilodeau, who repeated the feat four years later in Sochi. It has also supported, among others, moguls king Mikaël Kingsbury; long track speed skaters Isabelle Weidemann (who captured three Olympic medals, including a gold in Beijing) and Valérie Maltais (who shared the gold medal in Beijing with Isabelle Weideman and other members of Canada's Team Pursuit squad); and track stars such as Marco Arop, Aaron Brown, and Mohammed Ahmed (in addition to Damian Warner).
41. Personal interview, Gar Leyshon, January 10, 2023.
42. "PürInstinct," accessed December 12, 2024, https://purinstinct.com/learn/.
43. Personal interview, Gar Leyshon, January 10, 2023.
44. Personal interview, Gar Leyshon, January 10, 2023.
45. Personal interview, Gar Leyshon, January 10, 2023.
46. Personal interview, Gar Leyshon, January 10, 2023.
47. Vicki Hall, " 'You Need One Voice': Canadian Decathlete Damian Warner Trims Coaching Staff Ahead of Pivotal Season," *National Post*, December 20, 2016, https://nationalpost.com/sports/olympics/you-need-one-voice-canadian-decathlete-damian-warner-trims-coaching-staff-ahead-of-pivotal-season.
48. Personal interview, Gar Leyshon, January 10, 2023.
49. Personal interview, Gar Leyshon, January 10, 2023.
50. Personal interview, Gar Leyshon, January 10, 2023.
51. Personal interview, Gar Leyshon, January 10, 2023.
52. Ryan Pyette, "Inside London Decathlete Damian Warner's Pandemic Path to Glory," *London Free Press*, June 14, 2021, https://lfpress.com/sports/local-sports/it-took-quick-thinking-and-an-old-rink-to-get-damian-warner-back-on-track.
53. Personal interview, Gar Leyshon, January 10, 2023.
54. Personal interview, Gar Leyshon, January 10, 2023.
55. Personal interview, Damian Warner, January 13, 2023.
56. Personal interview, Gar Leyshon, January 10, 2023.
57. Personal interview, Damian Warner, January 13, 2023.
58. Personal interview, Damian Warner, January 13, 2023.
59. Personal interview, Gar Leyshon, January 10, 2023.
60. "Public Communications around COVID-19 and Games Postponement of IOC and Stakeholders—Knowledge Capture," March 2022. This document was produced by the IOC's Olympic Studies Centre in Lausanne, Switzerland, and was kindly provided to the authors by the Centre's head, Maria Bogner.
61. Personal interview, Gar Leyshon, January 10, 2023.
62. Personal interview, Damian Warner, January 13, 2023.
63. Personal interview, Damian Warner, January 13, 2023.

64. Personal interview, Gar Leyshon, January 10, 2023.
65. Personal interview, Damian Warner, January 13, 2023.
66. Doug Harrison, "Damian Warner Out of the Cold, into Temporary Training Home for Tokyo Olympics," *CBC*, October 31, 2020, https://www.cbc.ca/sports/olympics/summer/trackandfield/damian-warner-indoor-training-tokyo-olympics-1.5785135.
67. Harrison, "Damian Warner Out of the Cold."
68. Lori Ewing, "Damian Warner and Co., Built a Multi Events Training Facility in Old London Arena," *Toronto Star*, February 8, 2021, https://www.thestar.com/sports/2021/02/08/damian-warner-and-co-built-a-multi-events-training-facility-in-old-london-arena.html.
69. Personal interview, Damian Warner, January 13, 2023.
70. Personal interview, Kit McConnell, January 26, 2023, Lausanne, Switzerland.
71. Personal interview, Gar Leyshon, January 10, 2023.
72. Glynn Leyshon was the long-time wrestling coach at Western University and was named head coach of Canada's 1980 Olympic wrestling team, only to have the opportunity to serve in that capacity on site stripped from him when Canada joined the US-led boycott.
73. Personal interview, Scott Stafford, January 17, 2023, London, Ontario. Stafford is now retired.
74. Personal interview, Scott Stafford, January 17, 2023.
75. Personal interview, Scott Stafford, January 17, 2023; Scott Stafford, email to Stephen Wenn, February 13, 2023; personal interview, Gar Leyshon, January 10, 2023.
76. Personal interview, Gar Leyshon, January 10, 2023.
77. Personal interview, Scott Stafford, January 17, 2023. During this same period, Canadian swimming sensation and fellow Londoner, Maggie MacNeil, who captured three medals in Tokyo, including a gold in the 100 m butterfly, had access to the city's aquatic center.
78. Harrison, "Damian Warner Out of the Cold."
79. Personal interview, Scott Stafford, January 17, 2023; Scott Stafford, email to Stephen Wenn, February 13, 2023.
80. Personal interview, Gar Leyshon, January 10, 2023; personal interview, Damian Warner, January 13, 2023.
81. Pyette, "Damian Warner's Pandemic Path to Glory."
82. Pyette, "Damian Warner's Pandemic Path to Glory."
83. Pyette, "Damian Warner's Pandemic Path to Glory"; Harrison, "Damian Warner Out of the Cold."
84. Pyette, "Damian Warner's Pandemic Path to Glory"; personal interview, Gar Leyshon, January 10, 2023.
85. Personal interview, Gar Leyshon, January 10, 2023.
86. Personal interview, Scott Stafford, January 17, 2023; Pyette, "Damian Warner's Pandemic Path to Glory."
87. Ewing, "Damian Warner and Co."
88. Pyette, "Damian Warner's Pandemic Path to Glory."
89. Pyette, "Damian Warner's Pandemic Path to Glory"; personal interview, Gar Leyshon, January 10, 2023.
90. Personal interviews, Damian Warner, January 13, 2023; Gar Leyshon, January 10, 2023.
91. Personal interview, Gar Leyshon, January 10, 2023.
92. Personal interview, Damian Warner, January 13, 2023.
93. "Kevin Mayer Secures Olympic Qualifying Mark in Réunion," *Athletics Weekly*,

December 19, 2020, https://athleticsweekly.com/event-news/kevin-mayer-olympic-qualifying-mark-reunion-1039938663/; personal interview, Gar Leyshon, January 10, 2023, London, Ontario.
94. Personal interview, Damian Warner, January 13, 2023.
95. Personal interview, Gar Leyshon, January 10, 2023.
96. Personal interview, Damian Warner, January 13, 2023.
97. Personal interview, Gar Leyshon, January 10, 2023
98. Personal interview, Gar Leyshon, January 10, 2023.
99. Personal interview, Damian Warner, January 13, 2023.

CHAPTER 2

1. David Wharton, "Tokyo's Rough Road to 2020 Summer Olympics," *Los Angeles Times*, July 23, 2019, https://www.latimes.com/sports/story/2019-07-23/tokyos-rough-road-to-2020-summer-olympics.
2. Wharton, "Tokyo's Rough Road."
3. Stephen Wade, "Ticket Demand a Sign of Tokyo's Enthusiasm for 2020 Summer Games One Year Out," *Toronto Star*, July 22, 2019, https://www.thestar.com/sports/amateur/2019/07/22/ticket-demand-a-sign-of-tokyos-enthusiasm-for-2020-summer-games.html.
4. "Tokyo 2020 Olympics Logo Scrapped amid Plagiarism Claim," *BBC*, 1 September 2015, https://www.bbc.com/news/world-asia-34115750.
5. Wharton, "Tokyo's Rough Road."
6. Justin McCurry, "Japanese Olympic Official to Quit amid Corruption Allegations Scandal," *The Guardian*, March 19, 2019, https://www.theguardian.com/world/2019/mar/19/japan-olympic-committee-president-tsunekazu-takeda-to-resign-corruption-allegations-scandal; Associated Press, "Japanese Olympic Committee Head Resigns amid Tokyo Games Scandal," *Sportsnet*, March 19, 2019, https://www.sportsnet.ca/olympics/japanese-olympic-committee-head-resigns-amid-tokyo-games-scandal/.
7. "Chairman of the Japanese Olympic Committee Set to Quit," *CNN*, March 19, 2019, https://edition.cnn.com/2019/03/19/sport/tsunekazu-takeda-japanese-olympic-committee-spt-intl/index.html.
8. One of the two was Yahiko Mishima, a sprinter who was eliminated in the opening round of preliminary heats in both the 200 and 400 m events. See Bill Mallon and Ture Widland, *The 1912 Olympic Games: Results for All Competitors in All Events with Commentary* (McFarland & Company, 2002), 69, 72. The other was twenty-year-old Shizo Kanaguri, a marathon runner who failed to finish. Alluded to as "the Japanese Runner Who Disappeared," Kanaguri, suffering badly from the sweltering heat of the day, stopped exhausted at a garden some 20 km along the route. Deciding to retire from the race, without notifying officials, he returned to Stockholm by train. Years later, in 1967, by then seventy-five years old, he was invited to return to Stockholm, where he symbolically finished the race from the point of his garden visit. See Mallon and Widlund, *The 1912 Olympic Games*, 24. Kanaguri was no mere neophyte in marathon competition. He placed sixteenth in the event at the Antwerp Olympic Games eight years later.
9. For detailed biographical information on the life and career of Jigoro Kano, see, for instance, Brian N. Watson, *The Father of Judo: A Biography of Jigoro Kanō*, 1st ed. (Trafford Press, 2000).

10. The scenario of Tokyo's successful quest to bid for and be awarded the 1940 Summer Games of the XIIth Olympiad and Sapporo's award of the Vth Olympic Winter Games is told best by Sandra Collins in her celebrated monograph, *The 1940 Tokyo Games: The Missing Olympics, Japan, the Asian Olympics, and the Olympic Movement* (Routledge, 2007).
11. Here we refer to the statistics of Kamper and Mallon, noted chroniclers of Olympic performance records. See Erich Kamper and Bill Mallon, *The Golden Book of the Olympic Games* (Vallardi & Associati, 1992).
12. The notable Japanese 1928 Olympic swimmers were Katsuo Takaishi (bronze, 400 m freestyle) and Hiroshi Yoneyama, Nobuo Alai, Tokuhei Sada, and Katsuo Takaishi (silver, 4 × 200 m freestyle relay). See Kamper and Mallon, *The Golden Book of the Olympic Games*, 230, 237.
13. The much-celebrated 1932 Japanese men's Olympic swimming aggregation was composed of Yasuji Miyazaki (gold, 100 m freestyle), Tatsugo Kawaishi (silver, 100 m freestyle); Tsutomu Oyokota (bronze, 400 m freestyle); Kusuo Kitamora (gold, 1500 m freestyle); Shozo Makino (silver, 1500 m freestyle); Masaji Kiyokawa (gold, 100 m backstroke); Toshio Irie (silver, 100 m backstroke); Kentaro Kawatsu (bronze, 100 m backstroke); Yoshiyuki Tsuruta (gold, 200 m breaststroke); Reiso Koike (silver, 200 m breaststroke); and Yasuji Miyazaki, Mansanori Yusa, Takashi Yokoyama, and Hisakishi Toyoda (gold, 4 × 200 m freestyle relay). See Kamper and Mallon, *The Golden Book of the Olympic Games*, 230–37.
14. See Jason Farago, "The 1964 Olympics Certified a New Japan, in Steel and on the Screen," *New York Times*, July 30, 2020, https://www.nytimes.com/2020/07/30/arts/design/tokyo-olympics-1964-design.html.
15. For a general description of Japanese energy and resources in underwriting the Tokyo Olympics, see John Slater, "Tokyo 1964," in *Encyclopedia of the Modern Olympic Movement*, John F. Findling and Kimberly D. Pelle, eds. (Greenwood Press, 2004), 165–73.
16. Slater, "Tokyo 1964," 165.
17. For more on the 1972 Sapporo Olympic Winter Games, see Junko Tahara, "Sapporo 1972," in *Encyclopedia of the Modern Olympic Movement*, John F. Findling and Kimberly Pelle, eds. (Greenwood Press, 2004), 359–65.
18. For more on the 1998 Nagano Olympic Winter Games, see Naofumi Masumoto, "Nagano 1998," in *Encyclopedia of the Modern Olympic Movement*, John F. Findling and Kimberly Pelle, eds. (Greenwood Press, 2004), 415–19.
19. For a pre-COVID-19 assessment of the place of the Olympics and Tokyo 2020 within Japan's Olympic narrative, see Barbara Holthus et al., eds., *Japan Through the Lens of the Tokyo Olympics* (Routledge, 2020).
20. Personal interview, Kit McConnell, January 26, 2023, Lausanne, Switzerland.
21. Karolos Grohmann, "Tokyo 2020 Olympics: IOC Officially Bans AIBA from Amateur Boxing due to Finance and Government Issues," *The Independent*, June 26, 2019, https://www.independent.co.uk/sport/boxing/tokyo-2020-olympics-games-boxing-aiba-banned-latest-news-a8975326.html.
22. Grohmann, "Tokyo 2020 Olympics"; Matt Slater, "IOC Suspends AIBA and Appoints Special Task Force to Run 2020 Olympics Boxing Tournament," *The Independent*, May 23, 2019, https://www.independent.co.uk/sport/boxing/ioc-suspends-aiba-task-force-tokyo-2020-olympics-boxing-tournament-a8926596.html.

23. "China Pneumonia Outbreak: Mystery Virus Probed in China," *BBC*, January 3, 2020, https://www.bbc.com/news/world-asia-china-50984025.
24. Personal interview, Kit McConnell, January 26, 2023, Lausanne, Switzerland.
25. Daniel Matthews, " 'We Dodged a Bullet': The 'Crazy' Inside Story of How an Olympic Boxing Qualifier in Wuhan Almost Went Ahead as Covid First Broke Out," *Daily Mail*, July 30, 2021, https://www.dailymail.co.uk/sport/olympics/article-9831307/The-crazy-inside-story-Olympic-boxing-qualifier-Wuhan-went-ahead.html.
26. "Olympics: Boxing Qualifiers Set for Wuhan Nixed over Health Fears," *Reuters*, January 22, 2020, https://www.reuters.com/article/uk-olympics-2020-boxing-health-idUKKBN1ZL0H6.
27. "Olympic Boxing Qualifiers Moved to Jordan," *Japan Times*, January 25, 2020, https://www.japantimes.co.jp/sports/2020/01/25/more-sports/boxing-2/olympic-boxing-qualifiers-moved-jordan/.
28. Matthews, " 'We Dodged a Bullet.' "
29. "Public Communications around COVID-19 and Games Postponement of IOC and Stakeholders—Knowledge Capture," March 2022. This document was produced by the IOC's Olympic Studies Centre in Lausanne, Switzerland, and was kindly provided to the authors by the Centre's head, Maria Bogner.
30. Personal interview, Christophe Dubi, January 23, 2023, Lausanne, Switzerland.
31. 30 Personal interview, Richard Budgett, January 25, 2023, Lausanne, Switzerland.
32. Bogner shared this information with the authors following our interview with Christophe Dubi on January 23, 2023. Her memories of the event appear with her permission.
33. Personal interview, Christophe Dubi, January 23, 2023.
34. Personal interview, Kit McConnell, January 26, 2023.
35. Personal interview, Thomas Bach, January 24, 2023, Lausanne, Switzerland.
36. Personal interview, Timo Lumme, January 25, 2023, Lausanne, Switzerland; "See Inside China's Huoshenshan Hospital Built in 10 Days," *CBC*, 3 February 2020, https://www.cbc.ca/news/world/coronavirus-china-huoshenshan-hospital-photos-1.5450026.
37. Personal interview, Timo Lumme, January 25, 2023.
38. "The China Coronavirus: Time and Again," *The Economist*, January 25, 2020, 14, https://libproxy.wlu.ca/login?url=https://www.proquest.com/magazines/time-again/docview/2346435894/se-2.
39. "Coronavirus: How Bad Will It Get?" *The Economist*, 1 February 2020, 10, https://libproxy.wlu.ca/login?url=https://www.proquest.com/magazines/how-bad-will-get/docview/2349095209/se-2.
40. Eisuke Nakazawa et al., "Chronology of COVID-19 Cases on the Diamond Princess Cruise Ship and Ethical Considerations: A Report from Japan," *Disaster Medicine and Public Health Preparedness* 14, no. 4 (2020): 506–13, https://doi.org/10.1017/dmp.2020.50. The cost of construction is reported in Chris Baraniuk, "What the Diamond Princess Taught the World About Covid-19," *The BMJ*, April 27, 2020, https://www.bmj.com/content/369/bmj.m1632.
41. Doug Bock Clark, "Inside the Nightmare Voyage of the *Diamond Princess*," *GQ*, April 30, 2020, https://www.gq.com/story/inside-diamond-princess-cruise-ship-nightmare-voyage.

42. Clark, "Inside the Nightmare Voyage."
43. Chris Baraniuk, "What the Diamond Princess Taught." Nakazawa et al. place this number at 691 on February 23, 2020, when the final passengers remaining after the departure of passengers on a staggered basis beginning on February 15 departed the ship. See Nakazawa et al., "Chronology of COVID-19 Cases," 506. It is thought seven deaths were associated with the COVID-19 outbreak on the *Diamond Princess*. E. J. Mundell, "Diamond Princess Saga Began with One COVID Carrier," *WebMD*, July 29, 2020, https://www.webmd.com/lung/news/20200729/gene-study-shows-how-coronavirus-swept-through-the-idiamond-princessi#1.
44. Personal interview, Thomas Bach, January 24, 2023.
45. Stephen Wade, "Olympics to Continue amid Covid-19 Fears," *New York Times*, 14 February 2020, https://advance-lexis-com.libproxy.wlu.ca/api/document?collection=news&id=urn:contentItem:6058-SV11-JCRP-C23V-00000-00&context=1516831.
46. Wade, "Olympics to Continue amid Covid-19 Fears."
47. Ben Ellery and Richard Lloyd Parry, "Hopes Raised of Flight for Cruise Britons," *The Times*, February 18, 2020, https://advance-lexis-com.libproxy.wlu.ca/api/document?collection=news&id=urn:contentItem:5Y7G-NHH1-JCBW-N2Y9-00000-00&context=1516831; and, Clark, "Inside the Nightmare Voyage."
48. Wade, "Olympics to Continue amid Covid-19 Fears."
49. Sean Ingle, "Tokyo Marathon Cancels Mass Race over Coronavirus Scare," *The Guardian*, February 17, 2020, https://www.theguardian.com/sport/2020/feb/17/tokyo-marathon-restricted-to-elite-runners-over-coronavirus-scare-athletics.
50. Personal interview, Thomas Bach, January 24, 2023.
51. Personal interview, Thomas Bach, January 24, 2023.
52. Stephen Wade and Mari Yamaguchi, "Olympic Official: Virus Won't Cancel 2020 Games," *Chicago Daily Herald*, February 15, 2020, https://advance-lexis-com.libproxy.wlu.ca/api/document?collection=news&id=urn:ContentItem:5Y7B-G5N1-JBRC-V3PJ-00000-00&context=1516831.
53. Wade and Yamaguchi, "Olympic Official."
54. Martin Strydom, "Japan Slides Towards Recession After Typhoon," *The Times*, February 18, 2020, https://advance-lexis-com.libproxy.wlu.ca/api/document?collection=news&id=urn:contentItem:5Y7G-NHH1-JCBW-N2MW-00000-00&context=1516831.
55. Strydom, "Japan Slides Towards Recession"; Harry Wise, "Typhoon Hagibis and Sales Tax Rise Put Japan's Economy on Course for Recession . . . with the Coronavirus Outbreak Set to Make Things Worse," *This Is Money*, February 17, 2020, https://www.thisismoney.co.uk/money/markets/article-8012285/Typhoon-Hagibis-sales-tax-rise-causes-Japans-economy-slump-six-year-low.html.
56. Andrew Keh and Ben Dooley, "Grappling with Coronavirus, Tokyo Olympic Leaders Have No Good Options," *New York Times*, February 26, 2020, https://advance-lexis-com.libproxy.wlu.ca/api/document?collection=news&id=urn:contentItem:5Y9C-HH51-DXY4-X324-00000-00&context=1516831.
57. Eryk Bagshaw, "Olympic Fears Grow as Australian Team Doctor Warns Coronavirus 'a Significant Challenge'," *Sydney Morning Herald*, 25 February 2020, https://www.smh.com.au/national/olympic-fears-grow-as-australian-team-doctor-warns-coronavirus-significant-challenge-20200225-p54414.html.
58. Lori Ewing, "COVID-19 Fears Ahead of Tokyo Games Has Some Remembering Outbreak Prior to 2010 Olympics," *Globe and Mail*, February 20, 2020, https://

advance-lexis-com.libproxy.wlu.ca/api/document?collection=news&id=urn:contentItem:6o58-SV11-JCRP-C2RV-00000-00&context=1516831.
59. Stephen Wade, "Tokyo Olympics Could Be Cancelled if Virus Threat Is Too Serious, Pound Says," *Globe and Mail*, February 26, 2020, https://advance-lexis-com.libproxy.wlu.ca/document/?pdmfid=1516831&crid=765eb2bf-c4ca-40a3-a2fd-0c6df2a7ccd8&pddocfullpath=%2Fshared%2Fdocument%2Fnews%2Furn%3AcontentItem%3A6o58-SV11-JCRP-C3CB-0000000&pdcontentcomponentid=303830&pdteaserkey=sr10&pditab=allpods&ecomp=szznk&earg=sr10&prid=addc7be7-8087-478c-9990-1b66c51ed791.
60. Keh and Dooley, "Grappling with Coronavirus."
61. Chris Barrett, "Flickering Hope: Coates Confident the Games Will Go Ahead As Planned," *Sydney Morning Herald*, March 17, 2020, https://advance-lexis-com.libproxy.wlu.ca/api/document?collection=news&id=urn:contentItem:5YF9-5R31-FoJ6-JoDM-00000-00&context=1516831.
62. Dick Pound, "Olympic Webinar Program Series: (TBD) August, September, 2020 and 2021 Wrap-Up," American Bar Association Law Section, 6. Pound shared this draft document with the authors of this book in June 2020. Brackets ours.
63. Personal interview, Kit McConnell, January 26, 2023.
64. Personal interview, Kit McConnell, January 26, 2023.
65. Personal interview, Thomas Bach, January 24, 2023.
66. Personal interview, Christophe Dubi, January 23, 2023.
67. Pound, "Olympic Webinar Program Series," 6.
68. "FOCUS: Experts Foresee Tokyo Games Without Spectators if Virus Lingers," *Japan Economic Newswire*, March 13, 2020, https://advance-lexis-com.libproxy.wlu.ca/api/document?collection=news&id=urn:contentItem: 5YDK-KXB1-DYN6-WoX9-00000-00&context=1516831.
69. Pound, "Olympic Webinar Program Series," 6. Brackets ours.
70. Personal interview, Thomas Bach, January 24, 2023.
71. Dick Pound, "DRAFT—Possible Webinar Program(s) Regarding Postponement of 2020 Olympic Games," American Bar Association Section—Sports Law Committee, 1. Pound shared this draft document with the authors of this book in June 2020.
72. Pound, "DRAFT—Possible Webinar Program(s)."
73. Purchasers of apartments in 2019 would eventually sue the developers when it became clear that the contracted handover of the apartments in March 2023 would be delayed as a result of postponing the Olympics and Paralympics for a year. Andrew Dowdeswell, "Tokyo 2020 Developers Sued for Delayed Handover of Athletes' Village Apartments," *Inside the Games*, December 25, 2021, https://www.insidethegames.biz/articles/1117228/tokyo-2020-athletes-village-development.
74. Pound, "DRAFT—Possible Webinar Program(s)," 1–6.
75. "UPDATE2: Japan Adopts Basic Policy to Fight Coronavirus Outbreak," *Japan Economic Newswire*, February 25, 2020, https://advance-lexis-com.libproxy.wlu.ca/api/document?collection=news&id=urn:contentItem:5Y96-7JR1-JC65-520W-00000-00&context=1516831.
76. "UPDATE3: Japan Adopts Basic Policy to Fight Coronavirus Outbreak," *Japan Economic Newswire*, February 25, 2020, https://advance-lexis-com.libproxy.wlu.ca/api/document?collection=news&id=urn:contentItem:5Y96-7JR1-JC65-521F-00000-00&context=1516831.

77. Noriyuki Suzuki, "FOCUS: Coronavirus Response an Unexpected, Crucial Test for Abe," *Japan Economic Newswire*, February 29, 2020, https://advance-lexis.com.libproxy.wlu.ca/api/document?collection=news&id=urn:contentItem:5YB2-4841-DYN6-W06X-00000-00&context=1516831.
78. Koichi Nakano, "Japan Can't Handle the Coronavirus?" *New York Times*, February 26, 2020, https://advance-lexis-com.libproxy.wlu.ca/api/document?collection=news&id=urn:contentItem:5Y96-RCH1-DXY4-X1JB-00000-00&context=1516831.
79. Nakano, "Japan Can't Handle the Coronavirus."
80. Ben Dooley, "Shinzo Abe, Japan's Political Houdini, Can't Escape Coronavirus Backlash," *New York Times*, March 5, 2020, https://advance-lexis-com.libproxy.wlu.ca/api/document?collection=news&id=urn:contentItem:5YBY-PCS1-DXY4-X299-00000-00&context=1516831.
81. Nakano, "Japan Can't Handle the Coronavirus."
82. Dooley, "Shinzo Abe, Japan's Political Houdini."
83. "Banyan Flu Jabs," *The Economist*, March 7, 2020, 54, https://libproxy.wlu.ca/login?url=https://www.proquest.com/magazines/banyan-flu-jabs/docview/2372869987/se-2?accountid=15090.
84. Andrew Sharp, "The Turbulent Journey to the Opening of Tokyo 2020," *Asia Nikkei*, July 19, 2021, https://asia.nikkei.com/Spotlight/Tokyo-2020-Olympics/The-turbulent-journey-to-the-opening-of-Tokyo-2020.
85. Mireya Solís and David Dollar, "The 2020 Olympics Were Always Meant to Be a Story of Resilience," *Dollars & Sense*, podcast, The Brookings Institution, August 2, 2021, https://www.brookings.edu/podcast-episode/the-2020-tokyo-olympics-were-always-meant-to-be-a-story-of-resilience/.
86. Stephen Wade and Mari Yamaguchi, "Tokyo Olympics Say Costs $12.6B; Audit Report Says Much More," *Associated Press News*, December 20, 2019, https://apnews.com/article/asia-pacific-ap-top-news-tokyo-sports-general-japan-eb6d9e318b4b95f7e53cd1b617dce123; David Wharton, "2020 Tokyo Olympics Could Cost Japan More Than $26 Billion," *Los Angeles Times*, December 20, 2019, https://www.latimes.com/sports/olympics/story/2019-12-20/2020-tokyo-olympics-could-cost-japan-more-than-26-billion.
87. See for instance, "Japanese Olympic Committee Head Resigns."
88. Solís and Dollar, "The 2020 Olympics Were Always Meant."
89. Our source for much of Abe's background while writing this section is Wikipedia, "Shinzo Abe," https://en.wikipedia.org/wiki/Shinzo_Abe.
90. "Abenomics: How Shinzo Abe Aimed to Revitalise Japan's Economy," *BBC*, July 8, 2022, https://www.bbc.com/news/business-62089543.
91. Yuko Kato and Zubaidah Abdul Jalil, "Shinzo Abe: The Legacy of Japan's Longest-Serving PM," *BBC*, July 8, 2022, https://www.bbc.com/news/world-asia-53938094.
92. "Abenomics: How Shinzo Abe Aimed to Revitalise Japan's Economy."
93. Kato and Jalil, "Shinzo Abe."
94. Kato and Jalil, "Shinzo Abe."
95. Noriyuki Suzuki, "UPDATE1: Will Abe Declare Emergency over Coronavirus After Law Revision?" *Japan Economic Newswire*, March 13, 2020, https://advance-lexis-com.libproxy.wlu.ca/api/document?collection=news&id=urn:contentItem:5YDT-K441-DYN6-W0X4-00000-00&context=1516831.

CHAPTER 3

1. "Coronavirus: The First Three Months as It Happened," *Nature*, April 22, 2020, https://www.nature.com/articles/d41586-020-00154-w.
2. Personal interview, Richard Budgett, January 25, 2023, Lausanne, Switzerland.
3. Personal interview, Richard Budgett, January 25, 2023.
4. Personal interview, Richard Budgett, January 25, 2023. The independently-run ITA manages doping control at the Olympic Games and makes the decisions on which athletes to test, when, and where.
5. Personal interview, Richard Budgett, January 25, 2023.
6. "UPDATE4: Japan to Restrict Travel to and from China, S. Korea over Virus," *Japan Economic Newswire*, March 5, 2020, https://advance-lexis-com.libproxy.wlu.ca/api/document?collection=news&id=urn:contentItem:5YC4-06P1-JC65-50M7-00000-00&context=1516831.
7. "UPDATE1: Lower House Passes Virus Bill Allowing Abe to Declare Emergency," *Japan Economic* Newswire, March 12, 2020, https://advance-lexis-com.libproxy.wlu.ca/api/document?collection=news&id=urn:contentItem:5YDK-KXB1-DYN6-W103-00000-00&context=1516831; "UPDATE1: Japan's Diet Gives Abe Power to Declare Emergency amid Viral Fears," *Japan Economic Newswire*, March 13, 2020, https://advance-lexis-com.libproxy.wlu.ca/api/document?collection=news&id=urn:contentItem:5YDT-K441-DYN6-W10W-00000-00&context=1516831.
8. Matthew Futterman, "An Olympic Doctor Discusses the Effect of the Coronavirus on Sports," *New York Times*, March 8, 2020, https://advance-lexiscom.libproxy.wlu.ca/api/document?collection=news&id=urn:contentItem:5YCM-NSB1-JBG3-6002-00000-00&context=1516831.
9. Personal interview, Richard Budgett, January 25, 2023.
10. Victor Mather, "How the Coronavirus Is Disrupting Sports Events," *New York Times*, March 11, 2020, https://advance-lexis-com.libproxy.wlu.ca/api/document?collection=news&id=urn:contentItem:5YD8-3KF1-JBG3-61Y3-00000-00&context=1516831.
11. Andrew Keh, "Postpone the Olympics? Tokyo Official Backtracks After Causing Confusion," *New York Times*, March 11, 2020, https://advance-lexis-com.libproxy.wlu.ca/api/document?collection=news&id=urn:contentItem:5YD7-SBT1-JBG3-61V0-00000-00&context=1516831.
12. Personal interview, Timo Lumme, January 25, 2023, Lausanne, Switzerland.
13. Personal interview, Christophe Dubi, January 23, 2023, Lausanne, Switzerland.
14. Personal interview, Kit McConnell, January 26, 2020, Lausanne, Switzerland.
15. Keh, "Postpone the Olympics?"
16. Fred Imbert and Thomas Franck, "Dow Plunges 10% amid Coronavirus Fears for Its Worst Day Since the 1987 Crash," *CNBC*, March 11, 2020, https://www.cnbc.com/2020/03/11/futures-are-steady-wednesday-night-after-dow-closes-in-bear-market-traders-await-trump.html.
17. Keh, "Postpone the Olympics? Tokyo Official Backtracks After Causing Confusion."
18. Peter Baker, "U.S. to Suspend Most Travel from Europe as World Scrambles to Fight Pandemic," *New York Times*, March 11, 2020, https://advance-lexis-com.libproxy.wlu.ca/api/document?collection=news&id=urn:contentItem:5YD7-GFK1-DXY4-X0TV-00000-00&context=1516831.
19. "Visual Timeline of the Day That Changed Everything," *ESPN*, March 11, 2021, https://www.espn.com/espn/story/_/id/30546338/visual-line-day-changed-everything

-march-11; and Dayn Perry et al., "Timeline of How the COVID-19 Pandemic Has Impacted the 2020 Major League Baseball Season," *CBS Sports*, July 29, 2020, https://www.cbssports.com/mlb/news/timeline-of-how-the-covid-19-pandemic-has-impacted-the-2020-major-league-baseball-season/.
20. Keh, "Postpone the Olympics?."
21. "UPDATE4: Japan to Restrict Travel."
22. Noriyuki Suzuki, "Will Abe Declare Emergency over Coronavirus After Law Revision?" *Japan Economic Newswire*, March 13, 2020, https://advance-lexis-com.libproxy.wlu.ca/api/document?collection=news&id=urn:contentItem:5YDT-K441-DYN6-W10G-00000-00&context=1516831.
23. "UPDATE4: Abe Tells Trump Japan Prepping for Tokyo Olympics as Planned," *Japan Economic Newswire*, March 13, 2020, https://advance-lexis-com.libproxy.wlu.ca/api/document?collection=news&id=urn:contentItem:5YDT-K441-DYN6-W109-00000-00&context=1516831.
24. Munehisa Tokunaga, "UPDATE1: Nikkei Falls to Lowest Level in 3 Yrs as Market Routed amid Virus Fear," *Japan Economic Newswire*, March 13, 2020, https://advance-lexis-com.libproxy.wlu.ca/api/document?collection=news&id=urn:contentItem:5YDT-K441-DYN6-W0Y6-00000-00&context=1516831.
25. "UPDATE3: IOC Confirms Tokyo Olympics to Be Held as Planned," *Japan Economic Newswire*, 18 March 2020, https://advance-lexis-com.libproxy.wlu.ca/api/document?collection=news&id=urn:contentItem:5YFW-F0X1-DYN6-W3F0-00000-00&context=1516831.
26. "Europe Boxing Qualification for Tokyo 2020 Live from London on Olympic Channel," *AIPS Media*, March 13, 2020, https://www.aipsmedia.com/aips/pages/articles/2020/27356.html; "IOC Boxing Task Force Suspends European Qualifier in London and All Remaining Events Until May," *Olympics.com*, March 16, 2020, https://olympics.com/ioc/news/ioc-boxing-task-force-suspends-european-qualifier-in-london-and-all-remaining-events-until-may; and, Dan Roan and Laura Scott. "Coronavirus: Six Members of Boxing Teams Who Attended Qualifier Said to Have Tested Positive." *BBC*, March 26, 2020. https://www.bbc.com/sport/olympics/52047624.
27. Daniel Etchells, "IOC Boxing Taskforce Suspends European Qualifier in London," *Inside The Games*, March 16, 2020, https://www.insidethegames.biz/articles/1092014/ioc-boxing-taskforce-suspends-qualifiers.
28. Tariq Panja, "The I.O.C. Let an Olympic Boxing Qualifier Happen Despite Virus Warnings," *New York Times*, March 27, 2020, https://www.nytimes.com/2020/03/27/sports/olympics/coronavirus-ioc-boxing.html; Liam Morgan, "IOC Claim One Boxer Diagnosed with Coronavirus After European Qualifier Returned False Positive," *Inside The Games*, March 28, 2020, https://www.insidethegames.biz/articles/1092531/ioc-claim-one-boxer-false-covid-19-test.
29. Roan and Scott, "Coronavirus: Six Members of Boxing Teams Who Attended Qualifier Said to Have Tested Positive."
30. James Ellingworth, "Coronavirus Already Wreaking Havoc on Olympic Qualifying Schedule," *Globe and Mail*, March 11, 2020, https://advance-lexis-com.libproxy.wlu.ca/api/document?collection=news&id=urn:contentItem:6059-3X61-F06S-34V3-00000-00&context=1516831.
31. Andrew Keh, "Twenty-Four Hours When Sports Hit the Halt Button," *New York Times*, March 12, 2020, https://advance-lexis-com.libproxy.wlu.ca/api/document

?collection=news&id=urn:contentItem:5YDG-R431-DXY4-X2RK-00000-00&context=1516831.

32. Matthew Futterman and Talya Minsberg, "Boston and London Marathons Postponed Until Fall," *New York Times*, March 13, 2020, https://advance-lexis-com.libproxy.wlu.ca/api/document?collection=news&id=urn:contentItem:5YDN-CJ21-DXY4-X41T-00000-00&context=1516831.

33. Matthew Futterman and Talya Minsberg, "Boston and London Marathons Are Rescheduled for Fall," *New York Times*, March 14, 2020, https://advance-lexis-com.libproxy.wlu.ca/api/document?collection=news&id=urn:contentItem:5YDV-TCP1-DXY4-X51D-00000-00&context=1516831.

34. Lori Ewing, "As COVID-19 Halts Global Races, Canada's Marathoners Take It in Stride," *Globe and Mail*, March 14, 2020, https://advance-lexis-com.libproxy.wlu.ca/api/document?collection=news&id=urn:contentItem:6059-3X71-F06S-302J-00000-00&context=1516831.

35. Michael Gleeson, "Lack of Teams Will Force Olympics Delay: Top Coach Olympics," *Sydney Morning Herald*, March 17, 2020, https://advance-lexis-com.libproxy.wlu.ca/api/document?collection=news&id=urn:contentItem:5YF9-5R31-F0J6-J0CD-00000-00&context=1516831.

36. Matt Lawton, "Olympics Are '90% Certain' to Be Delayed, Training Is Almost Impossible,' Says KJT," *The Times*, March 18, 2020, https://advance-lexis-com.libproxy.wlu.ca/api/document?collection=news&id=urn:contentItem:5YFN-TRJ1-DYTY-C48X-00000-00&context=1516831.

37. Andrew Keh and Tariq Panja, "I.O.C.'s Reassurance About the Tokyo Olympics Rankles Some Athletes," *New York Times*, March 18, 2020, https://advance-lexis-com.libproxy.wlu.ca/api/document?collection=news&id=urn:contentItem:5YFS-CTH1-JBG3-632K-00000-00&context=1516831.

38. Personal interview, Richard Budgett, January 25, 2023.

39. Phil Lutton, "Games Medical Conference Falls Victim to Virus as Tokyo Fears Grow," *Sydney Morning Herald*, March 12, 2020, https://advance-lexis-com.libproxy.wlu.ca/api/document?collection=news&id=urn:contentItem:5YD7-7K61-F0J6-J4MK-00000-00&context=1516831.

40. Jules Boykoff, "Cancel. The. Olympics," *New York Times*, March 18, 2020, https://advance-lexis-com.libproxy.wlu.ca/api/document?collection=news&id=urn:contentItem:5YFP-92T1-JBG3-621J-00000-00&context=1516831.

41. Personal interview, Thomas Bach, January 24, 2023, Lausanne, Switzerland.

42. Personal interview, Christophe Dubi, January 23, 2023.

43. Personal interview, Timo Lumme, January 26, 2023.

44. Andrew Keh et al., "An Olympic Showdown: The Rising Clamor to Postpone the Tokyo Summer Olympics," *New York Times*, March 21, 2020, https://www.nytimes.com/2020/03/21/sports/olympics/tokyo-olympics-coronavirus-cancel.html.

45. Patients had to have a "fever of greater than 37.5 Celsius (99° F) for more than four days, unless the patients are elderly, have underlying conditions, or are connected to a previously confirmed case." Though the US testing system was not an overwhelming success story either, by March 20, the United States reached 313 tests per million people, while Japan lagged well behind at 118. Eric Margolis, "'This May Be the Tip of the Iceberg': Why Japan's Coronavirus Crisis May Just Be Beginning," *Vox*, March 28, 2020, https://www.vox.com/covid-19-coronavirus-explainers/2020/3/28/21196382/japan-coronavirus-cases-covid-19-deaths-quarantine.

46. Matt Futterman and Joe Ward, "Let the Games Begin. Or Not," *New York Times*, March 19, 2020, https://advance-lexis-com.libproxy.wlu.ca/api/document?collection =news&id=urn:contentItem:5YFX-M651-DXY4-X548-00000-00&context=1516831.
47. Martin Ziegler and Matt Lawton, "Coe's Fears over Level Playing Field at Games ... but Olympics Could Yet Start on Time in July. Gold Medal-Winner Expects Athletes to Withdraw," *The Times*, March 19, 2020, https://advance-lexis-com.libproxy.wlu.ca /api/document?collection=news&id=urn:contentItem:5YFW-SXM1-DYTY-C0W3 -00000-00&context=1516831.
48. Chris Barrett, "'I Can't See How Games Can Go On': Former Chef de Mission Casts Doubt over Tokyo Olympics," *Sydney Morning Herald*, March 19, 2020, https:// www.smh.com.au/sport/i-can-t-see-how-games-can-go-ahead-former-australia-chef -de-mission-casts-doubt-on-tokyo-20200318-p54bif.html.
49. Keh and Panja, "I.O.C.'s Reassurance About the Tokyo Olympics."
50. Ziegler and Lawton, "Coe's Fears over Level Playing Field."
51. Tony Minichiello, "Games Must Be Delayed to Save Integrity," *The Times*, March 20, 2020, https://advance-lexis-com.libproxy.wlu.ca/ api/document?collection=news &id=urn:contentItem:5YG3-S2S1-DYTY-C2PF-00000-00&context=1516831.
52. "Virus Briefs," *Chicago Daily Herald*, March 21, 2020, https://advance-lexis-com .libproxy.wlu.ca/api/document?collection=news&id=urn:contentItem:5YGT-91X1 -DY6F-J026-00000-00&context=1516831; Phil Lutton, "Swim Chiefs Query Value of Games Compromised by Coronavirus Chaos Olympics," *Sydney Morning Herald*, March 21, 2020, https://advance-lexis-com.libproxy.wlu.ca/api/document?collection =news&id=urn:contentItem:5YG5-0521-F0J6-J3X4-00000-00&context=1516831.
53. Barrett, "'I Can't See How Games Can Go On.'"
54. Barrett, "'I Can't See How Games Can Go On.'"
55. Alex Prewitt, "Standard of Caring," *Sports Illustrated*, May 2020, 22–24, https:// search-ebscohost-com.libproxy.wlu.ca/login.aspx?direct=true&AuthType=ip ,cookie,url,uid&db=rgm&AN=142960517&site=ehost-live; Alex Prewitt, "Hayley Wickenheiser Is Using Her Unique Platform in Global Fight Against COVID-19." *Sports Illustrated*, April 11, 2020, https://www.si.com/olympics/2020/04/11/hayley -wickenheiser-ice-hockey-medical-school-doctor-coronavirus.
56. Keh and Panja, "I.O.C.'s Reassurance About the Tokyo Olympics."
57. Andrew Webster, "Olympic Movement in a Bubble—but Not Immune to COVID-19," *Sydney Morning Herald*, March 20, 2020, https://advance-lexis-com.libproxy.wlu.ca /api/document?collection=news&id=urn:contentItem:5YFY-0Y81-F0J6-J402-00000 -00&context=1516831. The Olympics were canceled in 1916, 1940, and 1944 due to the world wars.
58. Personal interview, Thomas Bach, January 24, 2023.
59. Tariq Panja and Matthew Futterman, "Canada Withdraws from Summer Olympics as I.O.C. Weighs Postponement," *New York Times*, March 22, 2020, https://advance -lexis-com.libproxy.wlu.ca/api/ document?collection=news&id=urn:contentItem :5YGK-SJM1-DXY4-X533-00000-00&context=1516831.
60. Panja and Futterman, "Canada Withdraws from Summer Olympics"; Motoko Rich and Tariq Panja, "U.S. Olympic Committee Urges Postponing Summer Games in Tokyo"; Motoko Rich et al., "I.O.C. and Japan Agree to Postpone Tokyo Olympics," *New York Times*, March 24, 2020, https://advance-lexis-com.libproxy .wlu.ca/api/document?collection=news&id=urn:contentItem:5YH0-P7J1-DXY4-X 1PX-00000-00&context=1516831; "IOC to Consider Postponing Tokyo Games in 4 Weeks of Talks," *Chicago Daily Herald*, March 23, 2020, https://advance-lexis com

.libproxy.wlu.ca/api/document?collection=news&id=urn:contentItem:5YGT-91X1-DY6F-J0HK-00000-00&context=1516831; Matthew Futterman, "A Grand Vision of the Olympics Plays Catchup With the Rest of the World," *New York Times*, March 24, 2020, https://advance-lexis-com.libproxy.wlu.ca/api/document?collection=news&id=urn:contentItem:5YGY-ST01-JBG3-614W-00000-00&context=1516831.
61. Rich et al., "I.O.C. and Japan Agree to Postpone Tokyo Olympics."
62. Panja and Futterman, "Canada Withdraws From Summer Olympics"; Rich and Panja, "U.S. Olympic Committee Urges"; Rich et al., "I.O.C. and Japan Agree"; "IOC to Consider Postponing Tokyo Games"; Futterman, "A Grand Vision of the Olympics." Brackets ours.
63. "Coronavirus: The First Three Months as it Happened."
64. "UPDATE 4: IOC Exploring Scenarios for Tokyo Games, Including Postponement," *Japan Economic Newswire*, 22 March 2020, https://advance-lexis-com.libproxy.wlu.ca/api/document?collection=news&id=urn:contentItem:5YGR-9S21-JC65-50HG-00000-00&context=1516831.
65. Rich et al., "I.O.C. and Japan Agree."
66. Personal interview, Christophe Dubi, January 23, 2023. Capitals on "BAM!" ours as Dubi emphasized his comment by softly banging his fist on the table during the interview.
67. "Public Communications Around COVID-19 and Games Postponement of IOC and Stakeholders—Knowledge Capture," March 2022. This document was produced by the IOC's Olympic Studies Centre in Lausanne, Switzerland, and was kindly provided to the authors by the Centre's head, Maria Bogner.
68. Matthew Futterman and Andrew Keh, "Why the U.S. Lagged Behind in the Drive to Postpone the Summer Olympics," *New York Times*, March 26, 2020, https://advance-lexis-com.libproxy.wlu.ca/api/document?collection=news&id=urn:contentItem:5YHD-PX71-JBG3-611K-00000-00&context=1516831.
69. Futterman and Keh, "Why the U.S. Lagged Behind."
70. Stephen R. Wenn and Robert K. Barney, *The Gold in the Rings: The People and Events that Transformed the Olympic Games* (University of Illinois Press, 2020), 219–38. IOC–USOC relations are a major frame of analysis in the book, though the treatment of the Copenhagen Session and its fallout is found on the noted pages.
71. Dave Feschuk, "Olympic Athletes Should Bargain for Their Fair Share, Just Like the Pros—but It Won't Be Easy," *Toronto Star*, April 24, 2020, https://www.thestar.com/sports/amateur/olympic-athletes-should-bargain-for-their-fair-share-just-like-the-pros-but-it-won/article_8ae46d10-a509-5324-9155-93b20ad1e573.html; Han Xiao, "Han Xiao: Significant Changes Needed to Narrow the Power Gap Between Athletes' Commissions and Organisations," *Inside the Games*, February 18, 2021, https://www.insidethegames.biz/articles/1104425/han-xiao-athletes-commission-model. Several years ago, few people might have foreseen the NIL (Name, Image, Likeness) sea change in the NCAA. While the IOC remains opposed to direct funding of Olympic competitors from revenue generated by the Games themselves, the issue is unlikely to disappear and merits considered reflection. When World Athletics decided to award prize money to track and field gold medalists in Paris, Thomas Bach countered that such compensation should be supplied by "sponsors, governments or private institutions." See Rachel Axon, "World Athletics Introduces Prize Money Pool for Paris Gold Medal Winners," *Street & Smith's Sports Business Journal*, April 4, 2024, https://www.sportsbusinessjournal.com/Articles/2024/04/10/world-athletics-prize-money-track-and-field-olympic-competitions; "IOC Boss Critical of World Athletics Paying

Athletes," *Street & Smith's Sports Business Journal*, May 3, 2024, https://www.sportsbusinessjournal.com/Articles/2024/05/03/ioc-world-athletics-olympic-prize-money#:~:text=IOC%20President%20Thomas%20Bach%20suggested,role%20of%20an%20international%20sports; Brandon Marcello, "NIL Landscape in College Sports Changing: NCAA Losing Its Grip, Amateur vs. Employee Battle Looms," *CBS Sports*, April 23, 2024, https://www.cbssports.com/college-football/news/nil-landscape-in-college-sports-changes-as-ncaa-loses-grip-amateur-vs-employee-battle-looms/.

72. Chris Barrett, "'I Was Looking at Retiring': Delay Forces Rethink for Gold Hopeful OLYMPICS," *Sydney Morning Herald*, March 26, 2020, https://advance-lexis-com.libproxy.wlu.ca/api/document?collection=news&id=urn:contentItem:5YH6-V481-JD34-V181-00000-00&context=1516831.
73. Barrett, "'I Was Looking at Retiring.'"
74. Personal interview, Richard Budgett, January 25, 2023. Brackets ours.
75. World Health Organization, "COVID-19 Situation Update for the WHO African Region, External Situation Report 4," March 18, 2020, https://reliefweb.int/report/south-africa/covid-19-situation-update-who-african-region-external-situation-report-3-18; World Health Organization, "COVID-19 WHO African Region: External Situation Report 04/2020," accessed December 20, 2024, https://apps.who.int/iris/handle/10665/331587.
76. Personal interview, Thomas Bach, January 24, 2023.
77. Personal interview, Thomas Bach, January 24, 2023.
78. Personal interview, Christophe Dubi, January 23, 2023. Brackets ours.
79. Personal interview, Thomas Bach, January 24, 2023.
80. Personal interview, Thomas Bach, January 24, 2023.
81. Michael Stoneman, "Here We Go," *Olympic Review* 115 (April-May-June 2020), 31–32.
82. "UPDATE3: Abe Hints at Possibility of Postponing Tokyo Olympics," *Japan Economic Newswire*, 23 March 2020, https://advance-lexis-com.libproxy.wlu.ca/api/document?collection=news&id=urn:contentItem:5YGY-8YV1-JC65-52RB-00000-00&context=1516831.
83. Personal interview, Thomas Bach, January 24, 2023.
84. Stoneman, "Here We Go," 24.
85. Personal interview, Thomas Bach, January 24, 2023.
86. Mark Adams provided his thoughts while attending the interview we conducted with Thomas Bach on January 24, 2023. Brackets ours.
87. Personal interview, Thomas Bach, January 24, 2023.
88. Personal interview, Thomas Bach, January 24, 2023.
89. Personal interview, Thomas Bach, January 24, 2023.
90. Personal interview, Christophe Dubi, January 23, 2023.
91. Personal interview, Christophe Dubi, January 23, 2023. The time to the rescheduled opening of the Games was actually sixteen months; the Paralympics, however, would open in seventeen.

CHAPTER 4

1. Josh Cohen, "An Ode to Gregg Popovich, the Most Interesting Man in the NBA," *Bleacher Report*, May 31, 2013, https://bleacherreport.com/articles/1656735-an-ode-to-the-most-interesting-man-in-the-nba-gregg-popovich. Brackets ours.

2. Jack McCallum, "Why More Americans Aren't Happy for Gregg Popovich," *The Atlantic*, August 7, 2021, https://www.theatlantic.com/ideas/archive/2021/08/olympian-struggles-gregg-popovich/619673/.
3. McCallum, "Why More Americans Aren't Happy"; Drew Silverman, "Jerry Colangelo, Long-Time Architect of USA Basketball, Reflects on a Golden Career," *USA Basketball*, July 29, 2021, https://www.usab.com/news/2021/07/jerry-colangelo-feature; Marc Stein, "Also Postponed: A Coach's Quest for Olympic Gold," *New York Times*, March 28, 2020, https://advance-lexis-com.libproxy.wlu.ca/document/?pdmfid=1516831&crid=1e90ac33-eabc-475e-863e-598a1a49be91&pddocfullpath=%2Fshared%2Fdocument%2Fnews%2Furn%3AcontentItem%3A5YJ2-J2W1-DXY4-X45J-00000000&pdcontentcomponentid=6742&pdteaserkey=sr40&pditab=allpods&ecomp=zznyk&earg=sr40&prid=def6fdd8-6b6f-4583-9680-c61726f3b497.
4. Jacob Camenker, "Meet MyKayla Skinner, Who Finally Lived Out Olympic Dreams After Overcoming COVID," *Sporting News*, July 25, 2021, https://www.sportingnews.com/us/athletics/news/meet-mykayla-skinner-olympic-covid/jck75p8gk2t91p7d2u47q8lzu; Juliet Macur, " 'It's Just So Devastating': For Crestfallen Gymnasts, an Olympic Dream Deferred," *New York Times*, April 1, 2020, https://advance-lexis-com.libproxy.wlu.ca/api/document?collection=news&id=urn:contentItem:5YJR-SDY1-DXY4-X3MJ-00000-00&context=1516831.
5. Juliet Macur, "Take Coronavirus More Seriously, Say Olympic Rowers Who Got It," *New York Times*, July 24, 2020, https://advance-lexis-com.libproxy.wlu.ca/api/document?collection=news&id=urn:contentItem:60F0-JJS1-DXY4-X1WD-00000-00&context=1516831. Brackets ours.
6. Alice Thomson, "This Has Given My Body a Chance to Rest; Right Now, Tom Daley Should Have Been Preparing for the Olympics, but With the Pools Closed He's Spending Time with His Son," *The Times*, 9 June 2020, https://advance-lexis-com.libproxy.wlu.ca/api/document?collection=news&id=urn:contentItem:603C-7K81-DYTY-C3W5-00000-00&context=1516831. Brackets ours.
7. Isabel Reynolds and Josh Wingrove, "President Trump Suggests Tokyo Olympics Should be Postponed 1 Year," *Time*, March 12, 2020, https://time.com/5802271/trump-tokyo-olympics-coronavirus/; Annie Karni and Donald G. McNeil Jr., "Trump Wants U.S. 'Opened Up' by Easter, Despite Health Officials' Warnings," *New York Times*, March 24, 2020, https://advance lexiscom.libproxy.wlu.ca/api/document?collection=news&id=urn:contentItem:5YH4-TV21-JBG3-63DP-00000-00&context=1516831.
8. Karni and McNeil, "Trump Wants U.S. 'Opened Up' by Easter."
9. Ivan Pereira and Arielle Mitropoulos, "A Year of COVID-19: What Was Going On in the US in March 2020," *ABC News*, March 6, 2021, https://abcnews.go.com/Health/year-covid-19-us-march-2020/story?id=76204691.
10. Karni and McNeil, "Trump Wants U.S. 'Opened Up' by Easter."
11. "WHO Coronavirus 2019 (COVID-19): Situation Report—72 (April 1, 2020)," https://reliefweb.int/report/world/coronavirus-disease-2019-covid-19-situation-report-72-1-april-2020.
12. "WHO Coronavirus 2019 (COVID-19): Situation Report—41 (March 1, 2020)," https://reliefweb.int/report/china/coronavirus-disease-2019-covid-19-situation-report-41-1-march-2020.

13. Melina Delkic, "Coronavirus in Japan, New York Hospitals, Maduro Indictment: Your Friday Briefing," *New York Times*, March 26, 2020, https://advance-lexis-com.libproxy.wlu.ca/api/document?collection=news&id=urn:contentItem:5YHF-SRH1-DXY4-X026-00000-00&context=1516831.
14. Motoko Rich et al., "Japan Declares Emergency as Experts Fear 'Tip of the Iceberg,'" *New York Times*, April 8, 2020, https://advance-lexis-com.libproxy.wlu.ca/api/document?collection=news&id=urn:contentItem:5YM5-BKN1-DXY4-X4M9-00000-00&context=1516831.
15. Rich et al., "Japan Declares Emergency."
16. Rich et al., "Japan Declares Emergency."
17. Personal interview, Richard Budgett, January 25, 2023, Lausanne, Switzerland.
18. Personal interview, Richard Budgett, January 25, 2023.
19. Waseda University, "Faculty of Sport Sciences: AKAMA, Takao," https://dpt-healthpromotion.w.waseda.jp/wp/members/215/.
20. Personal interview, Richard Budgett, January 25, 2023.
21. Personal interview, Richard Budgett, January 25, 2023. Brackets ours.
22. Personal interview, Christophe Dubi, January 23, 2023, Lausanne, Switzerland.
23. "Public Communications around COVID-19 and Games Postponement of IOC and Stakeholders—Knowledge Capture," March 2022. This document was produced by the IOC's Olympic Studies Centre in Lausanne, Switzerland, and was kindly provided to the authors by the Centre's head, Maria Bogner.
24. "IOC and Tokyo 2020 Joint Statement—Framework for Preparation of the Olympic and Paralympic Games Tokyo 2020 Following Their Postponement to 2021," *Olympics.com*, April 16, 2020, https://olympics.com/ioc/news/ioc-and-tokyo-2020-joint-statement-framework-for-preparation-of-the-olympic-and-paralympic-games-tokyo-2020-following-their-postponement-to-2021.
25. "UPDATE2: Japan, IOC Agree to Postpone This Summer's Tokyo Olympics," *Japan Economic Newswire*, March 24, 2020, https://advance-lexis-com.libproxy.wlu.ca/api/document?collection=news&id=urn:contentItem:5YH5-82Y1-DYN6-W12J-00000-00&context=1516831.
26. Ryotaro Nakamaru, "FOCUS: Olympic Postponement Throws Wrench into Abe's Plans," *Japan Economic Newswire*, March 24, 2020, https://advance-lexis-com.libproxy.wlu.ca/api/document?collection=news&id=urn:contentItem:5YH5-82Y1-DYN6-W16F-00000-00&context=1516831.
27. Noriyuki Suzuki, "UPDATE4: Tokyo Olympics Postponed Until 2021 due to Coronavirus Pandemic," *Japan Economic Newswire*, March 24, 2020, https://advance-lexis-com.libproxy.wlu.ca/api/document?collection=news&id=urn:contentItem:5YH5-82Y1-DYN6-W14G-00000-00&context=1516831.
28. Joel Fitzpatrick, "FOCUS: Tokyo Games Postponement to Require Olympic-Scale Rethink," *Japan Economic Newswire*, April 1, 2020, https://advance-lexis-com.libproxy.wlu.ca/api/document?collection=news&id=urn:contentItem:5Y-JW-1NG1-JC65-51YP-00000-00&context=1516831.
29. "IOC and Tokyo 2020 Joint Statement."
30. "Olympics: Tokyo Organizers Securing Schedule, Venues for Delayed Games," *Japan Economic Newswire*, April 16, 2020, https://advance-lexis-com.libproxy.wlu.ca/api/document?collection=news&id=urn:contentItem:5YP2-K9H1-DYN6-W54J-00000-00&context=1516831.

31. "Tokyo, Olympic Organizers in Rough Waters 1 Month After Postponement," *Japan Economic Newswire*, April 24, 2020, https://advance-lexis-com.libproxy.wlu.ca/api/document?collection=news&id=urn:contentItem:5YRJ-CPG1-DYN6-W1D7-00000-00&context=1516831.
32. "IOC and Tokyo 2020 Joint Statement."
33. Personal interview, Thomas Bach, January 24, 2023, Lausanne, Switzerland.
34. Personal interview, Christophe Dubi, January 23, 2023.
35. Yuliya Talmazan, "New Dates Announced for Tokyo 2020 Olympics Postponed over Coronavirus Concerns," *NBC News*, March 30, 2020, https://www.nbcnews.com/news/world/new-dates-announced-tokyo-2020-olympics-postponed-over-coronavirus-concerns-n1171871.
36. Matthew Futterman, "Why Olympic Leaders Clung to the Plan to Have the Summer Games in Tokyo," *New York Times*, April 17, 2020, https://advance-lexis-com.libproxy.wlu.ca/api/document?collection=news&id=urn:contentItem:5YGY-MCG1-JBG3-610V-00000-00&context=1516831.
37. "FOCUS: Tokyo Games Dates Set, but Organizers Still Face Tests," *Japan Economic Newswire*, April 2, 2020, https://advance-lexis-com.libproxy.wlu.ca/api/document?collection=news&id=urn:contentItem:5YK3-0R41-DYN6-W24Y-00000-00&context=1516831.
38. "UPDATE1: Japanese Athletes Generally Positive to Tokyo Olympic Postponement," *Japan Economic Newswire*, March 25, 2020, https://advance-lexis-com.libproxy.wlu.ca/api/document?collection=news&id=urn:contentItem:5YHC-7BG1-DYN6-W534-00000-00&context=1516831.
39. "Olympics: Japanese Federations Hoping to Retain Help of Foreign Coaches," *Japan Economic Newswire*, May 4, 2020, https://advance-lexis-com.libproxy.wlu.ca/api/document?collection=news&id=urn:contentItem:5YTP-3DW1-DYN6-W0FX-00000-00&context=1516831.
40. "UPDATE2: Japan Approves Nearly $1 Tril. Package to Cushion Coronavirus Impact," *Japan Economic Newswire*, April 7, 2020, https://advance-lexis-com.libproxy.wlu.ca/api/document?collection=news&id=urn:contentItem:5YM4-VNP1-DYN6-W095-00000-00&context=1516831.
41. Personal interview, Richard Budgett, January 25, 2023. Brackets ours.
42. Personal interview, Timo Lumme, January 26, 2023. Brackets ours.
43. Personal interview, Timo Lumme, January 26, 2023. Brackets ours.
44. "Insurer Allianz Becomes Olympic sponsor," *France24*, September 18, 2018, https://www.france24.com/en/20180918-insurer-allianz-becomes-olympic-sponsor.
45. Personal interview, Timo Lumme, January 26, 2023.
46. Exarchos, as cited by Michael Payne, "The Cursed Olympics That Became the Miracle Games." Payne prepared this document as a post-Games report and shared it with the authors via email in January 2023.
47. Personal interview, Christophe Dubi, January 23, 2023. For the scope of the challenge for the Japanese, see also Motoko Rich and Ben Dooley, "Tokyo's New Challenge: Putting the Games in Mothballs," *New York Times*, March 26, 2020, https://advance-lexis-com.libproxy.wlu.ca/api/document?collection=news&id=urn:contentItem:5YHD-FJ11-DXY4-X4H3-00000-00&context=1516831.
48. Stephen Wilson, "The Tokyo Postponement: Lessons Learned for the Olympic Movement," *Olympic Review* 116 (June 2021), 69.
49. Personal interview, Christophe Dubi, January 23, 2023.

50. Personal interview, Christophe Dubi, January 23, 2023. Brackets ours.
51. Personal interview, Kit McConnell, January 26, 2023, Lausanne, Switzerland.
52. Personal interview, Christophe Dubi, January 23, 2023. Brackets ours.
53. "IOC Approves a Financial Envelope of up to USD 800 Million to Address the COVID-19 Crisis," *Olympics.com*, May 14, 2020, https://olympics.com/ioc/news/ioc-approves-a-financial-envelope-of-up-to-usd-800-million-to-address-the-covid-19-crisis.
54. Jocelyn Solis-Moreira, "How Did We Develop a COVID-19 Vaccine so Quickly?" *Medical News Today*, November 13, 2021, https://www.medicalnewstoday.com/articles/how-did-we-develop-a-covid-19-vaccine-so-quickly.
55. "IOC and Tokyo 2020 Joint Statement."
56. "IOC and Tokyo 2020 Joint Statement."
57. James Sutherland, "Tokyo 2020, IOC Look Toward Simplified Games, Present Progress Reports," *SwimSwam*, June 10, 2020, https://swimswam.com/tokyo-2020-ioc-look-toward-simplified-games-present-progress-reports/.
58. Sutherland, "Tokyo 2020, IOC."
59. Sutherland, "Tokyo 2020, IOC."
60. Solis-Moreira, "How Did We Develop"; Catherine Clifford, "How the Moderna Covid-19 mRNA Vaccine Was Made So Quickly," *CNBC*, July 3, 2021, https://www.cnbc.com/2021/07/03/how-moderna-made-its-mrna-covid-vaccine-so-quickly-noubar-afeyan.html.
61. Nicola Davis, "How Has a Covid Vaccine Been Developed So Quickly?" *The Guardian*, December 8, 2020, https://www.theguardian.com/society/2020/dec/08/how-has-a-covid-vaccine-been-developed-so-quickly.
62. Davis, "How Has a Covid Vaccine."
63. Solis-Moreira, "How Did We Develop."
64. Solis-Moreira, "How Did We Develop."
65. Solis-Moreira, "How Did We Develop."
66. Davis, "How Has a Covid Vaccine."
67. Personal interview, Thomas Bach, January 24, 2023.
68. Personal interview, Richard Budgett, January 25, 2023.
69. Personal interview, Thomas Bach, January 24, 2023.
70. Personal interview, Richard Budgett, January 25, 2023.
71. Personal interview, Richard Budgett, January 25, 2023.
72. Personal interview, Christophe Dubi, January 23, 2023.
73. Personal interview, Christophe Dubi, January 23, 2023.
74. Personal interview, Thomas Bach, January 24, 2023. Brackets ours.
75. Personal interview, Thomas Bach, January 24, 2023. Brackets ours.
76. Personal interview, Christophe Dubi, January 23, 2023.
77. Brian McCloskey, "Brian McCloskey: How Tokyo 2020 Paved the Way for Other Major Events," *Inside the Games*, August 6, 2022, https://www.insidethegames.biz/articles/1126658/blog-dr-brian-mccloskey; World Health Organization, "Biographies: IHR Emergency Committee for COVID-19," accessed December 23, 2024, https://www.who.int/docs/default-source/documents/ihr/ec-covid-19-biographies-combined-updated-october-2020bee6d4bde4b04b36a5f125a6e0970ef1.pdf?sfvrsn=7f569f7a_2; "Brian McCloskey," *Chatham House*, archived October 24, 2020, at https://web.archive.org/web/20201024035702/https://www.chathamhouse.org/about-us/our-people/brian-mccloskey.
78. McCloskey, "Brian McCloskey: How Tokyo 2020 Paved." Brackets ours.

79. "Project Crystal: Scenario Working Group," PowerPoint presentation, IOC Games Delivery Office, July 8, 2020. Olympic House, Lausanne, Switzerland. This PowerPoint was provided to the authors by Maria Bogner, head of the Olympic Studies Centre, Lausanne, Switzerland.
80. Personal interview, Richard Budgett, January 25, 2023.
81. McCloskey, "Brian McCloskey: How Tokyo 2020 Paved."
82. "Pfizer and BioNTech Announce Further Details on Collaboration to Accelerate Global COVID-19 Vaccine Development," *Pfizer*, April 9, 2020, https://www.pfizer.com/news/press-release/press-release-detail/pfizer-and-BioNTech-announce-further-details-collaboration.
83. Personal interview, Thomas Bach, January 24, 2023.
84. "GAVI—The Vaccine Alliance," archived October 1, 2022, at https://web.archive.org/web/20221001064353/https://www.who.int/europe/about-us/partnerships/partners/global-health-partnerships/gavi-alliance. "GAVI aims at accelerating access to vaccines, strengthening countries' health and immunization systems, and introducing innovative new immunization technology," primarily for children.
85. Personal interview, Thomas Bach, January 24, 2023.
86. Personal interview, Thomas Bach, January 24, 2023.
87. Andrew Keh, "First for Shots: Doctors, Nurses . . . Olympians?" *New York Times*, March 1, 2021, https://advance-lexis-com.libproxy.wlu.ca/api/document?collection=news&id=urn:contentItem:623X-0361-DXY4-X28P-00000-00&context=1516831.
88. Keh, "First for Shots." Brackets ours.
89. Personal interview, Thomas Bach, January 24, 2023.
90. Personal interview, Richard Budgett, January 25, 2023.
91. Keh, "Olympians Enter a Risky New Event: Line Jumping," *New York Times*, February 28, 2021, https://advance-lexis-com.libproxy.wlu.ca/api/document?collection=news&id=urn:contentItem:623R-34G1-DXY4-X1B0-00000-00&context=1516831.
92. Personal interview, Richard Budgett, January 25, 2023.
93. Personal interview, Christophe Dubi, January 23, 2023.
94. Personal interview, Thomas Bach, January 24, 2023.
95. Chris Medland, "Formula One Loses Nearly $400 Million in COVID-Hit 2020," *Racer*, February 26, 2021, https://racer.com/2021/02/26/formula-1-loses-nearly-400m-in-covid-hit-2020/; "Revenue Generated Worldwide by the Formula One Group for 2017–2020," *Statista*, December 9, 2022, https://www.statista.com/statistics/1137226/formula-one-revenue/.
96. Giles Richards, "Drive to Survive Documentary Helping Bring In New Generation of US F1 Fans," *The Guardian*, May 5, 2022, https://www.theguardian.com/sport/2022/may/05/drive-to-survive-documentary-helping-bring-in-new-generation-of-us-f1-fans.
97. Christian Sylt, "Why 2020 Could Be the Most Crucial Year in F1's History," *Forbes*, January 12, 2020, https://www.forbes.com/sites/csylt/2020/01/12/why-2020-could-be-the-most-crucial-year-in-f1s-history/?sh=209d1ecc308c.
98. Ian Parkes, "A Formula 1 Season Like No Other," *New York Times*, August 7, 2020, https://www.nytimes.com/2020/08/07/sports/autoracing/formula-1-season-coronavirus.html.
99. Its oversight duties encompass, among others, F1, Rally Racing, and Endurance Racing.
100. Personal interview, Pau Mota, January 23, 2023, Lausanne, Switzerland.
101. Personal interview, Pau Mota, January 23, 2023.

182 · NOTES

102. Personal interview, Pau Mota, January 23, 2023; Parkes, "A Formula 1 Season Like No Other."
103. Personal interview, Pau Mota, January 23, 2023.
104. Personal interview, Richard Budgett, January 25, 2023.
105. Personal interview, Pau Mota, January 23, 2023.
106. Personal interview, Richard Budgett, January 25, 2023.
107. Personal interview, Pau Mota, January 23, 2023.
108. Personal interview, Pau Mota, January 23, 2023.
109. Personal interview, Pau Mota, January 23, 2023.
110. Personal interview, Pau Mota, January 23, 2023.
111. Personal interview, Pau Mota, January 23, 2023.
112. Personal interview, Richard Budgett, January 25, 2023. Brackets ours.
113. Personal interview, Thomas Bach, January 24, 2023.

CHAPTER 5

1. Andrew Keh, "Power Game: Thomas Bach's Iron Grip on the Olympics," *New York Times*, July 20, 2021, https://www.nytimes.com/2021/07/20/sports/thomas-bach-tokyo-olympics.html. Brackets ours. Kirsty Coventry won seven Olympic medals in swimming across the 2004 and 2008 Olympics.
2. Keh, "Power Game."
3. Keh, "Power Game"; International Olympic Committee (IOC), "Mr. Thomas Bach," accessed December 24, 2024, https://olympics.com/ioc/mr-thomas-bach.
4. IOC, "Mr. Thomas Bach."
5. IOC, "Mr. Thomas Bach."
6. Keh, "Power Game."
7. Personal interview, Thomas Bach, January 24, 2023, Lausanne, Switzerland.
8. Keh, "Power Game."
9. Personal interview, Thomas Bach, January 24, 2023, Lausanne, Switzerland.
10. Personal interview, Thomas Bach, January 24, 2023.
11. Gary Smith, "Lessons from the Master: Emil Beck, the Obsessive West German Coach, Turns Out the World's Best Fencers at His Tauberbischofsheim Training Center," *Sports Illustrated*, September 14, 1988, https://vault.si.com/vault/1988/09/14/lessons-from-the-master-emil-beck-the-obsessive-west-german-coach-turns-out-the-worlds-best-fencers-at-his-tauberbischofsheim-training-center.
12. Keh, "Power Game."
13. Keh, "Power Game."
14. Personal interview, Thomas Bach, January 24, 2023. Brackets ours.
15. Keh, "Power Game."
16. Stephen R. Wenn and Robert K. Barney, *The Gold in the Rings: The People and Events That Transformed the Olympic Games* (University of Illinois Press, 2020), 215, 235–36, 242–44.
17. Nury Turkel, "Relocate the Olympics or Condone Genocide," *Foreign Policy*, June 2, 2021, https://foreignpolicy.com/2021/06/02/olympics-china-uyghurs-genocide-boycott/.
18. See, for instance, the work of Jules Boykoff, such as *Activism and the Olympics: Dissent at the Games in Vancouver and London* (Rutgers University Press, 2014) and *What Are the Olympics For?* (Bristol University Press, 2024).

19. "IOC President Bach Coy as Members Call for Rule Change to Extend Term," *France24*, October 15, 2023, https://www.france24.com/en/live-news/20231015-ioc-president-bach-coy-as-members-call-for-rule-change-to-extend-his-term; "IOC's Bach Doesn't Dismiss Proposal to Extend Term," *Street & Smith's Sport Business Journal*, October 1, 2023, https://www.sportsbusinessjournal.com/Articles/2023/10/16/thomas-bach-ioc-president-term-limits.aspx. A term limit for those serving as IOC president had been a key feature of the reform package passed by the IOC session in the wake of the 1998–1999 Salt Lake City bid scandal.
20. Keh, "Power Game."
21. Keh, "Power Game." Brackets ours.
22. Wong and Lewis also believe the planners of Tokyo 2020 missed an opportunity to share with the Japanese population that any decision to cancel the Games rested with the IOC alone—an action, if taken, that might have deflected a measure of criticism from the Tokyo Organizing Committee. Donna Wong and Yue Meng-Lewis, "The Good, the Bad, and the Ugly—Situational Crisis Communication and the COVID-19 Pandemic Tokyo 2020 Olympic Games," *Communication & Sport* 12, no. 1 (2023): 99–129. https://doi-org.libproxy.wlu.ca/10.1177/21674795231174188.
23. Personal interview, Kit McConnell, January 26, 2023, Lausanne, Switzerland.
24. Personal interview, Christophe Dubi, January 23, 2023, Lausanne, Switzerland. Brackets ours.
25. Personal interview, Richard Budgett, January 25, 2023, Lausanne, Switzerland. Brackets ours.
26. Personal interview, Christophe Dubi, January 23, 2023.
27. Personal interview, Thomas Bach, January 24, 2023. Brackets ours.
28. Ben Dooley and Makiko Inoue, "Olympics Delay Can Only Worsen Japan's Slump," *New York Times*, April 1, 2020, https://advance-lexis-com.libproxy.wlu.ca/api/document?collection=news&id=urn:contentItem:5YJP-5991-JBG3-635P-00000-00&context=1516831.
29. Ben Dooley, "Japan Falls into a Recession, with 'Ugly' Months to Come," *New York Times*, May 18, 2020, https://advance-lexis-om.libproxy.wlu.ca/api/document?collection=news&id=urn:contentItem:5YXP-VJ91-DXY4-X239-00000-00&context=1516831.
30. Dooley and Inoue, "Olympics Delay Can Only Worsen Japan's Slump."
31. "VOX POPULI: Bus Service in Ken Shimura's Hometown Steps Up to Help Locals," *Asahi Shimbun*, June 3, 2020, https://www.asahi.com/ajw/articles/13426149.
32. Wikipedia (Japanese), "Galaxy Express (Bus Company)," last modified December 21, 2024, https://ja.wikipedia.org/wiki/%E9%8A%80%E6%B2%B3%E9%89%84%E9%81%93_(%E3%83%90%E3%82%B9%E4%BC%9A%E7%A4%BE).
33. We are grateful for this update on the Galaxy Express company sent to us by our colleague, Kohei Kawashima (Waseda University). Kohei Kawashima, email message to Stephen Wenn, April 24, 2023.
34. Stephen Wilson, "The Tokyo Postponement: Lessons Learned for the Olympic Movement," *Olympic Review* 116 (June 2021), 69.
35. "IOC and Atos Extend Worldwide Olympic Partnership," *Olympics.com*, July 9, 2020, https://olympics.com/ioc/news/ioc-and-atos-extend-worldwide-olympic-partnership.
36. "The IOC and Procter & Gamble Announce an Extension to Their Worldwide Olympic Partnership Through 2028," *Olympics.com*, July 22, 2020, https://olympics

.com/ioc/news/the-ioc-and-procter-gamble-announce-an-extension-to-their-worldwide-olympic-partnership-through-to-2028.
37. Personal interview, Timo Lumme, January 26, 2023, Lausanne, Switzerland.
38. "IOC and Deloitte Announce Global Partnership to Advance the Olympic Movement," April 7, 2022, *Olympics.com*, https://olympics.com/ioc/news/ioc-and-deloitte-announce-global-partnership-to-advance-the-olympic-movement.
39. "IOC and Deloitte Announce Global Partnership."
40. Personal interview, Timo Lumme, January 26, 2023.
41. Personal interview, Timo Lumme, January 26, 2023; *The Playbook: Marketing Partners—Your Guide to a Safe and Successful Games*, vol. 3, June 2021, https://stillmed.olympics.com/media/Documents/Olympic-Games/Tokyo-2020/Playbooks/The-Playbook-Marketing-Partners-V3.pdf?_ga=2.77858004.1325720664.1677506866-2077939235.1666268141; *The Playbook: Broadcasters—Your Guide to a Safe and Successful Games*, vol. 3, June 2021, https://stillmed.olympics.com/media/Documents/Olympic-Games/Tokyo-2020/Playbooks/The-Playbook-Broadcasters-V3.pdf?_ga=2.80881623.1325720664.1677506866-2077939235.1666268141.
42. Personal interview, Timo Lumme, January 26, 2023. Brackets ours.
43. Personal interview, Timo Lumme, January 26, 2023.
44. "Top Olympic Broadcasters Reveal How COVID-19 Has Affected Plans for Tokyo 2020 and Beyond," *Olympics.com*, March 12, 2021, https://olympics.com/ioc/news/top-olympic-broadcasters-reveal-how-covid-19-has-affected-plans-for-tokyo-2020-and-beyond.
45. Personal interview, Kit McConnell, January 26, 2023.
46. Motoko Rich, "Tokyo's First Female Governor Sails to Re-election Even as Virus Cases Rise," *New York Times*, July 5, 2020, https://advance-lexis-com.libproxy.wlu.ca/api/document?collection=news&id=urn:contentItem:608Y-N151-DXY4-X417-00000-00&context=1516831.
47. Matthew Futterman et al., "The Tokyo Olympics Will Open a Year from Now. Maybe," *New York Times*, July 19, 2020, https://advance-lexis-com.libproxy.wlu.ca/api/document?collection=news&id=urn:contentItem:60CY-7M41-DXY4-X0NG-00000-00&context=1516831.
48. Futterman et al., "The Tokyo Olympics Will Open a Year From Now. Maybe."
49. "UPDATE2: Delayed Tokyo Olympics to Retain Same Venues, Competition Schedule," *Japan Economic Newswire*, July 17, 2020, https://advance-lexis-com.libproxy.wlu.ca/api/document?collection=news&id=urn:contentItem:60CJ-3CV1-DYMD-61D1-00000-00&context=1516831.
50. "Japan Marks 1 Year Until Delayed Olympics, but Virus Concerns Remain," *Japan Economic Newswire*, July 23, 2020, https://advance-lexis-com.libproxy.wlu.ca/api/document?collection=news&id=urn:contentItem:60DR-RNP1-DYMD-60GM-00000-00&context=1516831.
51. "Japan's Economy Shrinks 28.1% in the Second Quarter, More Than Initially Estimated," *CNBC*, September 7, 2020, https://www.cnbc.com/2020/09/08/japan-q2-revised-gdp-2020.html.
52. Motoko Rich, "Shinzo Abe, Japan's Longest-Serving Prime Minister, Resigns Because of Illness," *New York Times*, August 28, 2020, https://advance-lexis-com.libproxy.wlu.ca/api/document?collection=news&id=urn:contentItem:60PD-YXR1-DXY4-X2CD-00000-00&context=1516831.
53. Ryotaro Nakamaru, "FOCUS: Race to Succeed Abe Kicks Off with No Clear Favorite," *Japan Economic Newswire*, August 29, 2020, https://advance-lexis-com

.libproxy.wlu.ca/api/document?collection=news&id=urn:contentItem:60PN-6DN1-JC5B-G4FT-00000-00&context=1516831; Sayo Sasaki, "UPDATE2: Suga Elected as Successor to Japan PM Abe in Party Vote," *Japan Economic Newswire*, September 14, 2020, https://advance-lexis-com.libproxy.wlu.ca/api/document?collection=news&id=urn:contentItem:60V3-0931-DYMD-603K-00000-00&context=1516831.
54. Motoko Rich et al., "Japan's Next Prime Minister Emerges from Behind the Curtain," *New York Times*, September 14, 2020, https://advance-lexis-com.libproxy.wlu.ca/api/document?collection=news&id=urn:contentItem:60V2-MNY1-DXY4-X007-00000-00&context=1516831.
55. Motoko Rich, "Trump's Phone Buddy in North Korea Crisis: Shinzo Abe," *New York Times*, September 5, 2017, https://www.nytimes.com/2017/09/05/world/asia/japan-trump-north-korea-abe.html.
56. Rich et al., "Japan's Next Prime Minister Emerges."
57. "UPDATE3: Japan Holds 1st Meeting on COVID-19 Steps for Tokyo Olympics," *Japan Economic Newswire*, September 4, 2020, https://advance-lexis-com.libproxy.wlu.ca/api/document?collection=news&id=urn:contentItem:60S0-5S61-JC5B-G0BJ-00000-00&context=1516831.
58. Personal interview, Thomas Bach, January 24, 2023.
59. Motoko Rich and Matthew Futterman, "Tokyo Olympics Organizers Promote Games as Light at End of Pandemic Tunnel," *New York Times*, November 19, 2020, https://advance-lexis-com.libproxy.wlu.ca/api/document?collection=news&id=urn:contentItem:61B4-YGD1-DXY4-X07X-00000-00&context=1516831; Sayo Sasaki, "UPDATE5: Japan PM, IOC Head Agree Olympics to Happen as Planned Next Summer," *Japan Economic Newswire*, November 16, 2020, https://advance-lexis-6com.libproxy.wlu.ca/api/document?collection=news&id=urn:contentItem:619H-H5G1-JC5B-G051-00000-00&context=1516831.
60. Yuka Nakao, "FOCUS: Tokyo Stocks Seen Climbing in 2021 on Economic Recovery from Pandemic," *Japan Economic Newswire*, December 30, 2020, https://advance-lexis-com.libproxy.wlu.ca/api/document?collection=news&id=urn:contentItem:61MW-HP21-DYMD-60FW-00000-00&context=1516831.
61. Personal interview, Thomas Bach, January 24, 2023.
62. Personal interview, Thomas Bach, January 24, 2023.
63. "Japan Halts New Entry from Around World to Block New Virus Variant," *Japan Economic Newswire*, December 27, 2020, https://advance-lexis-com.libproxy.wlu.ca/api/document?collection=news&id=urn:contentItem:61MB-7M51-JC5B-G1S4-00000-00&context=1516831. The variant might have first appeared in South Africa. See Paul Waldie, "British Lockdown to Expand as Cases of Another COVID-19 Variant Surface in England," *Globe and Mail*, December 23, 2020, https://www.theglobeandmail.com/world/article-british-lockdown-to-expand-as-cases-of-another-covid-19-variant/?gad_source=1&gclid=EAIaIQobChMIt4OvvLujggMVVfjICh1HPw41EAAYAiAAEgK-DPD_BwE.
64. Motoko Rich and Makiko Inoue, "Japan Declares State of Emergency in Tokyo Area After Days of Hesitation," *New York Times*, January 7, 2021, https://advance-lexis-com.libproxy.wlu.ca/api/document?collection=news&id=urn:contentItem:61PK-D7S1-JBG3-61WM-00000-00&context=1516831.
65. Ayano Shimizu, "FEATURE: Pandemic Causing Uncertainty, Unease for Tokyo Olympic 'Host Towns,'" *Japan Economic Newswire*, December 7, 2020, https://advance-lexis-com.libproxy.wlu.ca/api/document?collection=news&id=urn:contentItem:61M7-8YV1-DYMD-60RK-00000-00&context=1516831.

66. Rich and Inoue, "Japan Declares State of Emergency." Brackets ours.
67. Rich and Inoue, "Japan Declares State of Emergency." Brackets ours.
68. Rich and Inoue, "Japan Declares State of Emergency."
69. Ayano Shimizu, "UPDATE2: IOC's Bach Says Tokyo Olympics Will Be Held, 'No Plan B,'" *Japan Economic Newswire*, January 21, 2021, https://advance-lexis-com.libproxy.wlu.ca/api/document?collection=news&id=urn:contentItem:61TM-39X1-JC5B-G271-00000-00&context=1516831.
70. Takumi Kato, "Opposition in Japan to the Olympics during the COVID-19 Pandemic," *Humanities and Social Sciences Communications* 8, December 16, 2021, https://www.nature.com/articles/s41599-021-01011-5.
71. Eryk Bagshaw, "Can Tokyo Cancel the Olympics?" *Sydney Morning Herald*, May 22, 2021, https://www.smh.com.au/world/asia/can-tokyo-cancel-the-olympics-20210520-p57tnn.html.
72. Annie K. Sparrow et al., "Protecting Olympic Participants from COVID-19—The Urgent Need for a Risk-Management Approach," *New England Journal of Medicine* 385, no. 1 (2021), https://www.nejm.org/doi/full/10.1056/NEJMp2108567. The article was published online on May 25, 2021.
73. Kazuki Shimizu et al., "Reconsider This Summer's Olympic and Paralympic Games," *BMJ* 373 (April 14, 2021), https://www.bmj.com/content/bmj/373/bmj.n962.full.pdf.
74. Dave Zirin and Jules Boykoff, "The Tokyo Olympics Are in Trouble," *The Nation*, April 21, 2021, https://www.thenation.com/article/society/tokyo-olympics-pandemic/.
75. Personal interview, Kit McConnell, January 26, 2023. Brackets ours.
76. Matthew Futterman, "Hopes for Tokyo's Summer Olympics Darken," *New York Times*, January 15, 2021, https://advance-lexis-com.libproxy.wlu.ca/api/document?collection=news&id=urn:contentItem:61S9-6V71-JBG3-64SR-00000-00&context=1516831.
77. For the composition of the All-Partner Task Force, see Maria Bogner, email message to authors, February 22, 2023.
78. Personal interview, Kit McConnell, January 26, 2023. Brackets ours.
79. Personal interview, Kit McConnell, January 26, 2023.
80. Personal interview, Pau Mota, January 23, 2023, Lausanne, Switzerland.
81. "First Playbook published outlining measures to deliver safe and successful Olympic and Paralympic Games Tokyo 2020," *Olympics.com*, February 3, 2021, https://olympics.com/en/news/first-playbook-published-outlining-measures-to-deliver-safe-and-successful-olymp.
82. Personal interview, Christophe Dubi, January 23, 2023.
83. "First Playbook Published Outlining Measures to Deliver Safe and Successful Olympic and Paralympic Games Tokyo 2020," *Olympics.com*, updated March 30, 2021, https://olympics.com/en/news/first-playbook-published-outlining-measures-to-deliver-safe-and-successful-olymp.
84. "First Playbook Published Outlining Measures."
85. Phil Lutton, "Games Test the Mettle and the Medals of Japan," *The Sun Herald*, January 31, 2021, https://advance-lexis-com.libproxy.wlu.ca/api/document?collection=news&id=urn:contentItem:61WH-SC01-JD34-V01M-00000-00&context=1516831.

86. *The Playbook: International Federations—Your Guide to a Safe and Successful Games*, February 2021, https://stillmedab.olympic.org/media/Document%20Library/OlympicOrg/Games/Summer-Games/Games-Tokyo-2020-Olympic-Games/Playbooks/The-Playbook-International-Federations.pdf, 6–8, 11.
87. *The Playbook: International Federations*, 4.
88. Melina Delkic, "Your Friday Briefing," *New York Times*, February 4, 2021, https://advance-lexis-com.libproxy.wlu.ca/api/document?collection=news&id=urn:contentItem:61XM-R401-JBG3-613R-00000-00&context=1516831.
89. Motoko Rich et al., "Olympics Chief Said Sorry for Demeaning Women. In Japan, That's Often Enough," *New York Times*, February 9, 2021, https://advance-lexis-com.libproxy.wlu.ca/api/document?collection=news&id=urn:contentItem:61YN-4T41-JBG3-6072-00000-00&context=1516831.
90. Motoko Rich, "Tokyo Olympics Chief Resigns over Sexist Comments," *New York Times*, February 11, 2021, https://advance-lexis-com.libproxy.wlu.ca/api/document?collection=news&id=urn:contentItem:6204-1K21-JBG3-62FM-00000-00&context=1516831.
91. Motoko Rich, "Tokyo Chief Expected to Resign over Sexism," *New York Times*, February 12, 2021, https://advance-lexis-com.libproxy.wlu.ca/api/document?collection=news&id=urn:contentItem:6209-27G1-JBG3-632G-00000-00&context=1516831; Melina Delkic, "Your Friday Briefing," *New York Times*, February 18, 2021, https://advance-lexis-com.libproxy.wlu.ca/api/document?collection=news&id=urn:contentItem:621M-9N21-DXY4-X01W-00000-00&context=1516831.
92. See, for instance, *The Playbook: Broadcasters*, 16, 21.
93. Personal interview, Pau Mota, January 23, 2023.
94. *The Playbook: Athletes and Officials—Your Guide to a Safe and Successful Games*," vol. 3, June 2021, https://stillmed.olympics.com/media/Documents/Olympic-Games/Tokyo-2020/Playbooks/The-Playbook-Athletes-and-Officials-V3.pdf?ga=2.139479667.1325720664.1677506866-2077939235.166626814145, 31; *The Playbook: Broadcasters*, 59.
95. Personal interview, Pau Mota, January 23, 2023.
96. Hidechika Akashi et al., "SARS-CoV-2 Infections in Close Contacts of Positive Cases in the Olympic and Paralympic Village at the 2021 Tokyo Olympic and Paralympic Games," *JAMA* 327, no. 10 (2022): 978–80, https://jamanetwork.com/journals/jama/fullarticle/2788895.
97. Motoko Rich et al., "Tokyo Olympics Playbook: Testing? Yes. Quarantines? No. Fans? Maybe," *New York Times*, February 3, 2021, https://advance-lexis-com.libproxy.wlu.ca/api/document?collection=news&id=urn:contentItem:61XC-SGG1-DXY4-X2F8-00000-00&context=1516831.
98. Jake Michaels, "Australian Open Projects Financial Hit Topping $78m, Tournament Director Says," *ESPN*, February 18, 2021, https://www.espn.com/tennis/story/_/id/30925928/australian-open-projects-financial-hit-topping-78m-tournament-director-says.
99. Stuart Fraser, " 'I Can't See Games Pulling Off What We Did'; Abuse from Players One of Many Tests for Craig Tiley in Organising the Australian Open," *The Times*, February 22, 2021, https://advance-lexis-com.libproxy.wlu.ca/api/document?collection=news&id=urn:contentItem:622C-W0M1-JCBW-N0HJ-00000-00&context=1516831.
100. Sparrow et al., "Protecting Olympic Participants from COVID-19."

101. Personal interview, Christophe Dubi, January 23, 2023.
102. Sho Mizuno, "WHO Remarks on Laxness Led to Stricter IOC Playbook," *Japan Times*, June 16, 2021, https://japannews.yomiuri.co.jp/sports/olympics-paralympics/20210616-52897/.
103. "We Need a Global Conversation on the 2020 Olympic Games," *The Lancet* 397, no. 10291 (2021), https://www.thelancet.com/journals/lancet/article/PIIS0140-6736(21)01293-9/fulltext.
104. "We Need a Global Conversation on the 2020 Olympic Games."
105. Personal interview, Richard Budgett, January 25, 2023.
106. Dan Palmer, "Number of COVID-19 Cases at Tokyo 2020 So Far 'As Expected' Says Doctor Advising IOC," *Inside the Games*, July 19, 2021, https://www.insidethegames.biz/articles/1110416/tokyo-2020-panel-mccloskey.
107. Michelle Ye Hee Lee, "South African Soccer Team Outbreak Tests Tokyo Olympics 'Covid-Safe' Strategy," *Washington Post*, July 19, 2021, https://www.washingtonpost.com/sports/olympics/2021/07/19/tokyo-olympics-south-africa-soccer-covid-outbreak/. Two players and a video analyst tested positive, but further spread was contained. "Tokyo Olympics: We Are on the Guillotine at the Moment, Says Covid-Hit South African Team Coach," *India Today*, July 19, 2021, https://www.indiatoday.in/sports/tokyo-olympics/story/covid-hit-south-african-football-team-coach-david-notoane-tokyo-2020-olympic-village-1830137-2021-07-19.
108. Nathan Fenno, "How Tokyo Olympic Organizers Managed to Keep COVID-19 Mostly in Check," *Los Angeles Times*, August 8, 2021, https://www.latimes.com/sports/olympics/story/2021-08-08/tokyo-olympics-overcame-challenges-poised-by-covid-19.
109. Brian McCloskey, "Tokyo 2020 Showed It Is Possible to Keep a Pandemic at Bay," *Olympics.com*, August 9, 2022, https://olympics.com/ioc/news/-tokyo-2020-showed-it-is-possible-to-keep-a-pandemic-at-bay.
110. Brian McCloskey et al., "The Tokyo 2020 and Beijing 2022 Olympic Games Held During the COVID-19 Pandemic: Planning, Outcomes, and Lessons Learnt," *The Lancet* 403, no. 10425 (2024): 493–502, https://www.thelancet.com/journals/lancet/article/PIIS0140-6736(23)02635-1/fulltext?uuid=uuid%3A24704d7e-2ebc-4e19-89a3-d8054d80af6d; see also McCloskey, "Tokyo 2020 Showed It Is Possible"; Tom Garlinghouse, "Keeping a Pandemic at Bay: Lessons for the Tokyo and Beijing Olympics," *High Meadows Environmental Institute*, January 18, 2024, https://environment.princeton.edu/news/lessons-from-the-tokyo-and-beijing-olympics/.
111. McCloskey, "Tokyo 2020 Showed It Is Possible."
112. Garlinghouse, "Keeping a Pandemic at Bay."
113. "New Data Shows No COVID-19 Spread Between Tokyo 2020 Participants and Local Population," *Olympics.com*, December 30, 2021, https://olympics.com/ioc/news/new-data-shows-no-covid-19-spread-between-tokyo-2020-participants-and-local-population. Daisuke Yoneoka (Infectious Disease Surveillance Center, National Institute of Infectious Diseases, Tokyo) and several colleagues reported that the number of COVID-19 cases in Japan during the Olympics (though data "lagged" by ten days) exceeded the number of expected cases, based on comparison with data from 42 control countries over the same period; however, they could not eliminate confounding variables such as the occurrence of two holidays in Japan during the period of the Games (which might have elevated the intermingling of Japanese citizens). They offer that the Japanese population might have let their guard down amid the Olympics because of the festive atmosphere,

thereby increasing the expected number of cases. Daisuke Yoneoka et al., "Effect of the Tokyo 2020 Summer Olympic Games on COVID-19 Incidence in Japan: A Synthetic Control approach," *BMJ Open* 12, no. 9 (2022), https://doi.org/10.1136/bmjopen-2022-061444. Norio Yamamoto (Department of Epidemiology, Graduate School of Medicine, Dentistry, and Pharmaceutical Sciences, Okayama University) and several fellow researchers assert that the Tokyo Olympics and Paralympics "likely" increased the number of COVID-19 cases in Tokyo, but they were constrained in offering precise data because the Games period coincided with the fifth wave of the Delta variant in Japan. Norio Yamamoto et al., "Causal Effect of the Tokyo 2020 Olympic and Paralympic Games on the Number of COVID-19 Cases Under COVID-19 Pandemic: An Ecological Study Using the Synthetic Control Method," *Journal of Personalized Medicine* 12, no. 2 (2022), https://www.mdpi.com/2075-4426/12/2/209.
114. H. J. Mai, "Overseas Spectators Will Be Banned from Tokyo Olympics Due to COVID-19 Risks," *National Public Radio*, March 20, 2021, https://www.npr.org/sections/coronavirus-live-updates/2021/03/20/979489573/overseas-spectators-will-be-banned-from-tokyo-olympics-due-to-covid-19-risks.
115. Ben Dooley and Makiko Inoue, "The Tokyo Olympics Will Allow Spectators Who Live in Japan, but With Restrictions," *New York Times*, June 21, 2021, https://www.nytimes.com/2021/06/21/world/tokyo-olympics-spectators.html.
116. Personal interview, Thomas Bach, January 24, 2023.
117. Personal interview, Thomas Bach, January 24, 2023.
118. Nancy Armour, "Tokyo Olympics to Be Held Without Fans After New COVID-19 State of Emergency Declared," *USA Today*, July 8, 2021, https://www.usatoday.com/story/sports/olympics/2021/07/08/2021-olympics-fan-not-allowed-attend-tokyo-games-due-covid-19/7899959002/.
119. Personal interview, Christophe Dubi, 23 January 2023.
120. Michael Payne, "The Cursed Olympics That Became the Miracle Games." Payne prepared this document as a post-Games report and shared it with the authors via email in January 2023.
121. Ben Dooley and Tiffany Hsu, "Toyota Pulls Its Olympics TV Ads in Japan," *New York Times*, July 19, 2021, https://advance-lexis-com.libproxy.wlu.ca/api/document?collection=news&id=urn:contentItem:635T-1411-DXY4-X1K5-00000-00&context=1516831.
122. Takashi Nakamichi and Yuki Furukawa, "More Companies Pull Out of Tokyo Olympics Opening Ceremony," *Bloomberg*, July 20, 2021, https://www.bloomberg.com/news/articles/2021-07-20/more-companies-pull-out-of-tokyo-olympics-opening-ceremony.
123. Eimi Yamamitsu and Maki Shiraki, "EXCLUSIVE Frustrated by Delays, Tokyo 2020 Sponsors Cancel Booths, Parties," *Reuters*, July 8, 2021, https://www.reuters.com/lifestyle/sports/exclusive-olympics-frustrated-by-delays-tokyo-2020-sponsors-cancel-booths-2021-07-08/.
124. Personal interview, Christophe Dubi, January 23, 2023. These quotes represent Dubi's recollection of the comments offered by Sparrow and McCloskey.
125. Personal interview, Christophe Dubi, January 23, 2023. Brackets ours.
126. Personal interview, Timo Lumme, January 26, 2023; and personal interview, Richard Budgett, January 25, 2023.
127. Merrit Kennedy et al., "Olympic Opening Ceremony Is a Delicate Mix of Celebration and Solemnity," *National Public Radio*, July 23, 2021, https://www.npr.org

/sections/tokyo-olympics-live-updates/2021/07/23/1019622003/tokyo-olympics-opening-ceremony.
128. "Tokyo Olympics Opening Ceremony," *CBS News*, July 23, 2023, https://www.cbsnews.com/pictures/tokyo-olympics-2021/.
129. Kennedy et al., "Olympic Opening Ceremony."
130. Personal interview, Thomas Bach, January 24, 2023. Brackets ours.

CHAPTER 6

1. Personal interview, Gar Leyshon, January 10, 2023, London, Ontario.
2. Personal interview, Gar Leyshon, January 10, 2023.
3. Personal interview, Damian Warner, January 13, 2023, London, Ontario.
4. Personal interview, Gar Leyshon, January 10, 2023.
5. Personal interview, Damian Warner, January 13, 2023.
6. Personal interview, Damian Warner, January 13, 2023.
7. Personal interview, Gar Leyshon, January 10, 2023.
8. Personal interview, Gar Leyshon, January 10, 2023.
9. Personal interview, Gar Leyshon, January 10, 2023.
10. Personal interview, Damian Warner, January 13, 2023.
11. Personal interview, Damian Warner, January 13, 2023; "Damian Warner Tops His Canadian Decathlon Record to Win Hypo Meeting," *CBC*, May 30, 2021, https://www.cbc.ca/sports/olympics/summer/trackandfield/damian-warner-hypo-meeting-may30-1.6046143.
12. Personal interview, Damian Warner, January 13, 2023.
13. Personal interview, Gar Leyshon, January 10, 2023.
14. Personal interview, Damian Warner, January 13, 2023.
15. Personal interview, Gar Leyshon, January 10, 2023.
16. Personal interview, Damian Warner, January 13, 2023.
17. Personal interview, Richard Budgett, January 25, 2023, Lausanne, Switzerland. Brackets ours.
18. Personal interview, Damian Warner, January 13, 2023.
19. "Ariarne Titmus Seals Legendary Status at Tokyo 2020 Olympics," *Olympics.com*, October 5, 2021, https://olympics.com/en/news/ariarne-titmus-seals-legendary-status-at-tokyo-2020.
20. Lee Hamilton, "Weightlifter Hidilyn Diaz Wins the Philippines' First-Ever Olympic Gold Medal," *Tatler Asia*, July 26, 2021, https://www.tatlerasia.com/lifestyle/sports/hk-hidilyn-diaz-weightlifter-wins-the-philippines-first-ever-olympic-gold-medal.
21. "How Olympic Champion Tom Daley Sealed a Golden Diving Legacy at Tokyo 2020," *Olympics.com*, October 5, 2021, https://olympics.com/en/news/tom-daley-seals-golden-legacy-at-tokyo-2020.
22. Barney Ronay, "Unassailable Thompson-Herah Strikes Second Gold in 200m Final," *The Guardian*, August 3, 2021, https://www.theguardian.com/sport/2021/aug/03/elaine-thompson-herah-strikes-second-gold-of-tokyo-2020-in-200m-final.
23. See "MyKayla Skinner Will Compete for Simone Biles in Women's Vault Finals," *National Public Radio*, July 31, 2021, https://www.npr.org/sections/tokyo-olympics-live-updates/2021/07/31/1023234130/mykayla-skinner-will-compete-for-simone-biles-in-womens-vault-finals; and "Gymnast MyKayla Skinner Wins Vault Silver

for U.S.," *Los Angeles Times*, August 1, 2021, https://www.latimes.com/sports/olympics/story/2021-08-01/us-gymnastics-mykayla-skinner-jade-carey-vault-uneven-bars.
24. "Barshim and Tamberi Share High Jump Success in Tokyo," *World Athletics*, August 1, 2021, https://worldathletics.org/competitions/olympic-games/news/tokyo-olympic-games-men-high-jump-report.
25. " 'Just Magical': Joy for Tamberi and Barshim As They Opt to Share Gold in Men's High Jump," *The Guardian*, August 2, 2021, https://www.theguardian.com/sport/2021/aug/02/tamberi-barshim-share-olympic-gold-mens-high-jump-reaction.
26. Personal interview, Kit McConnell, January 26, 2023, Lausanne, Switzerland.
27. Joseph Salvador, "Popovich Took Shot at Critics After Gold Medal Win: 'How the F— You Like Us Now?' " *Sports Illustrated*, August 16, 2021, https://www.si.com/nba/2021/08/16/gregg-popovich-calls-out-critics-in-speech-after-gold-medal-win.
28. Dylan Mickanen, "Christine Sinclair, Canada Win First Gold Medal in Soccer," *NBC Sports*, archived August 6, 2021, at https://web.archive.org/web/20210806192542/https://www.nbcsports.com/northwest/tokyo-olympics/toyko-olympics-christine-sinclair-canada-win-first-gold-medal-womens.
29. Dan Palmer, "Japan Win First Olympic Baseball Title to Complete Diamond Double in Tokyo," *Inside the Games*, August 7, 2021, https://www.insidethegames.biz/articles/1111355/baseball-tokyo-2020-gold-medal-game.
30. "Eliud Kipchoge Confirms All Time Greatness at Tokyo 2020," *Olympics.com*, October 5, 2021, https://olympics.com/en/news/eliud-kipchoge-confirms-all-time-greatness-at-tokyo-2020. The race was staged in Sapporo as a means of dealing with the hotter temperatures in Japan's capital.
31. "Allyson Felix By the Numbers," *Olympics.com*, October 5, 2021, https://olympics.com/en/news/athletics-allyson-felix-by-the-numbers.
32. Canada's Mandy Bujold Wins Battle to Box in Tokyo Olympics," *CBC*, June 30, 2021, https://www.cbc.ca/sports/olympics/summer/boxing/mandy-bujold-tokyo-olympics-1.6085623.
33. Doug Smith and Kerry Gillespie, "Mandy Bujold Falls Ill, Loses Quarter-Final at Rio Olympics," *Toronto Star*, August 16, 2016, https://www.thestar.com/sports/olympics/2016/08/16/canadian-mandy-bujold-loses-boxing-quarter-final-at-rio-olympics.html.
34. Devin Heroux, "Canadian Boxer Mandy Bujold Asking IOC to Change Qualifying Rules for Pregnant Women," *CBC*, April 26, 2021, https://www.cbc.ca/sports/olympics/summer/boxing/mandy-bujold-boxing-hires-lawyer-in-fight-to-qualify-for-tokyo-olympics-1.6002280.
35. "Canadian Boxer Bujold to Pursue Case at Court of Arbitration for Sport," *CBC*, April 30, 2021, https://www.cbc.ca/sports/olympics/summer/boxing/mandy-bujold-boxing-hires-court-of-arbitration-1.6009349.
36. Devin Heroux, "Heritage Minister Asks IOC to let Mandy Bujold to Compete After Boxer Missed Olympic Qualifying Events While Pregnant," *CBC*, May 17, 2021, https://www.cbc.ca/sports/olympics/olympics-canadian-government-letter-ioc-mandy-bujold-1.6030458.
37. Jamie Strashin, "Mandy Bujold's Olympic Fight Comes to Quick End After Legal Battle to Reach Tokyo," *CBC*, July 24, 2021, https://www.cbc.ca/sports/olympics/summer/boxing/olympics-mandy-bujold-boxing-july25-1.6116259.

38. Michael Pavitt, "Bujold Succeeds in Appeal to Compete at Tokyo 2020 Olympics," *Inside the Games*, July 1, 2021, https://www.insidethegames.biz/articles/1109660/bujold-boxing-tokyo-2020-appeal-win.
39. Jason Samenow, "Tokyo Faces Stifling Heat and Then a Tropical Storm as Olympics Near Their End," *Washington Post*, August 4, 2021, https://www.washingtonpost.com/weather/2021/08/04/tokyo-tropical-storm-heat-olympics/.
40. Personal interview, Damian Warner and Gar Leyshon, March 24, 2023, London, Ontario. Brackets ours.
41. Personal interview, Damian Warner and Gar Leyshon, March 24, 2023.
42. Personal interview, Damian Warner and Gar Leyshon, March 24, 2023.
43. Personal interview, Damian Warner and Gar Leyshon, March 24, 2023.
44. Personal interview, Damian Warner and Gar Leyshon, March 24, 2023.
45. Personal interview, Damian Warner and Gar Leyshon, March 24, 2023.
46. Personal interview, Damian Warner and Gar Leyshon, March 24, 2023.
47. "Coach Harry Marra," https://www.coachharrymarra.com/about (site discontinued). Eaton and Theisen-Eaton's success represents the first and only time in Olympic history that a coach had athletes in the decathlon and heptathlon win medals in the same competition.
48. Personal interview, Damian Warner and Gar Leyshon, March 24, 2023.
49. Eric Goodman, "Decathlon Tracker: Damian Warner Cracks 9000 Points, Takes Gold," *NBC Olympics*, August 3, 2021, https://www.nbcolympics.com/news/decathlon-tracker-live-updates-results-highlights-each-event.
50. Personal interview, Damian Warner and Gar Leyshon, March 24, 2023. Gar Leyshon expressed this opinion.
51. "Results: Hypo Meeting Gotzis 2021," *Watch Athletics*, accessed December 25, 2024, https://www.watchathletics.com/page/2419/results-hypo-meeting-gotzis-2021.
52. Personal interview, Damian Warner and Gar Leyshon, March 24, 2023.
53. Personal interview, Damian Warner and Gar Leyshon, March 24, 2023.
54. Goodman, "Decathlon Tracker."
55. Personal interview, Damian Warner and Gar Leyshon, March 24, 2023.
56. Personal interview, Damian Warner and Gar Leyshon, March 24, 2023.
57. Goodman, "Decathlon Tracker"; "Olympic Games, Olympic Stadium, Tokyo, 30 Jul–08 Aug 2021, Decathlon—1500 Meters Men, 05 Aug 2021 21:40," *World Athletics*, https://www.worldathletics.org/competitions/olympic-games/the-xxxii-olympic-games-athletics-7123391/results/men/decathlon/1500-metres/points.
58. Personal interview, Damian Warner and Gar Leyshon, March 24, 2023.
59. Devin Heroux, "Canadian Decathlete Pierce LePage Wins Silver at World Athletics Championships," *CBC*, July 24, 2022, https://www.cbc.ca/sports/olympics/summer/trackandfield/world-athletics-championships-decathlon-july-24-day-2-1.6530543. Brackets ours.
60. Personal interview, Damian Warner and Gar Leyshon, March 24, 2023.
61. Personal interview, Damian Warner and Gar Leyshon, March 24, 2023.
62. Personal interview, Damian Warner and Gar Leyshon, March 24, 2023; personal interview, Gar Leyshon, January 10, 2023; personal interview, Damian Warner, January 13, 2023, London, Ontario.
63. Jeff Fischer and Stephen Wenn were in the same program (Physical Education) at Western University, both graduating in June 1986. They knew each other well at this stage in their lives. Bob Barney had Jeff in one of his sport history classes. Sadly, Jeff

passed away in October 2022 at the age of fifty-nine due to cancer. The authors are dedicating their account of Damian Warner's Tokyo 2020 journey to his memory.
64. Personal interview, Damian Warner and Gar Leyshon, March 24, 2023.
65. Goodman, "Decathlon Tracker"; "Olympic Games, Olympic Stadium, Tokyo, 30 Jul–08 Aug 2021, Results, 110 Metres Hurdles," *World Athletics*, archived October 23, 2021, https://web.archive.org/web/20211023182952/https://worldathletics.org/competitions/Olympic-games/the-xxxii-olympic-games-athletics-7132391/results/men/decathlon/110-metres-hurdles/summary; and, "Results: Hypo Meeting Gotzis 2021."
66. Personal interview, Damian Warner and Gar Leyshon, March 24, 2023.
67. "Olympic Games, Olympic Stadium, Tokyo, 30 Jul–08 Aug 2021, Results, 110 Metres Hurdles."
68. Personal interview, Damian Warner and Gar Leyshon, March 24, 2023.
69. Goodman, "Decathlon Tracker."
70. Personal interview, Damian Warner and Gar Leyshon, March 24, 2023; Goodman, "Decathlon Tracker."
71. "Olympic Games, Olympic Stadium, Tokyo, 30 Jul–08 Aug 2021, Decathlon—Discus Throw Men, 05 Aug 2021 09:50," *World Athletics*, https://worldathletics.org/competitions/olympic-games/the-xxxii-olympic-games-athletics-7132391/results/men/decathlon/discus-throw/summary; Goodman, "Decathlon Tracker."
72. Personal interview, Damian Warner and Gar Leyshon, March 24, 2023.
73. Personal interview, Damian Warner and Gar Leyshon, March 24, 2023.
74. Personal interview, Damian Warner and Gar Leyshon, March 24, 2023.
75. "Olympic Games, Olympic Stadium, Tokyo, 30 Jul–08 Aug 2021, Decathlon—Pole Vault Men, 05 Aug 2021 12:45," *World Athletics*, https://worldathletics.org/competitions/olympic-games/the-xxxii-olympic-games-athletics-7132391/results/men/decathlon/pole-vault/summary.
76. Goodman, "Decathlon Tracker."
77. Personal interview, Damian Warner and Gar Leyshon, March 24, 2023.
78. Personal interview, Damian Warner and Gar Leyshon, March 24, 2023.
79. "Olympic Games, Olympic Stadium, Tokyo, 30 Jul–08 Aug 2021, Decathlon—Javelin Throw Men 05 Aug 2021, 19:15," *World Athletics*, https://worldathletics.org/competitions/olympic-games/the-xxxii-olympic-games-athletics-7132391/results/men/decathlon/javelin-throw/summary; Goodman, "Decathlon Tracker."
80. Personal interview, Damian Warner and Gar Leyshon, March 24, 2023.
81. "Olympic Games, Olympic Stadium, Tokyo, 30 Jul–08 Aug 2021, Decathlon—1500 Metres Men 05 Aug 2021 21:40," *World Athletics*, https://worldathletics.org/competitions/olympic-games/the-xxxii-olympic-games-athletics-7132391/results/men/decathlon/1500-metres/result.
82. Personal interview, Damian Warner and Gar Leyshon, March 24, 2023.
83. Goodman, "Decathlon Tracker."
84. Personal interview, Damian Warner and Gar Leyshon, March 24, 2023.

CHAPTER 7

1. Readers (and writers) of history would do well to read and heed the noted Brandeis University historian David Hackett Fischer's powerful arguments on the dangers often lurking when history is interpreted (see Fischer, *Historian's Fallacies: Towards*

a Logic of Historical Thought (Harper & Row, 1970). Borrowing from the critique of British historian Herbert Butterfield's *The Whig Interpretation of History* (G. Bell and Sons, 1931), in presenting what Fischer referred to as a "classic example" of such historians' fallacies, he argued that the Whig-bound explanation of history was, in essence, one that was written by historians who could not remove the conditions of the past, about which they wrote from their own contemporary sociopolitical beliefs. We argue that there is a tendency on the part of some Olympic activists and naysayers, similar to that of the old Whig historians, in their interpretation of Olympic history to link their "take" with a legitimation of their personally held sociopolitical points of view. For those interested in a recently published series of articles that espouses the view of critics of the Tokyo 2020 project, one might access volume 35, issue 1 of *Contemporary Japan* (2023).

2. Paul O'Shea and Sebastian Maslow, "The 2020/2021 Tokyo Olympics: Does Japan Get the Gold Medal or the Wooden Spoon?" *Contemporary Japan* 35, no. 1 (2023): 16–34, https://doi.org/10.1080/18692729.2023.2169819.
3. Barbara Holthus, Isaac Gagné, Wolfram Manzenreiter, and Franz Waldenburger clearly share our view of the "changing goalposts," and characterized assessing Tokyo 2020 in the following fashion: "If Japan—and the world—can truly pull off successful control of the virus, and if Tokyo 2020 in 2021 does in fact take place, the characterization of Tokyo 2020 as the 'Recovery Olympics' will take on a whole new meaning for the entire world." See Barbara Holthus et al., eds., *Japan Through the Lens of the Tokyo Olympics* (Routledge, 2020). For this specific quote, see https://www.routledge.com/Japan-Through-the-Lens-of-the-Tokyo-Olympics-Open-Access/Holthus-Gagne-Manzenreiter-Waldenberger/p/book/9780367471682. Urs Schöttli, a Swiss-born expert on Asian affairs who writes for the *Geopolitical Intelligence Services Report*, concluded, "The Tokyo 2020 Olympics were among the most successful games ever held. The performance of both organizers and athletes surpassed even the highest expectations," though he conceded this success came at a high financial cost. Urs Schöttli, "Japan after Tokyo 2020: Back to Power Politics," *GIS Reports*, September 10, 2021, https://www.gisreportsonline.com/r/tokyo-2020/.
4. "Prime Minister Abe's Participation in the 70th Session of the United Nations General Session," *Ministry of Foreign Affairs of Japan*, October 5, 2015, https://www.mofa.go.jp/mofaj/fp/unp_a/page3e_000395.html. This quote appears in Abe's speech, noted on the same web page.
5. Bach "stood for" and was awarded a second term as IOC president, one of four years under IOC protocol for IOC presidential terms of office. See "Thomas Bach Re-elected as IOC President for Second Term," *Olympics.com*, March 10, 2021, https://olympics.com/ioc/news/thomas-bach-re-elected-as-ioc-president-for-second-term.
6. "Thomas Bach Re-elected."
7. See Worldometer, "World/CoronaVirus/Countries/Japan," accessed December 26, 2024, https://www.worldometers.info/coronavirus/country/japan/.
8. Mike Chiari, "Japanese Prime Minister: IOC President '100% Agrees' to Postpone 2020 Olympics," *Bleacher Report*, March 24, 2020, https://bleacherreport.com/articles/2882723-japanese-prime-minister-ioc-president-100-agrees-to-postpone-2020-olympics.
9. Anthony Kuhn and Mark Kaktov, "Japan's Shinzo Abe Stepping Down as Prime Minister," *National Public Radio*, August 28, 2020, https://www.npr.org/2020/08/28/906945704/japans-shinzo-abe-is-stepping-down-as-prime-minister.

10. Abe's remark to Suga was quoted to the authors by Thomas Bach himself in a personal interview, January 24, 2023, Lausanne, Switzerland.
11. Mari Yamaguchi, "Abe Murder Suspect Says Life Destroyed by Mother's Religion," *Associated Press News*, August 26, 2022, https://apnews.com/article/shinzo-abe-religion-japan-social-media-68f18b50c5698bb65f024ff5c5d2c3ba.
12. See "President Bach Pays Final Respects to Former Prime Minister Abe Shinzo," *Olympics.com*, September 28, 2022, https://olympics.com/ioc/news/president-bach-pays-final-respects-to-former-prime-minister-abe-shinzo#:~:text=After%20the%20State%20Funeral%2C%20which,and%20Abe%20Shinzo's%20widow%2C%20Akie.
13. Personal interview, Thomas Bach, January 24, 2023, Lausanne, Switzerland.
14. "IOC President Thomas Bach Will Not Seek to Stay Beyond 2025," *NBC Olympics*, August 11, 2024, https://www.nbcolympics.com/news/ioc-president-thomas-bach-will-not-seek-stay-beyond-2025. Bach's successor will be chosen in March 2025 and will assume their duties in the summer.
15. See, for instance, "Tokyo Olympics: More Than 80% of Japanese Oppose Hosting Games—Poll," *The Guardian*, May 17, 2021, https://www.theguardian.com/world/2021/may/17/tokyo-olympics-more-than-80-of-japanese-oppose-hosting-games-poll#:~:text=More%20than%2080%25%20of%20Japanese%20people%20oppose%20hosting%20the%20Olympics,fourth%20wave%20of.
16. Mandelit del Barco, "The Japanese Public Begins to Embrace the Tokyo Olympics," *National Public Radio*, August 2, 2021, https://www.npr.org/sections/tokyo-olympics-live-updates/2021/08/02/1023606904/the-japanese-public-begins-to-embrace-the-tokyo-olympics; Tim Hornyak, "Even with No Tourists or Fans, Japan Is Already Seeing Economic Benefits from the $15.4 Billion Tokyo Olympics," *Time*, August 11, 2021, https://time.com/6089274/tokyo-olympics-economic-benefits/.
17. B. Fleitas, "The Other Numbers from the Olympic Games: 115 Million Viewers in Japan, 51,000 Covid Tests . . . ," *Marca*, September 8, 2021, https://www.marca.com/en/olympic-games/2021/08/09/61117b6846163f5b5e8b45de.html.
18. Stephen Wade, "Japan Has Its best Olympic Medal Haul: 27 Gold, 58 Overall," *Associated Press News*, August 8, 2021, https://apnews.com/article/2020-tokyo-olympics-japan-medals-a34e6a9c74600b9c5c1770f67efc8b38; and "TV Olympic Viewership for Opening Ceremony 56% in Tokyo Area," *Kyodo News*, July 2, 2021, https://english.kyodonews.net/news/2021/07/5d9fc4259ba7-breaking-news-tv-viewer-rating-for-tokyo-olympic-opening-ceremony-at-564.html.
19. While the country's mood shifted during the Games, buoyed by the success of the Japanese athletes, in some quarters IOC officials were still not embraced warmly. Though Abe and Bach enjoyed a positive relationship, and Bach and Suga found a collaborative path, Bach was not viewed favorably by the Japanese public, partly due to his push to stage the Games in the face of the population's concerns, a walking tour in Ginza that violated an active state of emergency, and his failure to abide by a three-day quarantine. "All of this," write Paul O'Shea and Jonathan Maslow, "earned him the nickname *Bottakuri danshaku* or Baron von Rip off." O'Shea and Maslow, "The 2020/2021 Tokyo Olympics"
20. Amy Gunia, "Japan's Prime Minister Yoshihide Suga Is Resigning. Here's What That Means," *Time*, September 3, 2021, https://time.com/6094995/japan-prime-minister-suga-resigns/.
21. The Wikipedia page describes concerns associated with the 2020 Summer Olympics under the following categories and headings. In the category "Organizational Issues and Controversies": (1) bribery and corruption, (2) Olympic sponsorship contract

scandals, (3) logo plagiarism, (4) stadium design plagiarism, and (5) environmental degradation. Under "Environment, Health and Safety Concerns," (1) COVID-19 pandemic and other contagion risks, (2) Fukushima radiation, (3) hot weather and air-conditioning, (4) water quality and temperatures, (5) asbestos in Olympic venues, (6) tropical storm Napartak, (7) Toyota self-driving car incident, and (8) damage of rooms by Australian athletes. Under "Political and Human Rights Issues," (1) worker rights, (2) acknowledgment of disputed territories, (3) rising sun flag, (4) South Korean team banner, (5) prohibition of political gestures, (6) mobilization of students for the Olympics, (7) cyber reconnaissance, (8) comments about Islam, (9) remarks by key figures, and (10) swim caps and women's uniforms. Under "Opening and Closing Ceremonies," (1) scandals of the directors of the ceremonies, including (2) Hiroshi Sasaki "Olympig" and (3) Kentaro Kobayashi holocaust jokes; (4) appointment and resignation of Keigo Oyamada; (5) absence of foreign leaders; (6) criticism from Latyr Sy; (7) music composed by Kochi Sugiyama; (8) Yasushi Akimoto (a member of the Olympics Organizing Committee who wrote a song perceived as misogynistic); (9) protests during the opening ceremony; (10) Tencent Video's broadcast of the opening ceremony; and (11) South Korean broadcast of the Opening Ceremony. Under "During the Games," (1) Belarusian athlete expulsion attempt, (2) suspected animal abuse in the modern pentathlon, (3) swimming timing system, (4) boycott in competing against Israeli athletes, (5) Iranian terrorist accusations, (6) Hong Kong shirt incidents, (7) Venezuelan medalist phone calls, (8) online abuse of athletes, (9) Raven Saunders' hand gesture, (10) Chinese athletes wearing Mao Zedong badges, (11) false claims of additional doping tests, (12) Russian reaction to results of the women's all-around rhythmic gymnastics, (13) medal count controversy, (14) German cycling director racist slur, (15) China–Taiwan tensions, (16) Chinese diplomacy, (17) British sprinter doping and demedaling, and (18) food waste. See Wikipedia, "Concerns and Controversies at the 2020 Summer Olympics," last modified November 28, 2024, https://en.wikipedia.org/wiki/Concerns_and_controversies_at_the_2020_Summer_Olympics.

22. Sheila A. Smith, "Here's Why Tokyo Is Hosting the Summer Olympics Despite COVID-19," *Council on Foreign Relations*, June 28, 2021, https://www.cfr.org/in-brief/heres-why-tokyo-hosting-summer-olympics-despite-covid-19#:~:text=For%20Prime%20Minister%20Shinzo%20Abe,from%20difficulty%2C%20and%20its%20hospitality.

23. For a brief but comprehensive analysis of the term "white elephant" and its application to mega-event history, including the Olympic Games, see Sarah Caitlin, "Sport's White Elephants: The Economic, Environment, and Human Cost of Mega-tournament Infrastructure," *McGill Daily*, January 16, 2023, https://www.mcgilldaily.com/2023/01/sports-white-elephants/#:~:text=The%20short%20term%20costly%20infrastructure,largely%20ounused%20after%20the%20event.

24. Amanda Shuman and Philippe Vonnard, "Taking Nature into Account? The International Olympic Committee Confronts Environmental Issues (1960s–1990s)," *Journal of Olympic Studies* 6 (forthcoming).

25. Jules Boykoff and Dave Zirin, "The Olympics Promise to Be Socially Responsible. How's That Working Out?" *Trib Live*, July 29, 2024, https://triblive.com/opinion/jules-boykoff-and-dave-zirin-the-olympics-promise-to-be-socially-responsible-hows-that-working-out/.

26. On behalf of the IOC Executive Board, IOC President Bach's enunciation of Olympic Agenda 2020 presented fifteen recommendations for action. Recommendation 2

dealt squarely with "the urgency of achieving sustainable development." For details of Recommendation 2, see "The Olympic Agenda 2020 + 5," https://stillmed.olympics.com/media/Document%20Library/OlympicOrg/IOC/What-We-Do/Olympic-agenda/Olympic-Agenda-2020-5-15-recommendations.pdf.

27. In 1955, IOC President Avery Brundage, in contemplating and rationalizing the IOC's first giant steps into revenue production, informed fellow Executive Board members of what "the huge potential value of television rights" could do in assisting the IOC's efforts "to promote Olympic ideals." See "Avery Brundage to Members of the Executive Board," August 3, 1955, Avery Brundage Collection, Box 114, Reel 62, International Centre for Olympic Studies, Western University, London, Ontario, Canada, as cited in Robert K. Barney et al., *Selling the Five Rings: The International Olympic Committee and the Rise of Olympic Commercialism*, rev. ed. (University of Utah Press, 2004), 59.

28. Of the "directly unpaid" Olympic family constituency, the athletes themselves rapidly come to mind. Normally, medal winners are recompensed through formula awards from their National Olympic Committees and Sports Federations, but the huge majority of Olympians live a competitive life of severe financial challenge. However, change may be in the air. Recently sanctioned measures enabling American intercollegiate athletes (the labor force of US intercollegiate sport) to engage in personal revenue-producing enterprise through the use of their image and likenesses has spilled over into the concept of similar application to Olympic athletes. This phenomenon, currently in the infant stage of consideration by both athletes and Olympic authorities, is likely to foster vigorous debate in the months and years ahead. For a preliminary "take" on the subject, see Dave Feschuk, "Olympic Athletes Should Bargain Their Fair Share, Just Like the Pros—but It Won't Be Easy," *Toronto Star*, April 24, 2020, https://www.thestar.com/sports/amateur/olympic-athletes-should-bargain-for-their-fair-share-just-like-the-pros-but-it-won/article_8ae46d10-a509-5324-9155-93b20ad1e573.html. A study completed at Toronto Metropolitan University estimated that a mere 4.1 percent of Olympic revenue flows to the athletes.

29. Jules Boykoff and Dave Zirin, "How the International Olympic Committee Fails Athletes," *Time*, August 8, 2024, https://time.com/7008621/ioc-olympics-fails-athletes/.

30. Brenda Elsey and Amira Rose Davis, hosts, *Burn It All Down*, podcast, "Interview: Jules Boykoff on the Politics, Power and Pain of the Beijing 2022 Winter Olympics," February 3, 2022, https://www.burnitalldownpod.com/episodes/interview-jules-boykoff-on-the-politics-power-and-pain-of-the-Beijing-2022-winter-olympics. Brackets ours.

31. Ryusei Takahashi, "We'll All Be Losers in 2020, Olympic Activists Say," *Japan Times*, July 23, 2019, https://www.japantimes.co.jp/news/2019/07/23/national/well-losers-2020-anti-olympic-activists-say/.

32. Shintaro Kano, "Economist Pours Cold Water on Tokyo's Hopes for Olympic Success in 2020," *Japan Times*, July 26, 2017, https://www.japantimes.co.jp/news/2017/07/26/national/no-success-story-tokyo-hosting-2020-games-economist/. Zimbalist was active in the bid by Boston, Massachusetts, for the 2024 Games eventually awarded to Paris. Boston, after being designated by the United States Olympic Committee as America's bid-city candidate, returned its designee status to the USOC after a public referendum reflected a resounding "no" toward proceeding with plans to host. Zimbalist was a vocal member of the activist group leading the

anti-Olympics initiative. See Andrew Zimbalist, "Boston Would Be Lucky to Lose the Competition," *Wall Street Journal*, January 9, 2015, https://www.wsj.com/articles/andrew-zimbalist-boston-would-be-lucky-to-lose-the-olympics-competition-1420847406. Zimbalist is the author of *Circus Maximus: The Economic Gamble Behind the Hosting of the Olympics and the World Cup* (Brookings Institution Press, 2020), now in its third edition, as well as coauthor with Chris Dempsey of *No Boston Olympics: How and Why Smart Cities Are Passing on the Torch* (University Press of New England, 2017).

33. Jules Boykoff, "Olympic Activism," Olympic and Paralympic Analysis, accessed December 26, 2024, https://olympicanalysis.org/section-5/anti-olympics-activism/.
34. Mike Francis, "Pacific Professor Boykoff in Forefront of Movement Against Tokyo Summer Olympics," *New York Times*, March 11, 2020, https://www.pacificu.edu/about/media/pacific-professor-boykoff-forefront-movement-against-tokyo-summer-olympics. The connotation "Pacific" refers to Boykoff's faculty appointment at Pacific University in Forest Grove, Oregon.
35. "Tokyo 2020 Reflects on Global Success, with Games Legacy Already Inspiring Future Generations," Olympics.com, February 3, 2022, https://olympics.com/ioc/news/tokyo-2020-reflects-on-global-success-with-games-legacy-already-inspiring-future-generations. One media poll indicated post-Games approval from 80 percent of the Japanese people.
36. Bulgaria's Ivan Slavkov was expelled as an IOC member by a vote of the IOC Session (82 in favor, 12 opposed, 5 abstentions) in July 2005. An episode of the BBC's *Panorama* showed Slavkov (on hidden camera) discussing ways to buy votes to secure the city of London the right to host the 2012 Olympics. "Ivan Slavkov, 70, Last Member Expelled from IOC," *Around the Rings*, July 12, 2012, https://www.infobae.com/aroundtherings/ioc/2021/07/12/ivan-slavkov-70-last-member-expelled-from-ioc/.
37. Much of this history has been delineated in the monograph authored by Stephen R. Wenn et al., *Tarnished Rings: The International Olympic Committee and the Salt Lake City Bid Scandal* (Syracuse University Press, rev. ed., 2022).
38. For a brief but in-depth article on this episode, see "Olympics: French prosecutors Believe Singaporean Tan Tong Han Played a Role in Bribing Voters for Tokyo 2020," *The Straits Times*, October 15, 2020, https://www.straitstimes.com/sport/olympics-french-prosecutors-believe-singaporean-tan-tong-han-played-a-role-in-bribing-voters.
39. Lamine Diack was a former IOC member (1999–2013) and former head of the International Association of Athletics Federations (1999–2015). A similar money-for-votes scheme hatched by the Diacks in Brazil had been unearthed in 2017. The investigation and legal proceedings wound their way through Brazil's courts for several years, resulting in a jail sentence of more than thirty years for Carlos Nuzman, chair of Rio 2016's bid committee and president of the 2016 Rio Olympic Organizing Committee. Duncan Mackay, "Nuzman Sentenced to More Than 30 Years in Prison for Rio 2016 Corruption," *Inside the Games*, November 26, 2021, https://www.insidethegames.biz/articles/ 1115967/carlos-nuzman-sentenced-to-30-years; "Rio Olympics Chief Sentenced to 30 Years in Prison for Buying 2016 Votes," *The Guardian*, November 26, 2021, https://www.theguardian.com/sport/2021/nov/26/rio-olympics-chief-sentenced-to-30-years-in-prison-for-buying-2016-votes. An appeals court overturned the conviction in March 2024 when it was determined that the presiding judge "did not have the authority to judge the case." Given that the

conviction was overturned on procedural grounds, the case awaits reassignment to a different court. Raúl Daffunchio Picazo, "Bribery Conviction of Rio 2016 Organizer Overturned," *Inside the Games,* March 9, 2024, https://www.insidethegames.biz/articles/1144147/rio-2016-organiser-conviction-overturned.

40. The Nagano bid committee allegedly spent an average of CAD$33,478 on sixty-two IOC member visits to Japan prior to the vote on the 1998 Olympic Winter Games site taken at the IOC's session in Birmingham, England, in June 1991. During the IOC Session in Birmingham, Nagano rented former British prime minister Neville Chamberlain's summer residence as an entertainment venue for IOC members. The cost of flying Nagano's 180-member delegation to Birmingham, and events staged in conjunction with its bid in Birmingham at Chamberlain's summer estate, was allegedly ¥24 million (more than $170,000). When the Salt Lake City bid scandal emerged in 1998, efforts to examine Nagano's bid, thought to have cost $14 million, were stymied by Japanese officials who, citing Japanese tradition and a "need to save" space, had burned Nagano's bid documents. John Watts, "Investigation Launched into Spiralling Allegations Concerning Nagano's Bid," *The Guardian,* 4 February 1999, https://www.theguardian.com/sport/1999/feb/04/olympic-bribes-nagano-bid-investigation; Mary Jordan and Kevin Sullivan, "Nagano Burned Documents Tracing Nagano's '98 Olympic Bid," *Washington Post,* January 21, 1999, https://www.washingtonpost.com/wp-srv/digest/daily/jan99/nagano21.htm; and, "Nagano Games Tainted by Scandal," *Toronto Star,* January 18, 1999, C8.

41. Ben Dooley and Hisako Ueno, "The Invisible Hand Behind the Tokyo Olympics," *New York Times,* July 20, 2021, https://www.nytimes.com/2021/07/20/business/tokyo-olympics-dentsu.html.

42. For a thorough understanding of Japan's Antimonopoly Law, see Mitsuo Matsushita and James Henderson, "The Antimonopoly Law of Japan—Relating to International Business Transactions," *Case Western Reserve Journal of International Law* 4, no. 2/3 (1972): 124.

43. The details of this scenario's history can be gleaned from Japanese media reports published during the legal proceedings attendant to the sordid circumstances bared to public view in early 2023. See, for instance, Eric Johnson, "The Continuing Saga of the Tokyo Games Scandal," *Japan Times,* February 15, 2023, https://www.japantimes.co.jp/news/2023/02/15/national/tokyo-olympics-bid-rigging-explainer/#:~:text=Tokyo%20prosecutors%20suspect%20that%20bid,total%20of%20%C2%A5538%20million.

44. In the wake of Tokyo 2020, Takahashi faced four criminal indictments for bribery in what became a sprawling scandal over the awarding of sponsorship contracts to domestic sponsors of the Tokyo Games. He posted bail set at $603,000 in December 2022 and awaited trial as 2023 closed. Allegations exist that Takahashi received bribes totaling $1.3 million. His legal issues remained unresolved in July 2024, though they received additional domestic press attention in November 2024. "Former Tokyo Olympics Executive Arrested over Bribes Released on Bail," *Japan Times,* December 26, 2022, https://www.japantimes.co.jp/2022/12/26/2022/12/26/national/crime-legal/haruyuki-takahashi-freed-bail/; "Ad Firm Hakuhodo Fined 200 Mil Yen Over Tokyo Olympics Bid-Rigging," *Japanese Economic Newswire,* July 11, 2024, https://advance-lexis-com.libproxy.wlu.ca/document/?pdmfid=1519360&crid=65917c00-c5e3-45e3-8a043bb2aed778ca&pddocfullpath=%2Fshared%2Fdocument%2Fnews%2Furn%3AcontentItem%3A6CFR-W4N1-JC5B-G3PX

-00000-00&pdcontentcomponentid=144760&pdteaserkey=sr19&pditab=allpods&ecomp=hc-yk&earg=sr19&prid=e539550a-c913-4edc-abc2-ba2d72630724; "Olympics: Japan's Biggest Ad Agency Indicted in Growing Games Scandal," *The Straits Times*, November 25, 2024, https://www.straitstimes.com/sport/japan-authorities-seek-criminal-charges-against-dentsu-others-over-olympics-contracts; "Publishing Executive Found Guilty in Tokyo Olympics Bribery Scandal Avoids Jail Time," *New York Post*, October 10, 2023, https://nypost.com/2023/10/10/publishing-executive-found-guilty-in-tokyo-olympics-bribery-scandal-but-avoids-jail-time/. Toshiyuki Yoshihara, an executive with publishing firm Kadokawa, was found guilty of bribing Takahashi with payments totaling $463,000. His two-year jail sentence was suspended for four years. If Yoshihara avoids criminal activity in that time, he will not serve the sentence. Fifteen others employed with five companies faced trial.

45. Mari Yamaguchi, "JOC, Sapporo Announce Decision to Abandon Bid, Seek Possible Bid from 2034 On," *Associated Press News*, October 11, 2023, https://apnews.com/article/japan-sapporo-olympic-bid-2030-tokyo-scandal-e1a46ba1ed7316121af0998271c0e03a. There was fallout for Dentsu beyond the courtroom. A third-party investigation of Dentsu's involvement in bid-rigging and its indictment tied to Tokyo 2020 attributed the company's situation to "factors such as a low regard for corporate compliance, mainly on the side of management, and an organizational culture in which results were seen to justify any means." *Yomiuri Shimbun*, "Dentsu's Complacency Said Behind Games Bid-Rigging Scandal," *Japan News*, June 10, 2023, https://japannews.yomiuri.co.jp/society/general-news/20230610-115474/. While facing indictment, Dentsu lost its standing as a major Olympic broadcast rights holder in Asia, as it had been from 2014 to 2024, when the IOC opted to sign a contract for a twenty-two-country territory (not including Japan, China, or South Korea) for 2026 to 2032 with Infront Sports & Media, a Chinese-owned company headquartered in Switzerland. Associated Press, "Amid Corruption Charges, Dentsu Out as IOC Broadcast Partner in Asia," *ESPN*, June 15, 2023, https://www.espn.com/olympics/story/_/id/37857144/amid-corruption-charges-dentsu-ioc-broadcast-partner-asia. In 2023, the Japanese government and the Tokyo Metropolitan Government and Osaka Prefecture also restricted Dentsu from bidding on government contracts for nine months and one year, respectively. Susan Lingeswaran, "Dentsu Barred from Bidding on Government Contracts amid Olympics Corruption Probe," *Sportcal*, February 16, 2023, https://www.sportcal.com/sponsorship/dentsu-barred-from-bidding-on-government-contracts-amid-olympics-corruption-probe/. Norihiro Kuretani, Dentsu's president, reassured shareholders that the company was committed to "thorough recurrence prevention measures and gaining the trust of sponsors" going forward, while foreseeing "limited impact" from the restrictions. Danielle Long, "Dentsu Japan Claims 'Extremely Limited' Impact from Bans on Government Tenders," *The Drum*, March 31, 2023, https://www.thedrum.com/news/2023/03/31/dentsu-japan-claims-extremely-limited-impact-bans-government-tenders.
46. "Tokyo 2020 Reflects on Global Success."

BIBLIOGRAPHY

"Ad Firm Hakuhodo Fined 200 Mil Yen Over Tokyo Olympics Bid-Rigging." *Japanese Economic Newswire*, July 11, 2024, https://advance-lexis.com.libproxy.wlu.ca/document/?pdmfid=1519360&crid=65917c00-c5e3-45e3-8a043bb2aed778ca&pddocfullpath=%2Fshared%2Fdocument%2Fnews%2Furn%3AcontentItem%3A6CFR-W4N1-JC5B-G3PX-00000-00&pdcontentcomponentid=144760&pdteaserkey=sr19&pditab=allpods&ecomp=hc-yk&earg=sr19&prid=e539550a-c913-4edc-abc2-ba2d72630724

Akashi, Hidechika, Satoshi Shimada, Toyomitsu Tamura, et al. "SARS-CoV-2 Infections in Close Contacts of Positive Cases in the Olympic and Paralympic Village at the 2021 Tokyo Olympic and Paralympic Games." *JAMA* 327, no. 10 (2022): 978–80. https://jamanetwork.com/journals/jama/fullarticle/2788895.

"Alison Levine and Iulian Ciobanu Cap off the Rio World Boccia Championships with a Bronze Medal." *Boccia Canada*, December 13, 2022. https://bocciacanada.ca/en/news/article/alison-levine-and-iulian-ciobanu-cap-off-the-rio-world-boccia-championships-with-a-bronze-medal/.

"Allyson Felix by the Numbers." *Olympics.com*, October 5, 2021. https://olympics.com/en/news/athletics-allyson-felix-by-the-numbers.

"Ariarne Titmus Seals Legendary Status at Tokyo 2020 Olympics." *Olympics.com*, October 5, 2021. https://olympics.com/en/news/ariarne-titmus-seals-legendary-status-at-tokyo-2020.

Armour, Nancy. "Tokyo Olympics to Be Held Without Fans After New COVID-19 State of Emergency Declared." *USA Today*, July 8, 2021. https://www.usatoday.com/story/sports/olympics/2021/07/08/2021-olympics-fan-not-allowed-attend-tokyo-games-due-covid-19/7899959002/.

Associated Press. "Amid Corruption Charges, Dentsu Out as IOC Broadcast Partner in Asia." *ESPN*, June 15, 2023. https://www.espn.com/olympics/story/_/id/37857144/amid-corruption-charges-dentsu-ioc-broadcast-partner-asia.

Axon, Rachel. "World Athletics Introduces Prize Money Pool for Paris Gold Medal Winners." *Street & Smith's Sports Business Journal*, April 4, 2024. https://www.sportsbusinessjournal.com/Articles/2024/04/10/world-athletics-prize-money-track-and-field-olympic-competitions.

B2ten. "Our History." Accessed December 12, 2024. https://b2ten.com/about-b2ten/.

Bagshaw, Eryk. "Can Tokyo Cancel the Olympics?" *Sydney Morning Herald*, May 22, 2021. https://www.smh.com.au/world/asia/can-tokyo-cancel-the-olympics-20210520-p57tnn.html.

Bagshaw, Eryk. "Olympic Fears Grow as Australian Team Doctor Warns Coronavirus 'a Significant Challenge.'" *Sydney Morning Herald*, February 25, 2020. https://www.smh.com.au/national/olympic-fears-grow-as-australian-team-doctor-warns-coronavirus-significant-challenge-20200225-p54414.html.

Baker, Peter. "U.S. to Suspend Most Travel from Europe as World Scrambles to Fight Pandemic." *New York Times*, March 11, 2020. https://advance-lexis-com.libproxy

. wlu.ca/api/document?collection=news&id=urn: contentItem:5YD7-GFK1-DXY4-X0TV-00000-00&context=1516831.

"Banyan Flu Jabs." *The Economist*, March 7, 2020, 54. https://libproxy.wlu.ca/login?url=https://www.proquest.com/magazines/banyan-flu-jabs/docview/2372869987/se-2?accountid=15090.

Baraniuk, Chris. "What the Diamond Princess Taught the World About Covid-19." *BMJ*, April 27, 2020. https://www.bmj.com/content/369/bmj.m1632.

Barney, Robert K., et al. *Selling the Five Rings: The International Olympic Committee and the Rise of Olympic Commercialism*, rev. ed. University of Utah Press, 2004.

Barrett, Chris. "Flickering Hope: Coates Confident the Games Will Go Ahead as Planned." *Sydney Morning Herald*, March 17, 2020. https://advance-lexis-com.libproxy.wlu.ca/api/document?collection=news& id=urn:contentItem:5YF9-5R31-F0J6-J0DM-00000-00&context=1516831.

Barrett, Chris. "'I Can't See How Games Can Go On': Former Chef de Mission Casts Doubt over Tokyo Olympics." *Sydney Morning Herald*, March 19, 2020. https://advance-lexis-com.libproxy.wlu.ca/api/document?collection=news&id=urn:contentItem:5YFR-1Y71-F0J6-J086-00000-00&context=1516831.

Barrett, Chris. "'I Was Looking at Retiring': Delay Forces Rethink for Gold Hopeful OLYMPICS." *Sydney Morning Herald*, March 26, 2020. https://advance-lexis-com. libproxy. wlu.ca/api/document?collection=news&id=urn:contentItem:5YH6-V481-JD34-V181-00000-00&context=1516831.

"Barshim and Tamberi Share High Jump Success in Tokyo." *World Athletics*, August 1, 2021. https://worldathletics.org/competitions/olympic-games/news/tokyo-olympic-games-men-high-jump-report.

Boykoff, Jules. *Activism and the Olympics: Dissent at the Games in Vancouver and London*. Rutgers University Press, 2014.

Boykoff, Jules. "Cancel. The. Olympics." *New York Times*, March 18, 2020. https://advance-lexis-com.libproxy.wlu.ca/api/document?collection=news&id=urn:contentItem:5YFP-92T1-JBG3-621J-00000-00&context=1516831.

Boykoff, Jules. "Olympic Activism." *Olympic and Paralympic Analysis*. Accessed December 26, 2024. https://olympicanalysis.org/section-5/anti-olympics-activism/.

Boykoff, Jules. *What Are the Olympics For?* Bristol University Press, 2024.

Boykoff, Jules, and Dave Zirin. "How the International Olympic Committee Fails Athletes." *Time*, August 8, 2024. https://time.com/7008621/ioc-olympics-fails-athletes/.

Boykoff, Jules, and Dave Zirin. "The Olympics Promise to Be Socially Responsible. How's That Working Out?" *Trib Live*, July 29, 2024. https://triblive.com/opinion/jules-boykoff-and-dave-zirin-the-olympics-promise-to-be-socially-responsible-hows-that-working-out/.

Brady, Rachel. "The Tokyo Olympics Challenge: How Can Canadian Athletes Aim for Gold at Games Compromised by COVID-19?" *Globe and Mail*, March 13, 2021. https://www. theglobeandmail.com/sports/olympics/article-the-tokyo-olympics-challenge-how-can-canadian-athletes-aim-for-gold-at/.

"Brian McCloskey." *Chatham House*. Archived October 24, 2020, at https://web.archive.org/web/20201024035702/https://www.chathamhouse.org/about-us/our-people/brian-mccloskey.

Bull, Andy. "Adam Peaty Wins GB's First 2020 Tokyo Gold and Makes Olympic History." *The Guardian*, July 25, 2021. https://www.theguardian.com/sport/2021/jul/26/adam-peaty-wins-gold-100m-breaststroke-tokyo-olympics-2020-swimming.

Butterfield, Herbert. *The Whig Interpretation of History* (G. Bell and Sons, 1931).
Caitlin, Sarah. "Sport's White Elephants: The Economic, Environment, and Human Cost of Mega-tournament Infrastructure." *McGill Daily*, January 16, 2023. https://www.mcgilldaily.com/2023/01/sports-white-elephants/#:~:text=The%20short%20term%20costly%20infrastructure,largely%20unused%20after%20the%20event.
Camenker, Jacob. "Meet MyKayla Skinner, Who Finally Lived Out Olympic Dreams After Overcoming COVID." *Sporting News*, July 25, 2021. https://www.sportingnews.com/us/athletics/news/meet-mykayla-skinner-olympic-covid/jck75p8gk2t91p7d2u47q8lzu.
Campbell, Charlie, Mayako Shibata, and Madeline Roache. "Tokyo's Olympics Trial." *Time*, January 18, 2021, 44–51. https://search-ebscohost-com.libproxy.wlu.ca/login.aspx?direct=true&AuthType=ip,cookie,url,uid&db=rgm&AN=147960786&site=ehost-live.
"Canada's Mandy Bujold Wins Battle to Box in Tokyo Olympics." *CBC*, June 30, 2021. https://www.cbc.ca/sports/olympics/summer/boxing/mandy-bujold-tokyo-olympics-1.6085623.
"Canadian Boxer Bujold to Pursue Case at Court of Arbitration for Sport." *CBC*, April 30, 2021. https://www.cbc.ca/sports/olympics/summer/boxing/mandy-bujold-boxing-hires-court-of-arbitration-1.6009349.
Canadian Paralympic Committee. "Alison Levine." Accessed December 27, 2024. https://paralympic.ca/team-canada/alison-levine.
"Chairman of the Japanese Olympic Committee Set to Quit." *CNN*, March 19, 2019. https://edition.cnn.com/2019/03/19/sport/tsunekazu-takeda-japanese-olympic-committee-spt-intl/index.html.
Charlesworth, David. "Tokyo Olympics: Adam Peaty Dismayed by Some Reaction Since Announcing Month-Long Break from Pool." *The Independent*, August 2, 2021. https://www.independent.co.uk/sport/olympics/adam-peaty-swimming-tokyo-break-b1894897.html.
Cheng, Maria, and Farai Mustaka. "Scientists Mystified, Wary, as Africa Avoids COVID-19 Disaster." *CTV News*, November 19, 2021. https://www.ctvnews.ca/health/coronavirus/scientists-mystified-wary-as-africa-avoids-covid-19-disaster-1.5673339.
Chiari, Mike. "Japanese Prime Minister: IOC President '100% Agrees' to Postpone 2020 Olympics." *Bleacher Report*, March 24, 2020. https://bleacherreport.com/articles/2882723-japanese-prime-minister-ioc-president-100-agrees-to-postpone-2020-olympics.
"The China Coronavirus: Time and Again." *The Economist*, January 25, 2020. https://libproxy.wlu.ca/login?url=https://www.proquest.com/magazines/time-again/docview/2346435894/se-2.
"China Pneumonia Outbreak: Mystery Virus Probed in China." *BBC*, January 3, 2020. https://www.bbc.com/news/world-asia-china-50984025.
Clark, Doug Bock. "Inside the Nightmare Voyage of the *Diamond Princess*." *GQ*, April 30, 2020. https://www.gq.com/story/inside-diamond-princess-cruise-ship-nightmare-voyage.
Clifford, Catherine. "How the Moderna Covid-19 mRNA Vaccine Was Made So Quickly." *CNBC*, July 3, 2021. https://www.cnbc.com/2021/07/03/how-moderna-made-its-mrna-covid-vaccine-so-quickly-noubar-afeyan.html.
"Coach Harry Marra." https://www.coachharrymarra.com/about (site discontinued).
Cohen, Josh. "An Ode to Gregg Popovich, the Most Interesting Man in the NBA." *Bleacher Report*, May 31, 2013. https://bleacherreport.com/articles/1656735-an-ode-to-the-most-interesting-man-in-the-nba-gregg-popovich.

Collins, Sandra. *The 1940 Tokyo Games: The Missing Olympics, Japan, the Asian Olympics, and the Olympic Movement.* Routledge, 2007.
"Coronavirus: How Bad Will It Get?" *The Economist*, February 1, 2020. https://libproxy.wlu.ca/login?url=https://www.proquest.com/magazines/how-bad-will-get/docview/2349095209/se-2.
"Coronavirus: The First Three Months as It Happened." *Nature*, April 22, 2020. https://www.nature.com/articles/d41586-020-00154-w.
"Crouser Breaks World Shot Put Record with 23.38m in Idaho." *World Athletics*, February 18, 2023. https://worldathletics.org/news/report/ryan-crouser-world-shot-put-record-2338m-idaho.
Daffunchio Picazo, Raúl. "Bribery Conviction of Rio 2016 Organizer Overturned." *Inside the Games.* March 9, 2024. https://www.insidethegames.biz/articles/1144147/rio-2016-organiser-conviction-overturned.
"Damian Warner Tops His Canadian Decathlon Record to Win Hypo Meeting." *CBC*, May 30, 2021. https://www.cbc.ca/sports/olympics/summer/trackandfield/damian-warner-hypo-meeting-may30-1.6046143.
Davis, Nicola. "How Has a Covid Vaccine Been Developed So Quickly?" *The Guardian*, December 8, 2020. https://www.theguardian.com/society/2020/dec/08/how-has-a-covid-vaccine-been-developed-so-quickly.
del Barco, Mandelit. "The Japanese Public Begins to Embrace the Tokyo Olympics." *National Public Radio*, August 2, 2021. https://www.npr.org/sections/tokyo-olympics-live-updates/2021/08/02/1023606904/the-japanese-public-begins-to-embrace-the-tokyo-Olympics.
Delkic, Melina. "Coronavirus in Japan, New York Hospitals, Maduro Indictment: Your Friday Briefing." *New York Times*, 26 March 2020. https://advance-lexis-com.libproxy.wlu.ca/api/document?collection=news&id=urn:contentItem:5YHF-SRH1-DXY4-X026-00000-00&context=1516831.
Delkic, Melina. "Your Friday Briefing." *New York Times*, February 4, 2021. https://advance-lexis-com.libproxy.wlu.ca/api/document?collection=news&id=urn:contentItem:61XM-R401-JBG3-613R-00000-00&context=1516831.
Delkic, Melina. "Your Friday Briefing." *New York Times*, February 18, 2021. https://advance-lexis-com.libproxy.wlu.ca/api/document?collection=news&id=urn:contentItem:621M-9N21-DXY4-X01W-00000-00&context=1516831.
Dempsey, Chris, and Andrew Zimbalist. *No Boston Olympics: How and Why Smart Cities Are Passing on the Torch.* University Press of New England, 2017.
Dickinson, Matt. "Project Immortal Is Not Boastful or an Ego Trip—I Just Want to Aim High." *The Times* (Edition 1 Ireland), December 30, 2020, 46–47.
Dooley, Ben. "Shinzo Abe, Japan's Political Houdini, Can't Escape Coronavirus Backlash." *New York Times*, March 5, 2020. https://advance-lexis-com.libproxy.wlu.ca/api/document? collection=news&id=urn:contentItem:5YBY-PCS1-DXY4-X299-00000-00&context=1516831.
Dooley, Ben. "Japan Falls into a Recession, With 'Ugly' Months to Come." *New York Times*, 18 May 2020. https://advance-lexis-com.libproxy.wlu.ca/api/document?collection=news&id=urn:contentItem:5YXP-VJ91-DXY4-X239-00000-00&context=1516831.
Dooley, Ben, and Tiffany Hsu. "Toyota Pulls Its Olympics TV Ads in Japan." *New York Times*, July 19, 2021. https://advance-lexis-com.libproxy.wlu.ca/api/document?collection=news&id=urn:contentItem:635T-1411-DXY4-X1K5-00000-00&context=1516831.

Dooley, Ben, and Makiko Inoue. "Olympics Delay Can Only Worsen Japan's Slump." *New York Times*, April 1, 2020. https://advance-lexis-com.libproxy.wlu.ca/api/document?collection=news&id=urn:contentItem:5YJP-5991-JBG3-635P-00000-00&context=1516831.

Dooley, Ben, and Makiko Inoue. "The Tokyo Olympics Will Allow Spectators Who Live in Japan, but with Restrictions." *New York Times*, June 21, 2021. https://www.nytimes.com/2021/06/21/world/tokyo-olympics-spectators.html.

Dooley, Ben, and Hisako Ueno. "The Invisible Hand Behind the Tokyo Olympics." *New York Times*, 20 July 2021. https://www.nytimes.com/2021/07/20/business/tokyo-olympics-dentsu.html.

Dowdeswell, Andrew. "Tokyo 2020 Developers Sued for Delayed Handover of Athletes' Village Apartments." *Inside the Games*, December 25, 2021. https://www.insidethegames.biz/articles/1117228/tokyo-2020-athletes-village-development.

"Eliud Kipchoge Confirms All Time Greatness at Tokyo 2020." *Olympics.com*, October 5, 2021. https://olympics.com/en/news/eliud-kipchoge-confirms-all-time-greatness-at-tokyo-2020.

Ellery, Ben, and Richard Lloyd Parry. "Hopes Raised of Flight for Cruise Britons." *The Times*, February 18, 2020. https://advance-lexis-com.libproxy.wlu.ca/api/document?collection=news&id=urn:contentItem:5Y7G-NHH1-JCBW-N2Y9-00000-00&context=1516831.

Ellingworth, James. "Coronavirus Already Wreaking Havoc on Olympic Qualifying Schedule." *Globe and Mail*, March 11, 2020. https://advance-lexis-com.libproxy.wlu.ca/api/document?collection=news&id=urn: contentItem:6059-3X61-F06S-34V3-00000-00&context=1516831.

Elsey, Brenda, and Amira Rose Davis, hosts. "Interview: Jules Boykoff on the Politics, Power and Pain of the Beijing 2022 Winter Olympics." *Burn It All Down*, podcast, February 3, 2022. https://www.burnitalldownpod.com/episodes/interview-jules-boykoff-on-the-politics-power-and-pain-of-the-Beijing-2022-winter-olympics.

Etchells, Daniel. "IOC Boxing Taskforce Suspends European Qualifier in London." *Inside The Games*, March 16, 2020. https://www.insidethegames.biz/articles/1092014/ioc-boxing-taskforce-suspends-qualifiers.

"Europe Boxing Qualification for Tokyo 2020 Live from London on Olympic Channel." *AIPS Media*, March 13, 2020. https://www.aipsmedia.com/aips/pages/articles/2020/27356.html.

Ewing, Lori. "As COVID-19 Halts Global Races, Canada's Marathoners Take It in Stride." *Globe and Mail*, March 14, 2020. https://advance-lexis-com.libproxy.wlu.ca/api/document? collection=news&id=urn:contentItem:6059-3X71-F06S-302J-00000-00&context=1516831.

Ewing, Lori. "COVID-19 Fears Ahead of Tokyo Games Has Some Remembering Outbreak Prior to 2010 Olympics." *Globe and Mail*, February 20, 2020. https://advance-lexis-com. libproxy.wlu.ca/api/document?collection=news&id=urn:contentItem:6058-SV11-JCRP-C2RV-00000-00&context=1516831.

Ewing, Lori. "Damian Warner and Co., Built a Multi Events Training Facility in Old London Arena." *Toronto Star*, February 8, 2021. https://www.thestar.com/sports/2021/02/08/damian-warner-and-co-built-a-multi-events-training-facility-in-old-london-arena.html.

Farago, Jason. "The 1964 Olympics Certified a New Japan, in Steel and on the Screen." *New York Times*, July 30, 2020. https://www.nytimes.com/2020/07/30/arts/design/tokyo-olympics-1964-design.

Fenno, Nathan. "How Tokyo Olympic Organizers Managed to Keep COVID-19 Mostly in Check." *Los Angeles Times*, August 8, 2021. https://www.latimes.com/sports/olympics/story/2021-08-08/tokyo-olympics-overcame-challenges-poised-by-covid-19.

Feschuk, Dave. "Olympic Athletes Should Bargain for Their Fair Share, Just Like the Pros—but It Won't Be Easy." *Toronto Star*, April 24, 2020. https://www.thestar.com/sports/amateur/olympic-athletes-should-bargain-for-their-fair-share-just-like-the-pros-but-it-won/article_8ae46d10-a509-5324-9155-93b20ad1e573.html.

"First Playbook Published Outlining Measures to Deliver Safe and Successful Olympic and Paralympic Games Tokyo 2020." *Olympics.com*. Updated March 30, 2021. https://olympics.com/en/news/first-playbook-published-outlining-measures-to-deliver-safe-and-successful-olymp.

Fischer, David Hackett. *Historian's Fallacies: Towards a Logic of Historical Thought*. Harper & Row, 1970.

Fitzpatrick, Joel. "FOCUS: Tokyo Games Postponement to Require Olympic-Scale Rethink." *Japan Economic Newswire*, April 1, 2020. https://advance-lexis-com.libproxy.wlu.ca/api/document?collection=news&id=urn:contentItem:5YJW-1NG1-JC65-51YP-00000-00&context=1516831.

Fleitas, B. "The Other Numbers from the Olympic Games: 115 Million Viewers in Japan, 51,000 Covid Tests...." *Marca*, September 8, 2021. https://www.marca.com/en/olympic-games/2021/08/09/61117 b6846163f5b5e8b45de.html.

"FOCUS: Experts Foresee Tokyo Games Without Spectators If Virus Lingers." *Japan Economic Newswire*, March 13, 2020. https://advance-lexis.com.libproxy.wlu.ca/api/document?collection=news&id=urn:contentItem: 5YDK-KXB1-DYN6-W0X9-00000-00&context=1516831.

"FOCUS: Tokyo Games Dates Set, but Organizers Still Face Tests." *Japan Economic Newswire*, April 2, 2020. https://advance-lexis-com.libproxy.wlu.ca/api/document?collection=news&id=urn:contentItem:5YK3-0R41-DYN6-W24Y-00000-00&context=1516831.

Francis, Mike. "Pacific Professor Boykoff in Forefront of Movement Against Tokyo Summer Olympics." *New York Times*, March 11, 2020. https://www.pacificu.edu/about/media/pacific-professor-boykoff-forefront-movement-against-tokyo-summer-olympics.

Fraser, Stuart. "'I Can't See Games Pulling Off What We Did'; Abuse from Players One of Many Tests for Craig Tiley in Organising the Australian Open." *The Times*, February 22, 2021. https://advance-lexis-com.libproxy.wlu.ca/api/document?collection=news&id=urn:contentItem:622C-W0M1-JCBW-N0HJ-00000-00&context=1516831.

Futterman, Matt, and Joe Ward. "Let the Games Begin. Or Not." *New York Times*, March 19, 2020. https://advance-lexis-com.libproxy.wlu.ca/api/document?collection=news&id=urn:contentItem:5YFX-M651-DXY4-X548-00000-00&context=1516831.

Futterman, Matthew. "A Grand Vision of the Olympics Plays Catchup With the Rest of the World." *New York Times*, March 24, 2020. https://advance-lexis-com.libproxy.wlu.ca/api/document?collection=news&id=urn:contentItem:5YGY-ST01-JBG3-614W-00000-00&context=1516831.

Futterman, Matthew. "Hopes for Tokyo's Summer Olympics Darken." *New York Times*. 15 January 2021. https://advance-lexis-com.libproxy.wlu.ca/api/document?collection=news&id=urn:contentItem:61S9-6V71-JBG3-64SR-00000-00&context=1516831.

Futterman, Matthew. "An Olympic Doctor Discusses the Effect of the Coronavirus on Sports." *New York Times*, March 8, 2020. https://advance-lexiscom.libproxy.wlu.ca/api/document?collection=news&id=urn:contentItem:5YCM-NSB1-JBG3-6002-00000-00&context=1516831.

Futterman, Matthew. "Why Olympic Leaders Clung to the Plan to Have the Summer Games in Tokyo." *New York Times*, April 17, 2020. https://advance-lexis-com.libproxy.wlu.ca/api/document?collection=news&id=urn:contentItem:5YGY-MCG1-JBG3-610V-00000-00&context=1516831.

Futterman, Matthew, and Andrew Keh. "Why the U.S. Lagged Behind in the Drive to Postpone the Summer Olympics." *New York Times*, March 26, 2020. https://advance-lexis-com.libproxy.wlu.ca/api/document?collection=news&id=urn:contentItem:5YHD-PX71-JBG3-611K-00000-00&context=1516831.

Futterman, Matthew, and Andrew Keh. "Boston and London Marathons Postponed Until Fall." *New York Times*, March 13, 2020. https://advance-lexis-com.libproxy.wlu.ca/api/document?collection=news&id=urn:contentItem:5YDN-CJ21-DXY4-X41T-00000-00&context=1516831.

Futterman, Matthew, and Talya Minsberg. "Boston and London Marathons Are Rescheduled for Fall." *New York Times*, March 14, 2020. https://advance-lexis-com.libproxy.wlu.ca/api/document?collection=news&id=urn:contentItem:5YDV-TCP1-DXY4-X51D-00000-00&context=1516831.

Futterman, Matthew, Motoko Rich, and Andrew Keh. "The Tokyo Olympics Will Open a Year From Now. Maybe." *New York Times*, July 9, 2020. https://advance-lexis-com.libproxy.wlu.ca/api/document?collection=news&id=urn:contentItem:60CY-7M41-DXY4-X0NG-00000-00&context=1516831.

Garlinghouse, Tom. "Keeping a Pandemic at Bay: Lessons for the Tokyo and Beijing Olympics," *High Meadows Environmental Institute*, January 18, 2024. https://environment.princeton.edu/news/lessons-from-the-tokyo-and-beijing-olympics/.

"GAVI—The Vaccine Alliance." Archived October 1, 2022, at https://web.archive.org/web/20221001064353/https://www.who.int/europe/about-us/partnerships/partners/global-health-partnerships/gavi-alliance.

Gleeson, Michael. "Lack of Teams Will Force Olympics Delay: Top Coach Olympics." *Sydney Morning Herald*, March 17, 2020. https://advance-lexis-com.libproxy.wlu.ca/api/document?collection=news&id=urn:contentItem:5YF9-5R31-F0J6-J0CD-00000-00&context=1516831.

Goldman, Tom. "Coronavirus Knocks U.S. Pole Vaulter Sam Kendricks Out of Tokyo Olympics." *National Public Radio*, July 29, 2020. https://www.npr.org/sections/tokyo-olympics-live-updates/2021/07/29/1022065062/coronavirus-knocks-u-s-pole-vaulter-sam-kendricks-out-of-tokyo-olympics.

Goldman, Tom. "USA's Ryan Crouser Sets Olympic Shot Put Record and Wins Olympic Gold Again." *National Public Radio*, August 5, 2021. https://www.npr.org/sections/tokyo-olympics-live-updates/2021/08/05/1025012458/usas-ryan-crouser-sets-olympic-shot-put-record-and-wins-gold-again.

Goodman, Eric. "Decathlon Tracker: Damian Warner Cracks 9000 Points, Takes Gold." *NBC Olympics*, August 3, 2021. https://www.nbcolympics.com/news/decathlon-tracker-live-updates-results-highlights-each-event.

Grohmann, Karolos. "Tokyo 2020 Olympics: IOC Officially Bans AIBA from Amateur Boxing due to Finance and Government Issues." *The Independent*, June 26, 2019.

https://www.independent.co.uk/sport/boxing/tokyo-2020-olympics-games-boxing-aiba-banned-latest-news-a8975326.html.

Gunia, Amy. "Japan's Prime Minister Yoshihide Suga is Resigning. Here's What That Means." *Time*, September 3, 2021. https://time.com/6094995/japan-prime-minister-suga-resigns/.

Hall, Kenji. "Tokyo Rift." *Sports Illustrated* 132, no. 4 (2021): 12–15. https://search-ebscohoscom.libproxy.wlu.ca/login.aspx?direct=true&AuthType=ip,cookieurl,uid&db=rgm&AN=149875978&site=ehost-live.

Hall, Vicki. "'You Need One Voice': Canadian Decathlete Damian Warner Trims Coaching Staff Ahead of Pivotal Season." *National Post*, December 20, 2016. https://nationalpost.com/sports/olympics/you-need-one-voice-canadian-decathlete-damian-warner-trims-coaching-staff-ahead-of-pivotal-season.

Hamilton, Lee. "Weightlifter Hidilyn Diaz Wins the Philippines' First-Ever Olympic Gold Medal." *Tatler Asia*, July 26, 2021. https://www.tatlerasia.com/lifestyle/sports/hk-hidilyn-diaz-weightlifter-wins-the-philippines-first-ever-olympic-gold-medal.

Harrison, Doug. "Reigning Olympic Champ Stefanidi Beats Alysha Newman in Virtual Pole Vault Event." *CBC*, May 16, 2020. https://www.cbc.ca/sports/olympics/summer/trackand field/ultimate-garden-clash-women-world-athletics-1.5573279.

Harrison, Doug. "Damian Warner Out of the Cold, into Temporary Training Home for Tokyo Olympics." *CBC*, October 31, 2020. https://www.cbc.ca/sports/olympics/summer/trackandfield/damian-warner-indoor-training-tokyo-olympics-1.5785135.

Henry, Matthew. "Peaty Tests Positive for Covid After Winning Silver." *BBC Sport*, July 29, 2024. https://www.bbc.com/sport/olympics/articles/crgl6nox39eo.

Heroux, Devin. "Canadian boxer Mandy Bujold asking IOC to change qualifying rules for Pregnant Women." *CBC*, 26 April 2021. https://www.cbc.ca/sports/olympics/summer/boxing/mandy-bujold-boxing-hires-lawyer-in-fight-to-qualify-for-tokyo-olympics-1.6002280.

Heroux, Devin. "Canadian Decathlete Pierce LePage Wins Silver at World Athletics Championships," *CBC*, July 24, 2022. https://www.cbc.ca/sports/olympics/summer/trackandfield/world-athletics-championships-decathlon-july-24-day-2-1.6530543.

Heroux, Devin. "Heritage Minister Asks IOC to Let Mandy Bujold to Compete After Boxer Missed Olympic Qualifying Events While Pregnant." *CBC*, May 17, 2021. https://www.cbc.ca/sports/olympics/olympics-canadian-government-letter-ioc-mandy-bujold-1.6030458.

Heroux, Devin. "Team Damian Warner: How 2 English Teachers Helped Turn a London Teen into the World's Greatest Athlete." *CBC*, July 19, 2022. https://www.cbc.ca/sports/olympics/summer/trackandfield/world-athletics-championships-damian-warner-feature-heroux-1.6524281.

Holthus, Barbara, Isaac Gagné, Wolfram Manzenreiter, and Franz Waldenberger, eds. *Japan Through the Lens of the Tokyo Olympics* (Routledge, 2020).

Hong, Hee Jung, and Justine Allen. "An Exploration of the Resources of High-Performance Athletes and Coaches to Cope with Unexpected Transitions." *Sport, Exercise, and Performance Psychology* 11, no. 4 (2022): 412–28. https://doi.org/10.1037/spy0000306. https://libproxy.wlu.ca/login?url=https://www.proquest.com/scholarly-journals/exploration-resources-high-performance-athletes/docview/2700773796/se-2;

Hornyak, Tim. "Even with No Tourists or Fans, Japan Is Already Seeing Economic Benefits from the $15.4 Billion Tokyo Olympics. *Time*, August 11, 2021. https://time.comcom/6089274/tokyo-olympics-economic-benefits/.

"Hosting Asian Games Will 'Wipe Away' Japanese Doubts, Says Top Official." *France24*, June 10, 2023. https://www.france24.com/en/live-news/20231006-hosting-asian-games-will-wipe-away-japanese-doubts-says-top-official.

"How Olympic Champion Tom Daley Sealed a Golden Diving Legacy at Tokyo 2020." *Olympics.com*, October 5, 2021. https://olympics.com/en/news/tom-daley-seals-golden-legacy-at-tokyo-2020.

Imbert, Fred, and Thomas Franck. "Dow Plunges 10% amid Coronavirus Fears for Its Worst Day Since the 1987 Crash." *CNBC*, 11 March 2020. https://www.cnbc.com/2020/03/11/futures-are-steady-wednesday-night-after-dow-closes-in-bear-market-traders-await-trump.html.

Ingle, Sean. "Tokyo Marathon Cancels Mass Race over Coronavirus Scare." *The Guardian*, February 17, 2020. https://www.theguardian.com/sport/2020/feb/17/tokyo-marathon-restricted-to-elite-runners-over-coronavirus-scare-athletics.

Ingle, Sean. "Duplantis and Lavillenie Scale the Heights in Ultimate Garden Clash." *The Guardian*, 3 May 2020. https://www.theguardian.com/sport/2020/may/03/duplantis-and-lavillenie-scale-the-heights-in-ultimate-garden-clash.

Ingle, Sean. "Ryan Crouser Leads Historic Olympic Podium Repeat in Shot Put." *The Guardian*, 5 August 2021. https://www.theguardian.com/sport/2021/aug/05/ryan-crouser-leads-historic-olympic-podium-repeat-in-shot-put.

"Insurer Allianz Becomes Olympic Sponsor." *France24*, September 18, 2018. https://www.france24.com/en/20180918-insurer-allianz-becomes-olympic-sponsor.

"IOC Approves a Financial Envelope of Up to USD 800 Million to Address the COVID-19 Crisis." *Olympics.com*, May 14, 2020. https://olympics.com/ioc/news/ioc-approves-a-financial-envelope-of-up-to-usd-800-million-to-address-the-covid-19-crisis.

"IOC and Atos Extend Worldwide Olympic Partnership." *Olympics.com*, July 9, 2020. https://olympics.com/ioc/news/ioc-and-atos-extend-worldwide-olympic-partnership.

"IOC Boss Critical of World Athletics Paying Athletes." *Street & Smith's Sports Business Journal*, May 3, 2024. https://www.sportsbusinessjournal.com/Articles/2024/05/03/ioc-world-athletics-olympic-prize-money#:~:text=IOC%20President%20Thomas%20Bach%20suggested,role%20of%20an%20international%20sports.

"IOC Boxing Task Force Suspends European Qualifier in London and All Remaining Events Until May." *Olympics.com*, March 16, 2020. https://olympics.com/ioc/news/ioc-boxing-task-force-suspends-european-qualifier-in-london-and-all-remaining-events-until-may.

"The IOC and Procter & Gamble Announce an Extension to Their Worldwide Olympic Partnership Through 2028." *Olympics.com*, July 22, 2020. https://olympics.com/ioc/news/the-ioc-and-procter-gamble-announce-an-extension-to-their-worldwide-olympic-partnership-through-to-2028.

"IOC and Tokyo 2020 Joint Statement—Framework for Preparation of the Olympic and Paralympic Games Tokyo 2020 Following their Postponement to 2021." *Olympics.com*, April 16, 2020. https://olympics.com/ioc/news/ioc-and-tokyo-2020-joint-statement-framework-for-preparation-of-the-olympic-and-paralympic-games-tokyo-2020-following-their-postponement-to-2021.

"IOC President Thomas Bach Will Not Seek to Stay Beyond 2025." *NBC Olympics*, August 11, 2024. https://www.nbcolympics.com/news/ioc-president-thomas-bach-will-not-seek-stay-beyond-2025.

IOC Press Release, June 18, 2008. "Olympic Education a Lasting Benefit for China's Schoolchildren." https://olympics.com/ioc/news/olympic-education-a-lasting-benefit-for-china-s-schoolchildren.

IOC Press Release, May 18, 2009: "Olympic Values Reach 400 Million Chinese Children" https://olympics.com/ioc/news/olympic-values-reach-400-million-chinese-children.

"IOC to Consider Postponing Tokyo Games in 4 Weeks of Talks." *Chicago Daily Herald*, March 23, 2020. https://advance-lexis-com.libproxy.wlu.ca/api/document?collection=news&id=urn:contentItem:5YGT-91X1-DY6F-J0HK-00000-00&context=1516831.

"Ivan Slavkov, 70, Last Member Expelled from IOC." *Around the Rings*, July 12, 2012. https://www.infobae.com/aroundtherings/ioc/2021/07/12/ivan-slavkov-70-last-member-expelled-from-ioc/.

"Japan Halts New Entry from Around World to Block New Virus Variant." *Japan Economic Newswire*, December 27, 2020. https://advance-lexis-com.libproxy.wlu.ca/api/document?collection=news&id=urn:contentItem:61MB-7M51-JC5B-G1S4-00000-00&context=1516831.

"Japan Marks 1 Year Until Delayed Olympics, but Virus Concerns Remain." *Japan Economic Newswire*, July 23, 2020. https://advance-lexis-com.libproxy.wlu.ca/api/document?collection=news&id=urn:contentItem:60DR-RNP1-DYMD-60GM-00000-00&context=1516831.

"Japan's Economy Shrinks 28.1% in the Second Quarter, More Than Initially Estimated." *CNBC*, September 7, 2020. https://www.cnbc.com/2020/09/08/japan-q2-revised-gdp-2020.html.

"Japan's Shinzo Abe Stepping Down as Prime Minister." *National Public Radio*, August 28, 2020. https://www.npr.org/2020/08/28/906945704/japans-shinzo-abe-is-stepping-down-as-prime-minister.

"Japanese Olympic Committee Head Resigns amid Tokyo Games scandal." *Sportsnet*, 19 March 2019. https://www.sportsnet.ca/olympics/japanese-olympic-committee-head-resigns-amid-tokyo-games-scandal/.

Johnson, Eric. "The Continuing Saga of the Tokyo Games Scandal." *Japan Times*, February 15, 2023. https://www.japantimes.co.jp/news/2023/02/15/national/tokyo-olympics-bid-rigging-explainer/#:~:text=Tokyo%20prosecutors%20suspect%20that%20bid,total%20of%20%C2%A5538%20million.

"Joint Statement from the International Olympic Committee and the Tokyo 2020 Organising Committee." *Olympics.com*, March 24, 2020. https://olympics.com/ioc/news/joint-statement-from-the-international-olympic-committee-and-the-tokyo-2020-organising-committee.

Jordan, Mary, and Kevin Sullivan. "Nagano Burned Documents Tracing Nagano's '98 Olympic Bid." *Washington Post*, January 21, 1999. https://www.washingtonpost.com/wp-srv/digest/daily/jan99/nagano21.htm.

" 'Just Magical': Joy for Tamberi and Barshim As They Opt to Share Gold in Men's High Jump." *The Guardian*, August 2, 2021. https://www.theguardian.com/sport/2021/aug/02/tamberi-barshim-share-olympic-gold-mens-high-jump-reaction.

Kamper, Erich, and Bill Mallon. *The Golden Book of the Olympic Games*. Vallardi & Associates, 1992.

Kano, Shintaro. "Economist Pours Cold Water on Tokyo's Hopes for Olympic Success in 2020." *Japan Times*, July 26, 2017. https://www.japantimes.co.jp/news/2017/07/26/national/no-success-story-tokyo-hosting-2020-games-economist/.

Karni, Annie, and Donald G. McNeil Jr. "Trump Wants U.S. 'Opened Up' by Easter, Despite Health Officials' Warnings." *New York Times*, March 24, 2020. https://advancelexiscom.libproxy.wlu.ca/api/document?collection=news&id=urn:contentItem:5YH4-TV21-JBG3-63DP-00000-00&context=1516831.

Kato, Takumi. "Opposition in Japan to the Olympics during the COVID-19 Pandemic." *Humanities and Social Sciences Communications* 8, December 16, 2021. https://www.nature.com/articles/s41599-021-01011-5.

Keh, Andrew. "First for Shots: Doctors, Nurses ... Olympians?" *New York Times*, March 1, 2021. https://advance-lexis-com.libproxy.wlu.ca/api/document?collection=news&id=urn:contentItem:623X-0361-DXY4-X28P-00000-00&context=1516831.

Keh, Andrew. "Olympians Enter a Risky New Event: Line Jumping." *New York Times*, February 28, 2021. https://advance-lexis-com.libproxy.wlu.ca/api/document?collection=news&id=urn:contentItem:623R-34G1-DXY4-X1B0-00000-00&context=1516831.

Keh, Andrew. "Postpone the Olympics? Tokyo Official Backtracks After Causing Confusion." *New York Times*, March 11, 2020. https://advance-lexis-com.lib proxy.wlu.ca/api/document?collection=news&id=urn:contentItem:5YD7-SBT1-JBG3-61V0-00000-00&context=1516831.

Keh, Andrew. "Power Game: Thomas Bach's Iron Grip on the Olympics." *New York Times*, July 20, 2021. https://www.nytimes.com/2021/07/20/sports/thomas-bach-tokyo-olympics.html.

Keh, Andrew. "Twenty-Four Hours When Sports Hit the Halt Button." *New York Times*, March 12, 2020. https://advance-lexis-com.libproxy.wlu.ca/api/document?collection=news&id=urn:contentItem:5YDG-R431-DXY4-X2RK-00000-00&context=1516831.

Keh, Andrew, and Ben Dooley. "Grappling With Coronavirus, Tokyo Olympic Leaders Have No Good Options." *New York Times*, February 26, 2020. https://advance-lexis-com.libproxy.wlu.ca/api/document?collection=news&id=urn:contentItem:5Y9C-HH51-DXY4-X324-00000-00&context=1516831.

Keh, Andrew, Matt Futterman, Tariq Panja, and Motoko Rich. "An Olympic Showdown: The Rising Clamor to Postpone the Tokyo Summer Olympics." *New York Times*, March 21, 2020. https://www.nytimes.com/2020/03/21/sports/olympics/tokyo-olympics-coronavirus-cancel.html.

Keh, Andrew, and Tariq Panja. "I.O.C.'s Reassurance About the Tokyo Olympics Rankles Some Athletes." *New York Times*, March 18, 2020. https://advance-lexis-com.libproxy.wlu.ca/api/document?collection=news&id=urn: contentItem:5YFS-CTH1-JBG3-632K-00000-00&context=1516831.

Kelly, Cathal. "Montreal-Based B2ten Is Giving Canadian Olympians a Better Run for Their Money." *Globe and Mail*, February 16, 2018. https://www.theglobeandmail.com/sports/olympics/montreal-based-b2ten-is-giving-canadian-olympians-a-better-run-for-their-money/article38013877/.

Kennedy, Merrit, and Leila Fadel. "She's Still Dealing with the Twisties, but Simone Biles Wins Another Medal in Tokyo." *National Public Radio*, August 3, 2021. https://www.npr.org/sections/tokyo-olympics-live-updates/2021/08/03/1024122723/simone-biles-return-balance-beam-gymnastics-olympics.

Kennedy, Merrit, Laila Fadel, and Tom Goldman. "Olympic Opening Ceremony Is a Delicate Mix of Celebration and Solemnity." *National Public Radio*, July 23, 2021. https://www.npr.org/sections/tokyo-olympics-live-updates/2021/07/23/1019622003/tokyo-olympics-opening-ceremony.

"Kevin Mayer Secures Olympic Qualifying Mark in Réunion." *Athletics Weekly*, December 19, 2020. https://athleticsweekly.com/event-news/kevin-mayer-olympic-qualifying-mark-reunion-1039938663/.

Lawton, Matt. "Olympics Are '90% Certain' to Be Delayed, Training Is Almost Impossible,' Says KJT." *The Times*, March 18, 2020. https://advance-lexis-com.libproxy.wlu.ca/api/document?collection=news&id=urn:contentItem:5YFN-TRJ1-DYTY-C48X-00000-00&context=1516831.

Lee, Michelle Ye Hee. "South African Soccer Team Outbreak Tests Tokyo Olympics 'Covid-Safe' Strategy." *Washington Post*, July 19, 2021. https://www.washingtonpost.com/sports/olympics/2021/07/19/tokyo-olympics-south-africa-soccer-covid-outbreak/.

"Levine Claims Gold While Dispaltro and Bussière Capture Bronze at the World Boccia Americas Regional Championships." *Boccia Canada*, December 12, 2021. https://bocciacanada.ca/en/news/article/levine-claims-gold-while-dispaltro-and-bussiere-capture-bronze-at-the-world-boccia-americas-regional-championships/.

Li, Yanyan. "Olympian Ashley Twichell Gives Birth to Baby Boy." *SwimSwam*, 28 May 2022. https://swimswam.com/olympian-ashley-twichell-gives-birth-to-baby-boy/#:~:text=Ashley%20Twichell%20announced%20via%20Instagram,revealed%20her%20pregnancy%20last%20November.

Lim, Harry B. T., Neha Malhotra, Shermaine Lou, and Jeevita Pillai. "The Impact of the Covid-19 Pandemic on Singapore National Youth Athletes' Mental Health and Potential Protective Factors." *International Journal of Sport and Exercise Psychology* 22, no. 7 (2023): 1569–87. https://doi.org/10.1080/1612197X.2023.2235593.

Lingeswaran, Susan. "Dentsu Barred from Bidding on Government Contracts amid Olympics Corruption Probe." *Sportcal*, February 16, 2023. https://www.sportcal.com/sponsorship/dentsu-barred-from-bidding-on-government-contracts-amid-olympics-corruption-probe/.

Long, Danielle. "Dentsu Japan Claims 'Extremely Limited' Impact from Bans on Government Tenders." *The Drum*, March 31, 2023. https://www.thedrum.com/news/2023/03/31/dentsu-japan-claims-extremely-limited-impact-bans-government-tenders.

Longman, Jeré. "The Pandemic's Secret Formula: Backyard Workouts and Lots of Sleep." *New York Times*, August 30, 2020.

Lundqvist, Carolina, Hannah Macdougall, Yoriko Noguchi, Anaëlle Malherbe, and Fabien Abejean. "When COVID-19 Struck the World and Elite Sports: Psychological Challenges and Support Provision in Five Countries during the First Phase of the Pandemic." *Journal of Sport Psychology in Action* 13, no. 2 (2022): 116–28. https://doi.org/10.1080/21520704.2021.1931594.

Lutton, Phil. "Games Medical Conference Falls Victim to Virus as Tokyo Fears Grow." *Sydney Morning Herald*, March 12, 2020. https://advance-lexis-om.libproxy.wlu.ca/api/document?collection=news&id=urn:contentItem:5YD7-7K61-F0J6-J4MK-00000-00&context=1516831.

Lutton, Phil. "Games Test the Mettle and the Medals of Japan." *The Sun Herald*, January 31, 2021. https://advance-lexis-com.libproxy.wlu.ca/api/document?collection=news&id=urn:contentItem: 61WH-SC01-JD34-V01M-00000-00&context=1516831.

Lutton, Phil. "Swim Chiefs Query Value of Games Compromised by Coronavirus Chaos Olympics." *Sydney Morning Herald*, March 21, 2020. https://advance-lexis-com.libproxy.wlu.ca/api/document?collection=news&id=urn:contentItem:5YG5-0521-F0J6-J3X4-00000-00&context=1516831.

Mackay, Duncan. "Nuzman Sentenced to More Than 30 Years in Prison for Rio 2016 Corruption." *Inside the Games*, November 26, 2021. https://www.insidethegames.biz/articles/1115967/carlos-nuzman-sentenced-to-30-years.

Macur, Juliet. " 'It's Just So Devastating': For Crestfallen Gymnasts, an Olympic Dream Deferred." *New York Times*, April 1, 2020. https://advance-lexis-com.libproxy.wlu.ca/api/document?collection=news&id=urn:contentItem:5YJR-SDY1-DXY4-X3MJ-00000-00&context=1516831.

Macur, Juliet. "Take Coronavirus More Seriously, Say Olympic Rowers Who Got It." *New York Times*, July 24, 2020. https://advance-lexis-com.libproxy.wlu.ca/api/document? collection=news&id=urn:contentItem:60F0-JJS1-DXY4-X1WD-00000-00& context=1516831.

Mai, H. J. "Overseas Spectators Will Be Banned from Tokyo Olympics Due to COVID-19 Risks." *National Public Radio*, March 20, 2021. https://www.npr.org/sections/coronavirus-live-updates/2021/03/20/979489573/overseas-spectators-will-be-banned-from-tokyo-olympics-due-to-covid-19-risks.

Maine, D'Arcy. "Olympics 2021—MyKayla Skinner's Gymnastics Career Ends at Tokyo Olympics with the Unlikeliest of Silver Medals." *ESPN*, August 1, 2021. https://www.espn.com/olympics/story/_/id/31934652/olympics-2021-mykayla-skinner-gymnastics-career-ends-tokyo-olympics-unlikeliest-silver-medals.

Mallon, Bill, and Ture Widland. *The 1912 Olympic Games: Results for All Competitors in All Events with Commentary*. McFarland & Company Publishers, 2002.

Marcello, Brandon. "NIL Landscape in College Sports Changing: NCAA Losing Its Grip, Amateur vs. Employee Battle Looms." *CBS Sports*, April 23, 2024. https://www.cbssports.com/college-football/news/nil-landscape-in-college-sports-changes-as-ncaa-loses-grip-amateur-vs-employee-battle-looms/.

Margolis, Eric. " 'This May Be the Tip of the Iceberg': Why Japan's Coronavirus Crisis May Just Be Beginning." *Vox*, March 28, 2020. https://www.vox.com/covid-19-coronavirus-explainers/2020/3/28/21196382/japan-coronavirus-cases-covid-19-deaths-quarantine.

Masumoto, Naofumi. "Nagano 1998." In *Encyclopedia of the Modern Olympic Movement*, edited by John F. Findling and Kimberly Pelle, 415–19. Greenwood Press, 2004.

Mather, Victor. "How the Coronavirus Is Disrupting Sports Events." *New York Times*, March 11, 2020. https://advance-lexis-com.libproxy.wlu.ca/api/document?collection=news&id=urn: contentItem:5YD8-3KF1-JBG3-61Y3-00000-00&context=1516831.

Matsushita, Mitsuo, and James Henderson. "The Antimonopoly Law of Japan—Relating to International Business Transactions." *Case Western Reserve Journal of International Law* 4, no. 2/3 (1972): 124–60.

Matthews, Daniel. " 'We Dodged a Bullet': The 'Crazy' Inside Story of How an Olympic Boxing Qualifier in Wuhan Almost Went Ahead as Covid First Broke Out." *Daily Mail*, July 30, 2021. https://www.dailymail.co.uk/sport/article-9831307/The-crazy-inside-story-Olympic-boxing-qualifier-Wuhan-went-ahead.html.

McCallum, Jack. "Why More Americans Aren't Happy for Gregg Popovich." *The Atlantic*, August 7, 2021. https://www.theatlantic.com/ideas/archive/2021/08/olympian-struggles-gregg-popovich/619673/.

McCloskey, Brian. "Brian McCloskey: How Tokyo 2020 Paved the Way for Other Major Events." *Inside the Games*, August 6, 2022. https://www.insidethegames.biz/articles/1126658/blog-dr-brian-mccloskey.

McCloskey, Brian. "Tokyo 2020 Showed It Is Possible to Keep a Pandemic at Bay." *Olympics.com*, August 9, 2022. https://olympics.com/ioc/news/-tokyo-2020-showed-it-is-possible-to-keep-a-pandemic-at-bay.

McCloskey, Brian, et al. "The Tokyo 2020 and Beijing 2022 Olympic Games Held During the COVID-19 Pandemic: Planning, Outcomes, and Lessons Learnt." *The Lancet* 403, no. 10425 (2024): 493-502. https://www.thelancet.com/journals/lancet/article/PIIS0140-6736(23)02635-1/fulltext?uuid=uuid%3A24704d7e-2ebc-4e19-89a3-d8054d80af6d.

McCurry, Justin. "Japanese Olympic Official to Quit amid Corruption Allegations Scandal." *The Guardian*, March 19, 2019. https://www.theguardian.com/world/2019/mar/19/japan-olympic-committee-president-tsunekazu-takeda-to-resign-corruption-allegations-scandal.

Medland, Chris. "Formula One Loses Nearly $400 Million in COVID-Hit 2020." *Racer*, February 26, 2021. https://racer.com/2021/02/26/formula-1-loses-nearly-400m-in-covid-hit-2020/.

Michaels, Jake. "Australian Open Projects Financial Hit Topping $78m, Tournament Director Says." *ESPN*, February 18, 2021. https://www.espn.com/tennis/story/_/id/30925928/australian-open-projects-financial-hit-topping-78m-tournament-director-says.

Mickanen, Dylan. "Christine Sinclair, Canada Win First Gold Medal in Soccer." *NBC Sports*. 6 August 2021. archived August 6, 2021, at https://web.archive.org/web/20210806192542/https://www.nbcsports.com/northwest/tokyo-olympics/toyko-olympics-christine-sinclair-canada-win-first-gold-medal-womens.

Miguel, Inês, Rui Sofia, and Cláudia Dias. "Portuguese Olympic and Paralympic Athletes' Experiences of the Covid-19 Pandemic and the Postponement of the Tokyo 2020 Olympic Games." *International Journal of Sport and Exercise Psychology* 22, no. 8 (2023): 1932–50. https://doi.org/10.1080/1612197X.2023.2238296.

Minichiello, Tony. "Games Must Be Delayed to Save Integrity." *The Times*, 20 March 2020. https://advance-lexis-com.libproxy.wlu.ca/api/document?collection=news&id=urn:contentItem:5YG3-S2S1-DYTY-C2PF-00000-00&context=1516831.

Mizuno, Sho. "WHO Remarks on Laxness Led to Stricter IOC Playbook." *Japan Times*, June 16, 2021. https://japannews.yomiuri.co.jp/sports/olympics-paralympics/20210616-52897/.

Moore, Sarah. "History of COVID-19." *News—Medical Life Sciences*, September 28, 2021, updated September 28, 2021. https://www.news-medical.net/health/History-of-COVID-19.aspx.

Morgan, Liam. "IOC Claim One Boxer Diagnosed with Coronavirus After European Qualifier Returned False Positive." *Inside The Games*, March 28, 2020. https://www.insidethegames.biz/articles/1092531/ioc-claim-one-boxer-false-covid-19-test.

"Mr. Thomas Bach." Accessed December 24, 2024. https://olympics.com/ioc/mr-thomas-bach.

Mundell, E. J. "Diamond Princess Saga Began with One COVID Carrier." *WebMD*, July 29, 2020. https://www.webmd.com/lung/news/20200729/gene-study-shows-how-coronavirus-swept-through-the-idiamond-princessi#1.

"Nagano Games Tainted by Scandal." *Toronto Star*, January 18, 1999. C8.

Nakamaru, Ryotaro. "FOCUS: Olympic Postponement Throws Wrench into Abe's Plans." *Japan Economic Newswire*, March 24, 2020. https://advance-lexis-com.libproxy.wlu.ca/api/document?collection=news&id=urn:contentItem:5YH5-82Y1-DYN6-W16F-00000-00&context=1516831.

Nakamaru, Ryotaro. "FOCUS: Race to Succeed Abe Kicks Off with No Clear Favorite." *Japan Economic Newswire*, August 29, 2020. https://advance-lexis-com.libproxy.wlu.ca/api/document?collection=news&id=urn:contentItem:60PN-6DN1-JC5B-G4FT-00000-00&context=1516831.

Nakamichi, Takashi, and Yuki Furukawa. "More Companies Pull Out of Tokyo Olympics Opening Ceremony." *Bloomberg*, July 20, 2021. https://www.bloomberg.com/news/articles/2021-07-20/more-companies-pull-out-of-tokyo-olympics-opening-ceremony.

Nakano, Koichi. "Japan Can't Handle the Coronavirus. Can It Host the Olympics?" *New York Times*, February 26, 2020. https://advance-lexis-com.libproxy.wlu.ca/api/document?collection=news&id=urn:contentItem:5Y96-RCH1-DXY4-X1JB-00000-00&context=1516831.

Nakao, Yuka. "FOCUS: Tokyo Stocks Seen Climbing in 2021 on Economic Recovery from Pandemic." *Japan Economic Newswire*, December 30, 2020. https://advance-lexis-com.libproxy.wlu.ca/api/document?collection=news&id=urn:contentItem:61MW-HP21-DYMD-60FW-00000-00&context=1516831.

Nakazawa, Eisuke, Hiroyasu Ino, and Akira Akabayashi. "Chronology of COVID-19 Cases on the Diamond Princess Cruise Ship and Ethical Considerations: A Report from Japan." *Disaster Medicine and Public Health Preparedness* 14, no. 4 (2020): 506–13. https://www.ncbi.nlm.nih.gov/pmc/articles/PMC7156812/.

"New Data Shows no COVID-19 Spread Between Tokyo 2020 Participants and Local Population." *Olympics.com*, December 30, 2021. https://olympics.com/ioc/news/new-data-shows-no-covid-19-spread-between-tokyo-2020-participants-and-local-population.

"New Zealand and Australia Were Covid Success Stories. Why Are They Behind on Vaccine Rollouts?" *CNN*, April 15, 2021. https://www.cnn.com/2021/04/15/asia/new-zealand-australia-covid-vaccine-intl-dst-hnk/index.html.

Nishida, Masaki, et al. "Mental Health Services at the Tokyo 2020 Olympic and Paralympic Games during the COVID-19 Pandemic." *Sports Psychiatry: Journal of Sports and Exercise Psychiatry* 1, no. 2 (2022): 36–38. https://doi.org/10.1024/2674-0052/a000005.

Nugent, Ciara. "Athletes on the Front Line." *Time*, July 19, 2021, 84–85. https://search-ebscohostcom.libproxy.wlu.ca/login.aspx?direct=true&AuthType=ip,cookie,url,uid&db=rgm&AN=151321354&site=ehost-live.

"Olympic Boxing Qualifiers Moved to Jordan." *Japan Times*, January 25, 2020. https://www.japantimes.co.jp/sports/2020/01/25/more-sports/boxing-2/olympic-boxing-qualifiers-moved-jordan/.

"The Olympic Agenda 2020 + 5." https://stillmed.olympics.com/media/Document%20Library/Olympic Org/IOC/What-We-Do/Olympic-agenda/Olympic-Agenda-2020-5-15-recommendations.pdf.

"Olympic Games, Olympic Stadium, Tokyo, 30 Jul–08 Aug 2021, Decathlon—1500 Meters Men, 05 Aug 2021 21:40." *World Athletics*. https://www.worldathletics.org/competitions/olympic-games/the-xxxii-olympic-games-athletics-7132391/results/men/decathlon/1500-metres/points.

"Olympic Games, Olympic Stadium, Tokyo, 30 Jul–08 Aug 2021, Results, 110 Metres Hurdles." *World Athletics*, archived October 23, 2021. https://web.archive.org/web/20211023182952/https://worldathletics.org/competitions/Olympic-games/the-xxxii-olympic-games-athletics-7132391/results/men/decathlon/110-metres-hurdles/summary.

"Olympic Games, Olympic Stadium, Tokyo, 30 Jul–08 Aug 2021, Decathlon—Discus Throw Men, 05 Aug 2021 09:50." *World Athletics*. https://worldathletics.org/competitions/olympic-games/the-xxxii-olympic-games-athletics-7132391/results/men/decathlon/discus-throw/summary.

"Olympic Games, Olympic Stadium, Tokyo, 30 Jul–08 Aug 2021, Decathlon—Pole Vault Men, 05 Aug 2021 12:45." *World Athletics*. https://worldathletics.org/competitions/olympic-games/the-xxxii-olympic-games-athletics-7132391/results/men/decathlon/pole-vault/summary.

"Olympic Games, Olympic Stadium, Tokyo, 30 Jul – 08 Aug 2021, Decathlon—Javelin Throw Men 05 Aug 2021, 19:15." *World Athletics*. https://worldathletics.org/competitions/olympic-games/the-xxxii-olympic-games-athletics-7132391/results/men/decathlon/javelin-throw/summary.

"Olympics: Qualifiers Set for Wuhan Nixed over Health Fears." *Reuters*, January 22, 2020. https://www.reuters.com/article/uk-olympics-2020-boxing-health-idUKKBN1ZL0H6.

"Olympics: French Prosecutors Believe Singaporean Tan Tong Han Played a Role in Bribing Voters for Tokyo 2020." *The Straits Times*, October 15, 2020. https://www.straitstimes.com/sport/olympics-french-prosecutors-believe-singaporean-tan-tong-han-played-a-role-in-bribing-voters.

"Olympics: Japanese Federations Hoping to Retain Help of Foreign Coaches." *Japan Economic Newswire*, May 4, 2020. https://advance-lexis-com.libproxy.wlu.ca/api/document?collection=news&id=urn:contentItem:5YTP-3DW1-DYN6-W0FX-00000-00&context=1516831.

"Olympics: Japan's Biggest Ad Agency Indicted in Growing Games Scandal." *The Straits Times*, November 25, 2024, https://www.straitstimes.com/sport/japan-authorities-seek-criminal-charges-against-dentsu-others-over-olympics-contracts.

"Olympics: Qualifiers Set for Wuhan Nixed over Health Fears." *Reuters*, January 22, 2020. https://www.reuters.com/article/uk-olympics-2020-boxing-health-idUKKBN1ZL0H6.

"Olympics: Tokyo Organizers Securing Schedule, Venues for Delayed Games." *Japan Economic Newswire*, April 16, 2020. https://advance-lexis-com.libproxy.wlu.ca/api/document?collection=news&id=urn:contentItem:5YP2-K9H1-DYN6-W54J-00000-00&context=1516831.

O'Shea, Paul, and Sebastian Maslow, "The 2020/2021 Tokyo Olympics: Does Japan Get the Gold Medal or the Wooden Spoon?" *Contemporary Japan* 35, no. 1 (2023): 16–34. https://doi.org/10.1080/18692729.2023.2169819.

Palmer, Dan. "Japan Win First Olympic Baseball Title to Complete Diamond Double in Tokyo." *Inside the Games*, August 7, 2021. https://www.insidethegames.biz/articles/1111355/baseball-tokyo-2020-gold-medal-game.

Palmer, Dan. "Number of COVID-19 Cases at Tokyo 2020 So Far 'As Expected' Says Doctor Advising IOC." *Inside the Games*, July 19, 2021. https://www.insidethegames.biz/articles/1110416/tokyo-2020-panel-mccloskey.

Panja, Tariq. "The I.O.C. Let and Olympic Boxing Qualifier Happen Despite Virus Warnings." *New York Times*, March 27, 2020. https://www.nytimes.com/2020/03/27/sports/olympics/coronavirus-ioc-boxing.html.

Panja, Tariq, and Matthew Futterman. "Canada Withdraws from Summer Olympics as I.O.C. Weighs Postponement." *New York Times*, March 22, 2020. https://advance-lexis-com.libproxy.wlu.ca/api/document?collection=news&id=urn:contentItem:5YGK-SJM1-DXY4-X533-00000-00&context=1516831.

Park, Alice, Mayako Shibata, and Leslie Dickstein. "The Pandemic Games." *Time*, July 19, 2021, 58–61. https://search-ebscohost-com.libproxy.wlu.ca/login.aspx?direct=true&AuthType=ip,cookie,url,uid&db=rgm&AN=151321306&site=ehost-live.

Parkes, Ian. "A Formula 1 Season Like No Other." *New York Times*, August 7, 2020. https://www.nytimes.com/2020/08/07/sports/autoracing/formula-1-season-coronavirus.html.

Pavitt, Michael. "Bujold Succeeds in Appeal to Compete at Tokyo 2020 Olympics." *Inside the Games*, July 1, 2021. https://www.insidethegames.biz/articles/1109660/bujold-boxing-tokyo-2020-appeal-win.

Pereira, Ivan, and Arielle Mitropoulos. "A Year of COVID-19: What Was Going On in the US in March 2020." *ABC News*, March 6, 2021. https://abcnews.go.com/Health/year-covid-19-us-march-2020/story?id=76204691.

Perry, Dayn, Katherine Acquavella, and R. J. Anderson. "Timeline of How the COVID-19 Pandemic Has Impacted the 2020 Major League Baseball Season." *CBS Sports*, July 29, 2020. https://www.cbssports.com/mlb/news/timeline-of-how-the-covid-19-pandemic-has-impacted-the-2020-major-league-baseball-season/.

"Pfizer and BioNTech Announce Further Details on Collaboration to Accelerate Global COVID-19 Vaccine Development." *Pfizer*, April 9, 2020. https://www.pfizer.com/news/press-release/press-release-detail/pfizer-and-biontech-announce-further-details-collaboration.

Pickman, Ben. "Water Wait." *Sports Illustrated*, May 2020, 480.

The Playbook: Athletes and Officials—Your Guide to a Safe and Successful Games, vol. 3. June 2021. https://stillmed.olympics.com/media/Documents/Olympic-Games/Tokyo-2020/Playbooks/The-Playbook-Athletes-and-Officials-V3.pdf?ga=2.139479667.1325720664.1677506866-2077939235.166626814145.

The Playbook: Broadcasters—Your Guide to a Safe and Successful Games," vol. 3. June 2021. https://stillmed.olympics.com/media/Documents/Olympic-Games/Tokyo-2020/Playbooks/The-Playbook-Broadcasters-V3.pdf?ga=2.80881623.1325720664.1677506866-2077939235.1666268141.

The Playbook: International Federations—Your Guide to a Safe and Successful Games. February 2021. https://stillmedab.olympic.org/media/Document%20Library/Olympic Org/Games/Summer-Games/Games-Tokyo-2020-Olympic-Games/Playbooks/The-Playbook-International-Federations.pdf.

The Playbook: Marketing Partners—Your Guide to a Safe and Successful Games, vol. 3. June 2021. https://stillmed.olympics.com/media/Documents/Olympic-Games/Tokyo-2020/Playbooks/The-Playbook-Marketing-Partners-V3.pdf?_ga=2.77858004. 1325720664.1677506866-2077939235.1666268141.

"President Bach Pays Final Respects to Former Prime Minister Abe Shinzo." *Olympics.com*, September 28, 2022. https://olympics.com/ioc/news/president-bach-pays-final-respects-to-former-prime-minister-abe-shinzo#:~:text=After%20the%20State%20Funeral%2C%20which,and%20Abe%20Shinzo's%20widow%2C%20Akie.

Prewitt, Alex. "Hayley Wickenheiser Is Using Her Unique Platform in Global Fight Against COVID-19." *Sports Illustrated*, April 11, 2020. https://www.si.com/olympics/2020/04/11/hayley-wickenheiser-ice-hockey-medical-school-doctor-coronavirus.

Prewitt, Alex. "Standard of Caring." *Sports Illustrated*, May 2020, 22–24. https://search-ebscohost-com.libproxy.wlu.ca/login.aspx?direct=true&AuthType=ip,cookie,url,uid&db=rgm&AN=142960517&site=ehost-live.

Price, Sam. "Covid 19: The Athlete Response." *Olympic Review* April/May/June 2020 (115). 36–42.

"Prime Minister Abe's Participation in the 70th Session of the United Nations General Session." *Ministry of Foreign Affairs of Japan*, October 5, 2015. https://www.mofa.go.jp/mofaj/fp/unp_a/page3e_000395.html.

"Project Crystal: Scenario Working Group." PowerPoint presentation. IOC Games Delivery Office, July 8, 2020.

Pyette, Ryan. "Inside London Decathlete Damian Warner's Pandemic Path to Glory." *London Free Press*, June 14, 2021. https://lfpress.com/sports/local-sports/it-took-quick-thinking-and-an-old-rink-to-get-damian-warner-back-on-track.

"Results: Hypo Meeting Gotzis 2021." *Watch Athletics*, accessed December 25, 2024. https://www.watchathletics.com/page/2419/results-hypo-meeting-gotzis-2021.

"Revenue Generated Worldwide by the Formula One Group for 2017–2020." *Statista*, December 9, 2022. https://www.statista.com/statistics/1137226/formula-one-revenue/.

Reynolds, Isabel, and Josh Wingrove. "President Trump Suggests Tokyo Olympics Should be Postponed 1 Year." *Time*, March 12, 2020. https://time.com/5802271/trump-tokyo-olympics-coronavirus/.

Rich, Motoko. "Shinzo Abe, Japan's Longest-Serving Prime Minister, Resigns Because of Illness." *New York Times*, August 28, 2020. https://advance-lexis-com.libproxy.wlu.ca/api/document?collection=news&id=urn:contentItem:60PD-YXR1-DXY4-X2CD-00000-00&context=1516831.

Rich, Motoko. "Tokyo Chief Expected To Resign Over Sexism." *New York Times*, February 12, 2021. https://advance-lexis-com.libproxy.wlu.ca/api/document?collection=news&id=urn: contentItem:6209-27G1-JBG3-632G-00000-00&context=1516831.

Rich, Motoko. "Tokyo's First Female Governor Sails to Re-Election Even as Virus Cases Rise." *New York Times*, July 5, 2020. https://advance-lexis-com.libproxy.wlu.ca/api/document?collection=news&id=urn:contentItem:608Y-N151-DXY4-X417-00000-00& context=1516831.

Rich, Motoko. "Tokyo Olympics Chief Resigns Over Sexist Comments." *New York Times*, February 11, 2021. https://advance-lexis-com.libproxy.wlu.ca/api/document?collection=news&id=urn:contentItem:6204-1K21-JBG3-62FM-00000-00&context=1516831.

Rich, Motoko. "Trump's Phone Buddy in North Korea Crisis: Shinzo Abe." *New York Times*, September 5, 2017. https://www-nytimes-com.libproxy.wlu.ca/2017/09/05/world/asia/japan-trump-north-korea-abe.html?searchResultPosition=1.

Rich, Motoko, and Ben Dooley, "Tokyo's New Challenge: Putting the Games in Mothballs." *New York Times*, March 26, 2020. https://advance-lexis-com.libproxy.wlu.ca/api/document?collection=news&id=urn:contentItem:5YHD-FJ11-DXY4-X4H3-00000-00&context=1516831.

Rich, Motoko, and Makiko Inoue. "Japan Declares State of Emergency in Tokyo Area After Days of Hesitation." *New York Times*, January 7, 2021. https://advance-lexis-com. libproxy.wlu.ca/api/document?collection=news&id=urn:contentItem:61PK-D7S1-JBG3-61WM-00000-00&context=1516831.

Rich, Motoko, Andrew Keh, and Matthew Futterman. "Tokyo Olympics Playbook: Testing? Yes. Quarantines? No. Fans? Maybe." *New York Times*, February 3, 2021. https://advance-lexis-com.libproxy.wlu.ca/api/document?collection=news&id=urn:contentItem: 61XC-SGG1-DXY4-X2F8-00000-00&context=1516831.

Rich, Motoko, and Matthew Futterman. "Tokyo Olympics Organizers Promote Games as Light at End of Pandemic Tunnel." *New York Times*, November 19, 2020. https://advance-lexis-com.libproxy.wlu.ca/api/document?collection=news&id=urn:contentItem:61B4-YGD1-DXY4-X07X-00000-00&context=1516831.

Rich, Motoko, Matthew Futterman, and Tariq Panja. "I.O.C. and Japan Agree to Postpone Tokyo Olympics." *New York Times*, March 24, 2020. https://www.nytimes.com/2020/03/24/sports/olympics/coronavirus-summer-olympics-postponed.html#:~:text=On%20 Tuesday%2C%20the%20virus%20won,in%20late%20July%2C%20until%202021.

Rich, Motoko, Makiko Inoue, and Ben Dooley. "Japan's Next Prime Minister Emerges From Behind the Curtain." *New York Times*, September 14, 2020. https://advance-lexis-com.libproxy.wlu.ca/api/document?.collection=news&id=urn:contentItem:60V2-MNY1-DXY4-X007-00000-00&context=1516831.

Rich, Motoko, Makiko Inoue, and Hikari Hida. "Olympics Chief Said Sorry for Demeaning Women. In Japan, That's Often Enough." *New York Times*, February 9, 2021. https://advance-lexis-com.libproxy.wlu.ca/api/document?collection=news&id=urn:contentItem:61YN-4T41-JBG3-6072-00000-00&context=1516831.

Rich, Motoko, Hisako Ueno, and Makiko Inoue. "Japan Declares Emergency as Experts Fear 'Tip of the Iceberg.'" *New York Times*, April 8, 2020. https://advance-lexis-com.libproxy.wlu.ca/api/document?collection=news&id=urn:contentItem:5YM5-BKN1-DXY4-X4M9-00000-00&context=1516831.

Rich, Motoko, and Tariq Panja. "U.S. Olympic Committee Urges Postponing Summer Games in Tokyo." *New York Times*, March 23, 2020. https://advance-lexis-om.libproxy.wlu.ca/api/document?collection=news&id=urn:contentItem: 5YGT-NG81-JBG3-6077-00000-00&context=1516831.

Richards, Giles. "Drive to Survive Documentary Helping Bring In New Generation of US F1 Fans." *The Guardian*, May 5, 2022. https://www.theguardian.com/sport/2022/may/05/drive-to-survive-documentary-helping-bring-in-new-generation-of-us-f1-fans.

"Rio Olympics Chief Sentenced to 30 Years in Prison for Buying 201 Votes." *The Guardian*, November 26, 2021. https://www.theguardian.com/sport/2021/nov/26/rio-olympics-chief-sentenced-to-30-years-in-prison-for-buying-2016-votes.

Roan, Dan, and Laura Scott. "Coronavirus: Six Members of Boxing Teams Who Attended Qualifier Said to Have Tested Positive." *BBC*, March 26, 2020. https://www.bbc.com/sport/olympics/52047624.

Rogers, Morgan, and Penny Werthner. "Gathering Narratives: Athletes' Experiences Preparing for the Tokyo Summer Olympic Games During a Global Pandemic." *Journal of Applied Sport Psychology* 35, no. 2 (2022): 330–48. https://doi.org/10.1080/10413200.2022.2032477.

Ronay, Barney. "Unassailable Thompson-Herah Strikes Second Gold in 200m Final." *The Guardian*, August 3, 2021. https://www.theguardian.com/sport/2021/aug/03/elaine-thompson-herah-strikes-second-gold-of-tokyo-2020-in-200m-final.

Rossiter, Antonia, Thomas M. Comyns, Ian Sherwin, Alan M. Nevill, Mark J. Campbell, and Giles D. Warrington. "Effects of Long-Haul Transmeridian Travel on Physiological, Sleep, Perceptual and Mood Markers in Olympic Team Support Staff." *Chronobiology International* 39, no. 12 (2022): 1640–55. https://doi.org/10.1080/07420528.2022.2139186.

Salvador, Joseph. "Popovich Took Shot at Critics After Gold Medal Win: 'How the F— You Like Us Now?'" *Sports Illustrated*, August 16, 2021. https://www.si.com/nba/2021/08/16/gregg-popovich-calls-out-critics-in-speech-after-gold-medal-win.

Sasaki, Sayo. "UPDATE2: Suga Elected as Successor to Japan PM Abe in Party Vote." *Japan Economic Newswire*, September 14, 2020. https://advance-lexis-com.libproxy

.wlu.ca/api/document?collection=news&id=urn:contentItem:60V3-0931-DYMD-603K-0000-00&context=1516831.
Sasaki, Sayo. "UPDATE5: Japan PM, IOC Head Agree Olympics to Happen as Planned Next Summer." *Japan Economic Newswire*, 16 November 2020. https://advance-lexis-6com.libproxy.wlu.ca/api/document?collection=news&id=urn:contentItem:619H-H5G1-JC5B-G051-00000-00&context=1516831.
Schöttli, Urs. "Japan After Tokyo 2020: Back to Power Politics." *GIS Reports*, September 10, 2021. https://www.gisreportsonline.com/r/tokyo-2020/.
"See Inside China's Huoshenshan Hospital Built in 10 Days." *CBC*, February 3, 2020. https://www.cbc.ca/news/world/coronavirus-china-huoshenshan-hospital-photos-1.5450026.
Sharp, Andrew. "The Turbulent Journey to the Opening of Tokyo 2020." *Asia Nikkei*, July 19, 2021. https://asia.nikkei.com/Spotlight/Tokyo-2020-Olympics/The-turbulent-journey-to-the-opening-of-Tokyo-2020.
Shimizu, Ayano. "FEATURE: Pandemic Causing Uncertainty, Unease for Tokyo Olympic 'Host Towns.'" *Japan Economic Newswire*, December 7, 2020. https://advance-lexis-com.libproxy.wlu.ca/api/document?collection=news&id=urn:contentItem:61M7-8YV1-DYMD-60RK-00000-00&context=1516831.
Shimizu, Ayano. "UPDATE2: IOC's Bach Says Tokyo Olympics Will Be Held, 'No Plan B.'" *Japan Economic Newswire*, January 28, 2021. https://advance-lexis-com.libproxy.wlu.ca/api/document?collection=news&id=urn:contentItem:61TM-39X1-JC5B-G271-00000-00&context=1516831.
Shimizu, Kazuki, Devi Sridhar, Kiyosu Taniguchi, and Kenji Shibuya. "Reconsider This Summer's Olympic and Paralympic Games." *BMJ* 372, April 14, 2021. https://www.bmj.com/content/bmj/373/bmj.n962.full.pdf.
Shuman, Amanda, and Philippe Vonnard. "Taking Nature into Account? The International Olympic Committee Confronts Environmental Issues (1960s–1990s)." *Journal of Olympic Studies* 6 (forthcoming).
Smith, Doug, and Kerry Gillespie. "Mandy Bujold Falls Ill, Loses Quarter-Final at Rio Olympics." *Toronto Star*, August 16, 2016. https://www.thestar.com/sports/olympics/2016/08/16/canadian-mandy-bujold-loses-boxing-quarter-final-at-rio-olympics.html.
Silverman, Drew. "Jerry Colangelo, Long-Time Architect of USA Basketball, Reflects on a Golden Career." *USA Basketball*, July 29, 2021. https://www.usab.com/news-events/news/2021/07/jerry-colangelo-feature.aspx
Slater, John. "Tokyo 1964." In *Encyclopedia of the Modern Olympic Movement*, edited by John F. Findling and Kimberly Pelle, 165–73. Greenwood Press, 2004.
Slater, Matt. "IOC Suspends AIBA and Appoints Special Task Force to Run 2020 Olympics Boxing Tournament." *The Independent*, May 23, 2019. https://www.independent.co.uk/sport/boxing/ioc-suspends-aiba-task-force-tokyo-2020-olympics-boxing-tournament-a8926596.html.
Smith, Evan. "Penn State Basketball's Lamar Stevens, the 'Heart and Soul' of Cavaliers." *Victory Bell Rings*, January 2022. https://victorybellrings.com/2022/01/14/psus-lamar-stevens-the-heart-and-soul-of-the-cleveland-cavaliers/.
Smith, Gary. "Lessons from the Master: Emil Beck, the Obsessive West German Coach, Turns Out the World's Best Fencers at His Tauberbischofsheim Training Center." *Sports Illustrated*, September 14, 1988. https://vault.si.com/vault/1988/09/14/lessons-

from-the-master-emil-beck-the-obsessive-west-german-coach-turns-out-the-worlds-best-fencers-at-his-tauberbischofsheim-training-center.

Smith, Sheila A. "Here's Why Tokyo Is Hosting the Summer Olympics Despite COVID-19." *Council on Foreign Relations*, June 28, 2021. https://www.cfr.org/in-brief/heres-why-tokyo-hosting-summer-olympics-despite-covid-19#:~:text=For%20Prime%20Minister%20Shinzo%20Abe,from%20difficulty%2C%20and%20its%20hospitality.

Solís, Mireya, and David Dollar. "The 2020 Olympics Were Always Meant to Be a Story of Resilience." *Dollars & Sense*, podcast, Brookings Institution, August 2, 2021. https://www.brookings.edu/podcast-episode/the-2020-tokyo-olympics-were-always-meant-to-be-a-story-of-resilience/.

Solis-Moreira, Jocelyn. "How Did We Develop a COVID-19 Vaccine So Quickly?" *Medical News Today*, November 13, 2021. https://www.medicalnewstoday.com/articles/how-did-we-develop-a-covid-19-vaccine-so-quickly.

Sparrow, Annie K., Lisa M. Brosseau, Robert J. Harrison, and Michael T. Osterholm, "Protecting Olympic Participants from COVID-19—The Urgent Need for a Risk-Management Approach." *New England Journal of Medicine* 385, no. 1 (2021). https://www.nejm.org/doi/full/10.1056/NEJMp2108567.

Spezia, Mark. "Denied Three Times, Ashley Twichell Clinches a Spot (Maybe More) at 2020 Tokyo Olympics." *ESPN*, September 20, 2019. https://www.espn.com/espnw/life-style/story/_/id/27643598/denied-three-s-ashley-twichell-clinches-spot-maybe-more-2020-tokyo-olympics.

Stein, Marc. "Also Postponed: A Coach's Quest for Olympic Gold." *New York Times*, 28 March 2020. https://advance-lexis-com.libproxy.wlu.ca/document/?pdmfid=1516831&crid=1e90ac33-eabc-475e-863e-598a1a49be91&pddocfullpath=%2Fshared%2Fdocument%2Fnews%2Furn%3AcontentItem%3A5YJ2-J2W1-DXY4-X45J-00000000&pdcontentcomponentid=6742&pdteaserkey=sr40&pditab=allpods&ecomp=zznyk&earg=sr40&prid=def6fdd8-6b6f-4583-9680-c61726f3b497.

Stoneman, Michael. "Here We Go." *Olympic Review* 115 (April-May-June 2020), 31–32.

Strashin, Jamie. "Mandy Bujold's Olympic Fight Comes to Quick End After Legal Battle to Reach Tokyo." *CBC*, July 24, 2021. https://www.cbc.ca/sports/olympics/summer/boxing/olympics-mandy-bujold-boxing-july25-1.6116259.

Stead, Aiden George. "The Pandemic Olympics: A Thematic Analysis of COVID-19 and the Tokyo Olympic Games." M.A. (Human Kinetics), University of Ottawa, 2022. https://ruor.uottawa.ca/server/api/core/bitstreams/649c17fb-0f64-420a-881d-f1a77e28e864/content.

Strydom, Martin. "Japan Slides Towards Recession After Typhoon." *The Times*, February 18, 2020. https://advance-lexis-com.libproxy.wlu.ca/api/document?collection=news&id=urn:contentItem:5Y7G-NHH1-JCBW-N2MW-00000-00&context=1516831.

Sutherland, James. "Tokyo 2020, IOC Look Toward Simplified Games, Present Progress Reports." *SwimSwam*, June 10, 2020. https://swimswam.com/tokyo-2020-ioc-look-toward-simplified-games-present-progress-reports/.

Suzuki, Noriyuki. "FOCUS: Coronavirus Response an Unexpected, Crucial Test for Abe." *Japan Economic Newswire*, February 29, 2020. https://advance-lexis-com.libproxy.wlu.ca/api/document?collection=news&id=urn:contentItem:5YB2-4841-DYN6-W06X-00000-00&context=1516831.

Suzuki, Noriyuki. "UPDATE1: Will Abe Declare Emergency over Coronavirus After Law Revision?" *Japan Economic Newswire*, March 13, 2020. https://advance-lexis-com.libproxy.wlu.ca/api/document?collection=news&id=urn:contentItem:5YDT-K441-DYN6-W0X4-00000-00&context=1516831.

Suzuki, Noriyuki. "UPDATE4: Tokyo Olympics Postponed Until 2021 Due to Coronavirus Pandemic." *Japan Economic Newswire*, March 24, 2020. https://advance-lexis-com.libproxy.wlu.ca/api/document?collection=news&id=urn:contentItem:5YH5-82Y1-DYN6-W14G-00000-00&context=1516831.

Suzuki, Noriyuki. "Will Abe Declare Emergency over Coronavirus After Law Revision?" *Japan Economic Newswire*, March 13, 2020. https://advance-lexis-com.libproxy.wlu.ca/api/document?collection=news&id=urn:contentItem:5YDT-K441-DYN6-W10G-00000-00&context=1516831.

Sylt, Christian. "Why 2020 Could Be the Most Crucial Year in F1's History." *Forbes*, January 12, 2020. https://www.forbes.com/sites/csylt/2020/01/12/why-2020-could-be-the-most-crucial-year-in-f1s-history/?sh=209d1ecc308c.

Tahara, Junko. "Sapporo 1972." In *Encyclopedia of the Modern Olympic Movement*, edited by John F. Findling and Kimberly Pelle, 359–65. Greenwood Press, 2004.

Takahashi, Ryusei. "We'll All Be Losers in 2020, Olympic Activists Say." *Japan Times*, July 23, 2019. https://www.japantimes.co.jp/news/2019/07/23/national/well-losers-2020-anti-olympic-activists-say/.

Talmazan, Yuliya. "New Dates Announced for Tokyo 2020 Olympics Postponed over Coronavirus Concerns." *NBC News*, March 30, 2020. https://www.nbcnews.com/news/world/new-dates-announced-tokyo-2020-olympics-postponed-over-coronavirus-concerns-n1171871.

"Thomas Bach Re-elected as IOC President for Second Term." *Olympics.com*, March 10, 2021. https://olympics.com/ioc/news/thomas-bach-re-elected-as-ioc-president-for-second-term.

Thomson, Alice. "This Has Given My Body a Chance to Rest; Right Now, Tom Daley Should Have Been Preparing for the Olympics, but With the Pools Closed He's Spending Time with His Son, He Tells Alice Thomson." *The Times*, June 9, 2020. https://advance-lexis-com.libproxy.wlu.ca/api/document?collection=news&id=urn:contentItem:603C-7K81-DYTY-C3W5-00000-00&context=1516831.

Thornton, Jane. "How the COVID-19 Delay of the Tokyo Olympics Helped Some Athletes Break Records." *The Conversation*, July 20, 2021. Jane Thornton, "How the COVID-19 Delay of the Tokyo Olympics Helped Some Athletes Break Records," *The Conversation*, July 20, 2021, https://theconversation.com/how-the-covid-19-delay-of-the-tokyo-olympics-helped-some-athletes-break-records-163861. https://theconversation.com/how-the-covid-19-delay-of-the-tokyo-olympics-helped-some-athletes-break-records-163861.

Tokunaga, Munehisa. "UPDATE1: Nikkei Falls to Lowest Level in 3 Yrs as Market Routed Amid Virus Fear." *Japan Economic Newswire*, March 13, 2020. https://advance-lexis-com.libproxy.wlu.ca/api/document?collection=news&id=urn:contentItem:5YDT-K441-DYN6-W0Y6-00000-00&context=1516831.

"Tokyo 2020 Reflects on Global Success, with Games Legacy Already Inspiring Future Generations." *Olympics.com*, February 3, 2022. https://olympics.com/ioc/news/tokyo-2020-reflects-on-global-success-with-games-legacy-already-inspiring-future-generations.

"Tokyo, Olympic Organizers in Rough Waters 1 Month After Postponement." *Japan Economic Newswire*, April 24, 2020. https://advance-lexis-com.libproxy.wlu.ca/api/document?collection=news&id=urn:contentItem:5YRJ-CPG1-DYN6-W1D7-00000-00&context=1516831.

"Tokyo Olympics: More Than 80% of Japanese Oppose Hosting Games—Poll." *The Guardian*, May 17, 2021. https://www.theguardian.com/world/2021/may/17/tokyo-olympics-more-than-80-of-japanese-oppose-hosting-games-poll#:~:text=More%20than%2080%25%20of%20Japanese%20people%20 oppose%20hosting%20the%20Olympics,fourth%20wave%20of.

"Tokyo Olympics Opening Ceremony." *CBS News*, July 23, 2023. https://www.cbsnews.com/pictures/tokyo-olympics-2021/.

"Tokyo Olympics: We Are on the Guillotine at the Moment, Says Covid-Hit South African Team Coach." *India Today*, July 19, 2021. https://www.indiatoday.in/sports/tokyo-olympics/story/covid-hit-south-african-football-team-coach-david-notoane-tokyo-2020-olympic-village-1830137-2021-07-19.

"Top Olympic Broadcasters Reveal How COVID-19 Has Affected Plans for Tokyo 2020 and Beyond." *Olympics.com*, March 12, 2021. https://olympics.com/ioc/news/top-olympic-broadcasters-reveal-how-covid-19-has-affected-plans-for-tokyo-2020-and-beyond.

"Tracking Covid-19's Global Spread." *CNN*, April 5, 2022. https://edition.cnn.com/interactive/2020/health/coronavirus-maps-and-cases/.

Turner, Abigail. "The Importance of Preserving the History of the COVID-19 Pandemic." *Global News*, March 12, 2021. https://globalnews.ca/news/7692671/coronavirus-covid-19-pandemic-preserve-history/.

"TV Olympic Viewership for Opening Ceremony 56% in Tokyo Area." *Kyodo News*, July 2, 2021. https://english.kyodonews.net/news/2021/07/5d9fc4259ba7-breaking-news-tv-viewer-rating-for-tokyo-olympic-opening-ceremony-at-564.html.

"UPDATE1: Japanese Athletes Generally Positive to Tokyo Olympic Postponement." *Japan Economic Newswire*, March 25, 2020. https://advance-lexis-com.libproxy.wlu.ca/api/document?collection=news&id=urn:contentItem:5YHC-7BG1-DYN6-W534-00000-00&context=1516831.

"UPDATE1: Japan's Diet Gives Abe Power to Declare Emergency amid Viral Fears." *Japan Economic Newswire*, March 13, 2020. https://advance-lexis-com.libproxy.wlu.ca/api/document?collection=news&id=urn:contentItem:5YDT-K441-DYN6-W10W-00000-00&context=1516831.

"UPDATE1: Lower House Passes Virus Bill Allowing Abe to Declare Emergency." *Japan Economic Newswire*, March 12, 2020. https://advance-lexis-com.libproxy.wlu.ca/api/document?collection=news&id=urn: contentItem:5YDK-KXB1-DYN6-W103-00000-00&context=1516831.

"UPDATE2: Delayed Tokyo Olympics to Retain Same Venues, Competition Schedule." *Japan Economic Newswire*, July 17, 2020. https://advance-lexis-com.libproxy.wlu.ca/api/document?collection=news&id=urn:contentItem:60CJ-3CV1-DYMD-61D1-00000-00&context=1516831.

"UPDATE2: Japan Adopts Basic Policy to Fight Coronavirus Outbreak." *Japan Economic Newswire*, February 25, 2020. https://advance-lexis-com.libproxy.wlu.ca/api/document?collection=news&id=urn:contentItem:5Y96-7JR1-JC65-520W-00000-00&context=1516831.

"UPDATE2: Japan Approves Nearly $1 Tril. Package to Cushion Coronavirus Impact." *Japan Economic Newswire*, April 7, 2020. https://advance-lexis-com.libproxy.wlu.ca/api/document?collection=news&id=urn:contentItem:5YM4-VNP1-DYN6-W095-00000-00&context=1516831.

"UPDATE3: Abe Hints at Possibility of Postponing Tokyo Olympics." *Japan Economic Newswire*, March 23, 2020. https://advance-lexis-com.libproxy.wlu.ca/api/document?collection=news&id=urn:contentItem:5YGY-8YV1-JC65-52RB-00000-00&context=1516831.

"UPDATE3: IOC Confirms Tokyo Olympics to Be Held as Planned." *Japan Economic Newswire*, March 18, 2020. https://advance-lexis-com.libproxy.wlu.ca/api/document?collection=news&id=urn:contentItem:5YFW-F0X1-DYN6-W3F0-00000-00&context=1516831.

"UPDATE3: Japan Adopts Basic Policy to Fight Coronavirus Outbreak." *Japan Economic Newswire*, February 25, 2020. https://advance-lexis-com.libproxy.wlu.ca/api/document?collection=news&id=urn:contentItem:5Y96-7JR1-JC65-521F-00000-00&context=1516831.

"UPDATE3: Japan Holds 1st Meeting on COVID-19 Steps for Tokyo Olympics." *Japan Economic Newswire*, September 4, 2020. https://advance-lexis-com.libproxy.wlu.ca/api/document?collection=news&id=urn:contentItem:60S0-5S61-JC5B-G0BJ-00000-00&context=1516831.

"UPDATE4: Abe Tells Trump Japan Prepping for Tokyo Olympics as Planned." *Japan Economic Newswire*, March 13, 2020. https://advance-lexis-com.libproxy.wlu.ca/api/document?collection=news&id=urn:contentItem:5YDT-K441-DYN6-W109-00000-00&context=1516831.

"UPDATE4: IOC Exploring Scenarios for Tokyo Games, Including Postponement." *Japan Economic Newswire*, March 22, 2020. https://advance-lexis-com.libproxy.wlu.ca/api/document?collection=news&id=urn:contentItem:5YGR-9S21-JC65-50HG-00000-00&context=1516831.

"UPDATE4: Japan to Restrict Travel to and from China, S. Korea over Virus." *Japan Economic Newswire*, March 5, 2020. https://advance-lexis-com.libproxy.wlu.ca/api/document? collection=news&id=urn:contentItem:5YC4-06P1-JC65-50M7-00000-00&context=1516831.

"Virus Briefs." *Chicago Daily Herald*, March 21, 2020. https://advance-lexis-com.libproxy.wlu.ca/api/document?collection=news&id=urn:contentItem:5YGT-91X1-DY6F-J026-00000-00&context=1516831.

"Visual Timeline of the Day That Changed Everything." *ESPN*, March 11, 2021. https://www.espn.com/espn/story/_/id/30546338/visual-line-day-changed-everything-march-11.

"VOX POPULI: Bus Service in Ken Shimura's Hometown Steps Up to Help Locals." *Asahi Shimbun*, June 3, 2020. https://www.asahi.com/ajw/articles/13426149.

Wade, Stephen. "Japan Has Its Best Olympic Medal Haul: 27 Gold, 58 Overall." *Associated Press News*, August 8, 2021. https://apnews.com/article/2020-tokyo-olympics-japan-medals-a34e6a9c74600b9c5c1770f67efc8b38.

Wade, Stephen. "Olympics to Continue amid Covid-19 Fears Tokyo Committee Isn't Considering Cancellation Despite Hundreds of Cases in Japan Already." *New York Times*, February 14, 2020. https://advance-lexis-com.libproxy.wlu.ca/api/document?collection=news&id=urn: contentItem:6058-SV11-JCRP-C23V-00000-00&context=1516831.

Wade, Stephen. "Ticket Demand a Sign of Tokyo's Enthusiasm for 2020 Summer Games One Year Out." *Toronto Star*, July 22, 2019. https://www.thestar.com/sports

/amateur/2019/07/22/ticket-demand-a-sign-of-tokyos-enthusiasm-for-2020-summer-games.html.

Wade, Stephen. "Tokyo Olympics Could Be Cancelled if Virus Threat Is Too Serious, Pound Says." *Globe and Mail*, February 26, 2020. https://advance-lexis-com.libproxy.wlu.ca/document/?pdmfid=1516831&crid=765eb2bf-c4ca-40a3-a2fd-0c6df2a7ccd8&pddocfullpath=%2Fshared%2Fdocument%2Fnews%2Furn%3AcontentItem%3A6058-SV11-JCRP-C3CB-00000-00&pdcontentcomponentid=303830&pdteaserkey=sr10&pditab=allpods&ecomp=szznk&earg=sr10&prid=addc7be7-8087-478c-9990-1b66c51ed791.

Wade, Stephen, and Mari Yamaguchi. "Olympic Official: Virus Won't Cancel 2020 Games." *Chicago Daily Herald*, February 15, 2020. https://advance-lexis-com.libproxy.wlu.ca/api/document?collection=news&id=urn:Content.Item:5Y7B-G5N1-JBRC-V3PJ-00000-00&context=1516831.

Wade, Stephen, and Mari Yamaguchi. "Tokyo Olympics Say Costs $12.6B; Audit Report Says Much More." *Associated Press News*, December 20, 2019. https://apnews.com/article/asia-pacific-ap-top-news-tokyo-sports-general-japan-eb6d9e318b4b95f7e53cd1b617dce123.

Waldie, Paul. "British Lockdown to Expand as Cases of Another COVID-19 Variant Surface." *Globe and Mail*, December 23, 2020. https://www.theglobeandmail.com/world/article-british-lockdown-to-expand-as-cases-of-another-covid-19-variant/?gad_source=1&gclid=EAIaIQobChMIt4OvvLujggMVVfjICh1HPw41EAAYAiAAEgK-DPD_BwE.

Waseda University, "Faculty of Sport Sciences: AKAMA, Takao," https://dpt-healthpromotion.w.waseda.jp/wp/members/215/.

Watson, Brian N. *The Father of Judo: A Biography of Jigoro Kanō*. 1st ed. Trafford Press, 2000.

Watts, John. "Investigation Launched into Spiralling Allegations Concerning Nagano's Bid." *The Guardian*, February 4, 1999. https://www.theguardian.com/sport/1999/feb/04/olympic-bribes-nagano-bid-investigation.

"We Need a Global Conversation on the 2020 Olympic Games." *The Lancet* 397, no. 10291 (2021). https://www.thelancet.com/journals/lancet/article/PIIS0140-6736(21)01293-9/fulltext.

Webster, Andrew. "Olympic Movement in a Bubble—but Not Immune to COVID-19." *Sydney Morning Herald*. 20 March 2020. https://advance-lexis-com.libproxy.wlu.ca/api/document?collection=news&id=urn: contentItem:5YFY-0Y81-F0J6-J402-00000-00&context=1516831.

Wenn, Stephen R., and Robert K. Barney. *The Gold in the Rings: The People and Events That Transformed the Olympic Games*. University of Illinois Press, 2020.

Wenn, Stephen R., Robert K. Barney, and Scott G. Martyn. *Tarnished Rings: The International Olympic Committee and the Salt Lake City Bid Scandal*. Rev. ed. Syracuse University Press, 2022.

Wharton, David. "Tokyo's Rough Road to 2020 Summer Olympics." *Los Angeles Times*, July 23, 2019. https://www.latimes.com/sports/story/2019-07-23/tokyos-rough-road-to-2020-summer-olympics.

Wharton, David. "2020 Tokyo Olympics Could Cost Japan More Than $26 billion." *Los Angeles Times*, December 20, 2019. https://www.latimes.com/sports/olympics/story/2019-12-20/2020-tokyo-olympics-could-cost-japan-more-than-26-billion.

"WHO Coronavirus 2019 (COVID-19): Situation Report—41 (March 1, 2020)." https://reliefweb.int/report/china/coronavirus-disease-2019-covid-19-situation-report-41-1-march-2020.

"WHO Coronavirus 2019 (COVID-19): Situation Report—72 (April 1, 2020)." https://reliefweb.int/report/world/coronavirus-disease-2019-covid-19-situation-report-72-1-april-2020.

Wikipedia, "Concerns and Controversies at the 2020 Summer Olympics," last modified November 28, 2024. https://en.wikipedia.org/wiki/Concerns_and_controversies_at_the_2020_Summer_Olympics#:~:text=Notable%20safety%20concerns%20for%20athletes,Sun%20Flag%20at%20Olympic%20venues.

Wilson, Stephen. "The Tokyo Postponement: Lessons Learned for the Olympic Movement." *Olympic Review* 116 (2021). 69.

Wise, Harry. "Typhoon Hagibis and Sales Tax Rise Put Japan's Economy on Course for Recession . . . with the Coronavirus Outbreak Set to Make Things Worse." *This Is Money*, February 17, 2020. https://www.thisismoney.co.uk/money/markets/article-8012285/Typhoon-Hagibis-sales-tax-rise-causes-Japans-economy-slump-six-year-low.html.

Wong, Donna, and Yue Meng-Lewis. "The Good, The Bad, and The Ugly – Situational Crisis Communication and the COVID-19 Pandemic Tokyo 2020 Olympic Games." *Communication & Sport* 12, no. 1 (2023), 99-129. https://doi-org.libproxy.wlu.ca/10.1177/21674795231174188.

World Health Organization. "Biographies: IHR Emergency Committee for COVID-19." Accessed December 23, 2024. https://www.who.int/docs/default-source/documents/ihr/ec-covid-19-biographies-combined-updated-october-2020bee6 d4bde4b04b36a5f125a6e0970ef1.pdf?sfvrsn=7f569f7a_2.

World Health Organization. "COVID-19 Situation Update for the WHO African Region, External Situation Report 4." March 18, 2020. https://reliefweb.int/report/south-africa/covid-19-situation-update-who-african-region-external-situation-report-.

World Health Organization. "COVID-19 WHO African Region: External Situation Report 04/2020." Accessed December 20, 2024. https://apps.who.int/iris/handle/10665/331587.

Worldometer. "World/CoronaVirus/Countries/Japan," accessed December 26, 2024, https://www.worldometers.info/coronavirus/country/japan/.

Yamaguchi, Mari. "Abe Murder Suspect Says Life Destroyed by Mother's Religion." *Associated Press News*, August 26, 2022. https://apnews.com/article/shinzo-abe-religion-japan-social-media-68f18b50c5698bb65f024ff5c5d2c3ba.

Yamaguchi, Mari. "JOC, Sapporo Announce Decision to Abandon Bid, Seek Possible Bid from 2034 On." *Associated Press News*, October 11, 2023. https://apnews.com/article/japan-sapporo-olympic-bid-2030-tokyo-scandal-e1a46ba1ed7316121af0998271c0e03a.

Yamamitsu, Eimi, and Maki Shiraki. "EXCLUSIVE Frustrated by Delays, Tokyo 2020 Sponsors Cancel Booths, Parties." *Reuters*, July 8, 2021. https://www.reuters.com/lifestyle/sports/exclusive-olympics-frustrated-by-delays-tokyo-2020-sponsors-cancel-booths-2021-07-08/#:~:text=TOKYO%2C%20July%208%20(Reuters),be%20allowed%2C%20sources%20told%20Reuters.

Yamamoto, Norio, et al. "Causal Effect of the Tokyo 2020 Olympic and Paralympic Games on the Number of COVID-19 Cases under COVID-19 Pandemic: An Ecological Study Using the Synthetic Control Method." *Journal of Personalized Medicine* 12, no. 2 (2022). https://www.mdpi.com/2075-4426/12/2/209.

Yomiuri Shimbun. "Dentsu's Complacency Said Behind Games Bid-Rigging Scandal." *Japan News,* June 10, 2023. https://japannews.yomiuri.co.jp/society/general-news/20230610-115474/.

Yoneoka, Daisuke, et al. "Effect of the Tokyo 2020 Summer Olympic Games on COVID-19 Incidence in Japan: A Synthetic Control approach," *BMJ Open* 12, no. 9 (2022). https://bmjopen.bmj.com/content/12/9/e061444.info.

Ziegler, Martin, and Matt Lawton. "Coe's Fears over Level Playing Field at Games . . . but Olympics Could Yet Start on Time in July. Gold Medal-Winner Expects Athletes to Withdraw." *The Times,* March 19, 2020. https://advance-lexis-com.libproxy.wlu.ca/api/document?collection=news&id=urn:contentItem:5YFW-SXM1-DYTY-C0W3-00000-00&context=1516831.

Zimbalist, Andrew. "Boston Would Be Lucky to Lose the Competition." *Wall Street Journal,* January 9, 2015. https://www.wsj.com/articles/andrew-zimbalist-boston-would-be-lucky-to-lose-the-olympics-competition-1420847406.

Zimbalist, Andrew. *Circus Maximus: The Economic Gamble Behind the Hosting of the Olympics and the World Cup.* Rev. ed. Brookings Institution Press, 2020.

Zirin, Dave, and Jules Boykoff. "The Tokyo Olympics Are in Trouble." *The Nation,* April 21, 2021. https://www.thenation.com/article/society/tokyo-olympics-pandemic/.

INDEX

A

Abe, Kan, 45
Abe, Shintaro, 45–46, 47
Abe, Shinzo: and Bach relationship, xiv, 45, 47, 103, 144–45, 146–47; background, 45–46; and bid for Games, 28; commitment to original date, 53; commitment to rescheduled Games, 74, 144, 145, 146–47; COVID-19 response, 43–44, 47, 50–51, 72–73, 76, 103; death of, 46, 146–47; economic policy, 46–47, 76, 143; images, 28; importance of Games to, 44–45, 47; and new date selection, 75, 102; postponement decision, x–xi, 3, 64–67, 146, 147; public support for, 43–44, 103; resignation of, 46, 146
Adams, Mark, 64, 65, 104
Africa and COVID-19, x, 63
Ahmed, Mohammed, 163n40
AIBA (Association Internationale de Boxe Amateur), 29–30, 54
Akama, Takao, 73, 145
Akimoto, Katsuhiro, 156
Alai, Nobuo, 166n12
Alibaba, 77
Allianz, 77
All-Partner Task Force, 60, 108
Amsterdam Games (1928), 27
Anson, Andy, 59
Antwerp Games (1920), 27
Aochi, Seiji, 29
ARD, 101
Arma, Gennaro, 35
Arop, Marco, 163n40
Association Internationale de Boxe Amateur (AIBA), 29–30, 54
athletes: cancellation concerns, 41–42; and COVID infections, 7, 70–71, 115–16, 127; expectation of postponement or cancellation, 56–58; Games highlights, xiv, 5–10, 126–30; importance of Games to, xiv–xv, 128–29, 156–57; and March 18 call, 58; as medical providers, 8, 57–58; and playbooks criticism, 112–13; reactions to postponement, 69–72, 75–76; revenue and funding of, 12–13, 14, 151, 175n71; and social media, 9–10; training adaptations, 5–10, 71–72; and travel restrictions, 6; and vaccination, 85–87
Athletes' Commission, 64, 93
Athletics Canada, 13, 20, 136
Atlanta Games (1996), 40, 154
Atos, 100
Australia: COVID-19 response, 43, 62, 112; COVID deaths, x; Grand Prix, 87, 88
Australian Olympic Committee, 59

B

B2ten, 12–13
Bach, Thomas: and Abe relationship, xiv, 45, 47, 103, 144–45, 146–47; and Bujold case, 130; career, 93; commitment to original date, 36, 37–38, 41, 55–56, 58, 59; commitment to rescheduled Games, 144, 145, 146–47; communication as priority, 95–97; on communication challenges, 102; on comparing Games, 90–91; confidence in rescheduled Games, 97, 98, 106–7, 108, 109; and cost reductions, 81; criticism of, 96; on direct funding of athletes, 175n71; dislike of, 195n19; and early news of COVID-19, 34; elections of, 93, 145; images, 66, 86, 105; as interviewee, xii; leadership on rescheduled Games, 79, 97, 98, 147–48; March 18 call, 58; and new date selection, 75; as Olympian, 93, 94, 95, 147; and Opening Ceremony, 120, 121; postponement decision, x–xi, 64–67, 146, 147; priorities as IOC president, 95–96;

Bach, Thomas *(continued)*
    and qualification event adaptations, 56; shift to remote work, xiii; and spectator decision, 116–17; and Suga, 104–5, 195n19; and vaccine development, 81–82, 84–87, 104–5
Bancel, Stéphane, 82
Barshim, Mutaz, 128, 129
basketball and Popovich, 70, 129
Battle, Talor, x
Beck, Emil, 94
Behr, Matthias, 94
Beijing Winter Games (2022), ix–x, xvi, 4, 148, 150, 157
Berlin Games (1916), 27
Berlin Games (1936), 27
Bideau, Nic, 55
bids: and costs, 44, 150–51; decline of, 32, 61, 148, 157; and environmental issues, 150–51; scandals and unethical conduct, 25–26, 45, 148, 154–56
Biles, Simone, 70, 127–28
Bilodeau, Alexandre, 163n40
BioNTech, 81, 82, 84–85, 104
Black, Dustin Lance, 71
Blackmun, Scott, 61
Black Tidings, 16, 154, 155
Blanco, Alejandro, 55
Blumenthal, Richard, 52–53
Bogner, Maria, xii–xiii, 31–32
Boston bid for 2024 Games, 197n32
Bourla, Albert, 84–85
boxing: cancellation of events, 53–54; gender equity and qualification events, 130–31; IOC and AIBA governance, 29–30
Boxing Task Force, 30, 53–54, 130
Boykoff, Jules, 4, 107, 151, 152, 153
Brazil: COVID deaths, x; COVID response, 119. *See also* Rio Games (2016)
British Olympic Association, 59
Bronfman, Stephen, 12
Brown, Aaron, 163n40
Brown, Abdul Hakim Sani, 76
Brown, Larry, 70
Brundage, Avery, 90–91, 93, 147, 197n27
Budgett, Richard: and Bach, 98; background, 49–50; commitment to original date, 36, 49; confidence in rescheduled Games, 97–98; and early news of COVID-19, 31; images, 113; as interviewee, xii; March 18 call, 58; on McCloskey, 84; and medical facility readiness, 73–74; and Mota, 89–90, 112; and Opening Ceremony, 119; on pandemic declaration, 62–63; and playbooks, 84, 108, 115; on postponement as right decision, 73; postponement/cancellation, shift to, 51, 55; and postponement dates, 76; relationships with Japanese officials, 145; on safety controls, 126; on Şahin, 82
Bujold, Mandy, 130–31
Burns, Terrence, 39–40

C

Canada: COVID cases and deaths, x; COVID restrictions, 8; funding of Canadian athletes, 12–13, 14
Canadian Olympic Committee, 58
Cancan, Ren, 130
cancellation of Games: and athletes' concerns, 41–42; calls for, 5, 153; and cancellation of other world sporting events, 30, 37, 52, 53–54, 55, 56; expectations of, 39–44, 51–52, 55–62; and Host City Contract, 40–41, 59; and insurance, 40; *vs.* postponement, 40, 42, 63–64; public opinion in Japan, 53, 102, 104, 106, 149; during WWI/WWII, 4, 27, 90–91, 157
Carey, Jade, 127, 128
CBC, 101
Centers for Disease Control (CDC), 114
Ceresto, 156
Chase, Kendall, 71
Cheptegai, Joshua, 6
China: and COVID-19, 30–36, 38, 44, 49, 60, 81; human rights issues, 96; Olympic Education program, ix–x; tourists from, 50
Ciobanu, Iulian, 9
civil rights, 151–52
Closing Ceremony, 99, 140
Coach's Eye app, 23
Coates, John: commitment to original date, 36, 37, 38–39; images, 37; and postponement, 40, 65, 75, 160n1

INDEX · 231

Cobb, Max, 54–55
Coe, Sebastian, 56, 58, 59
Colangelo, Jerry, 70
Collins, Dave, 11, 12
commercialism, 151, 152
communication: Bach as prioritizing, 95–97; Bach on challenges in, 102; and COVID-19 safety during Games, 78, 79; crisis communication evaluation, 97; and playbooks, 109
costs: and bids, 44, 150–51; and criticism of Olympics, 150–51; and postponement, 65–66, 75, 79, 80–81; reductions, 80–81, 99; of Tokyo Games, 25, 44–45, 150
Cotten, Jen, 13, 17, 23–24, 124, 137
Coubertin, Pierre de, 26, 90–91, 151, 152, 157
Court of Arbitration for Sport, 130–31
Coventry, Kirsty, 93, 148
COVID-19: athletes' infections, 7, 70–71, 115–16, 127; authors and, ix–x, xi; and China, 30–36, 38, 44, 49, 60, 81; global cases, x, 38, 60, 72; global deaths, x, 49, 60, 72; global spread of, 34–35, 49, 60; pandemic declaration, 17, 52, 62–63, 72; at Tokyo Games (2020), 115–16. *See also* Japan and COVID-19; safety of Games, planning; testing, COVID-19
Croley, Vickie, 11–12, 13, 20, 21
Cross, Martin, 50
Crouser, Ryan, 5–6

D
Daley, Tom, 71–72, 127
Daly, Chuck, 70
deaths from COVID-19: China, 38, 49, 60; global, x, 49, 60, 72; Japan, 106, 145; US, x, 72
Deighton, Paul, 84
Deiss, Joseph, 32–33
De Kepper, Christophe, 58, 61, 63, 64, 65, 160n1
Deloitte, 100
Dentsu, 43, 155–56
Desmarais, André, 12
Diack, Lamine, 16, 154, 155
Diack, Papa Massata, 16, 154, 155
Diamond Princess (ship), 35–36, 38, 43–44

Diaz, Hidilyn, 127
Doan, Ritsu, 76
Doncic, Luka, 132
Donofrio, Ed, 93
doping, 50, 57, 74, 96, 148, 157
Douglas, Gabby, 70
Dressel, Caeleb, 126–27
Drive to Survive (tv series), 87
Dubi, Christophe: and Bach, 98; on Bach's leadership, 79; background, 31, 32–34; on cancellation, 63–64; commitment to original date, 37, 41, 56; confidence in rescheduled Games, 97; on Hidemasa, 109; images, 31, 37; as interviewee, xii; on IOC functionality, 67; on IOC goodwill, 82, 83; and Mota, 90; and new date selection, 75; and Opening Ceremony, 119; and playbooks, 108, 109, 114; and postponement decision, 51–52, 60, 63–64, 65, 160n1; relationships with Japanese officials, 144–45; and rescheduled planning, 67, 74, 75, 77–79, 108, 109, 114; and Sparrow interview, 118–19; and vaccines, 82, 117; and Youth Olympic Games, 31
Dubi, Gerard, 31, 33, 119
Ducrey, Pierre, 108, 111, 119
Duplantis, Armand, 9

E
Eaton, Ashton, 133
Edström, Sigfrid, 90–91
Ehrhardt, Taylor, 20
Elite Athletic Training Facility, 14
Ellison, Adrian, 50
environmental impact of Olympics, 150–51
Erdener, Uğur, 82
European Center for Disease Prevention, 114
Exarchos, Yiannis, 77

F
Farquharson Arena, 19–23
Fauci, Anthony, 52
Fédération Internationale de l'Automobile (FIA), 88–89, 90
Felix, Allyson, 129
Felli, Gilbert, 33
Fichtel, Anja, 94

Finnoff, Jonathan, 51
Fischer, Jeff, 137
Formula 1, 37, 87–89, 90
Frijia, Vito, 14, 20
Frodeno, Jan, 9
Futterman, Matthew, 112

G
Galaxy Express, 98–99
Games Delivery Plan, 80
Garside, Harry, 30
Gauthier, Dominick, 12
GAVI Alliance, 85
gender equity and qualification events, 130–31
Germany, vaccination of athletes, 86
Ghebreyesus, Tedros Adhanom, 49, 52, 60, 86
Gifu City facility, 125–26
Global Athlete, 151
Glover, Helen, 8
Gobert, Rudy, 52
Gold in the Rings, The (Wenn & Barney), xi
Gómez, Iñaki, 56
Götzis Hypo-Meeting, 123–24, 133
Gőzgec, Eyűp, 54
Gramantik, Les, 13
Green, Nick, 56–57
Guilbault, Steven, 130

H
Hachimura, Rui, 76
Hadid, Zaha, 25
Hakuhodo, 156
Hamilton, Lewis, 87
Harada, Munehiko, 41
Harris, Tobias, 106
Harvey, Alex, 163n40
Hashimoto, Seiko: commitment to original date, 51, 53; on legacy of Games, 156–57; and Mori comments, 110; and postponement decision, 74, 160n1; as Tokyo 2020 president, 110, 118
Hassan, Sifan, 127
heat: and Farquharson Arena, 20, 23; and Tokyo Games (2020), 8, 76, 131, 132, 136, 138
Heil, Jennifer, 163n40

Here We Go Task Force, 60, 74
Hernandez, Laurie, 70
Hidemasa, Nakamura, 109
Hinchey, Tim, 57, 61
Hirano, Hiroshi, 43
Hirshland, Sarah, 59, 61, 86
Holmes, Andy, 50
Host City Contract, 40–41, 59
housing: and Olympic Village, 42, 77; and Paris Games (2024), 151
Huber, Christoph, 82
Hughes, David, 40
human resources: and personnel retention, 73, 74–75; training and COVID-19 safety, 78
human rights, 96, 151–52
Hungary: COVID deaths, x; vaccination of athletes, 87

I
Independent Expert Panel, 84, 108
India: COVID response, 72; vaccination of athletes, 87
insurance, 40
International Broadcast and Main Press Centers, 78, 101
International Management Group, 14
International Olympic Committee (IOC): All-Partner Task Force, 60, 108; archives, xi, xii–xiii; Boxing Task Force, 29–30, 53–54, 130; commitment to original date, 36–39, 41, 49, 51, 53, 55–56, 58–59; criticism of, 149–54; functionality of, 67; goodwill for, 82, 83; Here We Go Task Force, 60, 74; and human rights, 96, 151–52; inter-organizational relations, 61, 96; New Launch Task Force, 74–75; pressure on, 52, 54; relationships with Japanese officials, 42, 45, 59, 144–45; revenue, 28, 61, 96, 99, 148, 151; role of, 5; scandals and unethical conduct, 25–26, 45, 148, 154–56; shift to remote work, xiii, 99, 100, 147–48; social media campaign, 9. *See also* Bach, Thomas; postponement of Games; postponement planning; safety of Games, planning

International Paralympic Committee, 153
International Sport Federations (ISFs): commitment to original date, 49, 51; and COVID-19 protocols, 110, 111; and date selection, 65, 75, 80; funding and revenue, 28, 79, 148, 151; and postponement/cancellation expectations, 51, 63; and postponement decision, 64; qualification adaptations, 56; relations between, 95; and rescheduled planning, 42, 79, 84, 108, 109; role of, 5
International Testing Agency, 50
interviews, list of, xii
IOC. *See* International Olympic Committee (IOC)
IOC World Conference on Prevention of Illness and Injury in Sport, 55
Irie, Toshio, 166n13
ISFs. *See* International Sport Federations (ISFs)
Israel: COVID-19 response, 43; vaccination of athletes, 87

J

Jackson, Phil, 69–70
Japan: bid for 2030 Games, 156; economic disruption from COVID-19, 39, 53, 98–99, 103, 104; economic policy, 46–47, 76, 98, 104; medal count, Tokyo Games (2020), 149; medal count, total, 27; Olympic history and affinity, 26–29. *See also* Sapporo Winter Games (1940); Tokyo Games (1940); Tokyo Games (2020)
Japan and COVID-19: case counts, 36, 53, 56, 60, 72, 105–6, 145; deaths, 106, 145; and *Diamond Princess*, 35–36, 38, 43–44; first case, 43; response and Abe, 43–44, 47, 50–51, 72–73, 76, 103; response and Koike, 102; response and Suga, 103–8, 117, 149; state of emergency declarations, 47, 50–51, 72, 105, 117; and testing, 43–44, 56, 73; vaccination policy, 104–5, 117; vaccination rates, 5, 113
Japan Doctors Union, 5
Johnson, Boris, 54
ju-jitsu, 26

K

Kanaguri, Shizo, 165n8
Kano, Jigoro, 26–27
Kasaya, Yukio, 29
Kasumi, Yuki, 118
Kato, Katsonobu, 72
Kato, Yasuyuki, 40, 41
Kawabuchi, Saburo, 36, 37, 110
Kawaishi, Tatsugo, 166n13
Kawatsu, Kentaro, 166n13
Keh, Andrew, 112
Kendricks, Sam, 9–10
Killy, Jean-Claude, 82
King, Billie Jean, 130
Kingsbury, Mikaël, 163n40
Kipchoge, Eliud, 129
Kishi, Nobusuke, 45, 46
Kishida, Fumio, 103, 149
Kitamora, Kusuo, 166n13
Kiyokawa, Masaji, 166n13
Kocian, Madison, 70
Koike, Reiso, 166n13
Koike, Yuriko: commitment to rescheduled Games, 102; images, 118; and lack of Olympic symbols in Tokyo, 117; and Mori comments, 110; and postponement decision, 74, 160n1; reelection of, 102; and rescheduled planning, 74, 104; on ticket sales, 25
Konno, Akitsugu, 29
Kono, Taro, 106
Kovacs, Joe, 6
Krzyzewski, Mike, 70
Kuma, Kengo, 25
Kuretani, Norihiro, 200n45

L

Lalovic, Nenad, 30
Lancet, The, 114–15
Lausanne Youth Olympic Games (2020), 30–34
Lavillenie, Renaud, 9
Ledecky, Katie, 126
Lee, Matty, 127
LePage, Pierce, 133, 134, 135–36, 138–39, 141
Levine, Alison, 8–9
Levins, Cam, 55
Lewis, Carl, 129

Lewis, Lennox, 130
Leyshon, Gar: coaching style, 14; and COVID-19 in family, 17; early coaching by, 10–13; as interviewee, xv; and PürInstinct event, 12–13; Tokyo Games (2020) experience, 125–26, 131–40; training adaptations, 18–20, 22–24; training plan, original, 14–15, 16; travel issues, 123–24
Leyshon, Glynn, 19
Liberty Media, 87
Lillehammer Winter Games (1994), 29
logo issue, 25
London Games (2012): and Budgett, 50; and Marra, 133; and McCloskey, 83; records at, xiv; scandals and unethical conduct, 154; sponsorships, 25; and Warner, xv, 12
London-Western Track and Field Club, 19
Loosemore, Mike, 30
Los Angeles Games (1932), 27
Los Angeles Games (1984): and Beck, 94; and Budgett, 31, 50
Lumme, Timo: and Bach, 98; commitment to original date, 56; confidence in rescheduled Games, 100; and early news of COVID-19, 34, 51; images, 101; as interviewee, xii; and Opening Ceremony, 119; and playbook development, 100; relationships with Japanese officials, 145; and rescheduled planning, 76–77, 99–100; and revenue, 96
Lyons, Susanne, 59, 61

M

MacDonald, Scott, 20
Mack, Kris, 14–15, 124
MacNeil, Maggie, 126, 164n77
Makino, Shozo, 166n13
Maltais, Valérie, 163n40
Manfred, Rob, 52
Marra, Harry, 133, 134
Marshall, Mel, 6
Martin, Paul, 87
Mayer, Kevin: decathlon organization, 23; and Paris Games (2024), 141; and Tokyo Games (2020), 134, 135, 137, 138, 139, 140

McBean, Marnie, 140
McCloskey, Brian: background, 83–84; confidence in rescheduled Games, 97–98; images, 111, 114; and playbook development, 84, 108, 111, 114, 115–16; relationships with Japanese officials, 145; and testing, 115–16, 119
McConnell, Kit: on athletes, importance of event to, 128–29; on athletes' concerns, 41; and Bach, 98; and boxing governance, 30; career, 29–30; on commitment to rescheduled Games, 107; confidence in rescheduled Games, 97; and first news of COVID-19, 29–30, 33–34; images, 111; as interviewee, xii; on Koike's support for rescheduled Games, 102; on lack of information on COVID-19, 33–34; and playbook development, 108, 110, 111; and postponement decision, 64; on pressure on IOC, 52, 54; relationships with Japanese officials, 144–45; and rescheduled planning, 79, 108, 110, 111; on uncertainty, 18, 54
McCulloch, Kaarle, 62
media: criticism of Abe, 103; and methodology, xiii; and postponement/cancellation speculation, 3, 5, 52, 58–59; pressure on IOC president, 96; and rescheduled Games, 79, 107, 112, 117; social media, 9–10
Meng-Lewis, Yue, 97
methodology and resources, xi, xii–xiii, xv
Mexico, vaccination of athletes, 87
Miller, J. D., 163n40
Minichiello, Tony, 57
Mishima, Yahiko, 165n8
Miyamoto, Tetsuya, 73
Miyazaki, Yasuji, 166n13
Moderna, 81, 82, 83
Moir, Scott, 163n40
Moloney, Ashley, 134–35, 138, 139, 140
Mondo track, 20, 21, 22
Montreal Games (1976), 91, 93, 94, 95
Moran, Jerry, 52–53
Mori, Yoshiro: commitment to original date, 36, 37, 38–39, 51; confidence in rescheduled Games, 108; images, 37;

and new date selection, 75; and postponement decision, 60, 63, 74, 160n1; and rescheduled planning, 75; sexist remarks by, 110

Mota, Pau: background, 88; and Budgett, 89–90, 112; and FIA, 88–89, 90; as interviewee, xii; and playbook development, 90, 108, 109, 111, 112; relationships with Japanese officials, 145; testing by, 89, 90

MRI machines, 74

Munich Games (1972), 40, 91, 147

Muto, Toshiro, 37, 38–39, 75

N

Nagano Winter Games (1998), 27, 29, 154–55

Nageotte, Katie, 10

Nakahara, Hideomi, 41

Nakamori, Yasuhiro, xiv

Nakano, Koichi, 43–44

Naruhito (emperor), 120, 121

National Olympic Committees (NOCs): commitment to original date, 49, 51; and COVID-19 protocols, 110, 111; funding and revenue, 28, 79, 148, 151; and inter-organizational relations, 61, 96; postponement/cancellation expectations, 51, 57, 58, 59, 63; and postponement decision, 64; qualification adaptations, 56; role of, 5; and sponsorships, 77; and vaccination of athletes, 85

NBCUniversal, 38, 101

Nedasekau, Maksim, 128

New Launch Task Force, 74–75

Newman, Alysha, 10

Nidemasa, Hideki, 144–45

Nielsen, Dennis, 11, 20, 137

Nishikori, Kei, 75–76

Nishiura, Hiroshi, 73

NOCs. *See* National Olympic Committees (NOCs)

Noguchi, Akiyo, 76

Nowak, Mark, 71

Nuzman, Carlos, 154

O

OCOGs (Organizing Committees for the Olympic Games), 5, 28, 151

O'Connor, Kate, 57

Ogasawara, Hiroki, 153

Olympic Broadcasting Services (OBS), 76–77, 108

Olympic Charter, 96, 151, 154

Olympic Partners, The. *See* TOP (The Olympic Partners)

Olympic Polyclinic, 73–74

Olympic Program, The. *See* TOP (The Olympic Partners)

Olympics: Japanese history and affinity for, 26–29; skepticism/criticism of, 149–54. *See also* athletes; International Olympic Committee (IOC); International Sport Federations (ISFs); National Olympic Committees (NOCs); *specific Games*

Olympic Stadium (Tokyo), 25, 119

Olympic Village: apartments, 42, 77; COVID-19 cases, 115, 116; rescheduled planning, 76, 77–78; safety planning, 103, 111, 114, 126; Warner at, 126; welcoming ceremony cuts, 99

Omega, 77

Omi, Shigeru, 39, 106

Opening Ceremony, 99, 118, 119–21, 149

Organizing Committees for the Olympic Games (OCOGs), 5, 28, 151

Osaka, Naomi, 110

Oshitani, Hitoshi, 40, 73

Osterholm, Michael, 5

Oyokota, Tsutomu, 166n13

P

Panasonic, 118

Paralympic Games (2021), 8–9, 153

Paris Games (2024): bid investigation, 154; Russian participation in, 96; and sustainability, 150–51; and Warner, 18, 141

Paul, Barry, 93

Payne, Michael, 94, 117

Peaty, Adam, 6–7

Pfizer, 81, 82, 83, 84–85, 104

Philippines: first gold medal, 127; vaccination of athletes, 87

playbooks: criticism of, 112–15; development of, 4, 80–81, 84, 90, 100, 108–12; and sponsors and broadcasters, 100; versions of, 4, 108

Popovich, Gregg, 69–70, 129

postponement of Games: announcement, 3, 65–66, 146; athletes' reactions to, 17, 69–72, 75–76; *vs.* cancellation, 40, 42, 63–64; cancellations leading up to, 52, 53–54; decision, x–xi, 60, 64–67, 146, 147; first public IOC discussion of, 42; March 24 call, 3, 65–66; and name of Games, 65; and relationship between IOC and Japan, 42, 45, 59; relief at, 60–61; shift to expectation of, 51–52, 55–62; and Takahashi comments, 51; and television schedules, 38; Warner's reaction to, 17

postponement planning: challenge of organizing, 67; and costs, 65–66, 75, 79, 80–81, 99; date selection, 65, 69, 75; and personnel retention, 73, 74–75; schedule approval, 80; task forces, 60, 74–75, 108; vaccine prospects, 78–79, 81–82, 84–87, 90. *See also* playbooks; safety of Games, planning

Pound, Dick, 40–41, 42

Princess Cruise Line. *See Diamond Princess* (ship)

Proctor & Gamble, 100

public: concerns about holding Games, 53, 102, 104, 106–8, 115, 145–46, 149; decision to not allow spectators, 116–18; effect of Games on, xiv, xv, 140–41, 149, 157; polls, 4–5, 102, 104, 106

Public Health England, 53–54

PürInstinct, 12–13

Pusch, Alexander, 94

Q

qualification events: adaptations by, 56; cancellations of, 30, 53–54, 55, 56; concerns about lack of, 23, 61–62, 65; and gender equity, 130–31; and travel restrictions, 18, 52, 54–55

R

Radovanović, Nina, 131

Rakhimov, Gafur, 30

Redgrave, Steven, 50

Reisman, Aly, 70

relationships: importance of Bach/Abe, xiv, 45, 47, 103, 144–45, 146–47; between IOC and Japanese officials, 42, 45, 59, 144–45; as priority for Bach, 95–96; role in success, 144–48

remote work, shift to, xiii, 43, 99, 100, 147–48

revenue: and athletes, 151, 175n1; and commercialism, 151; and IOC, 28, 61, 96, 99, 148, 151

Rich, Motoko, 112

Rio Games (2016): athletes ending in same position at Tokyo Games, 6; and Bach, 148; and Bujold, 130; and Marra, 133; records at, xiv; scandals and unethical conduct, 154; and Warner, xv, 12, 13

Rodrigue, Sylvie, 130

Rodríguez Gacio, Susana, 8

Rogge, Jacques, xi, 33, 93

Russell, Leigh, 57

S

Sada, Tokuhei, 166n12

safety of Games, planning: challenges of, 78; and communication, 78, 79; and concerns about Japan's COVID-19 response, 103–8; and concerns about spread from athletes, 126; COVID-19 reporting app, 110; and health system capacity, 106, 107, 115; and host towns, 106; public opinion and concerns, 4–5, 53, 102, 104, 106–8, 115, 145–46, 149; and Sparrow, 113–14, 118–19; and spectators decision, 116–18; and testing, 89, 90, 111–12, 114, 115–16, 119, 125–26; and training, 78; and transparency, 79; and virulence projections, 82; and Warner at Gifu City facility, 125–26. *See also* playbooks

Şahin, Uğur, 82, 83

Sakamoto, Fumie, 106

Salt Lake City Games (2002): and McConnell, 29; scandals and unethical conduct, 148, 154, 183n19

Samaranch, Juan Antonio, 91, 93, 95

Sapporo bid for 2030 Games, 156

Sapporo Winter Games (1940), 27

Sapporo Winter Games (1972), 27, 29, 119

Scantling, Garrett, 134, 138–39

Schiller, Harvey, 75
Schirp, Michael, 86
Seoul Games (1988), 94
Serbia, vaccination of athletes, 87
Shibuya, Kenji, 72
Shimada, Satoshi, 112, 145
Shimizu, Kazuki, 107
Shiseido Co., 43
Siegel, Max, 61
Sinclair, Christine, 129
Skinner, Callum, 57
Skinner, MyKayla, 70–71, 127–28
Slavkov, Ian, 154
Smith, Seyi, 58
Sochi Winter Games (2014), 101, 148, 150
Sparrow, Annie, 113–14, 118–19
spectators, decision to not allow, 116–18
Spence, Craig, 111
sponsors: authors' interest in, xi–xii; and commercialism, 151; concerns about cancellation, 40–41; dropping out by, 118; and early news of COVID-19, 34; London Games (2012), 25; playbooks for, 100; postponement concerns and questions, 39, 42, 69; and rescheduled planning, 76–77, 99–101; and revenue, 61, 148; scandals and unethical conduct, 154, 155–56; and Warner, 18. *See also* TOP (The Olympic Partners)
SportAccord Conference, 37
Stafford, Ryan, 18–19
Stafford, Scott, 18–19
Stanning, Heather, 8
Stefanidi, Katerina, 10
Stern, David, 70
Stevens, Lamar, ix, x
Stockholm Games (1912), 26–27, 93
Strathroy District Collegiate Institute, 16, 17
Suga, Yoshihide: approval ratings, 106; and Bach, 104–5, 195n19; calls on to stop Games, 115; commitment to original date, 53; commitment to rescheduled Games, 105, 106–7, 146; and COVID-19 response, 103–8, 117, 149; election of, 103; and Mori comments, 110; and Olympic planning, 103–4; resignation of, 149

Sugita, Kazuhiro, 103
Swann, Polly, 8
Sydney Games (2020), 29, 33, 154

T

Takahashi, Haruyuki, 51, 53, 155–56
Takaishi, Katsuo, 166n12
Takeda, Tsunekazu, 25–26, 45, 154
Tamberi, Gianmarco, 128, 129
Tan, Tong Han, 155
Tashima, Kozo, 57
Taylor, Christian, 60–61
Taylor, Rohan, 109
Television and Marketing Services (TMS), 76–77, 96, 99, 100
television broadcasts: and cloud, 77; and commercialism, 151; concerns about postponement/cancellation, 38, 40–41, 42; facilities for, 78, 101; first color, 29; and Japanese audience for Opening Ceremony, 149; Olympic Broadcasting Services (OBS), 76–77, 108; and planning for rescheduled Games, 76–77, 99–101; playbooks for, 100; revenue from, 28, 61, 96, 99, 148, 151; satellite, 28, 29; and unethical conduct, 155–56
Tennis Australia, 112–13
terrorism, 40
testing, COVID-19: on arrival, 111–12, 125–26; at Games, 89, 90, 112, 119, 125; and Japan, 43–44, 56, 73; and playbook development, 111–12, 114, 115–16; in US, 173n45
testing, doping, 50, 57, 74
Theisen-Eaton, Brianne, 133
Thomas, Geraint, 9
Thompson-Herah, Elaine, 127
Thornton, Jane, 161n17
tickets and ticket sales, 25, 39, 42
Tiley, Craig, 112–13
Titmus, Ariarne, 126
Todt, Jean, 88
Tokyo Big Sight, 75
Tokyo Games (1940), 27
Tokyo Games (1964), 27–28
Tokyo Games (2020): athlete highlights, xiv, 5–10, 126–30; awarding of, xiv;

Tokyo Games (2020) *(continued)*
commitment to original date, 36–39, 41, 49, 51, 53, 55–56; costs of, 25, 44–45, 150; and heat, 8, 76, 131, 132, 136, 138; importance of to Abe, 44–45, 47; legacy of, 143–44, 156–57; logo, 25; medal count, 149; problematic incidents, 150; records at, xiv, 6; scandals and unethical conduct, 25–26, 45, 154–56; skepticism on benefits of hosting, 25; as success, 143–44, 153, 154, 156–57; ticket sales, 25; unethical conduct, 154–56. *See also* postponement of Games; postponement planning; safety of Games, planning

Tokyu, 156

Tomjanovich, Rudy, 70

TOP (The Olympic Partners): authors' interest in, xi–xii; cycle overlap concerns, 77; and early news of COVID-19, 34; postponement questions and concerns, 39, 69; and rescheduled planning, 76–77, 99–101; revenue and Bach, 148. *See also* sponsors

Toyoda, Akio, 118

Toyoda, Hisakishi, 166n13

Toyota, 118

training and training facilities: adaptations by athletes, 5–10, 17–24, 71–72; closures and concerns about ability to perform, 57, 58; at Games, 132; inequities in, 55, 56, 61–62; and Warner, xv, 15–24

transportation at Games: and cost cutting, 99; and Warner, 125, 136–37

travel restrictions: in Australia and New Zealand, x; effect on athletes, 6; in Japan, 105; lack of in early days, 30; and qualification events, 18, 52, 54–55

Trump, Donald, 52, 53, 54, 72, 103

Tsuruta, Yoshiyuki, 166n13

Türeci, Özlem, 82, 83

Twichell, Ashley, 7

U

Ukraine: COVID deaths, x; Ukraine War, 96

"Ultimate Garden Clash" competition, 9

United Kingdom: COVID-19 response, 43, 54, 72; COVID deaths, x

United States: COVID-19 cases and deaths, x, 72; testing in, 173n45; vaccination of athletes, 86

United States Olympic and Paralympic Committee (USOPC): and calls for postponement/cancellation, 59, 60–61; criticism of, 60, 61; and vaccination of athletes, 86

V

vaccines: development of, 80, 81–87, 104; and distribution to athletes, 85–87; Japan's vaccination rate, 5, 113; Japan's vaccine rollout, 104–5, 117; prospects and rescheduled planning, 78–79, 81–82, 84–87, 90

Van der Plaetsen, Thomas, 133

Vandertuin, Mike, 19

venues: Olympic Stadium redesign, 25; and rescheduled planning, 42, 69, 75, 76–78, 80; and white elephants, 150

Virtue, Tessa, 163n40

visas, 42

Voumard, Anne-Sophie, 101

W

Wall, Derek, 7

Walsh, Tomas, 6

Warner, Damian: and coaching changes, 13–14; early awareness of COVID-19, 16–18; early sports career, 10–12; as father, 23–24, 123; funding for, 12–13, 14, 18, 19; and Gifu City facility, 125–26; goal of 9000 points, 124, 133, 139–40; and Götzis Hypo-Meeting, 123–24; images, 15, 16, 21, 22, 135; injuries, 15–16, 141; as interviewee, xv; and London Games (2012), xv, 12; and medal ceremony, 140; and Paris Games (2024), 18, 141; and postponement decision, 17; and PürInstinct event, 12–13; and Rio Games (2016), xv, 12, 13; Tokyo Games (2021) experience, 125–26, 131–40; training and training facilities, xv, 15–24; travel issues, 123–24

Warner, Theo, 23–24, 134, 137

Watanabe, Morinari, 30

Weidemann, Isabelle, 163n40

Wenger, Peter, 71
Western University, 15, 16–17, 18, 20
White, John, 20
WHO (World Health Organization): and COVID-19 in Africa, 63, 159n5; early COVID-19 response, 30, 48, 49, 60; and GAVI Alliance, 85; pandemic declaration, 17, 52, 62–63, 72; and rescheduled planning, 78, 86, 89, 108, 114
Wickenheiser, Hayley, 57–58
Wilkens, Lenny, 70
Winter Youth Olympic Games (YOG) (Lausanne, 2020), 30–34
Wong, Donna, 97
World Athletics, 9, 175n71
World War I/II: and cancellation of Games, 4, 27, 90, 91, 157; and Shintaro Abe, 45–46

X
Xi, Jinping, 44
Xiao, Han, 58, 60, 61

Y
Yager, Eric, 81
Yamaguchi, Kaori, 107
Yamamoto, Hiroaki, 98–99
Yamashita, Yasuhiro, 156
Yao, Ming, 132
Yokoyama, Takashi, 166n13
Yoneyama, Hiroshi, 166n12
Yoshihara, Toshiyuki, 200n44
Youth Olympic Games (YOG) (Lausanne, 2020), 30–34
Yusa, Mansanori, 166n13

Z
ZDF, 101
Zenkel, Gary, 101
Zika, 148
Zimbalist, Andrew, 152–53
Zirin, Dave, 107, 151

www.ingramcontent.com/pod-product-compliance
Lightning Source LLC
Chambersburg PA
CBHW032213230426
43672CB00011B/2537